The Complete Illustrated Book of
GARDEN MAGIC

The Complete Illustrated Book of GARDEN MAGIC

ROY E. BILES

COMPLETELY REVISED AND EDITED

By MARJORIE J. DIETZ

ILLUSTRATED BY CATHERINE HOPKINS

Published by J. G. Ferguson Publishing Company *Chicago*

Distributed to the Book Trade by Doubleday & Company, Inc.

ISBN: 0-385-06497-7

Library of Congress Catalog Card Number 70–95239
Printed in the United States of America

ACKNOWLEDGMENTS

The publishers wish to express their appreciation to the following photographers whose photographs appear in THE COMPLETE ILLUSTRATED BOOK OF GARDEN MAGIC: Molly Adams, Guy and Lorraine Burgess, Marjorie J. Dietz, Herman Gantner, Paul E. Genereux, Nelson Groffman, Gottscho-Schleisner, Hilda and Gottlieb Hampfler, Margaret C. Ohlander, Margaret C. Perry, Jack and Mary Alice Roche, George Taloumis, Helen S. Witty.

Photographs were also contributed by All-America Rose Selections; C. C. Mpelkas of Sylvania Electric Products, Inc.; California Redwood Association; Lord and Burnham; O. M. Scott & Sons; Spaeth Displays; United States Department of Agriculture; Western Wood Products Association.

Some of the material in Chapter 20, "City Garden," first appeared in WOMAN'S HOME COMPANION GARDEN BOOK, edited by John C. Wister © 1947 by P. F. Collier, Inc., and is used by permission of Crowell Collier and Macmillan, Inc.

The quotation at the beginning of Chapter 1 is from FROM A NEW GARDEN by Mrs. Francis King and is used by permission of Alfred A. Knopf, Inc.

Contents

COLOR ILLUSTRATIONS

SPRING

Guy Burgess Top left
Molly Adams Top right
Nelson Groffman Bottom

Molly Adams

Marjorie J. Dietz
Marjorie J. Dietz
Marjorie J. Dietz
Marjorie J. Dietz

Nelson Groffman Top
Roche Bottom

Guy Burgess

Gottlieb Hampfler

Roche Top
Guy Burgess Bottom

Gottlieb Hampfler Top left
Nelson Groffman Top right
Gottlieb Hampfler Bottom left
Nelson Groffman Bottom right

FALL

Nelson Groffman Top left
Gottlieb Hampfler Top right
Marjorie J. Dietz Bottom

Roche

Roche
Roche

Roche
Roche

Roche

Nelson Groffman
Nelson Groffman

Guy Burgess

Roche

SUMMER

All-America Rose Selection Top left
Nelson Groffman Top right
Gottlieb Hampfler Bottom

Gottlieb Hampfler Top
Nelson Groffman Bottom left
Gottlieb Hampfler Bottom right

Roche

Nelson Groffman Top
Gottlieb Hampfler Bottom left
Roche Bottom right

Guy Burgess

Gottlieb Hampfler
Gottlieb Hampfler

Guy Burgess Top left
Roche Top right
Roche Bottom left
Molly Adams Bottom right

Roche Top left
Roche Top right
Gottlieb Hampfler Bottom

WINTER

Roche Top left
Gottlieb Hampfler Top right
Roche Bottom

Roche
Roche

Roche
Roche

Roche
Roche

Roche

Gottlieb Hampfler

Guy Burgess Top left
Nelson Groffman Top right
Molly Adams Bottom

Guy Burgess

Introduction

In the more than 30 years since Roy Biles' *Garden Magic* was first published, the fashion among writers, in their understandable zeal to introduce new generations to gardening, has been to adopt a matter-of-fact, common sense approach. There should be no aura of mystery or magic surrounding gardening. Of course, common sense *is* involved in the creation of beautiful gardens and landscapes, as it is in the achievement of growing one potted plant to flowering perfection. Yet anyone who has observed the wonders of plant growth in its many phases must be stirred by less tangible senses than common sense alone.

As Roy Biles wrote in his first edition of *Garden Magic:*

> There is magic in the garden. I cannot create a daffodil in all its colors and grace. No man can. I do not know how a daffodil is created. Yet each spring thousands and thousands of them are seen dancing in our gardens. There is law in the garden. It is the law of creation. If we follow that law we deal in magic. We cannot see the stuff of which the daffodil is made – we need not care by what process it comes into being. If we take the dark brown bulb, plant it according to that law at the right time – we achieve a miracle.

So miracle or magic, marvel or mystery – a sense of these must remain in gardening pursuits along with knowledge of the rules and methods, as Roy Biles knew so well. And in preparing and editing this new edition of *Garden Magic*, this essential balance has been retained. The joys of gardening are here as well as the detailed, practical information needed by today's homeowners and gardeners.

MARJORIE J. DIETZ

The Complete Illustrated Book of
GARDEN MAGIC

This formal outdoor-living area is in complete harmony with the house's architecture; it is both garden and terrace.

CHAPTER 1

Planning for Garden Enjoyment

Charm in a garden is an intangible subtle attraction, and it comes usually from a certain individuality in planning and planting.

– *Mrs. Francis King*

There are several ways to approach the planning and basic landscaping around your property. All of them should take into consideration the needs and interests of you and your family, whether you are moving into a brand new home that is as bare outside as in, or whether you have an older house with a planting that needs renovating or doesn't suit your gardening interests or taste.

Of course, not all new houses are bare of landscaping. The developer may have planted a lawn, some shrubs around the foundation, and he may have had the good sense to leave some of the property's original trees – if such had existed. Or, if you selected the property, *you* took care that some of the existing trees were saved and protected during construction.

Whatever kind of new homeowner you are, you will be as anxious to improve the outside of your property as you have been to decorate and furnish the inside of the house. Interrelation of house and garden is the keynote of today's landscaping. To achieve this, always against the background of your special requirements and interests as an individual family, use one of the three following approaches:

1. Employing landscape architects or consultants.

The amount of outside help that you seek in the planning stage depends, of course, on the budget! Employing a landscape architect (a professional with a degree in landscape architecture from an accredited school) or landscape designer or consultant to make a basic plan of your property can be a most worthwhile expenditure, especially for larger places complicated by varying terrain. A professionally landscaped property provides permanent satisfaction, increased value, and should be free from mistakes of judgment and taste that can be wrought by an enthusiastic but inexperienced owner. In addition to planning the landscape, professional consultants may recommend contractors and nurseries that will do the later work and may themselves supervise the plantings and necessary preliminary operations, such as earth moving to change grades, and installation of driveways, parking areas, terraces, and other components of the landscape.

Of course not all improvements need be accomplished at once. Projects can be carried on over several years to spread out the costs. The important point is that a near-perfect basic plan exists and is being followed to give relationship and meaning to the property as a whole.

2. Nurseries that plan and plant.

If you use neither a landscape architect nor landscape consultant, you can still get professional outside help by directly approaching a local nursery that specializes in planning landscaping as well as selling trees and shrubs. Such nurseries usually maintain a landscaping department and give you a plan without charge so long as you let them do the actual work with their own materials. Often, such an arrangement is entirely satisfactory, both financially and artistically. The new homeowner no longer has to worry about his naked-appearing house and lot (the nurseryman may lay turf instead of planting grass seed to give the homeowner a green lawn virtually overnight). Now all that remains for the homeowner is to maintain the plantings and concentrate on the details of the landscape – a rose garden, a perennial border, vegetables – in short, the pleasures of gardening which this book is about.

Before: The owners of this new house elected to do their own landscaping.

Seven years later: Foundation planting is crowded, but mugo pines and junipers have covered the unsightly bank between lawn and road.

One caution: Be careful to choose a reliable nursery, especially if you are new in the area, and know what you are contracting for. Again, be sure the plan and subsequent layout suit you and your family's needs rather than the convenience of the nursery. Some nurseries, unless encouraged otherwise, tend to repeat successful landscaping formulas so that many communities are composed of look-alikes – houses and landscapes all from the same cookie cutter. Unless you prefer your landscaping to be like that of every other in the area, be wary of package landscaping deals. Also, don't encourage the nurseryman to fill every inch of your property with plants! It is better to have a lean appearance at first then later overcrowding. Besides, you will want to add plants of your own choosing.

3. Planning and planting your own landscape.

If you do not wish to hire a landscape architect, consultant, or nursery service, then you must be your own designer. The risks vary according to the complexity of your site, your taste, skill, and knowledge of design and gardening and family requirements. It should be faced from the start that the new homeowner will probably make some mistakes, but few that can't be remedied.

First of all, you can learn from the mistakes as well as accomplishments of other homeowners by studying existing plantings and solutions to landscaping challenges. The work of good landscape architects is on public display around university buildings, public buildings, industrial complexes, shopping centers, parks, botanic gardens, and even state highways. While each property must be treated individually, you can utilize much of what you observe about the importance of texture, balance, and composition in arranging plants. Some of the books recommended in the month-by-month calendar at the end of this book will help, too.

Features that Make a Landscape

Before starting to make a plan of your proposed landscape design on paper, think about the garden components you want and their requirements and what existing features, if any, can be used to advantage.

Here are lists of landscaping features and other garden adjuncts that can go into a landscape plan (your special interest may be lacking, and of course some of these may not fit into your family's living scheme at all):

LANDSCAPING FEATURES

Open lawn
Foundation and public or front plantings
Trees
Shrubs
Terrace or patio
Fencing and hedges for privacy
Walks, steps, walls
Rock garden
Garden pool

PLANT INTERESTS

Roses and rose garden
Flower garden (annuals and/or perennials)
Special flowers (irises, day lilies, daffodils)
Dwarf fruit trees
Vegetable garden
Herb garden
Wild flowers (for shade and under existing trees)
Heaths and heathers (and other plants for special soil conditions)

UTILITY, RECREATIONAL AREA

Service area (laundry, garbage cans)
Toolhouse
Greenhouse, nursery and cold frame
Swimming pool, sandbox and recreation
Driveway and parking area (if not laid out by builder)

Open lawn: Nothing sets off the beauty of your house and garden like a stretch of well-kept, weedless lawn. (see Chapter 3.) With the advent of the power mower, new grass seed mixtures, and preemergent weed inhibitors, lawn maintenance is no longer a discouraging or backbreaking affair. Keep your lawn area open in the center, and use it as a setting for the various other things of which your garden is composed. Except in extremely small plans, the lawn should dominate all other features. It should be at least two or three times the width of the borders surrounding it.

(Minimum Maintenance Schematic Plan) A minimum maintenance plan with emphasis on outdoor living. Other garden components can be added to fit owners' tastes and interests.

Foundation and front plantings: These reflect the taste of the occupants to every passerby. This outward appearance may enhance, or lower, the value of the property. Most builders plant a few evergreens in the front before the house is sold, but when possible it is better to make a deal to do your own planting. In fact, it is sensible to scrutinize the builder's planting very carefully! Except in very unusual circumstances, the plants are a mere bonus and should be transplanted to a boundary corner to which they may be better suited. A planting in the front can mark the boundaries of the lot, frame the house, and correct architectural weaknesses or emphasize outstanding features.

As for the planting around the base of the house, usually called a foundation planting, there has been a definite and welcome revolution in its style. No longer is it considered fashionable to bury the house base in a mass of greenery. Gone are the coniferous evergreens planted as young plants that soon soared up to the second story, and the vogue that followed for broad-leaved evergreens that also soon outgrew their quarters. Now the emphasis is on restraint – the use of ground covers or very low shrubs with only an occasional larger shrub or small tree for accent.

Of course not all houses are suited to this spare foundation treatment. Almost all old houses are set too high and too much of their foundation is exposed. If your house has this fault, plantings at the corners will give the illusion of width, helping to bring the house down to earth. The architecture of some dwellings does present a special planting problem, and in such cases, seeking professional advice may be the best solution.

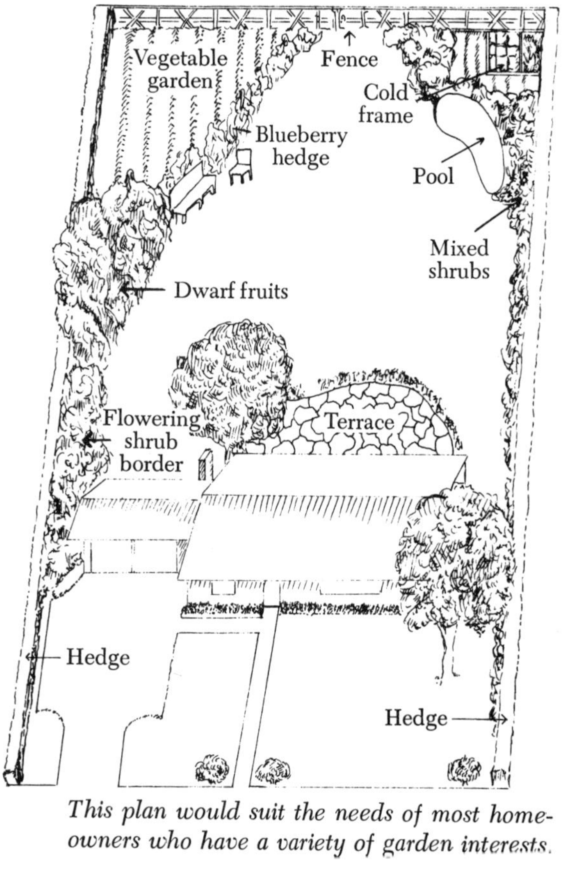

This plan would suit the needs of most homeowners who have a variety of garden interests.

Another problem in landscaping the front or public area of your home is the prevalence of the picture window. If you have any choice in the matter, consider the possibility of not having your home face the street. A living room with large windows overlooking the back garden is far more desirable than a picture window facing a busy thoroughfare or your neighbor's parking area and gaping garage. The problem of a front picture window, that is, providing *something* to look at that is decorative in most seasons, can sometimes be very simply resolved by the placement of one ornamental tree – not as a part of the foundation planting but far enough back so that it can grow properly. Another solution, especially for colonial-type or cottage dwellings, is to make a portion of the front area into a terrace, perhaps enclosed by a picket fence or evergreen hedge. Such an arrangement becomes a dooryard or entrance garden. It is an example of more traditional treatment than the landscaping with less front planting mentioned above.

Here are some additional points to guide you in planning the front or public part of your landscaping: Shrubbery for the front yard should be selected more for foliage effects than flowers. Many plants with con-

Sometimes the best place for a flower garden is near the house, where it becomes a dooryard garden.

spicuous flowers should generally be avoided. Trees should be used to frame the house, so the house will be seen between them. A large tree set directly in front of the house may throw the plan off balance. While variations in form, color, and texture are desirable, repetition is the keynote of a pleasing design. Plan to avoid a spotty appearance by using fewer varieties.

Ultimate height of the plants and an adequate supply of moisture are also important factors to consider. It is costly to keep plants down to proper size for the location; besides, severe pruning ruins their natural shape. Plantings under overhanging roofs may not receive the benefit of rainfall. Keeping them watered is expensive and time-consuming.

Use low-growing plants around steps and at the entrance of the home. Tall plants are apt to crowd, making access rather difficult.

Trees: Trees, especially those with flowers and fruit, are planted for the dual purpose of providing decoration and shade – shade for a terrace or part of the house during the warmest part of the day. Specimen trees (see Chapters 4 and 5) can be used in detached positions about the property for particular emphasis; for instance, on either side of the entrance to a walk. Low-growing trees can be strategically located to provide privacy inside the house or, as mentioned above, they can become the picture for a picture window. (Generally, though, don't dot trees haphazardly about the lawn in a cluttering manner; their positioning should have a purpose.)

Small lots may not have much space for many trees. Perhaps one tree, properly located to shade a terrace, with large shrubs instead of trees used elsewhere, may be all that is required. In planting shade trees, always remember that in five or six years they will make considerable growth, and try to imagine what your property will look like when they are full-sized.

A very nice way of providing future shade in a small garden is to plant a group of trees to approximate a small woodland. The planting of half a dozen trees, from 6 to 8 feet apart, gives quicker and better results than planting one tree and waiting for it to grow to maturity. Let the trees grow together and force each other upward. Trim them where they rub together and of course, trim off the lower branches so they are considerably above your head. If you wish, you may cut out the weaker trees as they mature, leaving only the strongest ones for permanent effect. For this project, select the easiest growing, most pest-resistant trees of your locality. Suggestions include shadblow (*Amelanchier*), birch (*Betula*), dogwood (*Cornus florida*), linden (*Tilia*), willow oak (*Quercus phellos*), box elder (*Acer negundo*), or others. An interesting variation is to plant a white-blossoming tree such as wild cherry, wild plum, white-flowering peach, pear, or apple, with a redbud (Judas tree). These, planted on the edge of the group facing the lawn, will bloom together in spring, giving a beautiful effect.

If the grove is in the corner of the property, a screen or hedge of regel privet, forsythia, or evergreen plants that grow in shade can be used to insure privacy and background.

Shrubs: Today's properties provide ample excuse to feature the superior shrubs – both evergreen and leaf-losing – that are available. Broad-leaved evergreen shrubs (see Chapters 4 and 6) in small groups, perhaps with one small tree as an accent, can be used at property corners, as screens near entrances and outdoor living areas, and to separate various sections of the property. In planting shrubs or trees, try to get an equal amount of bulk, height, or width on either side of an imaginary line (axis) down the middle of the lot.

Gravel surfacing instead of grass makes sense for heavy traffic areas near entrances.

Terraces and Other Components

Terrace, patio, or outdoor living room: All are names for the same feature, a modern development of yesterday's porch and garden house. Most terraces are adjacent to the house and usually can be approached from the living room or dining area and, ideally, also directly from the kitchen. In regions with year-round mild climates and elsewhere in summer the terrace should seem to be a part of the house itself, and nothing defeats this so thoroughly as having to step down to it from inside the house. Its surface can be paved with concrete, flagstone, brick, gravel, or irregularly shaped flat stones, as well as other materials. While it is best to have the terrace as nearly level as possible with the flooring of the dwelling, it is not at all necessary – and often quite impossible – to have a terrace level with the lawn and garden beyond.

The size, shape, and character of a terrace are determined by the architecture of the house, the nature and design of the garden, the general landscape beyond and

Start of construction of free-form terrace of concrete and flagstone. Large circle is for pool.

This attractively designed terrace of generous proportion makes outdoor living a pleasure.

surrounding it, and the interests and needs of the owner and family.

A terrace may be rectangular and extend along the entire length of a house and beyond, or be a more intimate, enclosed area shielded from both the elements and neighbors. American families like to spend as much time as possible outdoors and the creation of an attractive terrace area can provide an enjoyable challenge to the homeowner.

Fences and hedges for privacy: Boundaries of a property are the logical locations for fences and hedges of varying kinds and heights. They can also be used to enclose, totally or partially, service, terrace, and other sections of the garden. If a lot is of ample size, a shrubbery border may act as a screen, but if it is narrow, such as a 50-foot lot, it is really too small for masses of shrubbery. A fence may be the answer with a few plants used along it as accent. Putting a hedge (see Chapter 7) around the front of a property may dwarf it and give the owners a shut-in feeling. On the other hand, houses close to a busy road require some screening from the noise and activity going on in front.

Walks and steps: Do not make walks or paths more extensive than necessary. Walks and steps should lead somewhere and should bear some relationship in their composition and size to the rest of the landscape and house. They should not meander needlessly, but on the other hand, there is no reason why the user shouldn't expect pleasant encounters such as plantings along the way. Before surfacing a walk or path with concrete, consider that bright, glaring paths cut up and dwarf a property. Steppingstones or walks with grass between the stones are usually the least conspicuous.

The informal, brick-surfaced terrace reflects the informality of the naturalistic landscape.

Rough-hewn logs or railroad ties make simple yet adequate steps in a rustic setting.

Rock gardens: If you have on your grounds a small natural slope, fairly well exposed to the light and sun, it is the place to locate a rock garden. Large stones placed as outcroppings will make it look like a natural formation. It is seldom that a rock garden can be artistically successful as a mound in the center of the yard. Rock gardens nearly "on the flat" can be constructed, though, and are described in Chapter 12.

Garden pool and water garden: Water plants (see Chapter 13) are easily grown and very adaptable. All they need is sunlight and food. A little shade on the north may be had for background, but any shading directly over the pool will interfere with the number, size, and health of the water-lilies themselves. Informal pools may be used in connection with almost any feature, but formal pools must be located very carefully so that they are in complete balance with the rest of the plan.

The mirror or reflecting pool is another means of bringing water into the garden and also will be a bird attraction if it is shallow. As a rule it has few or no water plants growing in it, but is supposed to reflect the sky and the surrounding foliage. It may be located in the shade or semishade, where water-lilies will not grow well. It should be flush with the turf, and fancy

Substantial steps of brick and flagstone make an easy access from lower level to terrace.

edging should be avoided. It should be more of a mirror than a planting and can range in diameter from about 3 feet to much larger.

Rose garden: A rose garden must not be too close to a wall or hedge and must have sunlight for at least half the day and air all around it. Confined rose gardens are invitations to all the pests to which roses are heir. Roses (see Chapter 11) need a well-drained soil. The beds must not be too wide, or it will be necessary to tramp upon them to cut blooms or attend to them, thus undoing the effects of cultivation. Climbing roses need an area of at least 3 square feet of ground per plant. The same ground conditions apply as in the rose garden. For successful growth they should have the sunlight upon them for at least two-thirds of the day.

Flower gardens: Along with roses and other flowering shrubs, annuals and perennials give the homeowner the opportunity to be creative with color, using it as lavishly or sparingly as he pleases.

Most annuals and perennials (see Chapter 9) need full sun, but a few will do well in part shade. They can be combined in a border – the traditional way – usually about 5 feet wide and about 3 times as long

Solution for picture window: a tiny garden court enclosed by screen of cedar 2 x 2s gives privacy as well as attractive view from within house.

as wide, or used as color accents – the more contemporary way – around the terrace and in front of shrubbery groupings.

The amount of actual space you allow for a flower garden depends on your own enthusiasm and the time you have to take care of it. The nice thing about a flower garden is that usually it can be expanded or reduced in size, according to the whim of the gardener.

Special flowers: The above remarks are also true of any special plant group. If you find that you derive more pleasure from growing bearded iris, day lilies, or daffodils, you can allow space for them according to their needs. (see Chapters 9 and 10.)

Fruit trees: Standard fruit trees, of course, require a considerable area. However, dwarf fruit trees (see Chapter 15) of various kinds can be included at the edge of the vegetable garden, in the borders, and used for ornamental effect elsewhere on the property. They have the advantage of giving blossoms in the spring and a harvest of full-sized fruit in the fall.

Vegetable garden: Even though small, a vegetable garden can be most satisfying, especially to the gourmet cook of the family. The vegetable garden needs full sun. Place it in a corner, or at the end of the property behind some low-growing shrubbery. Although it is not a part of the garden scene, it need not be unsightly. It may be developed along a formal or semiformal plan, with beds of vegetables surrounded by grass walks or separated by flower borders. Or it may be kept strictly utilitarian and made on the straight row system as described in Chapter 14.

Herb garden: Herbs may be grown in the vegetable garden, but they are decorative enough to be made into a small garden that can be placed near the terrace and kitchen. Herbs, either in combination or as individuals, can be grown in pots and planters near outdoor living areas where they are ornamental to look at and convenient for snipping for culinary purposes.

Wild flowers: Many homes may end with partial woodland as part of the property, providing the correct environment for a wild-flower garden. Many native plants may already be in existence there. Others can be introduced from nearby woods or ordered from specialists who propagate such plants for retail sale.

Heaths and heathers: If you find that your home is in a region where the soil is especially peaty, sandy, or acid (see Chapter 6), you will discover an intriguing family of plants especially suitable for these conditions. They include the familiar rhododendron and azalea, shrubs tolerant of more average garden conditions, as well as bearberry (*Arctostaphylos uva-ursi*), an evergreen ground cover (see Chapter 8) native to sandy regions from coast to coast.

Inexpensive reed screening covers stucco garage to form background for plants in California garden.

The beloved Scottish heather (*Calluna*) and its relative (*Erica*) also belong here.

Service area: If you really want privacy, the service entrance to the house (the kitchen door) should be screened somewhat from the garden, and another entrance, either from the living room or the dining room, should be constructed for entrance onto the terrace and garden. If the garden is to remain intimate, it is hardly gracious to drag friends around from the front of the house, or to take them out through the kitchen. Therefore another entrance besides the kitchen door is essential.

A service area should also contain garbage and disposal cans and a collapsible clothes rack or revolving device on a pole.

If your lot is too small for much of a service area, there are removable metal clothes posts that drop into sockets temporarily for airing and drying clothes.

Service areas can be screened by shrubs or fences. Many attractive prefabricated fences are available through local lumber yards. Choose a material that is in harmony with the architecture of your home.

Toolhouse: Few garages offer adequate space for full storage of gardening supplies and tools. The toolhouse can be an elaborate structure, serving also as a modern version of yesterday's potting shed, or a simple place to store the lawn mower and a few hand tools. Whatever form it takes should be attractive rather than an eyesore.

Greenhouse, nursery area, and cold frame: All should be provided for in the planning stage if they fit in with your gardening interests.

Swimming pool, sandbox, and other recreational features: A play area for small children will save a lot of wear and tear on the rest of the garden area. A sandbox and room enough to play may be provided. Screen it off with a little shrubbery, and have it within calling distance of the house.

Most swimming pools are too large for their property and dominate the area. There is no way that high-above-ground pools can artistically be integrated with the rest of the landscape, but ground-level or sunken pools of rectangular or free-form shape can often be made to appear less out of place with the use of shrubs, roses, and potted plants.

Driveway and parking area: These days the garage is usually attached to the home; but if it is a separate unit, it should be as near the house as possible.

Adequate space must be allowed for maneuvering and parking the car. Sometimes this space can be made a part of the play area. Driveways surfaced with a sheet of solid concrete can be glaring. Gravel is often less obnoxious.

Trees and shrubs should not interfere with the moving car along the driveway nor obstruct the view at the entrance. A good deal of thought goes into highway landscaping to avoid obstructing the view of oncoming cars. Homeowners should be equally alert in keeping driveways clear.

Formal or Informal Landscaping?

Next comes the question: What type of garden? If your property is a small lot, it has almost been cut out for you as a formal or semiformal garden. However, if it is an irregular lot or one having more than one level, it will lend itself very well to development along informal or "naturalistic" lines. Informal or semiformal does not mean a hodgepodge of planting and layout. Before deciding what type of landscaping to adopt, you should have an idea of the features previously discussed that you want to incorporate in your plan, and the degree of your gardening interest. Some types of formal landscaping require more rigid maintenance (but sometimes the reverse is true) than informal layouts. Outside help, even when your budget permits, is scarce, and so you must always consider how much maintenance – outdoor housekeeping is an apt description – you wish to do as opposed to the more pleasurable hobby of actual gardening.

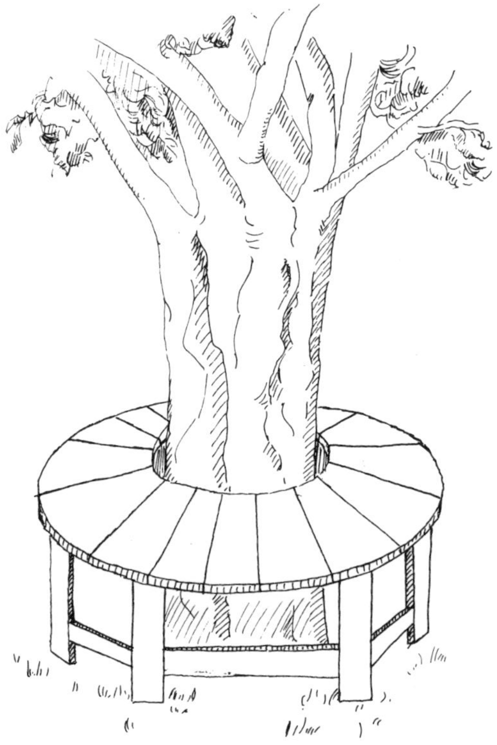

A tree bench is an inviting garden feature.

Whatever design you select, plan for a vista from the house, and keep in mind the imaginary line (axis) by which you balance your planting. The vista may be down this line. There should be an object of interest or accent just off the end of it but not exactly in the center. The object of interest may be a planting, pool, a bench, or some garden ornament.

Some Simple Principles of Design

1. A landscape should conform to the architecture of the house, grade or slope of the lot, existing trees, and any other permanent features.

2. If your lot is long and narrow, cut off the rear for special features; and use narrow borders.

Foundation planting "don't": Don't plant young evergreens that will soon shoot upward under windows unless you don't want to look out!

3. Borders with straight or slightly curved edges will give an appearance of length and greater scale. Sharp curves dwarf beds and lawn. Keep the curves simple and easy.

If your lot is short and wide, use wide borders and a shallow border along the rear of the property. A single row of shrubs is never as good as a broad belt or a "staggered" row.

4. Even the most informal planting must have balance. Draw an imaginary line (called an axis) down the center of your planting. Lawn on one side should approximately balance the area of lawn on the other side and as nearly as possible, shrubbery border against perennial border, feature against feature. Do not make curved borders on either side correspond. Stick to irregularity but get balance.

5. An informal general plan with a formal intimate garden such as a cutting garden or rose garden goes very well. The generally informal plan requires less upkeep, less strict attention to detail of design. However, the plantings must be good as the interest centers on them rather than the design.

6. In using shade trees, place them where you may look into the shade, as well as out from the shade. Trees, flower beds, or other large features placed in the middle of your lawn dwarf its size and spoil the vista. Unless you are building your plan around them, as in the case of existing trees, use them only as separate features, for accent or to frame a view.

Making the Plan

You should now be ready for the final phase of planning your basic landscaping, making a plan to scale on paper. You can use plain or cross-ruled paper available from stationery stores. Use the scale most convenient to you. If you decide on a scale of one-eighth inch equaling a foot, and your lot is 50 by 60 feet, you will draw a rectangle of 6¼ inches by 7½ inches on paper.

Sometimes it is difficult to envision the landscape from a flat plan on paper. A variation is to cut out the various components to scale and shape from colored construction paper and then move them about on the plan before pasting until they seem to fall into proper place. Matching the col-

These windows will never become obscured because the cotoneasters and low hollies never grow tall.

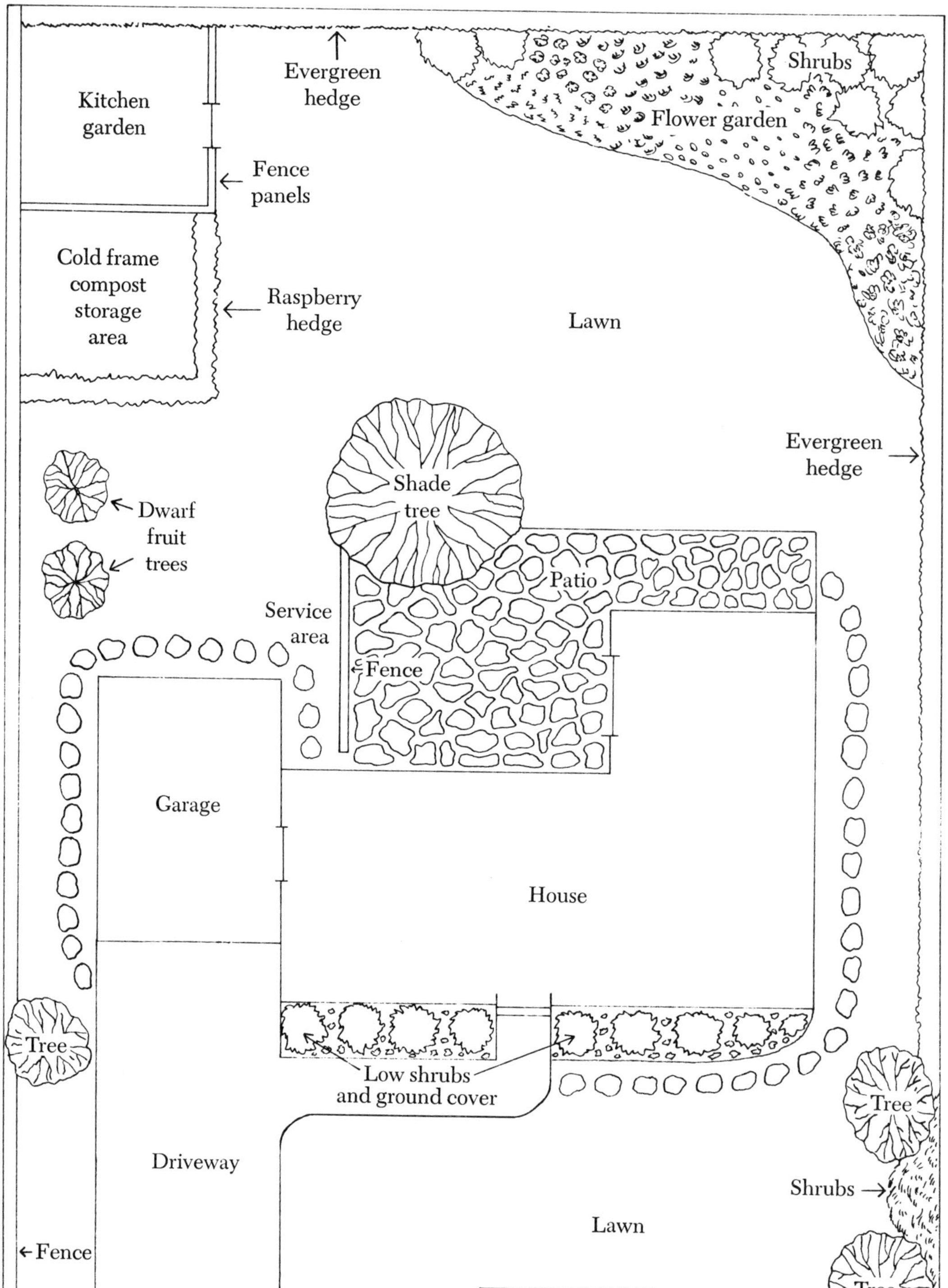

The informal plan requires less upkeep; less attention to design details.

Steps in laying a brick walk: The level of bricks placed in firm, crushed-stone base is checked, and then the joints between the bricks are filled with sand.

Brick can be laid in a variety of patterns.

ors of the construction paper with your landscape components will give you an idea of the final color effects you can achieve in your garden.

An even better method and one that will give you full spatial effect is to use small blocks and objects to represent trees, house, flower beds. A dimensional model of your landscaped property can become a project unto itself but one that can very readily expose the weaknesses as well as the strengths of your plan.

Here is the order of procedure when making a plan:

1. Draw a sketch of your property to scale.
2. Locate the house, garage, and permanent features.
3. Locate the walks, drives, fences, and terrace areas.
4. Trees should be marked to show the approximate spread of the foliage, the approximate area and pattern of the shade thrown by them.
5. Decide what views in the neighborhood you wish to screen out, and plan your planting accordingly.
6. Try to arrange for an easy entrance to your rear garden from your house and a handy place for service and storage.
7. Mark where shady plants will grow and sun-loving plants will grow.
8. Take some pictures of the different sides of your house. Study them and visualize how you would like the planting to look in regard to the house.

Improvement of sandy soil. A cover crop of rye grass has been sown in the fall. In the spring, when it is several inches high, it is cultivated back into the soil, where its roots and tops decay to become humus.

CHAPTER 2

Soil and Its Fertility

And the earth brought forth grass, And herb yielding seed, and the fruit tree yielding fruit.
– Gen. 1:12

One can expect more success with plants when he has learned something about what makes plants grow – what makes them healthy in certain locations and sickly in others.

A great many people think that improving fertility means merely placing in the soil chemical elements which are part of and necessary to plants. This is but a very small part of it.

The first necessity in growing plants is water. Plants use about 300 pounds of water to produce 1 pound of solid matter. That is to say, for every pound of lumber from the forest, hay or hemp from the field, it took 300 pounds of water to sustain the plant while it was manufacturing this pound of solid matter. Plants do not eat, they only drink. The food must be in very weak solution in order for the tiny fiber roots to take it up into the chemical laboratory of the plant. The leaves allow the excess moisture to evaporate while retaining the things which they need to sustain life. Even after the fiber roots (food-absorbing part of the plant) take up the solution, it must still be in liquid form to be able to circulate.

It stands to reason that, as plants themselves are made up for the most part of water (69 to 90 percent), this water needs frequent renewing. In the desert all elements of fertility are present, but the country is arid. As soon as water is supplied, vegetation springs into life.

At the other extreme are marshes where there is plenty of water; temperature and climate are ideal, and yet the usual kinds of vegetation do not grow because of lack of other essentials.

Suppose, for instance, that we have achieved the ideal combination of all elements of fertility. What then goes on in the soil to transform this into stalk, leaves, and blossoms of the plant?

In your garden there are countless workers – working for you day and night, enriching the earth and making possible all plant life. These organisms are so minute that a row of 25,000 of them may be contained in an inch.

These bacteria are for the most part living in the decaying organic matter – the humus – in the soil. If there is little humus there are few bacteria. The increase of bacteria ceases when there is only 2 or 3 percent moisture and is most notable when there is 25 to 40 percent. Warmth, too, is necessary, and the bacteria have been found to increase enormously after a warm summer rain.

This friendly army has a means of preserving itself under adverse conditions by producing spores. These spores may be called seed. In other words, a spore is a young plant that has surrounded itself with a sort of armor, hard cell, or wall, so that it may retain life amid uncongenial surroundings for years. When conditions again become suitable, this shell breaks open; and the bacteria multiply in the usual manner.

These spores, lying frozen all winter in our gardens, are only waiting for the sun and rain of the springtime to awaken them to activity. This is why the character of our soil is important. If it is sand, little water is retained in it; and the air is circulated rather freely. Under these conditions it is almost impossible to keep bacteria alive because of evaporation and the easy passage of water to the lower level of the soil. Again, there is the fine-grained soil (clay), that is so compact that there is practically no space for circulation of air, and bacterial life is smothered.

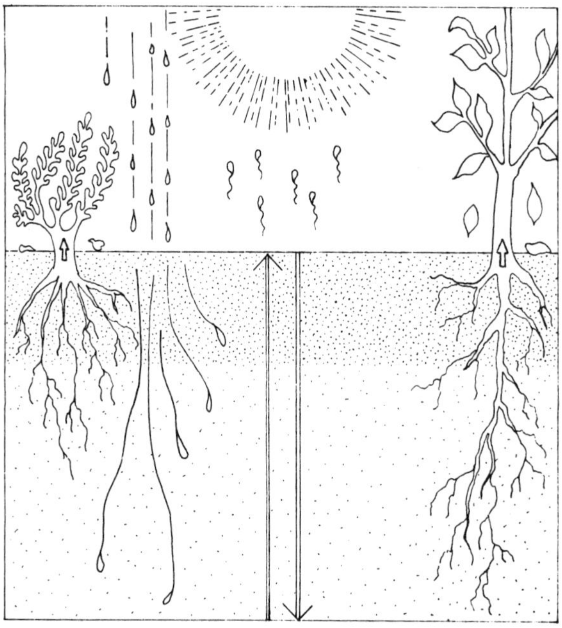

The water cycle. Rainfall percolates downward through soil, is drawn upward again by capillary attraction and, if not used by plants, is evaporated from the surface. Water taken in by plant roots is used by leaves in food-forming process, then passes, as vapor, into air through transpiration from leaves.

This is why it is necessary to make it possible for water to enter the soil in such a manner that some of it is retained for a long period of time. Too much water is just as bad as not enough, and so it must be allowed to filter through the soil, and away from the plant. This is called drainage. By taking the two opposite kinds of soil, sand and clay, and mixing them together, using one to remedy the defects of the other, a happy solution to a drainage problem can be reached. Then if a proper amount of vegetable matter – humus – is added to this mixture, the ideal soil for most types of plants results.

Your garden should consist of good garden loam, made up of about 20 percent sand, 40 percent clay, and 40 percent decaying vegetable matter or humus. This humus may be placed in your soil as manure, peat moss, leaf mold, or homemade compost. If your soil is mainly clay that is sticky when wet and has the tendency to bake and crack, it needs sand for drainage and humus for conditioning. If it is sandy and water runs from it too freely, it needs the addition of humus and clay to keep the water in the soil ready for the plant.

Soil Drainage

Water is essential to plant life, but it must be present in the soil in such form that the plants can take it up. To be available, it must be stored in the tiny spaces between the soil particles; that is, it forms a thin film around each particle. But too much moisture, for most plants, is as undesirable as too little. Some plants, of course, live in water, but they are especially adapted to do so. On land, an excess of water around the soil particles keeps out the air that plant roots must obtain; it prevents the growth and activity of bacteria; and it may dissolve and wash away valuable plant food. For these reasons, surplus moisture must be removed by drainage.

Spring

Spring's official herald is the crocus. For many weeks of bloom, plant several kinds.

A few clumps of an early daffodil help to give color and life to an otherwise unawakened terrace.

Yellow tulips contrast with trees and shrubs in the outdoor-living area of a city garden.

Tulips in the Darwin and Cottage classes supply the major form and color for these large island borders separated by a sea of grass.

In a Long Island, N.Y. garden: white azalea 'Palestrina' and red azalea 'Buccaneer.'

Carolina rhododendron pure pink hybrids catch filtered sunshine in spring garden.

Dexter Hybrid rhododendron 'Scintillation' in early bud-and-flower stage.

Bluebells (Scilla) bloom with the yellow deciduous azalea 'Director Moerlands.'

Garden pools can be frankly artificial or deceptively natural. Either way they must be part of the landscape.

Right: *Lavish use of yellow crocuses transforms this frontyard lawn into a spring garden.*

The art of rock and water gardening is shown to perfection in the Knippenburg garden in New Jersey.

Red flowering dogwoods harmonize with a brick wall. Rock garden plants, yellow alyssum and white candytuft, spill over retaining wall.

An artfully trained tree stands as a piece of living sculpture among massed groups of evergreen azaleas.

Garden furniture today should be chosen as much for its decorative contribution to the landscape as for its functional application.

A *flowering fruit tree and pink dogwood frame a suburban home. Neither will outgrow its alloted space.*

The loveliness of an old apple orchard. Dwarf apple trees give similar effect in less space.

Golden-chain tree (Laburnum), *which flowers in late spring, is ideal for small properties.*

The various white-barked birch trees are important ornamentals for every season of the year.

Water which enters soil during rains seeps either downward or horizontally through porous soil toward lower levels. When it reaches a layer of rock, hardpan, shale, or clay which is impervious or only slightly porous, the passage of water is stopped or slowed up. The point at which this happens is called the water table.

The depth of the growing soil above this table determines, to a large extent, what plants will grow on the land and how well they will grow. Attention must be given both to surface runoff, so that excess water will not stand on top of the soil, and to subdrainage, so that it will seep out of the growing layer.

Drainage does many things, but the first and most important reason for it is the fact that plant roots will not enter saturated soil. Almost all cultivated plants must have air in the soil to complete root growth and feeding processes.

In land where the water table is close to the top of the ground, the growing layer is too shallow to allow the deep rooting necessary for healthy plant growth. In heavy soil with a fairly deep growing area in summer, the water does not percolate fast enough during spring rains, and as a consequence the water table is temporarily raised.

In either of these cases, the shallow root systems that plants are able to develop in spring are unable to reach water during the summer dry spells. Such land is given a constant and desirably lower water table if drained with farm tile.

The Installation of Drainage Tile

Drainage tile quickly lowers the water table after a rain and holds it at the proper level. The plants root deeply in the spring and are able to withstand drought in summer. No fear should be felt that it will dry out the soil too much, for it only drains to the depth at which it is placed and leaves available plenty of moisture where the roots can get it.

Some signs which indicate a need of drainage are often apparent upon the surface. Inspection should be made at the wettest season of the year. When water stands upon the surface after rains, or if a saturated soil fails to dry out promptly during subsequent favorable weather, it can be taken as a definite sign that something is wrong.

The type of vegetation which grows upon the ground naturally is also a good indication. The absence of normal grasses coupled with the presence of coarse wire grass, rushes, mint, willow, or spruce can be a sign of too much moisture. Frequent winter-killing of fruit trees or shrubbery is an indication of shallow rooting. Often they show rank growth in the spring when

Soil which remains constantly waterlogged can be drained by installing underground tiles. Note the level line for measuring the depth of slope. With level line and tile in place, measure the depth of the drain tiles from the line.

the water is high in the ground and a yellowing of their overgrown foliage during the summer when it recedes.

To be sure of the character of the soil, it is customary to take samples at various depths with a ground auger or a posthole digger. This will show the depth of the topsoil and many times reveal the cause of the difficulty. Before proceeding with the actual work of draining, be sure that there is no water trapped upon the top of the ground by uneven grading of the slope. Also, remove any nearby causes of wetness by intercepting and tiling hillside springs. Such springs can be traced by surface vegetation or by a series of borings starting at the edge of the wet spot.

Directions for laying tile depend on the slope of the land and character of the soil. Unless the lines are very long or the land is very wet, 4-inch tile is large enough. Keep the lines as straight as possible, and always avoid abrupt corners or right angles, as they interfere with the free flow of the water.

Lateral joints with a main sewer, or main line of tile, are often called "Y branches" or "slants," because they come in at an angle of about 30 degrees to the line of flow. Where lines of tile connect, wrap heavy paper strips about the joints and cover with concrete after tile is in the trench. It is not necessary to have concrete or paper on the bottom of the joints.

To avoid excessive digging through hills, tile should go around them, following the natural slope of the land. For this reason, a system takes many forms over a large area. All lines must have adequate slope or fall. The greater the fall, the faster the tile works. Six inches of fall to 100 feet of tile may be used if the line is carefully and firmly laid to maintain an even slope. One foot of fall to 100 feet of tile is safer.

Any great amount of tiling should be laid out with a leveling instrument, but small operations can be done with a line.

In hand digging much labor will be saved if only a short section of tile is laid at a time. About 6 to 8 feet of trench are opened and the tile is placed in it. When the next length of trench is dug, it is easy to dig off the top soil and toss it forward into the first strip on top of the tile. The soil in the bottom can then be thrown into the trench being filled to complete it, saving the labor of throwing it to the surface and handling it again.

How deep to place the tile depends upon the kind of soil and the kind of plants to be grown upon it. Grass grows well with a water table 2 feet from the surface. Trees and shrubbery need 4 feet or more. For general garden use a good depth is about 4 feet in ordinary soil.

The deeper the tile is laid the farther apart the tile lines may be placed. The distance varies with the density of the soil. In sandy or open soil, lay the lines deeper and farther apart. In clay soil, lay them closer to the surface and closer together. In sandy or very porous soil, the lines will attain maximum efficiency at once, but in heavier soil, effectiveness increases each year as the finer particles are washed out and the soil becomes more open.

Start at the outlet and lay the tile upgrade. Screen any exposed outlets to prevent rodents from entering, building nests, and clogging them. Place tile ends closely together to avoid stoppage by entrance of soil – one-eighth inch is the proper distance. Place in a straight line, and secure them on either side with earth so that they will not roll out of place when filling is done. All broken or cracked tile should be discarded.

If you have a problem of water-bearing soil or land that is so heavy it makes gardening difficult, a line of tile, 4 feet or more deep, down the middle of a lot will be certain to help. Well-placed tile will in time improve almost any land for 50 feet on either side of it. Its presence will be shown by the brighter and more intense green of the vegetation above it which spreads from year to year as its efficiency increases.

Soil Texture

All soils are composed of particles of varying sizes which determine their texture. In some soils each particle acts as a separate unit; in other soils various minute particles become grouped together and act as single units. The arrangement of soil particles is called a soil's structure.

These mechanical characteristics are of great importance in determining the moisture movement in soils. An ideal structure permits easy and rapid movement of air and water as well as retention of the optimum moisture supply.

Soil "puddling" occurs in a heavier soil when small soil particles are forced or floated in between larger particles. Such soils become compact and tight because of excessive moisture, or because they have been worked when wet to a heavy, gummy mass. This soil will dry very fast with the advent of warm weather. As the soil loses so much water, its volume shrinks greatly, making large cracks. The cracks cause more loss of moisture from the subsoil by evaporation, so the condition is slowly but continually aggravated.

To improve compact soils, some provision for adequate surface and underground drainage must be made. The former can be taken care of by surface grading, while the installation of tile drainage is about the only means of improving underground drainage. To become more friable, heavy soils should be broken up with coarse sand and a liberal supply of organic matter. This furnishes a home for the needed friendly bacteria, and retains moisture and plant food. Organic matter also improves a sandy soil, but a very porous sandy soil may also need the addition of some soil of heavier texture.

It is essential that the soil contain all the elements found in the plant itself, and that it retain them long enough for the plant to absorb them during its life. The chemical elements most needed by plants and most liable to rapid exhaustion are nitrogen, phosphoric acid (phosphorus), and potash (potassium).

Time-tested method of determining whether soil is ready for spring spading and planting. If a squeezed handful of soil sticks to form a mudball, it is still too wet. Working soil at this stage can injure its structure. Wait a few weeks.

Soil is ready for digging or planting when a squeezed handful does not form a ball but breaks apart into a soft, crumbly mass.

NITROGEN:

Makes leaf and stem.
Promotes quick growth – weight and bulk.
Gives good color to foliage.

PHOSPHORUS:

Promotes fruits and flowers.
Makes strong roots.
Insures crop maturity.

POTASSIUM:

Promotes general health of plant and of flowers.
Strengthens stems or stalks.
Increases size and flavor of fruits.

There are, of course, other chemical elements, but they are used in such small quantities that they are lost from the soil only in exceptional cases. The elements are used by the plant only in solution.

Acidity and alkalinity of the soil also affect fertility and can be the determining factor as to which kinds of plants to grow. (See Chapter 6 for plants that can grow in acid soil.)

An acid soil exists when there are more hydrogen ions in a mixed soil and water sample than hydroxl ions. A soil is neutral when the soil-water mixture contains an equal number of both hydrogen ions (acid) and hydroxl ions (alkaline). This all makes perfect sense to the soil scientist, but the gardener need only concern himself with the pH scale, a system invented to express the acidity or alkalinity of solutions, such as a soil-water solution.

The pH Scale

Extremely acid	Below 4.5
Very strongly acid	4.5–5.0
Strongly acid	5.1–5.5
Medium acid	5.6–6.0
Slightly acid	6.1–6.5
Neutral	6.6–7.3
Mildly alkaline	7.4–7.8
Moderately alkaline	7.9–8.4
Strongly alkaline	8.5–9.0
Very strongly alkaline	9.1 and higher

Fortunately, most plants thrive in a slightly acid to neutral or slightly alkaline soil. While sometimes the degree of acidity or alkalinity of a soil can be the cause of poor growth or plant failure, it is wrong to assume that an application of limestone may correct the trouble. The soil should first be tested by the home gardener, using one of the kits available from garden centers or mail-order nurseries, or by a professional (consult your county agent or state agricultural experiment station). The results of the test, expressed in the terms of the pH scale (above), indicate how much lime must be added to raise the pH. (See Chapter 6 for amounts of sulfur to add to soils to make them more acid.)

To determine the nature of soil and its needs, use a soil-testing kit. Soil from individual garden sections, such as lawns, should be collected and tested separately.

Suggested Applications of Finely Ground Limestone To Raise the pH of a 7-Inch Layer of Several Textural Classes of Acid Soils, in Pounds per 1,000 Square Feet

	pH 4.5 to 5.5		*pH 5.5 to 6.5*	
Textural class	*Northern and Central States*	*Southern Coastal States*	*Northern and Central States*	*Southern Coastal States*
Sands and loamy sands	25	15	30	20
Sandy loams	45	25	55	35
Loams	60	40	85	50
Silt loams	80	60	105	75
Clay loams	100	80	120	100
Muck	200	175	225	200

Testing separate samples. Certain kinds of plantings – rhododendrons, vegetables, lawns – have different requirements as to fertility and degree of acidity.

Comparing the color of a soil sample solution to the chart. Test results tell the gardener whether to add lime, nitrogen or other substances to his soil.

While too much lime can be harmful to soils and plants, there are definite benefits it can give in addition to affecting the pH of the soil. It supplies calcium, makes porous soils more compact, and increases the activity of beneficial soil bacteria. These benefits may be partially at the root of the popular notion that "liming the lawn" is an essential spring activity. In truth, a light application of limestone, about 25 pounds per 1,000 square feet, can produce good effects on turf that is slightly acid, a condition preferred by most grasses.

In addition to testing for acidity, it is possible, by applying certain chemicals to a small amount of soil (or to water allowed to leach through it), and noting the reaction, to determine the amounts of the important plant food elements in that soil. To be really accurate and of most value, such tests should be made in a laboratory with complicated apparatus, and the results should be studied in connection with a careful examination of the physical condition of the land, the crops it bears, and its management. State agricultural experiment stations and sometimes county agents will make such tests. For gardeners, there are inexpensive kits with detailed instructions.

It is understood, of course, that certain plants desire shade; others, exposure to the sun. Such plants as roses prefer shelter from wind. Chemical and physical soil fertility is, therefore, worthless if we try to grow a sun-loving plant in deep shade, or vice versa.

Fertilizers and Humus

Plant foods or prepared chemical fertilizers come in salt form, readily available, easily soluble in water. They are balanced in various percentages to contain the elements necessary for the plant. For instance, on a bag of commercial plant food with the marking 10-6-4, the first figure (10) denotes the percentage of nitrogen; the second (6), the percentage of available phosphorus; and the third (4), the percentage of water-soluble potash. The other 80 percent of the fertilizer mixture may contain trace elements and filler material to keep the plant food in good working condition.

There are different fertilizers offered for various types of plants. For instance, a lawn fertilizer high in nitrogen is not as suitable for dahlias and other bulb or root plants, since roots are formed from phosphates and potash.

Use chemical fertilizers sparingly. Overstimulation is weakening to any plant. Young plants, especially, must be fertilized with care as the material is likely to be wasted if more is given than can be taken up by plants.

Chemical elements are held in solution for a longer time when water-holding, soil-conditioning humus has been added to the soil. Also the humus itself, having a quantity of slowly available chemical elements, helps to provide a balanced ration for the plant.

A good, almost universally available source of humus for small gardens is *peat moss,* derived from sphagnum moss. It is usually sold in bales and is low in nitrogen and highly acid. In appearance, it is brown, fibrous, crumbly, and light. It is especially suitable for acid-loving plants such as rhododendron and azalea, but is good for other plants as well.

Sedge peat is a marsh peat, made by the laying down of thousands of generations of grasses, sedges, and reeds under water. The product known as "Michigan peat" is a sedge peat and is usually very dark in color.

Other sources of *humus* are leaf mold (decomposed leaves) such as accumulates on the floor of a forest or wood lot; seaweeds, spent hops, decomposed sawdust, decomposed wood chips, ground sugar cane residue (bagasse), ground corn cobs, decomposed animal manures, and compost. The compost heap should be a feature of every garden. It is made of layers of vegetable refuse from garden and kitchen, alternating with layers of soil, old sods and manure, if obtainable. To increase the fertilizing value of home compost, the United States Department of Agriculture recommends adding the following per bushel of finished compost: 1 cup ammonium sulfate; ½ cup superphosphate; ⅔ cup ground dolomitic limestone or wood ashes.

Compost piles do not have to be complicated, nor must they be built in pits. In

Seedling plants should not receive chemical fertilizers until they have formed three or more true leaves about the pair of seedling leaves.

For perennials, scatter about a tablespoon of fertilizer around base, scratch in by cultivator. Make several applications a season, starting in the spring.

fact, it is better for decomposition if the pile is started at ground level and gradually raised as debris is collected. It should be kept flat, or slightly hollow on top, rather than rounded, so that moisture can collect in the center.

Animal manures make fine humus and fertilizers when properly decayed. Before they can be safely incorporated in the soil around a plant, they should be rotted, usually for a year, by composting. Fresh manure releases heat which will burn plant roots if they come in contact with it.

Cow manure is rich in plant-food elements. Being wet and heavy, it is therefore a first-class manure for light to medium loams. Horse manure is a dry manure which warms up the land and is excellent for heavy, cold, clay-like soils; there is, as a rule, a fairly large percentage of litter in it, and this also adds to its warming effects. It is best from stables where straw or peat is used for bedding. If wood shavings have been used, the manure is of less value in the garden, for the shavings, when incorporated with the soil, rot very slowly. Such manure is, however, good for liquid manure or surface mulching.

Pig manure is not unlike cow manure generally – a rich, strong manure, smelly to work with unless well rotted. It is most useful on light land. *Sheep, poultry,* and *pigeon manures,* when free of litter, are more like a bulky guano than manure. They should be stored under cover and kept dry, and, if to be stored for any length of time, they will benefit considerably if each day's accumulation is very lightly dusted with superphosphate. Use ½ to ¾ pound per square yard, and hoe it in lightly, applying at cropping time or as a top-dressing to plants. When mixed with an equal quantity of fine soil it forms a good top-dressing.

Even sandy seashore soils can be improved by manures or other humus-forming materials to support good plant growth.

Decayed farmyard manure should be dug into the ground in the spring and fresh manure in the autumn. Spread it in 2- to 3-inch layers.

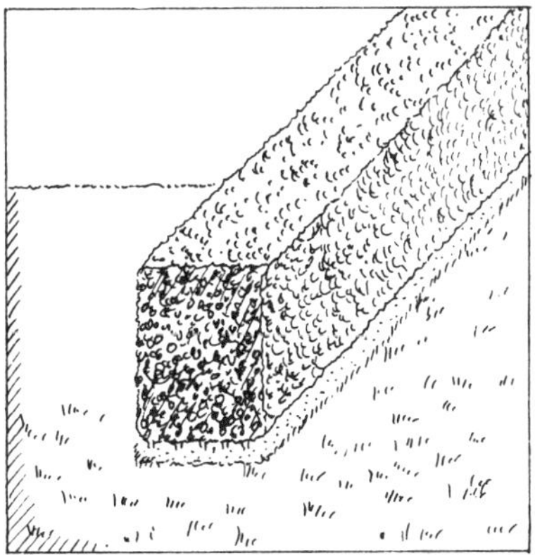

Hedges need about one lb. of fertilizer per 15 feet of hedge. Apply in spring. For most shrubs, apply about three ounces for every two square feet of area covered by shrub.

To fertilize trees, make holes about 18 inches apart, 18 inches deep, and 2 inches wide, in a circle around the full spread of branches. Fill holes with fertilizer.

Peat moss is the most available humus-forming material that can be bought. There is hardly a soil that can't be improved by it.

Lime or fertilizer or other substances added to the soil should be well mixed-in before any planting takes place.

No scientific gardener will allow his land to stand long vacant, but immediately sows it with a quick-growing and leafy plant; this is then allowed to grow and is dug in when partly grown. Italian rye grass, buckwheat, vetch, rye, soybeans, rape, and turnips make excellent *green manure,* as crops of this sort are called.

The various *bone meals* are fertilizers for general use and have more lasting effect than many; the finer they are ground, the more quickly they act. They are high in phosphate and contain some nitrogen. Bone meal is called the "safe" fertilizer because it does not burn and can be applied to almost any plant without injuring it. Use it with bulbs, dahlias, roses. Bone meal is usually more expensive and slower to become available to plants than superphosphate.

Nitrate of soda is rich in nitrogen, concentrated and quickly available. It is a powerful material and will kill many plants if used in quantity or applied directly on their tissues. Dissolve a tablespoonful in a little hot water and dilute to 2 gallons.

Sulfate of ammonia is one of the most powerful of all nitrogenous fertilizers. It is slightly acid and valuable when fast growth is desired. It is not as apt to be washed away by rain as the nitrates. Beware of letting this fertilizer come into contact with vegetation, as it is caustic. Use at rate of one-half to 1 ounce per square yard.

Urea-form nitrogen fertilizers release nitrogen slowly over a period of many weeks. They are especially valuable for lawns.

Sulfate of potash and *muriate of potash* are the two forms of potash most commonly in use. They are applied to the ground a week or two before the growing season or even as a top-dressing for crops which have already started their growth. Apply at the rate of 1 to 2 ounces per square yard or ½ pound to 100 square feet.

Superphosphate, sometimes called *acid phosphate,* supplies phosphoric acid that is more quickly available than that in bone meal. Apply at the rate of 2 to 3 ounces per square yard.

Wood ashes, the ashes left after vegetable matter of any kind is burned, help to loosen and "sweeten" soil, and the fine dust has a percentage of potash in a most useful

Lumpy soil can sometimes be best pulverized for seed sowing by pushing an overturned rake back and forth across it.

Enterprising gardeners collect any materials locally available for mulching or soil improvement. Seaweed can be used for both purposes.

form. Use at cropping time or later, as a top-dressing around established plantings and on lawns.

Dried blood, when available, is fine, especially for rhododendrons and water plants. It contains nitrogen. Use at the rate of 2 to 3 ounces per square yard. It is also a rabbit repellant.

Cottonseed meal is slow to decompose and is excellent for acid-loving plants. *Tankage,* a slaughter-house by-product, is a variable material and less used than it formerly was. *Sewage sludge* (the product "Milorganite") is a good all-purpose fertilizer, especially high in nitrogen.

Soil Preparation

Careful tilling of the soil is one of the first essentials in making a flower bed or, in fact, in any kind of gardening.

Turning the ground, or ordinary digging, is done with a spade, garden fork or mechanical tiller. Ground is turned one spit deep (a spit means the depth of soil that can be conveniently moved in one spadeful). In this operation, any soil conditioner such as humus or fertilizer should be first spread over the ground and then worked through the soil. If the ground is to lie through cold weather, the clods should not be broken up but left rough. All roots, woody weeds and large stones should be gathered and removed.

Wood chips, a shredded mixture of branches, twigs and sometimes leaves, are often left in places accessible to gardeners by tree-trimmers from utility companies. The chips, which eventually decay, make a fine mulch.

A power tiller, which greatly simplifies soil preparation, is a worthwhile investment for many gardeners. Machines can also be rented.

Double digging is a lot more trouble, but is well worth the effort for long-term results. A line is stretched 2 feet from the end across the plot to be dug. A trench one spit deep and 2 feet wide is then dug, the soil being wheeled to the opposite end of the area and piled near the last strip to be dug. On the bottom of the open trench may be thrown a quantity of sand, stones or similar rubbish, together with leaves, straw, manure, or other conditioning material. This is spaded into the second spit of ground or subsoil. If the subsoil is sandy, use more humus, leaf mold or peat moss. The garden line is then moved 2 feet more, and the topsoil from this strip, mixed with suitable conditioning materials as in simple digging, is used to fill the first trench. The process is then repeated until the soil first removed is used to fill the last trench.

Mulching is also an essential aspect of soil management for the home gardener. Most mulching materials not only help prevent weed growth and retain moisture, but also gradually decompose and end by contributing humus to the soil.

A variety of annual flowers formed this colorful border planted in soil improved by manures and other humus-forming materials.

A healthy, weed-free lawn is America's favorite setting for either cottage or mansion.

CHAPTER 3

Lawns and Grading

A child said, "What is the grass?" fetching it to me with full hands;
How could I answer that child? I do not know what it is any more than he.

– *Walt Whitman*

The first requisite of a lawn is adequate drainage. The ground must have sufficient slope to carry off the surface water, or be sufficiently open and porous to absorb it; otherwise, it must be drained with agricultural tile (see Chapter 2.). A good lawn can never grow upon waterlogged soil.

Secondly, a good lawn requires a suitable topography, not too steep nor broken with irregularities or changes of level, partly for appearance's sake, but largely to make the maintenance of good sod easier. A rise of 1 foot in 4 is about the limit for a successful lawn. If this does not take care of the elevation it may be necessary to use one or more terraces or stone retaining walls.

It is hard to keep grass growing on steep grades. When extensive regrading is impracticable to correct steep grades, instead of grass, use ground-cover plants such as English ivy, periwinkle, Japanese spurge (pachysandra), or evergreen-bittersweet, all of which are also useful for covering bare spots beneath trees and other shady places where it is hard to grow grass of any kind. (see Chapter 8, Vines and Ground Covers.) However, in most cases, especially where the grounds are being laid out and developed around a new house, it is practical and most successful to take care of lawn and other garden problems by means of grading, carefully planned and carried out.

It should not be a great deal of trouble for your contractor to scrape off the topsoil when making your cellar excavation. Also, he can arrange to protect the topsoil around the house or to remove it so that the excavated material may go on the bottom, and the topsoil be respread in its proper place. If it is mixed up with the excavated material, it is usually lost; and considerable time and money must be spent to bring it to a point where it will successfully support vegetation.

Changing a Grade

Complicated grade changes require the help of a professional who makes a topographic survey and then a plan on paper. He will also supervise the actual grading operation later. However, comparatively simple changes in grade can be determined with an ordinary chalk line or heavy cord. Fasten the string at the highest point in your grade and continue it to the lowest point. If there are humps in the grade which do not permit this, a trench a few inches wide may be dug so that the line is stretched straight and tight. This line will enable you to see how much you will have to remove or fill. Stakes should then be driven into the ground in the bottom of the trench, leaving them exposed about 6 inches above the level string.

This will enable you to explain to whoever is doing the work that the grade is to be 6 inches below the tops of these stakes. Repeat this sort of check every 5 to 10 feet. When the lawn does not slope evenly to the street or other boundary of your lot, the grade must be warped, so to speak, to fit the sidewalks along the street or the shifting grade of your neighbor's lawn. The grade along your foundation planting should be level if possible, and all grades should start from this point.

By the above method, as you will change your grade every 5 or 10 feet, your stakes will be set correctly at every point along the line. It is only necessary to have two fixed points – the top and bottom of the grade.

If you do not want an even grade, and would prefer a rolling one, it is always safe to use what is known as the OG curve. An OG curve is simply a compensated curve; that is, if your grade curves several inches or feet above your line at the starting point, it should be hollowed out an equal number of inches or feet below your line at the bottom of the grade. Both of these curves should be approximately the same length. Do not have a long mound and then have a little short curve at the bottom. This may look all right, but the balanced curve is always safe.

Fall-sown lawns are best

Late August or early September are ideal times for sowing seed, but even a planting in October is better than waiting until spring. (Many of the Southern lawn grasses – Bermuda, carpet, St. Augustine, and centipede – may be planted in spring or summer.) The warm days of fall are sufficient for the grass but not hot enough to sprout weed seeds. Some weeds may grow at this point, but few seeds will sprout. Fall-sown grass also has the benefit of fall rains. Once the seed is germinated and established in the fall, the grass seems to toughen and develop a sturdy root system; it is ready in the spring to spread into a good, thick turf and hold its own against the weeds.

The most important fact to be remembered in grass seed germination is that the seeding must be kept moist for 3 or 4 weeks. Seed requires from 10 to 14 days to germinate, and once allowed to dry the process stops. The difficulty of holding moisture in the late spring or summer is one of the obstacles to any great success at those times.

Despite all the advice about sowing lawn grasses in the fall, man is a stubborn

Where grass will grow and where it will not: The too-steep slope in the rear has been planted with a ground cover instead of lawn.

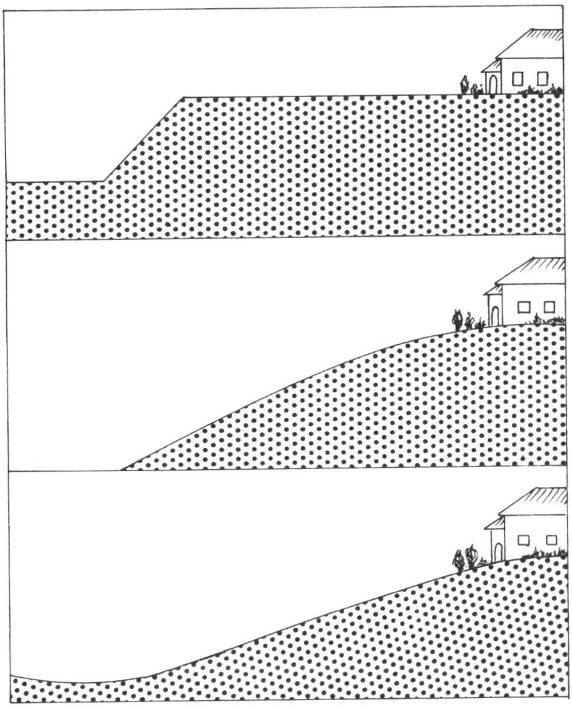

Top: *poor grading. Steepness of slope will cause rapid water runoff and mower will "scalp" crest.* Center: *fair grading. Maximum slope should be one foot in four.* Bottom: *good grading. Rolling grade (OG curve) makes lawn seem larger.*

creature who enjoys planting lawn seed in the spring. If for one reason or another, you must sow grass in the spring, do it as early as possible.

The Kinds of Lawn Grasses

Most lawn grasses are available in mixtures, and there are many combinations as well as varying proportions of the many varieties sold in local outlets or through mail-order nurseries. In sowing seed for a new lawn, it pays to buy a good mixture, especially if you have gone to some trouble and expense in preparing the seed bed. Where a mere green covering is desired, less expensive blendings of short-lived grasses may prove satisfactory. Remember that in buying grass seed, you truly get what you pay for!

Kentucky bluegrass has long been the most desirable lawn grass for the northern section of the country. Kentucky bluegrass has long roots which penetrate deep into the soil, forming a heavy, thick turf. It will grow well in any good soil, either acid or alkaline, but grows best in a cool climate. Where the summers are hot and humid, bluegrass tends to go into dormancy and the tops brown. Sow 2½ pounds to 1,000 square feet.

Newer strains of bluegrass are vastly superior, not only in resistance to leaf-spot disease, but when properly fed and mowed, they resist drought and remain green all summer.

Merion is the best-known strain and, next to Kentucky bluegrass, is about the most popular grass over much of the country. It produces a much heavier root system and grows more rapidly than ordinary bluegrass. It requires regular feeding. Merion bluegrass can be cut close, from ½ to 1½ inches. Although it is expensive in comparison with most other bluegrasses, less seed can be sown. The usual recommendation is 1½ pounds to 1,000 square feet.

Other selections of bluegrass can be planted and include *Delta, Arboretum, Prato, Newport, Windsor,* and *Park.* Park bluegrass (from the University of Minne-

Some homeowners may prefer no lawn. Here pebble cover complements a modern house.

A perfect lawn of Merion bluegrass sets off this flower border. Note graceful curve of the edges.

sota) is considered even more vigorous and faster-growing than Merion. It is less expensive than Merion bluegrass, but the recommended sowing rate is higher – about 3 pounds to 1,000 square feet. It is recommended for areas of the Midwest where Merion bluegrass has been especially susceptible to rust. Windsor bluegrass makes a beautiful turf but is expensive, slow to germinate, and comparatively slow growing. Once past these hurdles, it makes an aristocratic, weed-free lawn for most northern areas.

Fescues (Chewings, creeping red) are next in importance and are tolerant of adverse growing conditions such as shade and poor soil. They will also thrive in full sunlight. They spread by rhizomes. The improved varieties are the same color as bluegrass. Chewings fescue, the older kind, is cheaper, but many object to the deep green color. Pennlawn fescue is the best of the improved varieties.

There are two tall-growing fescues, *Alta* and *Kentucky 31,* which may be included in cheap mixtures. Both are coarse and should be used for play areas. They do have enduring qualities and will thrive most anywhere.

Redtop (a kind of bent grass) and *ryegrass* (perennial ryegrass and Italian or

This Monterey-style California house has its garden in the dooryard. Lawn sweeps down to street.

annual ryegrass) germinate quickly, which is one reason for seedsmen including them in their mixtures. Both are coarse in texture and not permanent but have their value under certain circumstances. A good lawn seed mixture should not contain more than 10 percent of these nurse grasses – preferably 5 percent.

Many owners insist upon *white clover* in their lawn mixture. Where a lawn is to be left to shift for itself, it may have some uses, but in a well-kept lawn, it has many drawbacks and few advantages. It leaves a bare spot to carry through the winter, and its texture and many white flower heads spoil the velvety appearance of any lawn. Its advantage is that it may, in conjunction with bluegrass, survive sandy, alkaline conditions where redtop burns out.

The *creeping bent grass* is a very particular plant, susceptible to drought and pests, and most successful only on the northern Pacific and on the northeastern coasts. Unless you live in these areas or are willing to expend a large amount of intelligent care on your lawn, including almost daily watering, don't attempt its cultivation. If you are intrigued by its velvety appearance, ask the manager of a golf course concerning the cost of construction and care of bent grass putting greens!

Meyer zoysia, which originated at the United States Department of Agriculture station at Beltsville, Maryland, received widespread publicity when it was introduced. Although weeds and crabgrass cannot get a toehold in the thick mat of roots, the tops brown when frost strikes and it does not show green color until late in the spring. In northern gardens a green lawn during the bulb season in the early spring is a prime requisite. For this reason, it is not likely to take the place of bluegrass.

In the South, Meyer zoysia makes a beautiful lawn, responding to regular fertilization and care. Under certain situations in the North, zoysia lawns have their place. It is an excellent choice for lawns for a second or vacation home and grows well in sandy soils that dry out fast. It is also suitable for play areas isolated from a spring garden.

The handsome lawn is a healthy one: dense, well-fed and watered, weed-free, and mowed not too short.

Zoysia and most Bermuda grass as well as St. Augustine and other southern grasses must be made with plugs or stolons of the plants. Among the strains of these grasses are U3 Bermuda-grass, zoysia 52, and emerald zoysia. Dichondra is a grass substitute planted in the Southwest. However, the near-universal bluegrasses such as Newport, Prato and Windsor are being grown up and down the West Coast.

Whereas most of the grasses described above will be planted as part of a mixture (in a mixture, different kinds of grasses share the burden of adapting to a variety of climatic, exposure, and soil conditions), lawns of one kind of grass, usually a bluegrass, are fairly common, too. A good mixture should contain not less than 75 percent of good perennial grasses; the elite of mixtures can contain 90 percent. Examples of mixtures that give a high-quality lawn are Merion bluegrass, 60 percent, Newport bluegrass, 20 percent, and Pennlawn fescue, 20 percent; Merion bluegrass, 25 percent, Newport bluegrass, 25 percent, Pennlawn fescue, 30 percent, Kentucky bluegrass, 20 percent. Any lawn seed you buy lists the ingredients and percentages of

Hummocky mascarene-grass (Zoysia tenuifolia) *makes a lawn suitable for mild climates.*

each on the label. Often it is possible to buy special mixtures formulated for your region that are the results of tests by state agricultural experiment stations. County agents can be helpful in problem areas.

Making a New Lawn

There are several approaches to follow in making a brand-new lawn, and to say that one way is the only way or is foolproof is nonsense. First, there is the "topsoil" method. In this method, a load of topsoil or even several loads are contracted for and are spread over the area to be seeded. The layer of topsoil added can be from 2 to 3 inches or even 6 inches – the amount depending on your pocketbook and the kind of soil you had originally. The new soil can be spread very quickly these days by a small bulldozer although it is usually still necessary to do some final grading with hand rakes.

Most lawn grasses do best in a slightly acid soil so it may be necessary to add limestone. (About 50 pounds of limestone to 1,000 square feet if your soil tests below pH 5.5. Add 25 pounds per 1,000 feet for tests of about 6.0.) A lawn fertilizer high in nitrogen should be spread before the final raking and seeding. As lawn fertilizers differ in their formulations, it is necessary to apply them at the rate recommended on the bag. Use a spreader for even distribution. Seeding can be done by hand or by spreader. Whisk over the surface very lightly with a bamboo rake to put the seed in contact with the soil, but do not bury all the seed. Or if you have access to a lawn roller, give a light rolling after the seeds are sown. Generally this operation is unnecessary and may be harmful. Rolling tends to pack the soil, making it difficult for grass plants to grow. After seeding, be sure that the soil does not dry out before the seeds begin to germinate.

A second method for starting a new lawn is to sow on the existing soil. In many cases, this method will be perfectly satisfactory *if* there is reasonable fertility and a regular feeding schedule can be followed and the soil has the ability to retain moisture.

An especially sandy soil may support spring and fall growth of grass seed when

A tiller is invaluable in lawn making. Use it to break up soil, mix in needed supplements.

The back of a lawn rake being used to pulverize surface and work in plant food.

the weather is cool and rains are adequate, but this same soil during summer and drought offers little moisture solace to the grass when it needs it most. Much of the same trouble may result in a heavy clay that bakes so hard that moisture and fertilizer cannot penetrate. Grass seed usually will not germinate well in such soils. The remedy for both types of soil is to add organic matter – Michigan peat and peat moss are the most universally available sources of humus – but any material offered locally is satisfactory. (At this point the new lawnmaker may decide that topsoil, after all, is the best solution!)

Use a power tiller to break up the soil, and incorporate any added materials lightly into the soil. These materials – organic matter, fertilizer – should remain in the top 3 or 4 inches rather than lower down so the new grass can benefit from them. Such lawns can often turn out to be

Applying fertilizer evenly is important in making a new lawn or feeding a very well established one.

Purchased from a turf farm, sod is unrolled like carpet on prepared soil bed. Use roller to settle sod.

Sod may also be laid over old lawn. Use lawn roller to insure adequate contact between turf and underlayer.

quite adequate once the grass becomes established and a regular feeding schedule is followed.

There is a third method for making a new lawn; and as costs decrease, it may well be the most satisfactory. It is the laying of sod or turf. The sod is grown by turf farms that supply it in convenient rolls. By following this method, it is possible to have a full-blown lawn in one day. However, the same soil preparation (tilling and raking to make a smooth, firm foundation and liming and fertilizing) is as necessary as for seeding. And as with seeding, constant, even moisture must be supplied to get the grass established in its new situation.

When you think about the constant punishment a lawn takes, you can sympathize with its great need for moisture and nourishment. Regular fertilizing is the key to success with any kind of grass – zoysia, perennial rye, or bluegrass and fescue. After all, there are only a few months when grass is not growing, and during a good part of that time it is being trod upon and constantly mowed.

Always apply a fertilizer high in nitrogen (in amounts according to directions on the bag). The modern formulations, with some nitrogen in the slow-release form of urea, are less likely to burn than once was the case with regular forms. Usually two applications, one in spring and one in late summer or fall, are recommended.

Lawn Renovation

A neglected lawn that may be thin in its turf covering and weed-choked, especially by crabgrass, can be brought back to the proper degree of function and beauty. Mow it very close, then rake. If it is especially sandy, spreading a 1-inch-or-more layer of peat moss mixed with topsoil or compost (or any organic material available), and raking, and scratching this lightly in – so it is in some contact with the existing soil – may be necessary and probably will benefit most soils anyway. Apply

A rotary mower will cut long grass without tearing or matting it. Mowing height is easily adjusted.

lime, as suggested previously, and a lawn fertilizer. Rake and scratch these materials into existing soil. Then sow seed and water regularly until the seed germinates. Lawn renovation of a major sort should be done in fall. The second best time is early spring – and this means March in most areas of the North, a time when many soils are hardly thawed.

About Mowing and Watering

The first mowing of a new lawn should be given when the grass is about 2 to 3 inches high with the blades set 2 inches high. Be sure the grass is dry and the blades of the mower are sharp – especially important in soft new grass which can be easily torn and injured by dull blades.

Power mowers have taken the drudgery out of keeping the grass cut. But as with other modern equipment, they may require the services of a skilled mechanic to keep them in good repair.

Before using a power mower in the spring, the entire lawn area should be gone over carefully for rocks and debris which will do the blades no good and may cause an accident.

Opinions on the need for raking grass clippings off the lawn have changed. While clippings can return some humus to the soil if left on the lawn, clippings that do not rot and instead form a thick matting (called thatch) shut out air, moisture, and food, and eventually choke the living grass. A heavy once-a-year raking (there are thatch-removal machines that can be rented), usually in spring, may be in order on established lawns. The use of a grass catcher on the mowing machine helps keep thatch to a minimum.

Can a lawn be overwatered? Surprisingly, it can, especially if the turf is heavy and the soil is predominantly of clay. Under such conditions the turf gradually suffocates from lack of aeration. Also, certain fungus diseases thrive when the soil is overly moist.

The need for regular watering is most vital in the seeding and seedling stages and after the application of fertilizer. Of

This fertilizer spreader leaves a trail of flour from a special bin, making even coverage easy.

Thatch rake removes accumulated cuttings, dead stems. Mechanical thatch removers are available.

Underground watering systems can be set for automatic operation. Note wide coverage of spray.

course, during periods of drought, all kinds of lawn grasses need watering, but even lawns that turn brown usually revive and turn green when the drought ends. Although during drought, any amount of water, however slight, will help a parched lawn, it is generally best to evenly and thoroughly soak a lawn. This may mean an hour for a clay soil and 10 minutes for a sandy soil. Then the lawn should dry out before the next thorough soaking. The idea that watering should not be done in sunlight is wrong. If enough water is applied – naturally if the water is rationed, there will be less evaporation in the evening – it can be done at any time.

Weeds in the Lawn

In the battle to keep weeds out of turf, the homeowner owes a great debt to the chemist. Research has provided the knowledge and means for everyone to have a weedless lawn.

Along with regular feeding and watering (for healthy, vigorous turf offers no toehold to alien weeds like crabgrass and *Poa annua*), there are preemergent weed inhibitors that prevent crabgrass seed from sprouting. There is also 2-4-D, a chemical that selects only broad-leaved weeds like plantain and dandelion for oblivion, leaving the narrow-bladed grasses alone. (Garlic and wild onion plants can be destroyed by 2-4-D in spring.) Always follow directions and remember that 2-4-D can kill all broad-leaved plants besides weeds, including your choicest ornamentals that may be touched by spray drift when using it on a lawn.

Bluegrass (*Poa annua*) has become a nuisance in lawns where summer weather alternates between droughts and periods of humidity by turning yellow and leaving large bare patches. Because it constantly reseeds, control is difficult. Consult authorities in your area.

Perennial coarse grasses like quack grass are being attacked by turf specialists; but until a selective killer has been found, a nonselective kind which destroys other plants on contact is about the only solution.

Quack grass is called "arm under the soil," for the roots spread out in all directions. It is next to impossible to dig out; even a tiny rootlet left in the soil will send forth a new crop. It is not nearly as bothersome in the lawn as in flower beds.

There are several preemergent chemicals against crabgrass on the market, and all must be applied in the spring. Again, follow directions carefully. There is not much point to applying killers to crabgrass plants after they have formed seed, as the plants are only annuals and will soon die anyway. It is the seeds that are the culprits, and the best way to stop them is before they germinate. This they start to do as apple blossoms fade. They are famous for their longevity in the soil and can lurk there for years. For this reason it is best to apply preemergent chemicals every year.

Many lawn fertilizers now contain various weed treatments that can be applied to established lawns as you feed. Consult garden centers and other outlets for garden supplies.

Some Other Lawn Problems

Few people are willing to put forth the effort necessary to keep grass growing under trees. The grass is competing with the tree for food and moisture, and there is also the problem of shade. Before sowing a special shade mixture of lawn grasses (predominantly fescues), condition the soil as thoroughly as possible, adding organic matter in the form of peat moss and a complete lawn food. Then water well and thereafter as needed. Continue regular feeding. If your grass languishes or dies under trees, give up and plant a ground cover like English ivy (*Hedera helix baltica*) or Japanese spurge (*Pachysandra terminalis*). (See Ground Covers and Vines, Chapter 8.)

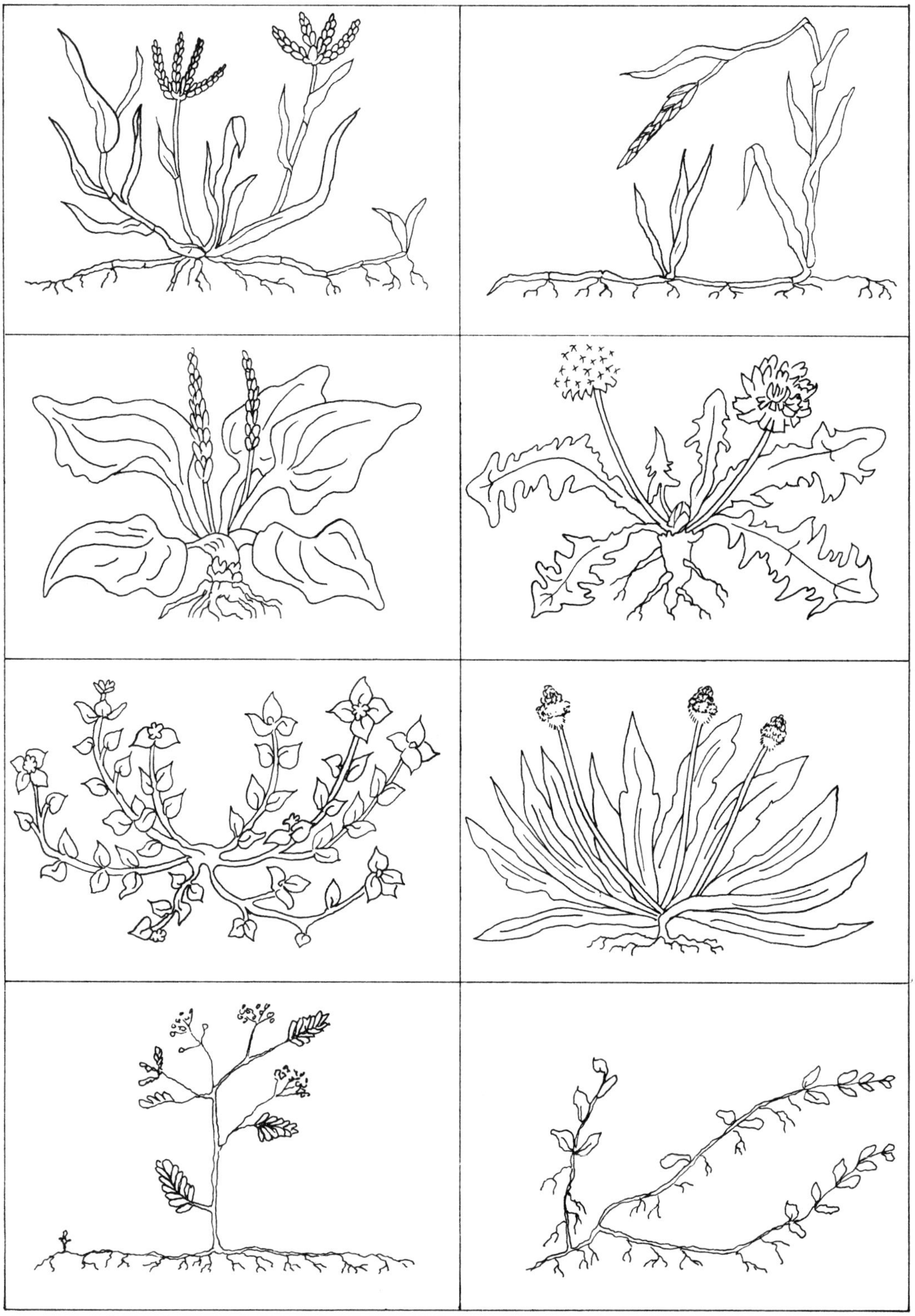

Lawn weeds. Left: *top to bottom, crabgrass, plantain, chickweed, yarrow.* Right: *top to bottom, quack grass, dandelion, buckhorn, thyme-leaved speedwell.*

Where grass and ground-cover plants won't grow, as under this maple, consider a pebble bed.

The growth of moss on lawn areas is an indication that the soil is impoverished. Spade the soil; incorporate peat moss or compost (if available); apply a lawn fertilizer; and resow.

It can be quite a shock to a happy and proud lawnmaker to wake up some summer morning and find that his beautiful, smooth lawn has been undermined by an invasion of moles. Sometimes the moles disappear as suddenly as they arrived. But when they don't, the best remedy is to destroy the grubs that attracted them in the first place. (Moles, contrary to common belief, are not vegetarians. They do not eat roots and bulbs. Mice, which often use the runways of moles, are the destroyers of plant parts.)

There are several chemicals that destroy grubs of the Japanese and Asiatic beetles and others that spend part of their life cycle in the soil. The main chemicals are dieldrin, heptachlor, diazinon, and chlordane, and they are available under various trade names. All are highly poisonous and should be used with great caution and strictly according to directions. These chemicals also kill ants, chiggers, worms, chinch bugs, sod webworms, and other annoying turf pests.

The sycamore is truly a tree for all seasons. The mottled effect of the bark of a mature tree is magnificent when the tree is bare or in leaf.

CHAPTER 4

Trees and Shrubs

"Jock, when ye hae naething else to do, ye may be aye sticking in a tree; it will be growing, Jock, when ye're sleeping."

– Sir Walter Scott

The difference between trees and shrubs is not very clearly marked. A tree has been described as having but one stem or trunk whereas a shrub has several. Most trees are considerably larger than most shrubs, but all are woody plants and in general have the same growth habits. Some trees and shrubs are deciduous or leaf-losing – they drop their foliage in the fall. Others are evergreen and include the coniferous or cone-bearing, needle-leaved plants like the pine. (They are discussed in more detail in the next chapter.) Evergreen shrubs (rhododendron, azalea, andromeda, and others) are discussed in Chapter 6.

The three principal parts of a tree are the roots, the stem or trunk, and the crown. Roots have three main functions. They anchor the tree to the ground, absorb water and dissolved food from the soil, and transport these to the stem and then to branches, twigs, leaves, and other parts of the crown. The principal work of the big roots near the stem is to help the trees stand up, while the fine root hairs at the end of the rootlets are the ones that absorb the water from the soil.

The stem of a tree, also called trunk or bole, is the main axis extending from the roots to the crown, or to the tip in case of an unbranched stem. Tree stems range from long to short, straight to crooked, and from erect to prostrate. A cross section of a stem will show three parts – bark, wood, and pith. In the central part is the pith, which in an old tree trunk may not be noticeable. About it is the wood, which in many trees can be divided into the darker heartwood and the lighter sapwood. Between the wood and the bark is a very thin layer of growing cells known as the cambium. This is the most vital part of a tree, for it is here that all new wood and bark are made. When a tree is girdled, the ring of cambium is severed and this helps to kill the tree.

The most valuable part of a forest tree is the stem, for it produces the wood that is used so extensively by man. The stem supports the tree crown, transports food and water, and stores food. During the winter months considerable food is stored in the stem for use early in spring when growth starts.

Trees grow bigger from year to year. In order for them to grow, they must feed. The raw material out of which trees make their food comes from two sources – the soil and the air. The rootlets with their many small root hairs absorb water and with it the food substances that are held in solution. During the growing season there

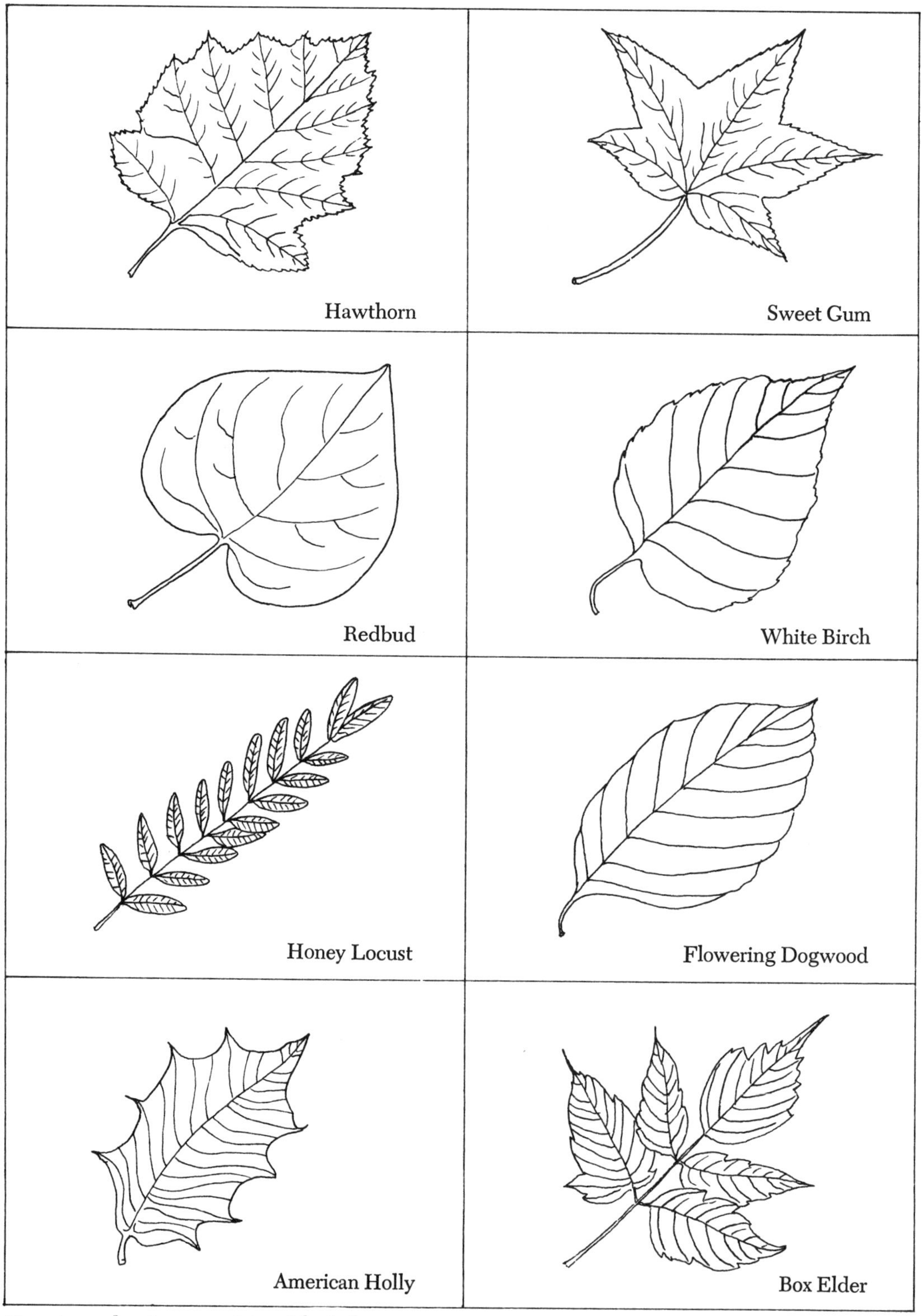

Drawings showing a variety of leaf shapes.

is a continuous flow of sap from the roots through the stems to the leaves, where it is converted into nutritious tree food.

Some trees reach a great size and become very old, while others remain small and die young. And some trees remain small and compact but still live to a ripe old age. Of our native trees, the white oak, buttonwood, white pine, and hemlock are long-lived trees, while the poplar, willow, birch, sassafras, and locust are short-lived.

By counting the growth rings, it has been found that trees are probably the oldest living things on earth. The famous "great tree of Tule," a cypress near Oaxaca, Mexico, is apparently close to its reputed age of 4,000 years. A giant sequoia (*Sequoia gigantea*) in King's Forest, California, was found by John Muir to be over 4,000 years old, and in 1947 a fallen redwood (*S. sempervirens*) was found to be 2,200 years old.

Whereas all trees share the same growth functions and have similar basic needs, they, of course, differ very much in their outward appearances. After all, they belong to different families and genera. (See Chapter 20 for an explanation of plant families and genera.) The homeowner usually looks for a tree of graceful habit, pleasing foliage, or showy bloom. Some of the finest small lawn trees qualify on all these points.

Trees for Shade and Ornament

Of our native trees the redbud or Judas tree (*Cercis canadensis*), producing lavender-rose flowers before the leaves appear, and the flowering dogwood (*Cornus florida*) are both popular for spring flowers. The various hawthorns usually have more or less horizontal branches so that they have a distinctive appearance in a planting as well as producing colorful fruit in the fall.

Of the larger trees for extensive lawns and meadows, the oaks and maples have

The Moraine locust is a thornless variety of the fast-growing honey locust. It is a good lawn subject.

While the weeping willow is a favorite tree for waterside planting, it thrives easily in other situations.

few rivals. The pin oak (*Quercus palustris*) has a graceful, drooping habit, and its autumn foliage color is bright red. Among the maples, the Norway, sugar, and red are known for their ability to grow into well-formed trees. The lindens or basswoods are symmetrical and handsome in flower and foliage.

The bolleana and Lombardy poplars form pyramids of growth to screen unsightly places and to improve the skyline. The sycamores and birches are famous for their white bark. The purple beech makes a magnificent lawn tree where there is adequate space. The ginkgo (sometimes called the maidenhair tree because of the odd shapes of its leaves) is a useful street tree but can also be planted on larger home grounds.

There are many other lawn trees that can be planted by the homeowner for shade and ornament. Hardy over a large part of the country are various improved forms and selections of the honey locust (*Gleditsia triacanthos*). Among those listed by most nurserymen are the Moraine locust and Sunburst locust. The latter has gold-splashed foliage at the ends of its branches. There are improvements in the linden and maple, and whereas it is no longer sensible to plant the American elm because of the Dutch elm disease, several elm substitutes are available. Two include the Hamburg and Christine Buisman elms. A member of the elm family. *Zelkova serrata,* is being widely planted as a substitute for the hapless American elm.

Flowering Fruit Trees and Shrubs

The flowering fruit trees offer great value to the homeowner who wants a floral effect along with his trees. As they have been developed for flowering qualities, their fruit is negligible but often ornamental. They usually take the form of a shrub or dwarf tree and are appropriate for a small place.

Among the most popular are the decorative kinds of plum, cherry, almond, apricot, and peach, and no genus (*Prunus*) of trees adds more to the beauty of spring. Against a background of evergreens they show to great advantage. The blossoms appear on the stems before the leaves in the early spring, and in cold climates they are often in jeopardy from frost. It is best when possible to plant them on the north side of the house where development is retarded until the spring frosts are likely to be over.

This position must not deprive them of a number of hours of sunlight each day. Shelter from prevailing winds in the form of taller shrubbery is also helpful, as an exceptionally severe winter may kill the flower buds just as it freezes those of fruit trees.

The first and best-known is the flowering almond (*Prunus glandulosa*), a hardy shrub usually growing to 4 feet. It is offered in single and double varieties. When grafted it must be watched for suckers which should be cut off at ground level. The flowering apricot (*Prunus mume*) has double white and pink flowers – very decorative on its small tree frame, but they are quite susceptible to spring frost.

Flowering peach (*Prunus persica*) is a small showy tree with double pink-and-white-flowered forms coming into flower after the almond. Plum comes in a number of flowering forms. Japanese plum is a larger tree cultivated in several varieties. Favorite among decorative plums is the purple-leafed plum (*Prunus cerasifera atropurpurea*) a free-growing and highly ornamental subject. It presents double pink flowers with reddish or bronze-purple foliage which makes it different as well as ornamental when the flowers are gone.

The flowering cherry (*Prunus cerasifera*) gives an exotic touch suggesting century-old gardens. It is much publicized because of the planting of a number of them in Washington D.C. The Yoshina cherry (*Prunus yedoensis*) is also a part of this display and is the major tree in the Tidal Basin in Washington. Its pale pink flowers

Flowering fruit trees, especially weeping forms, make ideal accents for terrace and patio.

harmonize with the white Sargent cherry (*Prunus sargenti*, the hardiest and tallest of the Orientals) which blooms at almost the same time. The Yoshina is more spreading and unfit for planting in a small space.

The most widely planted of these flowering stone fruits by home gardeners is the single-flowered Higan cherry (*Prunus subhirtella*), especially free flowering in habit. It is the spring cherry tree of Japan and bears a profusion of pink flowers so that the branches often are literally hidden from sight. It is of bushy growth and has the advantage of usually staying small, a desirable quality in a suburban garden. There is a variety (*autumnalis*) of the Higan cherry that blooms again in lesser degree in the fall. The weeping cherry is a form of the Higan, and there are white or rose-colored varieties. It has been used in this country for 50 years, which is a tribute to its beauty and hardiness. It remains popular today and is most useful on limited suburban properties because of its 15-foot height. It is especially effective near a terrace.

The flowering crabapple (*Malus*) is one of the most satisfactory small trees for home grounds. The crabapples are extremely hardy and will grow in exposures which would be fatal to the cherries. They offer a profusion of bloom in a wide color range from white to deep pink. Trees vary in height according to varieties, and in the autumn they are adorned with fruits in shades of green, yellow, orange, scarlet, and crimson. Newer varieties are quite immune or resistant to disease.

Best known is the Bechtel's crab (*Malus ioensis flora plena*). The tree grows about 10 feet tall, and when in bloom the double

Crabapple 'Katherine' in bloom with tulips in the White House Rose Garden. Its flowers are white, the fall fruit, yellow.

The hawthorns are noted for their abundant bloom in late spring. They are small trees, desirable as lawn accents.

pink flowers resemble small roses. It is susceptible to a rust disease. 'Dorothea,' which was originated in Arnold Arboretum, and 'Charlotte,' from Waukegan, Illinois, are improved varieties of the Bechtel.

The Hopa crab is another hybrid. It has attractive pink flowers and bright red fruits, and the rich maroon foliage offers contrast in the border throughout the growing season.

Malus 'Red Jade,' from the Brooklyn Botanic Garden, is a semiweeping tree with blush-white flowers that appear with the leaves. It is more famous for the colorful display of bright red fruits in the fall. The first to bloom in the spring is the Manchurian crab (*Malus baccata mandshurica*). Buds are deep pink and open into large, fragrant, white blossoms.

Next comes the flowering quince or Japanese quince, a "firebush" in early May when it is covered with clusters of bright scarlet flowers. Its foliage develops soon after flowering. It reaches a height of 4 to 6 feet. Grown against a wall with southern exposure, it often blooms as early as January, but elsewhere as late as June. There are several fine varieties of flowering quince (*Chaenomeles japonica* or *C. lagenaria*), ranging from bright red to orange, pink, and white. (The fruiting quince is *Cydonia oblonga,* and it, too, is ornamental in both flower and fruit.)

All flowering fruits flourish under the care given other fruits (see Chapter 15). They can be planted in spring or fall. Choose sunny positions with a little shelter from prevailing winds. Dig deep, large holes (2 feet deep), put old manure or peat moss in the bottom and refill with good soil. In acid soils, mix in limestone generously, for flowering fruit trees love a near-neutral condition. If the soil is acid, relime yearly.

Prune out the oldest wood to stimulate growth of new wood. Members of the *Prunus* genus, especially, bear their flowers on shoots of the previous year, so young wood coming along means a more floriferous plant. Prune, if possible, in November. The *Prunus* varieties bleed in the spring, and the cuts should be coated with a tree paint, a good practice in all pruning.

Bare-root trees or shrubs can be stored temporarily in shallow trenches for days or a week or so before planting.

A dormant spray (garden centers now carry complete fruit sprays) applied just before the buds open is a safeguard against a host of ills. It is the easiest way of all to prevent pest injury.

Planting Suggestions

The majority of trees and shrubs for home planting come from local outlets – garden centers and nurseries – and from mail-order nurseries, but occasionally there is opportunity to dig and move plants that are growing wild. Small plants are not hard to lift and transplant successfully, but large plants with sprawling root systems may not recover from the shock. Such large plants taken from the wild should first be root pruned, which may take at least two years. A part of the circle is completed one spring, and the balance of the trench is dug out the following spring. This causes the roots to make a fine growth close to the trunk; and when it is finally moved, the ball is filled with fine roots. The tree is then

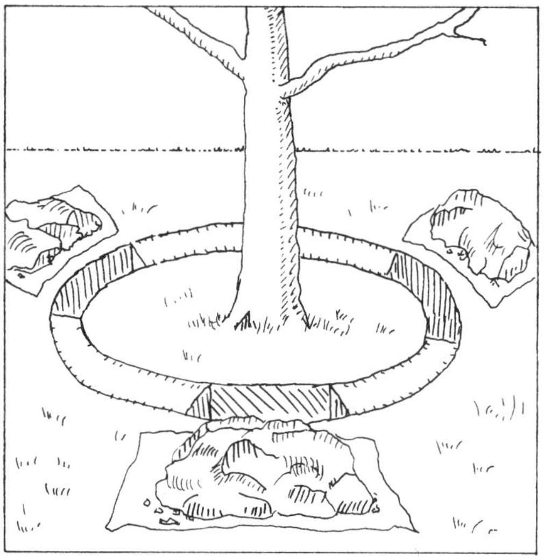

Transplanting established tree from the wild or elsewhere: tree must be root pruned in advance, one to two years before digging. First year, three trenches are dug as shown, fertilizer is added to trenches before soil is replaced. Second year, remaining trenches around tree are dug. Tree can be moved third year in spring or fall.

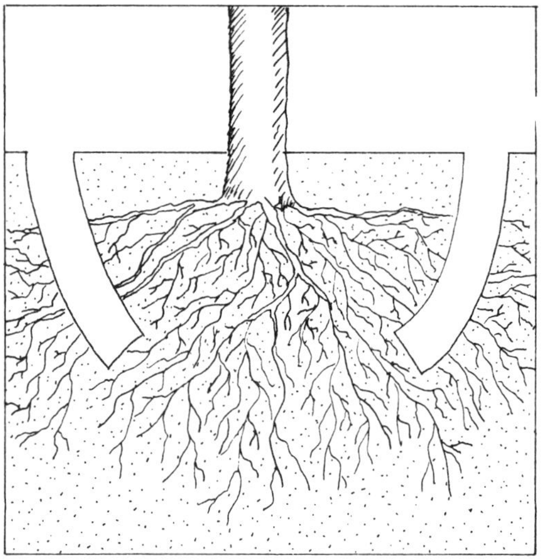

Profile of tree roots after pruning to compact root ball.

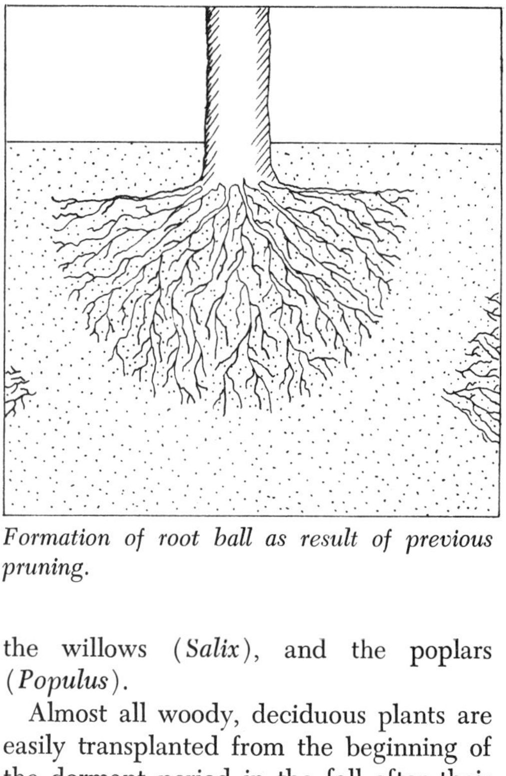

Formation of root ball as result of previous pruning.

pulled over and the bottom roots cut, and in this way the root shock is divided into three parts. The moving of large trees is a job for experts or someone with patience and equipment and requires the preparation of a hole of great size and depth.

There are a number of trees which can only be transplanted successfully when very young. They have a "tap" root, a strong center root which grows straight down. Special root treatment is given such trees in the nursery.

It is heartening to know that trees and shrubs in small sizes, in addition to being good buys for budget reasons, also recover rapidly from the shock of transplanting and in a few years will have reached a size of landscape value. Of course, some trees (and shrubs) grow much faster than others. Some, not all, pay a penalty for this quick growth by ending up at maturity with brittle wood that is easily broken in wind storms. A few fast-growing trees include the Chinese or Asiatic elm (*Ulmus pumila*), silver maple (*Acer saccharinum*), the willows (*Salix*), and the poplars (*Populus*).

Almost all woody, deciduous plants are easily transplanted from the beginning of the dormant period in the fall after their leaves drop until spring before new foliage unfolds. Spring planting is considered preferable for a few trees: examples include apple, dogwood, magnolia, birch, tulip tree, and poplar.

If the planting is done in spring it is best to wait until the soil warms up a little.

Modern power equipment has reduced large-tree moving and planting to a science but for homeowners it is still a matter of brains and brawn, boards to use as levers and makeshift methods.

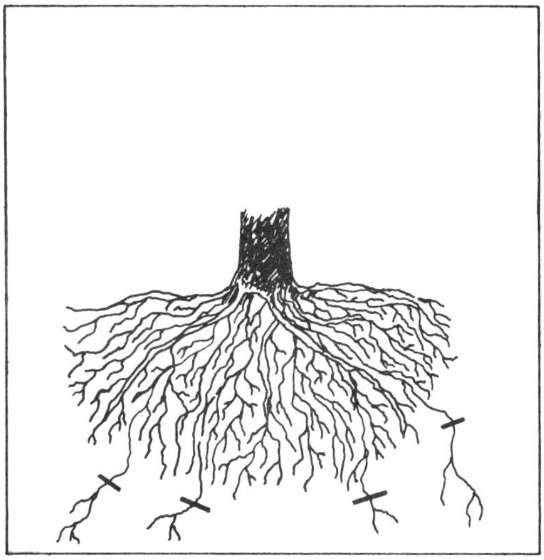

Before planting bare-root trees or shrubs, cut off straggly or broken roots.

Light soil permits planting earlier than heavy clay soil, and, of course, no planting should be done when the ground is lumpy or frozen.

Balled-and-burlapped plants can be delivered from the nursery and planted at the gardener's leisure. Occasionally the ball may have to be soaked if it appears to be drying out. Material, especially bare-root, shipped from a mail-order source, should be unpacked as soon as possible and heeled into a vacant flower bed as soon as you receive it. It may be kept there as long as it is dormant or until you are ready to plant it.

When taking a tree bare-root from the soil, it is best to dip it into a bath of mud, which is called "puddling." This protects the roots from exposure to the air before planting, and also from any air pockets which may exist after planting. It enables it to get into quicker and closer contact with the planting soil.

The planting hole should be excavated about 2 feet deep and should be at least one foot wider each way than the full spread of the roots. Any increase in these dimensions will be repaid by quicker growth and plant health. The bottom of the hole should be broken up with a fork

Dipping bare roots into a mud bath before planting coats them with a protective layer to prevent drying out.

and thoroughly mixed with water-holding material, such as peat moss, leaf mold, thoroughly rotted manure, or vermiculite. The hole must drain readily.

The excavated soil should be placed upon a piece of burlap, boards, or go into a wheelbarrow – with the best soil separated from the subsoil. If the plant is one which grows in acid soil (see Chapter 6), work in a generous quantity of peat moss and powdered sulfur, if your soil lacks the proper

The bare roots of trees and shrubs must be soaked for at least 24 hours in a pail of water before planting.

Measure the balled-and-burlapped roots of a tree before digging and setting the plant in the hole.

Before planting a group of trees and shrubs, put them in place to see if the arrangement is pleasing.

Soaking a newly set-out birch clump before completion of planting assures saturation of roots, and helps settle the soil to eliminate air pockets.

It's usually impossible and unnecessary to remove burlap around roots after planting, but it is a good practice to open it and loosen at the top.

acidity, and place the best soil in the bottom of the hole. (If your soil is very acid, you may want to add several handfuls of limestone for most trees and shrubs.)

The balance of the soil should also be well mixed with peat moss, leaf mold, or vermiculite. If it is hard clay, sand or vermiculite will help to break it up. (Sometimes it is well to abandon the soil altogether and bring in some good garden loam for the planting.) After filling the hole to the depth required by the roots of the plant, flood it with water to settle the bottom soil. When this has drained away, place the tree in the position in which it is to grow and work the soil about it. Be sure that there are no air pockets; use a stick or shovel handle, as well as your hands and feet, to work the soil under and around all roots. But use care in doing this to see that the roots are not injured. Never tramp on the burlapped ball of a plant in such a way as to rock it so that roots get broken. The roots are important, as the fine fiber-like ones are feeders for the plant. If the tree is bare-root, any broken or diseased roots should be cut off clean.

Plant the tree at approximately the same depth as it grew in the nursery. You can gauge this by the ring on the trunk. Lay the roots out naturally if the tree is bare-root. When the hole is two-thirds filled, tramp it firmly with the feet and again flood it with water to compact the soil and

Transplanting a dormant tree: first measure the size of the future root ball.

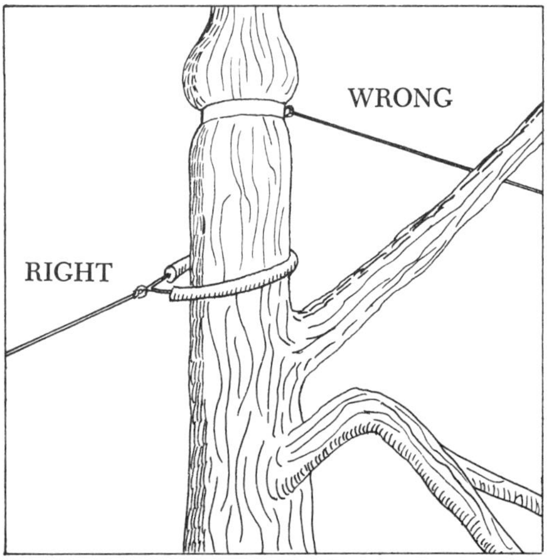

The "rights and wrongs" of guying a tree. Too tight a noose chokes trunk, may lead to later breaking in strong wind. Right method allows tree to grow and move naturally but still yields support.

Transplanting a dormant tree: removing soil to start formation of the root ball.

Transplanting a dormant tree: after digging and removing soil to desired depth, shovel is used to sever roots under ball.

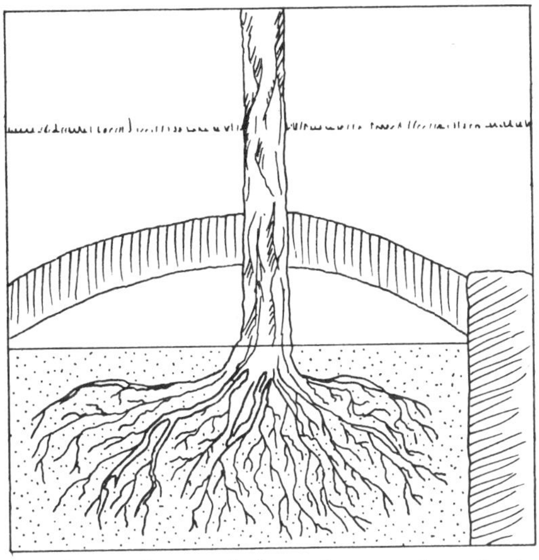

Profile of planting hole and roots after planting. Roots should be spread out naturally and soil tramped firmly.

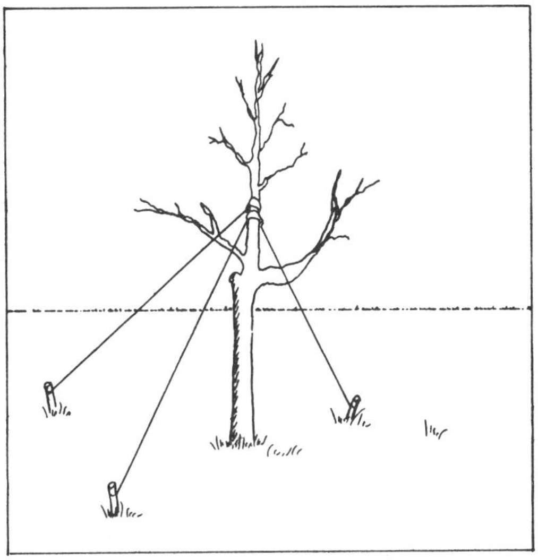

After planting, prune to a single leader. Put in guy wires as necessary to hold tree against wind.

Transplanting a dormant tree: by carefully rocking and tipping tree, burlap is worked under ball.

Transplanting a dormant tree: small trees like this can be carried to new planting locations without closing up burlap. Larger plants may need burlap closed with cord and nails to prevent disturbing root ball in transporting and planting operations.

destroy air pockets. Now place the balance of the soil loosely in position. Do not tramp or firm it, but grade it so that any water will drain toward the trunk of the tree. The crown of the tree should now be cut back considerably, perhaps at least one-third, if this pruning has not been done by the nursery. (Most nurseries send out their plants properly pruned.) If it has only one leader or principal stem, it should not be topped.

If the tree has any size it should be braced with guy wires run through pieces of old rubber hose where they touch the tree so as not to injure the bark.

On younger trees it is good practice to apply a mulch each fall, cultivating it into the soil in the spring. If the planting is done in the spring, a mulch of straw or leaves will hold the moisture in the ground. Strawy manure is good, but hard to obtain these days. Use anything that is available – compost, leaf mold or rotting leaves, wood chips, pine needles.

It is essential that young trees and shrubs obtain a ready supply of moisture. Excellent results can be obtained from placing a piece of tile upright in the planting hole. A hose may be placed in this and the roots supplied with water by allowing it to run for 10 or 15 minutes slowly. Or, better still, put a "Y" in your hose and supply several trees at the same time. Chemical fertilizer can also be supplied by pouring it in solution into this hole.

Fertilizer Requirements

Few people realize the spread of the roots of a tree. Fifty feet is not unusual for a root to travel to reach water and nourishment. Many feeding roots, however, are just under the edge of the branches where the drip of the water falls upon them. Nature has arranged the tree to conserve for its own use almost all moisture which falls upon its surface. Part of the rainfall is siphoned down the stem of the leaf upon the branch, and then down the trunk. If the ground is properly graded, this water flows deep into the soil where it is held for the use of the taproot during dry weather. The water which drips off the edge of the leaves falls directly upon the feeding roots where it can be used by the tree at once.

Most people know that the tree breathes through its leaves, but few realize the necessity for air around its feeding roots. In the forest, trees are fed under natural conditions by a decaying litter of leaves returning to the soil food and water-holding material previously taken from it.

Under most home garden conditions, trees are brought into competition with grass from which all leaves are carefully raked. They are often planted in ground in which all topsoil has been stripped or hopelessly lost in the building of a house. They may require feeding by artificial means; and if they show signs of distress, the soil should be loosened under their branches to prevent the smothering of the feeding roots by tight, heavy clay. In dry weather the lawn should be kept well watered. If the trees appear to be dying in the top during the summer, if the foliage is pale and thin, or if the leaves have a slightly wilted appearance in the morning, they may be dying of hunger and thirst. Other possibilities to consider are that they have received some wound or that they have been attacked by insect or disease pests.

Feeding trees is just as important as providing the right diet for other plants in the garden. Well-fed trees are better able to withstand insect attacks, diseases, storm damage, and drought conditions. But tree roots have little chance of absorbing the plant food if it is placed on the surface of the soil. Either it is consumed by grasses and plants under the branches or it is washed away before it has a chance of going down into the ground.

Holes should be made with a punch bar or soil auger, from 18 to 24 inches deep and about 2 feet apart, starting from about 2 feet from the trunk (depending on the size of the tree) and extending to the outer branches. A rule of thumb is to measure the diameter of the tree trunk a foot above ground, then start feeding at the same distance from it. For instance, if the tree trunk measures 12 inches, the feeding would start 12 inches from the trunk. It is not necessary or advisable to make all the holes the same depth; tree roots may be at various levels under the soil.

While there are especially prepared fertilizers for trees, any plant food high in nitrogen such as 10-8-6 or 10-6-4, will be satisfactory. Use about 2 to 4 pounds of the fertilizer for each inch in diameter of the tree trunk at breast height. Small trees, less than 6 inches in diameter will require only half of the dosage.

A method of restoring to the ground some of the natural growing conditions is to mulch the area as suggested earlier. Don't expect your trees to continue to grow in a 4-foot space between curb and sidewalk unless you feed and care for them and also prepare a space beyond the sidewalk where they may feed. In almost all cities there is a process available by which the ground can be broken up and fertilizer injected by compressed air.

If your tree has suffered the loss of a part of its root system by the installation of gas, sewer, or water pipes or by the paving of a street or walk, feed it well until it has time to form new roots. If they have enough stored vitality they will send their roots 200 feet under walks and paving in search of food, but unless they find it they simply dry up.

Insects and Diseases

If the leaves of your trees are full of small holes or eaten away, you need a stomach poison spray applied as soon as this is discovered. The chewing insect eats this stomach poison with the leaves. If tiny insects (scale) form along the trunk and branches they are best eradicated by spraying with an oil emulsion in winter or with lime sulfur in the spring before the buds start to open.

Borers sometimes attack the trunk and branches, leaving holes and, many times, sawdust where they enter. Puncture the borer by running a wire into the hole; or, if the tree is young (5 to 15 years old), dig it out carefully, disinfect the wound with creosote oil and seal with tar or grafting wax. Tubes of chemicals to squeeze into borer holes are sold by garden centers.

Never cut a branch if it can be avoided. Do not let butchers mutilate your trees or shrubs. Do not cut them back to make them thicker. Coat all wounds with a good tree paint, liquid asphaltum, a good grade shellac, or even a good lead house paint. Do not coat the entire trunk.

There is a trend – perhaps a healthy one on the whole – toward less use of poisons in the garden. Trees can show the same resiliency as do humans in bouncing back to full health from various ailments. The heavy infestations of certain pests, the canker worm for instance, are cyclical occurrences that the home gardener can hardly hope to affect.

Some of the best friends that the tree has are insectivorous birds. For this reason they should be encouraged to stay in the garden. Have water available for them to bathe in and drink, houses for them to live in and include in your planting small fruits, such as berries and cherries.

Repair Work

Most tree surgeons are university men who have made a lifetime study of trees. However, many so-called tree men are merely butchers who have taken up this line with no preparation. Any considerable amount of work calls for expert attention, but there are many small things which the gardener can do for his own trees.

The bark keeps out insects and diseases; therefore, keep the bark-growing tissue (the cambium) as healthy as possible. The removal of branches must be done so that new growth, called a callus, may completely heal over the wound before decay sets in.

Tree pruning series. First step in removing large limb from tree is to undercut the bark to prevent later tearing.

Make second cut on top a few inches outward from first half cut. Saw through.

It is important that all wounds drain; hence any cut upon a tree should be perpendicular, and as close to the bark as possible without injuring it. Large branches should be cut off in 3 sections. The first cut is to get rid of the weight, the second is to prevent any tearing below the branch to be removed, and the third is to finish the cut.

The filling of cavities is a job to be handled with great care. All diseased tissue must be removed, and a certain amount of apparently healthy tissue must also be taken to insure a complete removal of the diseased parts. This is done with a gouge chisel or knife after which all exposed sapwood is given a coat of good shellac. If the cavity is to be left unfilled, the surface can be given a protective coat of liquid asphalt, *not* creosote or any strong corrosive material. White lead or paint is not satisfactory.

Most people think that filling the cavities with cement is for the protection of the tree. It is usually done for appearance's sake. A cavity, if well waterproofed and drained, may be left open for inspection at any time.

When a new home is being built and existing trees have been marked for survival, it will probably be necessary to protect their trunks with boards wired together as otherwise they are bound to be mauled by the dumping of building materials and various comings and goings involved with the building. Any severe grading operation is bound to injure surface

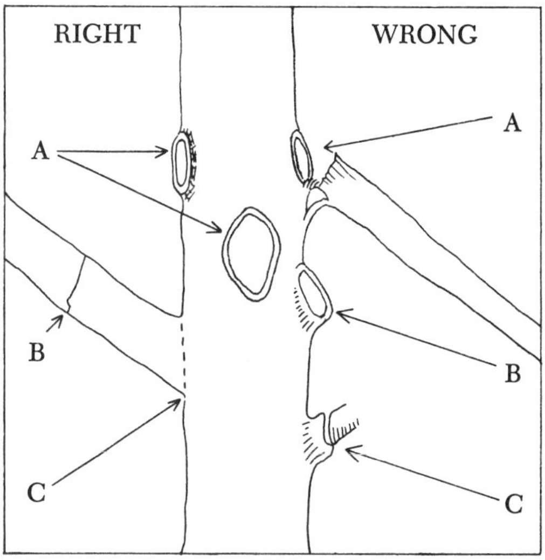

"Rights and wrongs" of pruning: Wrong "A" shows how bark can tear and wound when only one cut is made. Wrong "B" shows bad cut that can collect water and disease. Wrong "C" shows cut that is too far from trunk. Right "A" shows neat cut, flush with trunk, ready to form callus. Right "B" shows proper removal of heavy limb in three steps. Right "C" points to third and final cut in removing limb.

Final cut close to tree's trunk (outlined in chalk).

A clean cut close to trunk will heal smoothly. Use aerosol tree paint to cover cut.

roots. When grades are permanently changed so that the soil is raised or lowered a foot or more around trees, some sort of tree well must be constructed around the trunk.

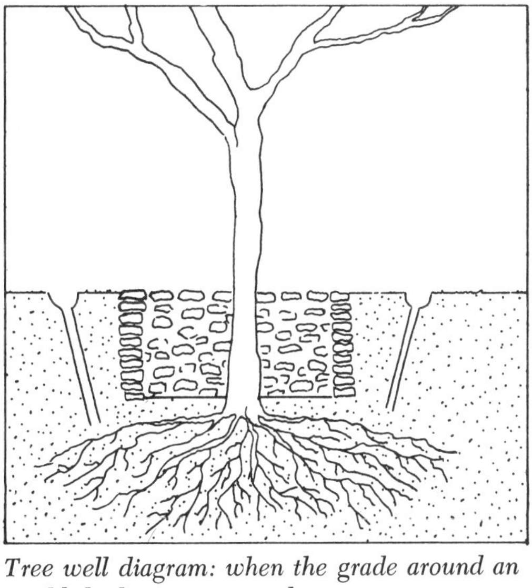

Tree well diagram: when the grade around an established tree is raised, it is necessary to construct a well around the trunk so air and moisture can continue to reach roots. Well is usually lined with stones or bricks. Installing tiles beyond the well, as shown, admits additional air and water to roots.

Landscaping with Shrubs

As important as trees are to the gardener and homeowner, perhaps even more vital today are shrubs, both deciduous and evergreen. (See Chapter 6 for Broad-Leaved Evergreens and Acid-Soil Plants.) As the cost of land goes up and as suburban lots become smaller and smaller, shrubs rather than trees have become the dominant planting.

The selection of deciduous shrubs available today for the home gardener is a remarkably varied one. The old standbys get better – there are several excellent improvements in forsythia – and every now and then a brand new shrub appears. One such introduction is the white forsythia (*Abeliophyllum distichum*), so called because its early spring white flowers resemble those of forsythia.

The majority of deciduous shrubs bloom in spring and early summer, but there are selections for summer, too. Like trees, some shrubs have attractive fall coloring before their leaves drop. Some shrubs with outstanding fall color include burning-bush (*Euonymus alatus*), alpine currant (*Ribes alpinum*), redvein enkianthus (*Enkianthus campanulatus*), and Japanese barberry (*Berberis thunbergi*).

Forsythia 'Lynwood Gold' has bright golden-yellow flowers in early spring. Its growth can be restricted by annual pruning after flowering.

The firethorn (Pyracantha) *has bright orange-red berries in fall. Its clustered white flowers in late spring are effective but not as showy.*

Other shrubs are known for their fine berry display which is attractive to look at and also keeps winter birds in the area. Some of the best shrubs for fruit effects are many of the barberries, cotoneasters, deciduous hollies, viburnums (*Viburnum wrighti* has outstanding red berries as well as red autumn foliage), sapphire-berry (*Symplocos paniculata*), firethorn (*Pyracantha coccinea*) and sea-buckthorn (*Hippophaë rhamnoides*).

The correct planting time for deciduous shrubs is the same as for trees – from late fall as the leaves drop to spring before new leaf growth starts. Of course, as with any woody plant, balled-and-burlapped shrubs can be planted when purchased (even if they are in leaf or flower as there is no root disturbance). Many nurseries offer shrubs in containers for planting from spring to fall. If the can is cut in two places so it can be pried apart, there is very little root disturbance, if any, at planting.

It is usual to select shrubs that grow well in your locality and for foolproof results this is the only way. For an adventure that often ends with success, experiment a little with plants that are not quite hardy in your area. If you can create a microclimate (a special, protected setting) that suits them, you will add much to your gardening enjoyment.

Landscaping with Shrubs

Shrubs should be selected carefully for height. A shrub which normally grows 6 feet high is very hard to keep pruned back to 3 feet. Care must be taken to give shrubs a reasonable amount of space. They usually appear best in groups and are rarely effective in single rows. Where space is available a border is best – on small properties it is better to fill the corners. Avoid straight lines both as to the shape of the border and the planting. Do not get too many of one variety in a group. Three or four are sufficient for the ordinary border. The taller plants should be in the rear, the

When transplanting a thorny or wide-spread shrub, it helps to tie up branches. Excavated soil can be placed in wheelbarrow or on burlap.

Trees and shrubs of all kinds are now available in cans from local outlets. Most tin cans are being replaced by plastic containers that are more easily slit for removal of plant.

medium in the middle, and the smaller at the front. Include broad-leaved evergreen shrubs in the border, too. Also, an occasional accent of a small tree or very tall shrub adds interest to the planting.

Straight top lines should also be avoided by keeping in mind the ultimate height of the various plants. Alternate the rows by high and low plantings. Where the border is deep, that is, from front to back, tall plants may be used in the background; but where the border becomes shallow, lower plants should be used. This gives an appearance of greater depth. Variety may be obtained by the introduction of groups of bulbs and ground cover in the foreground.

When a border or group of shrubs is to be planted in the same location, it pays to prepare the entire planting area rather than digging a series of holes. This is when a power tiller comes in so handily. If you don't own one (and don't plan on having a vegetable garden or extensive flower garden which would make it worthwhile for you to buy your own power cultivator), you can rent one from a local outlet. By running over the area several times, you can cultivate to a depth of 8 to 10 inches or more (depending on the structure of your soil). The various conditioning materials that you need to add (peat moss, leaf mold, a complete fertilizer) can be mixed with the soil by tilling. Later, you can use the tiller to dig deeper holes, if needed, for each shrub if there is maneuvering space. Planting distances between shrubs in a border depend, of course, on the ultimate spread of each shrub. Variations between 3 to 5 feet will suit the majority of shrubs.

See that the ground is firm about the roots to avoid air pockets, and settle the ground by watering. A mulch of whatever material is available will prevent weed growth and conserve moisture.

Pruning Shrubs

Do not prune early-flowering shrubs each spring unless you don't mind removing the flowering branches. The majority of flowering shrubs bloom on the new wood produced during the growing season of the previous year. Prune within a few weeks after the flowers fall to give new wood a chance to ripen for next year's bloom.

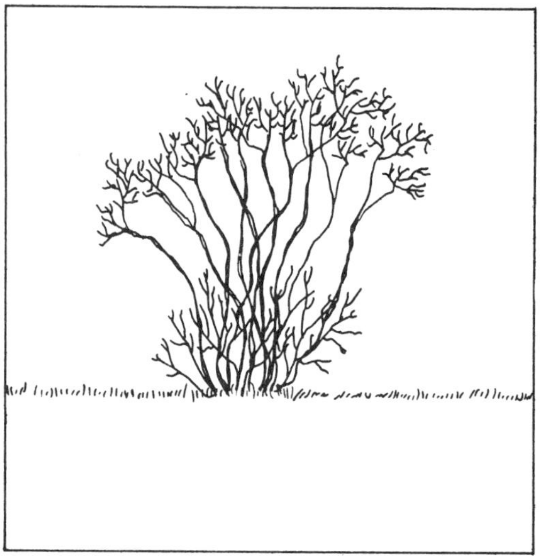

Overgrown, straggly shrubs are unsightly and give poor flower display.

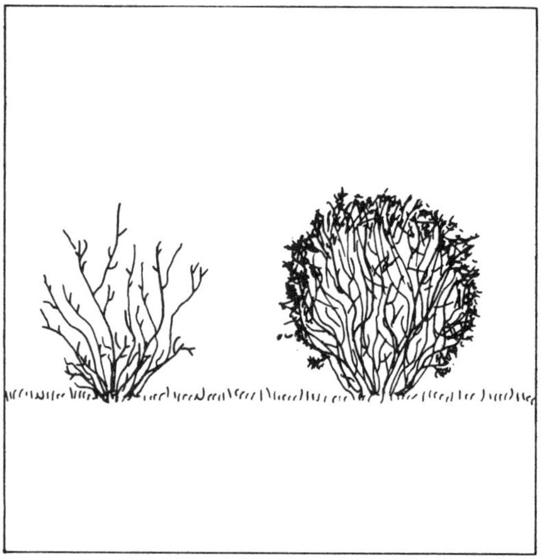

Correct pruning: properly pruned shrub (left) *results in balanced growth* (right).

The idea is to remove old wood, usually at the base, to shorten stray shoots and to shape those plants that need it. Often very little pruning is required other than the removal of old wood. The following shrubs are examples: forsythia, shrub dogwood, Japanese quince (trim also to improve form), kerria, fragrant honeysuckle, mock-orange, spring-blooming spirea, jetbead, lilac.

A few shrubs offer special problems in pruning to many gardeners because their flowering habits are not understood. The French or florist's hydrangea, with bright blue or pink flowers, is an example. There are many kinds of hydrangeas, and most of them can be cut back severely in early spring because they flower on new wood. But the French hydrangea (*Hydrangea macrophylla or hortensis*) produces its flowers from buds formed the previous season; so pruning in early spring naturally destroys these buds. Any necessary pruning should be done in summer after the flowers have faded.

Certain shrubs should be cut back to the ground in early spring to make a more compact habit. They include indigo bush, butterfly bush (except *Buddleia alternifolia* which flowers on wood of the previous season so should be pruned to shape the plant directly after flowering in early summer), certain varieties of shrub althea or rose of Sharon like 'Bluebird' and 'Vitex.'

The general rule is to trim early-flowering shrubs just after they bloom. Trim late-flowering (summer or fall) or berry-bearing shrubs in March.

Renovating Old Shrubs

Temper your shears with brains; do not just lop off a few outer branches. The neglected shrub may seem to be a hopeless mass of branches, but proceed gradually. Reach into the bush, and remove first all dead wood. This may be done at any season. Second, cut off some of the oldest branches right down to the base. Always keep some of the old wood and yet have new shoots coming from the bottom, not only on the outside of the plant, but in the center. This means that your trimming must admit light and air to the center to support this growth. Remember, shrubbery does not have to be pruned every year. It is more a process of thinning out than of trimming back, and, instead of being a seasonal flurry, it can be spread over the year or several years with benefit to the gardener as well as to the plant.

Overgrown screen and massed shrubs

Large shrubs which grow in clumps can be divided by hatchet or axe as shown.

Usual arrangement for informal shrub border is to plant large shrubs in rear, medium in center and low-growing shrubs in front. Stagger the plants rather than setting them in a straight line. Larger shrubs should be planted farther apart than smaller ones.

can be cut to the ground as a last resort, but if this would leave an ugly gap, the renovating, as described above, can be extended over several seasons. Shrubs with arching branches such as *Buddleia alternifolia, Forsythia, Kolkwitzia,* and *Spiraea vanhouttei* present a difficult problem if allowed to get out of hand, for they should not have their sweeping grace marred by the ugly stubs and laterals left by top cutting. They require thinning from the ground and careful heading in of the tops when removing the branches with their faded flowers.

Sometimes but not often, it may be worthwhile to revive an old shrubbery border (in fall or spring) by dividing the bushes which have outgrown their location. Their crowns may be split with a hatchet and the divisions pruned both as to roots and top. The oldest wood should be removed as should all broken or bruised roots.

Trees and Shrubs for Special Purposes

A SELECTION OF THE SMALLER TREES FOR ACCENT AND LIGHT SHADE

(f = flowers)

Acer ginnala (Amur maple) 15 ft.
Acer palmatum (Japanese maple) 6 to 20 ft.
Albizzia julibrissin (Silk tree) 35 ft. (f)
Amelanchier grandiflora (Shadbush) 25 ft. (f)
Betula papyrifera (Paper birch) 40 ft.
Betula pendula laciniata (Cutleaf weeping birch) 35 ft.
Cercis canadensis (Redbud) 30 ft. (f)
Chionanthus virginica (Fringetree) 20 ft. (f)
Cornus alternifolia (Pagoda dogwood) 20 ft. (f)
Cornus florida (Flowering dogwood) 25 ft. (f)
Cornus kousa (Chinese dogwood) 20 ft. (f)
Cornus nuttali (Western flowering dogwood) 75 ft.
Crataegus various (Hawthorn) 20 ft.
Davidia involucrata (Dove tree) 40 ft. (f)
Euonymus bungeanus (Spindle tree) 15 ft.
Euonymus europeus (Spindle tree) 10 ft.
Gordonia alatamaha (Franklin tree) 20 ft. (f)
Halesia monticola (Silverbell tree) 30 ft. (f)
Koelreuteria paniculata (Goldenrain tree) 30 ft. (f)
Laburnum anagyroides (Golden chain tree) 20 ft. (f)
Magnolia "Dr. Merrill" hybrid 10 ft. (f)

Magnolia soulangeana (Saucer magnolia) 20 ft. (f)
Magnolia stellata (Star magnolia) 8 ft. (f)
Malus various (Flowering crabapple) 15 to 30 ft. (f)
Oxydendrum arboreum (Sourwood) 20 ft. (f)
Prunus various (Flowering cherry, etc.) 15 to 30 ft.
Robinia pseudo-acacia fatigiata (Locust) 25 ft. (f)
Salix blanda (Wisconsin weeping willow) 40 ft.
Salix matsudana tortuosa (Corkscrew willow) 20 ft.
Saphora japonica (Japanese pagoda tree) 60 ft. (f)
Sorbus various (Mountain ash) 30 to 45 ft. (f)
Stewartia pseudo-camellia (Stewartia) 50 ft. (f)
Styrax japonica (Storax) 30 ft. (f)
Syringa amurensis japonica (Tree lilac) 30 ft. (f)
Wisteria sinensis (Chinese wisteria, tree form) 8 to 15 ft. (f)

A SELECTION OF TREES AND SHRUBS FOR FRAGRANCE

Abeliophyllum distichum (White forsythia) 6 ft.
Buddleia davidi (Butterfly-bush) 8 ft.
Calycanthus floridus (Strawberry shrub) 7 ft.
Chimonanthus praecox (Wintersweet) 4 to 6 ft.
Chionanthus virginica (Fringe tree) 15 ft.
Choisya ternata (Mexican-orange) 6 ft.
Cladrastus lutea (Yellow-wood) 45 ft.
Clethra alnifolia (Summersweet) 8 ft.
Corylopsis spicata (Winter hazel) 6 ft.
Daphne burkwoodi (Somerset daphne) 5 ft.
Daphne cneorum (Garland-flower) 1 ft.
Daphne mezereum (February daphne) 3 ft.
Daphne odora (Winter daphne) 4 ft.
Fothergilla gardeni (Dwarf fothergilla) 3 ft.
Fothergilla monticola (Fothergilla) 6 ft.
Gordonia alatamaha (Franklin tree) 10 ft.
Hamamelis mollis (Witch hazel) 6 to 10 ft.
Itea virginica (Sweet spire) 3 to 6 ft.
Ligustrum various (Privet 6 to 10 ft.
Lonicera fragrantissima (Winter honeysuckle) 6 ft.
Magnolia various (Magnolia) 10 to 50 ft.
Malus various (Flowering crab) 15 ft.
Philadelphus various (Mock-orange) 5 to 10 ft.
Pterostyrax hispida (Epaulette-tree) 40 ft.
Rhododendron arborescens (Sweet azalea) 8 ft.
Rho. molle (Chinese azalea) 6 ft.
Rho. nudiflorum (Pinxterbloom) 6 ft.
Rho. roseum (Roseshell azalea) 8 ft.
Rho. viscosum (Swamp azalea) 8 ft.
Ribes odoratum (Flowering currant) 6 ft.
Robinia pseudo-acacia (False-acacia) 80 ft.
Rosa various (Rose) 4 to 8 ft.
Syringa various (Lilac) 10 ft.
Viburnum burkwoodii (Fragrant V.) 8 ft.
Viburnum carlcephalum (Fragrant V.) 6 ft.
Viburnum carlesi (Pink snowball) 6 ft.
Viburnum fragrans (Fragrant V.) 8 ft.
Wisteria sinensis (Wisteria, tree form) 8 to 15 ft.

TREES AND SHRUBS THAT ENDURE SHADE

Amelanchier various (Shadbush)
Aronia melanocarpa elata (Glossy chokeberry)
Clethra alnifolia (Summersweet)
Cornus florida (Flowering dogwood)
Cornus racemosa (Gray dogwood)
Cornus sanguinea (Blood-twig dogwood)
Euonymus alatus (Winged euonymus)
Euonymus europaea (European burning-bush)
Forsythia suspensa (Weeping forsythia)
Hamamelis various (Witch hazel)
Hydrangea arborescens grandiflora (Snowhill hydrangea)
Hydrangea quercifolia (Oak-leaf hydrangea)
Ilex verticillata (Winterberry)
Ligustrum various (Privet)
Lonicera various (Honeysuckle)
Myrica pensylvanica (Bayberry)
Rhamnus frangula (Buckthorn)
Rhodotypos kerrioides (Jetbead)
Rhus canadensis (Fragrant sumac)
Ribes alpinum (Mountain currant)
Ribes odoratum (Flowering currant)
Symphoricarpos various (Snow- and coralberry)
Viburnum various (Viburnum)

SHRUBS FOR WINTER TWIG EFFECTS

Cornus alba siberica (Red-twig dogwood)
Cornus sanguinea (Blood-twig dogwood)
Cornus stolonifera flaviramea (Golden-twig dogwood)
Cytisus praecox (Broom)

The star magnolia (Magnolia stellata) *flowers so early in spring that its blooms are often frost-nipped.*

Forsythia intermedia spectabilis (Showy forsythia)
Kerria japonica (Kerria)
Poncirus trifoliata (Hardy orange)
Rosa virginiana (Virginia rose)
Rosa rubrifolia (Redleaf rose)
Salix purpurea (Purple osier)
Vaccinium corymbosum (Blueberry)

SHRUBS FOR BACKGROUND AND LARGE BORDERS

Aronia melonocarpa elata
Buddleia various
Cercis chinensis (Chinese redbud)
Chionanthus virginica (Fringetree)
Cornus mas (Cornelian cherry)
Cotoneaster dielsiana
Cotoneaster racemiflora
Deutzia scabra (Deutzia)
Euonymus alatus (Winged euonymus)
Forsythia various (Golden bell)
Kolkwitzia amabilis (Beauty-bush)
Ligustrum various (Privet)
Lonicera fragrantissima (Winter honeysuckle)
Lonicera korolkowi (Blueleaf honeysuckle)
Lonicera maacki (Amur honeysuckle)
Philadelphus various (Mock-orange)
Prunus tomentosa (Nanking cherry)
Prunus triloba plena (Double flowering plum)
Rhus cotinus (Smoke tree)
Syringa vulgaris hybrids (Lilac)
Viburnum burkwoodii (Fragrant viburnum)
Viburnum carlesi (Pink snowball)
Viburnum opulus (Cranberry bush)
Viburnum tomentosum (Doublefile viburnum)
Viburnum wrighti (Wright V.)
Vitex agnus-castus (Chaste tree)
Weigela various (Weigela)

SPREADING SHRUBS FOR BANKS AND ROUGH PLACES

Berberis thunbergi (Japanese barberry)
Cornus stolonifera flaviramea (Golden-twig dogwood)
Cotoneaster apiculata (Cranberry cotoneaster)
Cotoneaster horizontalis (Rockspray)
Cotoneaster salicifolia (Willowleaf C.)
Forsythia suspensa (Weeping forsythia)
Lonicera maacki (Amur honeysuckle)
Myrica pensylvanica (Bayberry)
Prunus pumila (Sand cherry)
Rhus various (Sumac)
Rosa wichuraiana (Memorial rose)
Spiraea tomentosa (Hardhack)
Stephanandra incisa (Cutleaf stephanandra)
Symphoricarpos albus (Snowberry)
Symphoricarpos chenaulti (Chenault coralberry)
Symphoricarpos orbiculatus (Coralberry)

TREES AND SHRUBS WITH RED BERRIES

Aronia arbutifolia (Red chokeberry)
Berberis thunbergi (Japanese barberry)
Cornus florida (Flowering dogwood)
Cotoneaster dielsiana (Diels cotoneaster)
Cotoneaster divaricata (Spreading cotoneaster)
Cotoneaster horizontalis (Rock cotoneaster)
Cotoneaster racemiflora (Racemed cotoneaster)
Crataegus coccinea (Thicket hawthorn)
Crataegus cordata (Washington hawthorn)
Crataegus crusgalli (Cockspur hawthorn)
Euonymus atropurpureus (Native wahoo)
Euonymus bungeanus (Winterberry euonymus)
Euonymus europaea (European burning-bush)
Ilex verticillata (Winterberry)
Lonicera maacki (Amur honeysuckle)
Lonicera morrowi (Morrow honeysuckle)

Photinia villosa (Redberried photinia)
Pyrancantha coccinea (Firethorn)
Rosa various (Shrub rose)
Sorbus americana (American mountain ash)
Sorbus aucuparia (European mountain ash)
Viburnum americanum (American cranberry bush)
Viburnum dilatatum (Linden viburnum)
Viburnum opulus (Cranberry bush)
Viburnum wrighti (Wright V.)

SHRUBS WITH WHITE BERRIES

Cornus alba (Tartarian dogwood)
Cornus racemosa (Panicle dogwood)
Cornus stolonifera (Red-osier dogwood)
Symphoricarpos albus (Snowberry)

SHRUBS WITH BLACK BERRIES

Aronia melanocarpa (Black chokeberry)
Ligustrum regelianum (Regel privet)
Ligustrum vulgare (European privet)
Rhamnus caroliniana (Indian cherry)
Viburnum lantana (Wayfaring tree)
Viburnum prunifolium (Black-haw)
Viburnum sieboldi (Siebold viburnum)

SHRUBS WITH BLUE-BLACK BERRIES

Viburnum cassinoides (Withe-rod)
Viburnum dentatum (Arrowwood)
Viburnum lentago (Nannyberry)
Viburnum molle (Kentucky viburnum)

SHRUBS WITH BLUE BERRIES

Ampelopsis brevipedunculata (Porcelain ampelopsis)
Callicarpa purpurea (Chinese beauty-berry)
Cornus amoenum (Silky dogwood)
Symplocos paniculata (Sweetleaf)

TREES AND SHRUBS FOR A SUCCESSION OF BLOOM

(Bloom time is approximate and depends on region and weather.)

January-February
Hamamelis japonica (Japanese witch hazel)
H. mollis (Chinese witch hazel)

February-March
H. vernalis (Spring witch hazel)
Chimonanthus praecox (Wintersweet)
Cornus mas (Cornelian cherry)

The Franklin tree (Gordonia altamaha) *produces its waxy white flowers in late summer. Its lush foliage turns bright red in autumn.*

C. officinalis (Japanese dogwood)
Corylopsis spicata (Winter hazel)
Daphne mezureum (February daphne)
Daphne odora (Winter daphne)
Lonicera fragrantissima (Winter honeysuckle)

April
Abeliophyllum distichum (White forsythia)
Amelanchier various (Shadbush)
Cercis canadensis (Redbud)
Chaenomeles japonica (Flowering quince)
Exochorda grandiflora (Pearlbush)
Forsythia various (Goldenbell)
Magnolia stellata (Star magnolia)
Prunus various (Flowering almond, etc.)
Viburnum burkwoodi (Burkwood viburnum)

May
Chionanthus virginica (Fringe tree)
Cornus florida (Flowering dogwood)
Crataegus various (Hawthorn)
Cytisus praecox (Warminster broom)
Daphne cneorum (Garland flower)
D. genkwa (Blue daphne)
Davidia involucrata (Dove tree)
Deutzia various (Deutzia)
Laburnum various (Goldenchain tree)
Malus various (Flowering crab)
Prunus various (Flowering cherry)
Rhododendron various (Rhododendron and azalea)
Rosa hugonis (Father Hugo rose)
Spiraea various (Bridalwreath, etc.)
Syringa various (Lilac)

The ethereal white flowers of the shadbush (Amelanchier) *are often the first signs of advancing spring in woods.*

Viburnum tomentosum (Doublefile V.)
Weigela various (Weigela)
June
Abelia grandiflora (Glossy abelia)
Aesculus parviflora (Bottlebrush buckeye)
Buddleia alternifolia (Fountain buddleia)
Cornus kousa chinensis (Chinese dogwood)
Kalmia latifolia (Mountain laurel)
Kolkwitzia amabilis (Beauty-bush)
Philadelphus various (Mock-orange)
Potentilla fruticosa (Shrub cinquefoil)
Rosa various shrub types (Rose)
July-August
Spiraea various (Spirea)
Syringa amurensis japonica (Tree lilac)
Buddleia davidi (Butterfly-bush)
September
Clethra alnifolia (Summersweet)
Gordonia alatamaha (Franklin tree)
Hibiscus syriacus (Rose of Sharon)
Hydrangea various (Hydrangea)
Rhododendron viscosum (Swamp azalea)
Rhus cotinus (Smoke tree)
Sophora japonica (Japanese pagoda tree)
Spiraea billiardi (Billiard spirea)
Spiraea bumalda (Anthony Waterer, etc.)
Spiraea sanssouciana (Spirea)
Tamarix various (Tamarisk)
Vitex agnus-castus (Chaste tree)
October-November
Hamamelis virginiana (Witch hazel)
Prunus subhirtella autumnalis (Flowering cherry)

A slow-growing form of white pine makes a handsome accent plant several feet across, wider than it is high. It needs sun and good soil.

CHAPTER 5

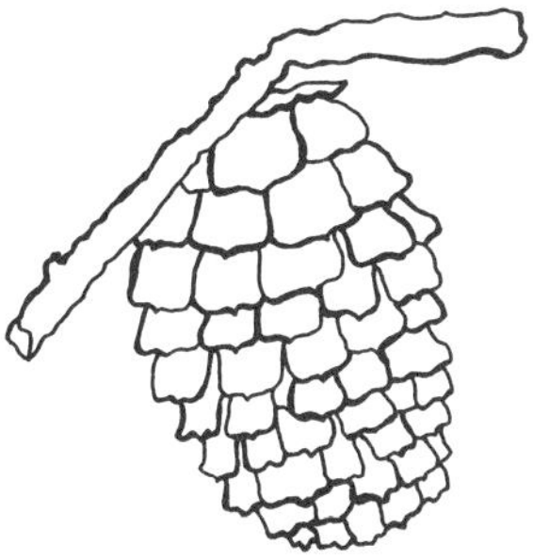

Coniferous Evergreens

Ah, happy, happy boughs! that cannot shed
Your leaves, nor ever bid the Spring adieu.
– John Keats

The range of trees covered by the term coniferous is wide. The name comes from the cone which is the "flower" of the plant and later its fruit. In size, conifers range from the little round Swiss mountain pine (*Pinus mugo*) in rock gardens to the giant sequoia of our Pacific Coast. Many conifers grow far into the North and, beyond their economic value, are of esthetic importance because often they are the only green plants visible during the long winter months.

One of the conifers (or cone-bearers) is the larch, which is not evergreen at all, but sheds its needle-like foliage in autumn the same as other deciduous plants. Another leaf-losing conifer is the fast-growing metasequoia, listed in nursery catalogs as "dawn redwood."

Included with the conifers because of their similar habits and uses and because they are narrow-leaved evergreens are the yews and the junipers or red cedars, even though they do not bear cones, but berry-like fruits. They are red and fleshy in the yews and bluish-gray and firm in the case of junipers.

The two seasons when transplanting and planting of evergreens may be most safely carried on are from late summer to early fall and from the time the frost is out of the ground in spring until the plants start to make new growth.

The advantage of late summer planting is that the roots get a chance to reestablish themselves before winter and are ready to make new growth promptly in the spring. The disadvantage is that the plants go into the rigors of winter in a weakened condition. The advantage of spring planting is that the plant gets the benefit of the most favorable growing season while weakened by the transplanting operation. However, the subsequent hot, dry days of summer may prove trying.

Larger trees may be handled more easily in February or March when a ball of frozen earth can be taken. The freezing of the soil to a solid mass makes possible the taking of the larger ball necessary to a tree of greater size.

There is a type of evergreen adaptable to almost every need, locality, and condition. Some varieties grow in swamps, at the water's edge, others upon rocky cliffs. However, the kinds used for ornament have for the most part two basic needs: good drainage and adequate moisture.

Evergreens are really never dormant and even in winter, when other plants are bare of leaves, constant transpiration is going on (in a lessened degree, of course) through

Pine hedge being set out in spring. Plants this large have screening value at once.

their foliage. Therefore, water must be supplied during a prolonged dry spell even if the weather is moderately cold and especially in late fall after a dry summer. Newly planted evergreens need special attention to their moisture needs in the fall.

Transplanting Tips

While it is usually preferable and more satisfying to go to a nursery and pick out a large, fully-formed evergreen that will immediately create the effect for which it has been selected, it can be equally satisfying and sometimes more practical to order "baby" evergreen plants through a mail-order nursery. There are many nurseries that specialize in growing evergreen seedlings, and it is possible to save money by buying these plants by the 10s, 20s or 100s.

They can be planted out in rows in a home nursery for later transplanting, or can be set out where they are to remain permanently. If space is no problem, this is one way to grow your own Christmas tree. Or, by interplanting evergreens with seedling oaks and other deciduous trees, you can start turning a portion of your home grounds into a woodland. The trees will grow faster than you might expect. Usually the nursery offers you a choice of 2- or 3-year or older seedlings, varying in size from 3 to 12 inches, depending on the kind of evergreen. Most will have been root pruned or transplanted – important because you will get a stockier, stronger root system. (Evergreen seedlings collected from the wild are quite another matter and often are hardly worth planting unless you have carefully collected them yourself.)

The young seedlings are mailed out in bundles at the right time for planting in spring or fall and of course are bare-root. They should be unpacked at once and their roots soaked overnight in a pail of water. During the actual planting process, the young plants should be protected from drying out. Keep them in a pail of water until they are planted.

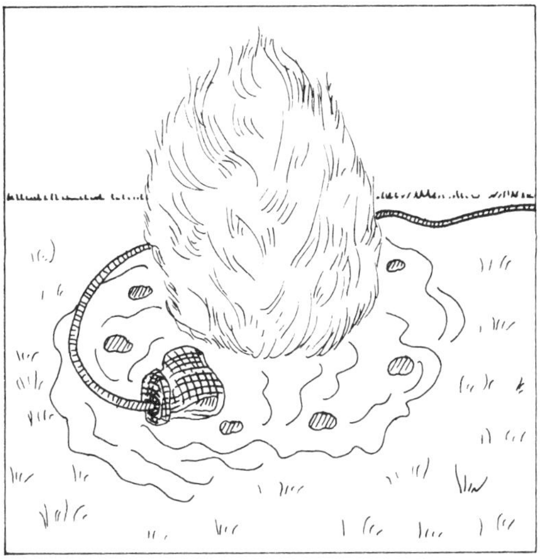

Preparing soil around plant to be dug: holes admit water applied daily for a week. Burlap tied over end of hose prevents washing of soil.

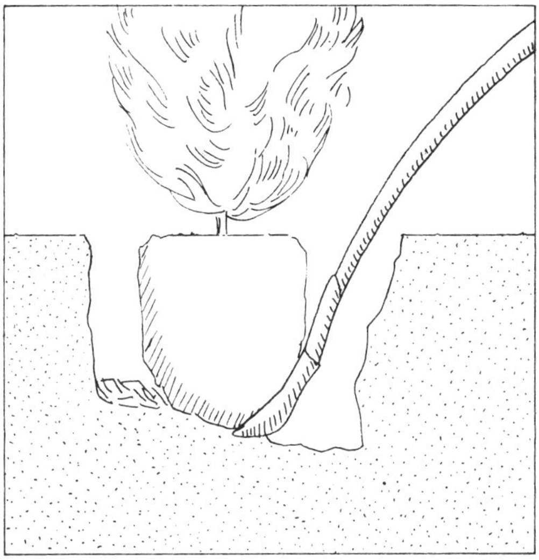

Digging a conifer to be moved. Cut trench, then work soil out from beneath roots.

Evergreens that are just beyond the seedling stage should be lifted with as much soil about their roots as possible and a large tree should always be transplanted with a ball of earth. The larger the ball, the quicker the recovery. Here is the right way to move large evergreens, as it is done in a nursery or on your own property:

If the season is at all dry, first cultivate the area around the tree, then force a bar into the ground in a series of holes 2 or 3 feet deep around the tree. This circle should be of the size of the ball which you intend to take. Water this for several hours daily with a gentle stream. Grade the ground to turn the water into the holes. Repeat for about a week and allow to dry for several days.

Now prepare the planting hole in the new location. Dig it twice as wide as the ball and half again as deep. If your soil is clay or is heavy, work a quantity of sand and gravel deeply into the bottom. Fill the hole with water and allow to drain away several times. If the soil removed is heavy, make it friable with sand, and work in some thoroughly rotted manure or peat moss and bone meal or superphosphate.

Dig a trench around the tree to be moved, sloping one side to admit a wooden platform. Work the earth from beneath the tree, cutting the bottom roots cleanly with a knife or saw and trimming all broken roots cleanly. Secure the burlap tightly around the root ball with strong cord and nails used as pins. (The tree's roots should be covered and kept moist at all times.) Tilt the burlapped ball against the platform and tie it securely in place with rope or heavy cord.

A rope handle can be fastened to the top

Using platform to move plant. Stout cords hold trunk and root ball to platform. Rope handle (top) facilitates lifting.

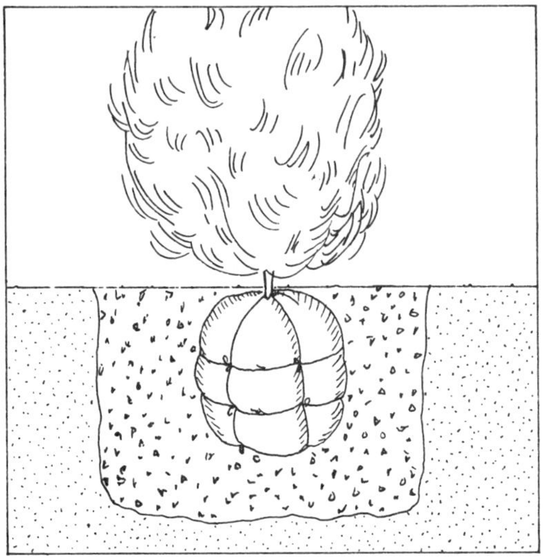

Relative size of root ball and well-prepared planting hole. Plant has been set lower than its previous growing level.

of the platform to facilitate lifting. The platform method allows moving a larger ball; if this is firmly secured in place, breakage and jar are minimized. Lower the ball into the new location, and then untie. Remove or loosen or carefully slit burlap and proceed to plant, using care to firm all earth to avoid future settling. Firming the soil around evergreen roots is second in importance only to watering. Keep soil from drying out for several weeks and until fall if the planting is done in the spring.

If you are buying an evergreen and if the tree is large it will come to you with the branches tied to avoid injury to them. If you are unable to plant the tree at once and the weather is warm, it is well to untie the branches until you are ready to plant. Also, wet the ball and cover it with straw, sacks, or other material to keep it from drying out.

When you are ready, place the tree, with its branches tied, at a convenient spot near the hole. You will notice upon the trunk a soil line which indicates the depth at which it was planted in the nursery. Your planting should be at the same level or an inch lower than the nursery planting. Be very careful to see that the tree is planted on a bed of well-firmed soil, so that it will

Handling a conifer during transplanting is easier if branches are tied with soft twine.

Young tree in place in a hole twice as wide as root ball. Soil under the plant has been firmed.

How to lift a root ball. This pine has been set into hole partly filled with prepared soil.

Firming the soil around conifers is essential. Tread soil down around root ball only.

not sink after it is wet. The preparation of the hole and the actual planting will be as already described. Some nurseries coat the roots with mud or clay by dipping them before shipment when they are not protected by a good ball. This coating should be softened by soaking before planting is done. Be sure that all broken or injured roots are cut off cleanly. Cracks or bad bruises may form a place for disease to enter and cause trouble later.

If the tree is of considerable size, it is important that its branches be kept tied during the planting so the ends will not become bruised or broken. However, it is difficult to set the tree in its proper position without knowing something of its shape. Therefore, the branches can be untied after the tree has been placed in the hole; then it may be turned about before the burlap is loosened to obtain the best position. Then tie them up again loosely to get them out of the way until the planting is finished.

If the planting location is exposed to strong winds, support the tree by tying some soft material about its trunk and fastening it to a stake or post driven into the ground. If the season is well advanced, a windbreak of some kind on the windward side may be necessary to prevent the drying out of the tender new foliage.

Tender foliage of newly planted evergreen sheltered by a windbreak.

Mulching the ground around evergreens with about 2 inches of some loose, porous material will help retain moisture and keep their roots cool. Use compost, pine needles, rotted strawy manure, leaf mold, pine bark, or whatever material is available. Be sure that the mulch stays loose and that air penetrates it easily.

Facts on Pruning Conifers

Balsam and concolor firs (*Abies*) may be thickened by judicious shearing when young, but the concolor fir should be planted where it can develop naturally, as its greatest charm is in the young growth as it fans out each spring.

The upright junipers (*Juniperus*) respond to light shearing when a formal effect is desired. The Canert red cedar makes a fine specimen and bears more berries when unsheared; for a tall hedge, it should be topped lightly as should the Keteleeri variety. Other upright forms are best allowed to follow their own habit of growth. All spreading varieties may need heading back to keep them under control in restricted places. The Pfitzer juniper makes a rapid growth and will give trouble if allowed to get out of hand. Take off the oldest branches by slipping the shears in under new shoots so the stubs will not show. The natural grace of the tree should be preserved.

The spruces (*Picea*) can be thickened by pinching off the center bud on each twig in early spring, or clipping off half of each new twig in June. They can be sheared when young, but, as with the firs, the leader must not be cut. Specimen trees, especially the blue spruces, must have room to develop without interference.

Swiss mountain pines (*Pinus mugo*) can be kept compact by shearing or by taking off one-half of each soft leader or "candle" in June.

The yews (*Taxus*) and arborvitaes (*Thuja*) respond readily to pruning if the shape of the plant is kept in mind. They shear readily into hedges when young. *Taxus media* hybrids can be trimmed into globes but the Hatfield variety should be left in its natural irregular form. Wire its upright stems together lightly with insulated electric wire to avoid snow damage, as is sometimes done with pyramidal arborvitae. This also makes formal shearing easier. To get the desired outline, shear horizontally around the bottom for a foot or so, then work to the top with vertical cuts. To trim globes, trim a zone around the middle, and work up and down to it.

The junipers in this Japanese garden have been trained formally and closely sheared.

Insects and Diseases

If ever we need visual evidence that the atmosphere of our major cities is polluted, we can look at parks that contain mature plantings of coniferous evergreens. The majority of these plants are decrepit, not from old age, but from the poisonous fumes and gases that are spewed into the air every day. So unless you live a reasonable distance from a big city and its miserable air, you cannot expect most conifers to grow well. Under poor growing conditions

Hemlock can be trained as an espalier. The light tips are early-summer growth.

The mugo pines in this planting can be kept low by shearing or by pinching tip "candles."

and when adequate moisture is lacking, they will be more susceptible to disease and insect pests. In cities and suburbs, frequently wash off the soot and grime deposited from the air. Evergreen foliage is sticky and impurities tend to smother it. An occasional shower is an excellent tonic and also helps suppress red spider mites, often a pest of evergreens.

The cedar-apple, or gall, is caused by the apple-rust fungus whose life cycle includes 4 to 5 months on the apple and 18 or more months on the red cedar (*Juniperus virginiana*). Its presence on the latter causes a brownish gall to form on the tree which becomes active after the warm spring rains and throws off spores from its soft orange-colored, gelatinous horns. These spores infect apple leaves, and there develop new spores which are carried by the wind to the same or other junipers. Hawthorns, native crabs, and their hybrids are also susceptible to this and other fungus pests, and in some sections cannot be grown with success. Actually, the junipers are not generally as harmed by this back-and-forth disease, but the apples and crabs can become debilitated, as severe attacks of the rusts cause defoliation. The Chinese crabs seem to be resistant and are replacing the Bechtels in many plantings. Control consists of destroying badly infected cedars and replacing them with less susceptible varieties, though the best plan is not to grow the alternate host plants within a mile or two of one another. The galls can be reduced by hand-picking throughout the year as they mature, and both cedars and apples can be sprayed in the spring with lime-sulfur or fermate.

Bagworms weave spindle-shaped bags on a foundation of the needles of the trees on which they live. In them the young are hatched in the spring to carry on in the same manner. They are found on many varieties of evergreens, but seem to prefer juniper, spruce, arborvitae, and larch. Hand-picking the bags and destroying them will take care of light infestations, but spraying all trees in the yard with arsenate of lead, carbaryl or malathion will kill the

Some dwarf conifers for the home garden. Left to right, hemlock, spruce, pine.

Pine windbreak on an exposed, sandy site shelters plantings of broom, spring bulbs, blue forget-me-nots.

young worms. Morning is the best time, when they come out to feed. The pests seem to like thick plantings with shade and northern exposures.

The red spider is really an 8-legged mite barely visible under a magnifying glass. It weaves fine webs (readily discernible) on the underside of branches and sucks the plant juices, causing a mottled, lackluster effect. Severe infestations can eventually kill a tree. Since the spider flourishes under hot, dry conditions where air drainage is poor, it can be discouraged by deep watering and by hosing off the tree each week.

The Living Christmas Tree

More live Christmas trees (which may be any of various kinds of conifers) are being used each year so that the tree can be planted after the holidays. The trees need special handling as they suffer severely from the hot, dry air of the average home; also, sudden changes from outdoors to a living room for approximately two weeks and then out again, are hard on them.

If you wish your live Christmas tree to grow after the holidays, keep it in a pan where its burlapped roots may be kept moist. Place it as far away from direct heat as possible. When indoor use is over, place it in the cool cellar or porch where its foliage may be washed off, its roots moistened and the plant hardened gradually to cold over a period of a week or two. Plant it outdoors with good drainage in mild weather; then water and mulch it well.

Conifers and Other Needle-Leaved Evergreens in General Use

(Heights are for aged, mature trees.)

Abies balsamea (Balsam fir) 60 to 70 ft. Narrow pyramidal growth; dark green fragrant needles. The traditional Christmas tree. For moist cool climates as windbreak, borders, specimen.

Abies concolor (White fir) 90 to 100 ft. Symmetrical; gray-blue needles. Tolerant of some drought and heat. Specimen, group, border use.

Abies koreana prostrata (Dwarf Korean fir). A dwarf plant of irregular, arching habit for Japanese and modern landscape effects among stones.

Cedrus atlantica (Atlas cedar) 120 ft. Broad pyramid. Hardy to Washington, D.C. Needs rich soil. *C. atlantica glauca* (Blue Atlas cedar) is hardy to New

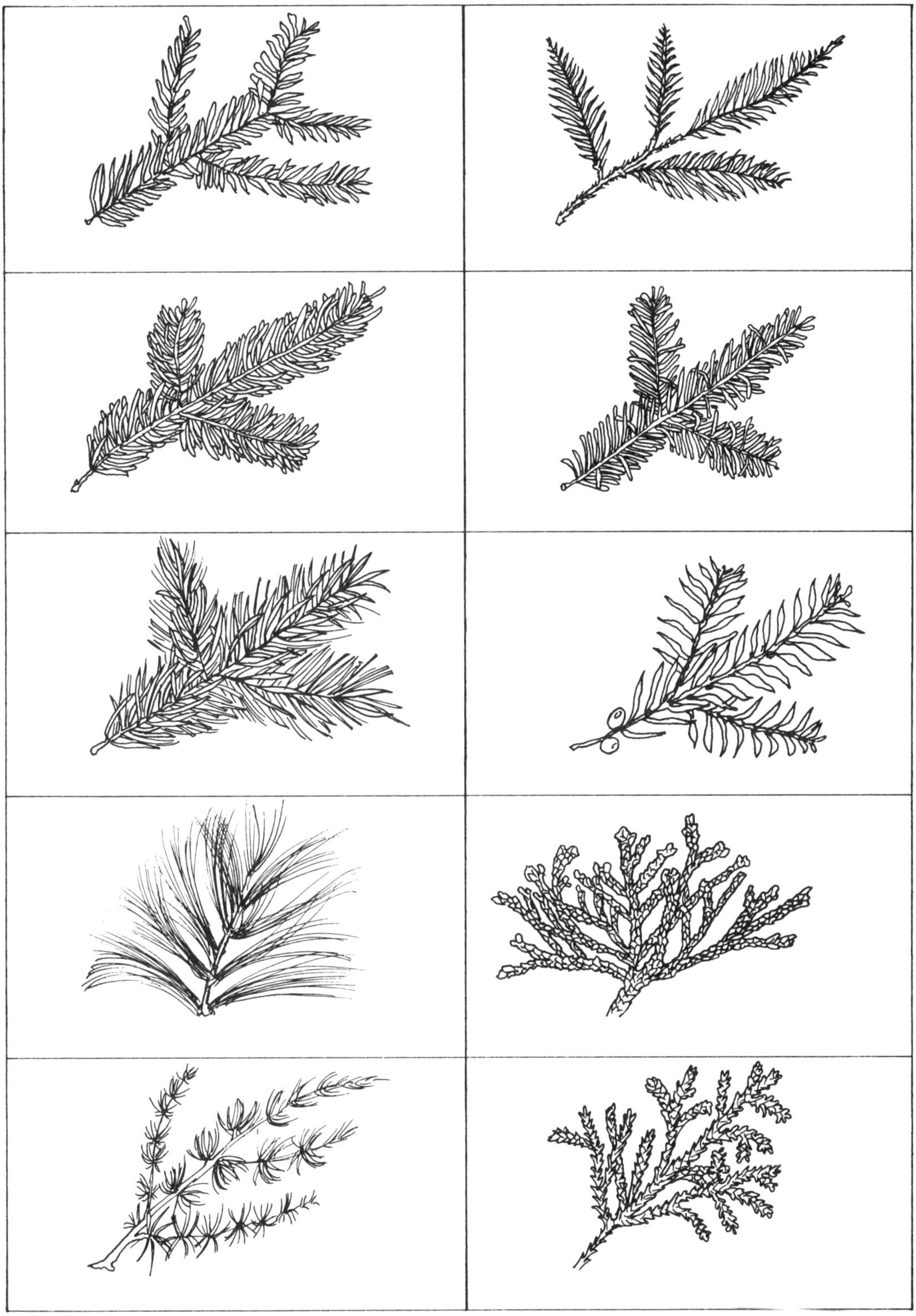

Foliage of coniferous evergreens. Left: *top to bottom, hemlock, spruce, Douglas fir, pine, larch.* Right: *top to bottom, redwood, balsam fir, yew, arborvitae, prostrate juniper.*

York and southern New England. For lawn specimens.

Cedrus deodara (Deodar cedar) 150 ft. Pyramidal with pendulous branches, dark green needles. For California and South.

Cedrus libani (Cedar of Lebanon) 120 ft. Pyramid, broadens with age. Green needles. Hardy to southern New England. Beautiful lawn specimen.

Chamaecyparis lawsoniana (Lawson false cypress) 120 ft. Many, many forms for mild climates.

Chamaecyparis obtusa (Hinoki false cypress) 120 ft. Broad pyramid. Very hardy; survives temperatures of −35 degrees. There is a dwarf form, *nana,* suitable for Japanese landscaping and rock gardens.

Chamaecyparis pisifera (Sawara false cypress) 150 ft. Narrow pyramid. Very hardy in North. Many forms, including dwarfs, available.

A small form of Hinoki cypress is suitable for a mixed shrub planting; others would soon outgrow site.

Chamaecyparis thyoides (White cedar) 75 ft. Native tree for moist soil, usually forming several trunks.

Cryptomeria japonica (Japanese cedar) 130 ft. Irregular pyramid. Hardy to New York City and southern New England. Accents and screens.

Juniperus chinensis (Chinese juniper) 60 ft. Light green to blue needles; columnar shape. For accent, group, border. Many forms including the following:

J. chinensis japonica (Japanese juniper) 8 to 12 inches. Spreading; blue-green, pointed leaves with white lines. Decorative.

J. chinensis pfitzeriana (Pfitzer juniper) Broad, spreading, ironclad, endures shade. Foundation, bank, group plantings.

J. chinensis sargenti (Sargent juniper) Low, creeping; blue-green, rugged ground cover.

J. excelsa stricta (Spiny Greek juniper) 60 ft. Pyramid. Blue needles; slow growth. For mild climates.

J. horizontalis plumosa (Andorra juniper) 15 to 18 inches. Low; silvery purple. For banks, steps, foundation, rock garden. Many other kinds.

J. scopulorum (Colorado red cedar) 20 to 25 ft. Columnar shape; silver whipcord foliage. For accent, groups, formal effects.

J. squamata meyeri (Meyer juniper) 3 to 4 ft. Irregular form; bright blue to pinkish needles. For specimen, accent, rock garden.

J. virginiana (Red cedar) 30 to 35 ft. Columnar form; grayish-green, purplish needles in winter. Hedge, background.

J. virginiana canaerti (Canert juniper or Canert red cedar) 12 to 15 ft. Deep green whipcord foliage; blue berries. For accent, hedge, specimen.

Larix leptolepis (Japanese larch) 90 ft. Deciduous conifer. Broad, conical form; soft, tufted needles; fresh spring color. Plant as specimen.

Libocedrus decurrens (Incense cedar) 100 ft. Columnar form. Needs pure air and

A dwarf blue spruce is a good foil for a boulder (as here) or a stone or masonry wall.

rich, acid soil that does not dry out. Hardy to southern New England. Handsome specimen.

Metasequoia glyptostroboides (Dawn redwood) 150 ft. Known only by fossil remains, this deciduous conifer came to life in 1945 when an expedition in China discovered it was far from extinct. It is a fast-growing tree from seed and is now offered by most major nurseries. Plant in moist, rich soil as a lawn specimen.

Picea abies (Norway spruce) 80 to 90 ft. Dark green needles; conical shape. Plant for windbreak and to form woodland. Very hardy north. Some of its many forms include:

P. glauca (White spruce) 60 to 70 ft. Compact pyramid; light green needles. Plant in groups for background, windbreak, screen.

P. glauca densata (Black Hills spruce) 50 to 60 ft. Compact, slow-growing; bluish-green needles. Specimen, naturalistic plantings. Very hardy.

P. glauca conica (Dwarf Alberta spruce) 4 to 6 ft. Dwarf compact cone; miniature needles. Formal and decorative for small areas.

P. pungens (Colorado spruce) 80 to 150 ft. Green to blue needles. Specimen, windbreak, woodland.

P. pungens kosteriana (Koster blue spruce) Silver-blue. Use as specimen, or in groups. There are many dwarf forms of *P. pungens.*

Pinus cembra (Swiss stone pine) 70 ft. Very dense pyramid. Slow-growing, very hardy. Valued as accent.

Pinus mugo (Swiss mountain pine) 4 ft. Shrubby; dense growth; dark green nee-

One of the choicest of conifers to use as a specimen is Swiss stone pine, Pinus cembra.

dles. Foundations, groups, accent, or ground cover. There are many forms, some more compact than others.

P. nigra (Austrian pine) 60 to 70 ft. Pyramidal, spreading; deep green needles. Tolerates city, seashore, forests. Fast-growing.

P. strobus (White pine) 75 ft. Pyramidal, spreading; soft, blue-green needles. Specimen, group, screen, forests.

P. sylvestris (Scotch pine) 60 to 75 ft. Irregular, rapid growth; gray-green needles. Plant to make woodland.

Pseudolarix amabilis (Golden larch) 60 to 100 ft. Deciduous conifer. Leaves turn yellow in fall, then drop. Excellent lawn specimen. More compact than Japanese larch.

Pseudotsuga taxifolia (Douglas-fir) 70 to 80 ft. Colorado-spruce type pyramid; green to blue needles. Hardy, useful; endures shade. Plant as a specimen or to form forest.

Sciadopitys verticillata (Umbrella pine) 100 ft. Distinctive narrow pyramid. Glossy green needles. Needs rich, moist soil. Plant as specimen. Hardy to lower New England.

Sequoia sempervirens (Redwood) 350 ft. Grows as narrow pyramid. Best on Pacific Coast.

Sequoiadendron gigantium (Giant sequoia) 300 ft. Narrow pyramid. This famous Pacific Coast native is hardy to lower New England. Soil should not dry out.

Taxus cuspidata (Japanese yew) 40 ft. Pyramidal, dense. This yew and the others below are popular ornamentals over much of the country. Deep green, waxy, flat foliage and scarlet berries. Grows in full sun or shade; thrives in various soils. Hardy and ordinarily free from disease. The various kinds can be pruned into many forms from straight hedges to topiary.

Taxus cuspidata nana (Dwarf yew) 2 to 3 ft. Slow-growing. Specimen, low hedge, tubs.

Taxus media (Intermediate yew) 40 ft. but usually lower. Hybrid of Japanese and English (*T. baccata*). Columnar to pyramidal; dense. Var. *hatfieldi,* bushy, and var. *hicksi* more columnar.

Thuja occidentalis (American arborvitae) 60 ft. Flattened, scaly leaves, yellow-tinted in winter. Suitable for light shade. Needs acid soil, well prepared with peat moss, that won't dry out. Not tolerant of air pollution. Use for hedges, sheared or unsheared, grouping, accent. There are many sizes and forms, some with yellow needles.

Thuja orientalis (Oriental arborvitae) 60 ft. Compact, erect habit. More tolerant of heat and drought than American arborvitae. There are many forms, including dwarfs and yellow-leaved kinds.

Tsuga canadensis (Canadian hemlock) 75 to 90 ft. Conical form, with drooping branches and soft green needles. Prefers shade, protection, and rich, moist soil. Use as specimen, hedge, formal and informal, background, and to form woodland. With good soil, fairly fast-growing. Sargent's weeping hemlock is *T. canadensis pendula,* a beautiful, slow-growing (but eventually very large) evergreen for large lawns.

Tsuga caroliniana (Carolina hemlock) 75 ft. Handsome pyramid with more glossy needles than Canadian hemlock. Hardy to New York City and like climates.

A great favorite among broad-leaved evergreen shrubs is the rhododendron. Its floral display in spring is superb, but in all seasons its habit of growth and foliage are outstanding.

CHAPTER 6

Broad-Leaved Evergreens and Acid-Soil Plants

As the holly groweth green,
With ivy all alone,
When flowerës can not be seen
And green wood leaves be gone.

– *Anonymous*

Broad-leaved evergreens include a wide assortment of trees and shrubs. Some require acid soil while others thrive in neutral or even slightly alkaline soil. Most of them prefer a "woodsy" soil that contains an abundance of leaf mold.

The broad-leaved evergreens ("broad-leaved" separates them from the coniferous or needle-leaved evergreens of the previous chapter) are most typically represented by holly, camellia, azalea, and rhododendron, but there are many more. Of course, not all of them are hardy in cold climates. Logically enough, mild climates offer a wider selection of broad-leaved evergreens. In the extreme North, the choice may be limited to small shrubs or such ground huggers as bearberry (*Arctostaphylos uva-ursi*) that survive only because they are protected over the winter by a snow blanket.

Hollies, the evergreen barberries, boxwood, and tea-olive are among those that are especially notable for their foliage. In addition, the barberries and some of the hollies stand out because of their winter-long berry display.

As for beautiful flowers, few plants rival those of the rhododendron and the camellia. Think how more valued the rose would be if it had the foliage of a camellia! The camellia offers flowers as perfect as the rose, yet has magnificent, waxy green foliage the year around. Two broad-leaved evergreens for mild climates are famous for their distinctive fragrance. Once encountered, who can forget the perfume from a gardenia or tea-olive?

Obviously, such multi-endowed plants are of tremendous importance in landscaping. Their role in the winter scene is invaluable but there is a practical reason for their recent and rising popularity. Once they are properly planted, most broad-leaved evergreens are easy to grow and demand little attention.

Hollies—True and False

The American and English hollies with their bright red berries have long been associated with Christmas. More recently their Oriental relations have been found even more suitable for the home grounds. Few plants are more widely used in modern landscaping than the Japanese holly (*Ilex crenata*)and its many forms.

American holly (*Ilex opaca*) is native from Massachusetts to Florida and west to Missouri and Texas. In its native habitat this tree can be very handsome. Growers

The American holly, a popular tree for home landscaping, grows naturally over a large section of the country.

Holly 'Blue Girl' and holly 'Blue Boy' (right) *are examples of improved forms of hardy hollies available.*

Some evergreen hollies have spineless foliage. Others have leaves so heavily spined that they become a form of living sculpture – best admired from afar!

The Japanese holly (Ilex crenata) *and its many compact forms is ideally suited to plant ing around foundations.*

have selected trees with better fruiting habits and finer foliage which are far superior to most wild growth. While the American holly prefers an acid soil, it will tolerate alkaline soil. In the latter, often the iron is inaccessible, but an application of iron sulfate or iron chelates may relieve the chlorosis which causes the leaves to turn yellow. In a congenial location the American holly grows quite large. Use it for accent, or plant several in a group. It is suitable for hedging. Plant in spring or early in the fall.

English holly (*Ilex aquifolium*) does very well in the Pacific Northwest and other mild, moist climates although specimens have survived in the Midwest and north of New York City along the coast. They need protection from the winter sun and winds. English hollies should be planted in the spring and should be carefully watered to keep their roots from drying out. Mix peat moss liberally with the soil before planting.

Japanese holly (*Ilex crenata*) resembles boxwood in habit of growth. Leaves are small and berries are black. The plants are low-growing and can be kept under 3 feet in height. There are many varieties such as *I. crenata convexa* and *I. crenata helleri*.

Chinese holly (*Ilex cornuta*) has the lovely prickly foliage of English holly and is hardy in Philadelphia, on Long Island and elsewhere in the North in sheltered positions.

Inkberry (*Ilex glabra*) is a native species found in acid bogs from Massachusetts to Florida. Its leaves are glossy, and the berries are black. In colder regions it may freeze back to the ground but will come up from the base. Since it has a graceful habit of growth and seldom attains more than 6 feet in height, it is useful for foundation plantings. It demands plenty of organic matter in the form of peat moss in its planting hole.

To insure a crop of holly berries it is usually necessary to have both male and female plants in the neighborhood. They should be of the same species so that blooming periods coincide. (Interesting hybrids can develop from the cross-pollination between different species and varieties when the resulting seeds germinate.) The distance between the male and female (the berry-producing plant) can be as far apart as one-half mile, but much closer proximity insures a bountiful crop of berries. Some hollies naturally produce more berries than others and some bear more heavily in alternate years.

Hollies are shallow-rooted. They should be mulched rather than cultivated, for digging around them may destroy many of the fine feeding roots. The Japanese hollies can be sheared in early spring as can any kind of holly grown as a formal hedge. Otherwise prune only as necessary to shape the plants.

Mahonias are often confused with hollies because of their prickly leaves. *Mahonia aquifolium*, commonly called Oregon holly-grape, is a handsome evergreen shrub for sun or shade and is useful in foundation

A mixed planting of evergreen azaleas and rhododendrons will eventually camouflage most of the fence.

plantings and on banks. It will grow well in any soil but is apt to get out of bounds in a congenial location. However, the Oregon holly-grape is more a shrub to welcome than to shun as it can be drastically pruned to keep it within bounds and to a height of 2 feet or so. It has clusters of bright yellow, fragrant flowers in early spring that are followed by grape-like bunches of edible, dark blue berries. This evergreen is native to the Pacific Northwest but is hardy in much colder climates. Its only problem may be burning of the leaves from winter wind and sun.

There are several other mahonias – all more fussy about climate and soil than *M. aquifolium.* One is *M. bealei,* almost exotic in habit, with stiff, compound leaves and large, showy flower clusters in spring. It needs rich, humus-like soil that does not dry out and resents disturbance once established. It is considered hardy to southern New England in protected situations.

Other mahonia species for mild climates include *M. japonica, M. napaulensis* and *M. nervosa,* the Oregon-grape. As hardy as *M. aquifolium* is a dwarf counterpart, *M. repens,* which may be grown as a ground cover.

Wintergreen barberry (*Berberis julianae*) is the hardiest of all evergreen barberries and perhaps the most popular. In the northern section it sometimes shows winter injury but recovers in the spring. Its spiny-toothed leaves and very dense growth make it an ideal shrub for hedges or barriers up to 6 feet. Other evergreen barberries worth planting in the home garden include the warty barberry (*B. verruculosa*), also with holly-like leaves similar to the wintergreen barberry; and Darwin's barberry (*B. darwini*), a handsome evergreen for mild climates. All of the evergreen barberries in spring bear a profusion of yellow or orange flowers that are followed by dark blue berries.

Still another holly-like, broad-leaved evergreen is osmanthus, the tea-olive. If it weren't that holly has alternate leaves and osmanthus, (page 88) it would be difficult to differentiate between *Osmanthus ilicifolius* and many forms of holly. All of the tea-olives are mild-climate subjects although *O. ilicifolius* does quite well on Long Island and similar tempered northern areas in sheltered situations. The most famed of tea-olives is *O. fragrans* which has a delectable perfume in its small flowers that appear in late winter and spring.

Popular Broad-Leaved Evergreens

There are few evergreen shrubs that can be considered everblooming, but glossy abelia (*Abelia grandiflora*) is in flower from early summer until late fall. The funnel-shaped pink flowers blend pleasantly with the bronze foliage which is reliably evergreen from Philadelphia south. In colder regions, the abelia should be classed as semi-evergreen. It is a superior landscaping shrub, its full, slightly arching branches of medium height making it suitable for a variety of uses.

Boxwood (*Buxus sempervirens*), though not a native plant, was used extensively in Colonial gardens. It is slow-growing and long-lived; some of the specimens in the East were planted before the Revolution. Boxwoods are one of the easiest of woody plants to propagate. Cuttings taken from mature new wood will root quickly in sand or Vermiculite.

Boxwood will thrive in any soil provided there is good drainage, in sun or partial shade. The plants are not heavy feeders; a mulch of rotted manure or rich compost in the spring will suffice. The roots are near the surface which makes boxwood easy to move.

There are many varieties of the common box (*Buxus sempervirens*) with better form and deep glossy leaves. Best known is the true dwarf box (*B. sempervirens suffruticosa*). The Korean box (*B. microphylla Koreana*) will stand lower temperatures. Boxwoods will not survive long, cold winters but will tolerate occasional subzero temperatures.

An especially dwarf, compact form of boxwood partially outlines these beds in the White House rose garden.

Mature specimens of boxwood show to best advantage when they are uncrowded and permitted to assume their natural, somewhat irregular shapes.

The camellia is a beautiful shrub for mild climates that causes surprise by sometimes thriving and flowering in such northern outposts as Long Island and Cape Cod. It likes a well-drained, acid soil that contains quantities of leaf mold and other humus-like material. It needs partial shade and, especially in the North, protection from cold, drying winds and direct sun. Most camellia varieties and hybrids are derived from *Camellia japonica*, *C. sasanqua* and *C. reticulata*. There are many named varieties. Consult catalogs or specialists for details and descriptions.

Low boxwood hedges define the geometric beds of this formal green garden. Myrtle is planted in each bed.

One of the really outstanding evergreen shrubs is Japanese privet, *Ligustrum japonicum*. It has waxy, bright green leaves from 2 to 4 inches long on a compact, rounded bush from 4 to 6 feet high. It has the typical privet spikes of fragrant white flowers in early summer followed by black berries. This privet is hardy to Philadelphia and grows well on Long Island.

Scarlet firethorn (*Pyracantha coccinea*) is one of the most widely-used of any berried shrub. It is especially colorful in West Coast gardens. The foliage is dark and glossy and borne on thorny stems. White flowers in spring are followed by scarlet or orange fruits which are abundant and showy in fall and winter. Pyracantha grows quite tall but can be pruned back to form a hedge or can be espaliered against a wall, fence, or house. It tolerates quite dry soils that are neutral, slightly acid or alkaline. The variety *P. coccinea lalandi*, with orange fruits, is hardy as far north as Minneapolis but should have a protected location in the northern regions.

One of the outstanding broad-leaved evergreen shrubs of borderline hardiness above Philadelphia is *Skimmia japonica.* It has leathery textured, bright green foliage rather similar to that of a rhododendron and clusters of small, powerfully fragrant white flowers in early spring. If you wish to enjoy skimmia's Christmas-red berries in the winter, you must plant both a male and female shrub in the same area. Give them humus-rich soil and shade and, of course, shelter from winter wind and sun in the North. It can be kept at a height and spread of 3 to 5 feet.

Leatherleaf viburnum (*Viburnum rhytidophyllum*) is one of the few members of this large genus with evergreen leaves. It is a bold, striking plant with long (7-inch), dark green, wrinkled leaves, with a woolly underside. While hardy in the North, it may be killed back in prolonged subzero weather. It prefers rich soil and partial shade.

The larger kinds of rhododendrons make attractive year-round screens, especially when combined with other trees and shrubs.

Rhododendrons and Other Acid-Soil Evergreens

When the term "broad-leaved evergreen" is mentioned, the first shrub that usually comes to mind is the rhododendron. (The azalea is in the same genus as rhododendron and has virtually the same culture but there are enough physical differences to enable us to consider them separately.)

The rhododendron and other members of the same family require an acid soil and will not tolerate lime. Every effort must be used to maintain soil acidity if your soil is not naturally acid. Along with the correct condition of acidity (from 4.5 to 5.5 pH), the soil should be well drained yet so rich in humus-forming materials (peat moss, leaf mold, compost, *decomposed* sawdust, or rotted, strawy manure) that the fine root systems never become dry.

Rhododendrons can be naturalized in open woods, thriving under the high shade of oaks and shadblow.

Special Soil Requirements

In the areas throughout the United States where acid soil exists, rhododendrons and other related plants can readily be grown providing climatic conditions are equitable. Where blueberries and huckleberries, oak, birch, larch, and white pine trees grow wild, we may be sure of success, for they are indicators of an acid soil. In other regions, it will be necessary to change the soil chemically, by adding ferrous sulfate or flowers of sulfur, and perhaps physically, by removing some of the existing clay or sand and replacing it with a mixture of peat moss and other humus-like ingredients. (The old method of acidifying the soil with aluminum sulfate is out of fashion and is considered harmful to both plants and soil.) You can test soil yourself (soil-testing kits are available from garden centers or mail-order sources) or seek assistance from your county agent in locating a soil-testing laboratory in your area. Most state agricultural stations test soil, too.

These tests will tell whether your soil is acid or alkaline. The symbol of measurement of this soil reaction is pH. Most plants do well in soil running from slightly alkaline (pH 7.5) to slightly acid (pH 6.0), but greater extremes are required for many of our popular acid or lime-loving plants.

If your soil tests 7.0 (neutral), to grow rhododendrons and other acid-soil plants properly, you will want to lower your soil pH to 5.5 by adding about 16½ pounds of ferrous sulfate per 100 square feet. Or you can add 5½ pints of sulfur. (See table.)

Other means to maintain soil acidity include incorporating large quantities of peat moss and/or leaf mold into the planting holes. Then keep a mulch around the

A group of rhododendrons has been used as a magnificent and effective screen to separate the front and rear of the property.

This specimen rhododendron acts as both landscape accent and privacy screen in front of large window.

Suggested Application of Ordinary Powdered Sulfur To Reduce the pH of an 8-Inch Layer of Soil, as Indicated in Pints per 100 Square feet

Original pH of soil	*Pints of sulfur for 100 square feet to reach pH of—* 4.5 Sand	4.5 Loam	5.0 Sand	5.0 Loam	5.5 Sand	5.5 Loam	6.0 Sand	6.0 Loam	6.5 Sand	6.5 Loam
5.0	⅔	2	...	...	...	...	...	...	..	..
5.5	1⅓	4	⅔	2	...	...	...	...	..	..
6.0	2	5½	1⅓	4	⅔	2	...	...	..	..
6.5	2½	8	2	5½	1⅓	4	⅔	2	..	..
7.0	3	10	2½	8	2	5½	1⅓	4	⅔	2

Before planting rhododendrons and other balled-and-burlaped shrubs, soak the root ball thoroughly.

Place boards over springy, freshly-dug soil to avoid compacting it during planting process.

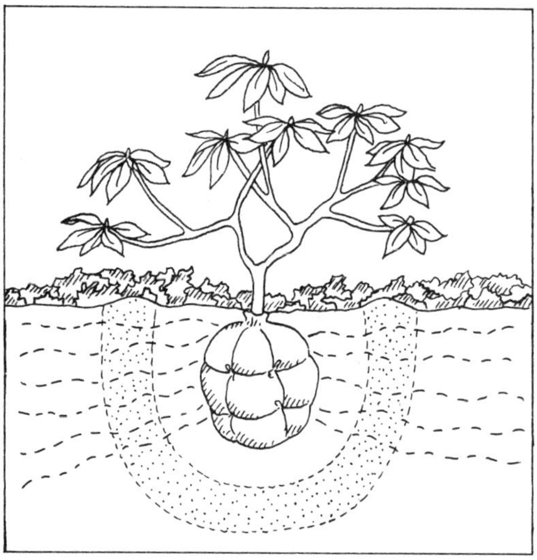

Make a generous-sized planting hole. Mix peat moss in soil. Untie and loosen burlap before adding final soil mixture. Water. Roots will grow horizontally and thrive under leaf mulch.

plants, using leaf mold, decayed sawdust (for each bushel of sawdust used as mulch, add one-half pound ammonium sulfate to restore nitrogen), pine needles, or compost. Apply organic, acid-residue fertilizers like cottonseed meal or commercial fertilizers formulated for acid-soil plants.

For these special broad-leaved evergreens like the rhododendron and azalea, exposure is almost as important as soil. They welcome neither full shade nor full sunshine and need shelter from drying winter winds. They are wonderful woodland plants and do especially well under the filtered canopy provided by deep-rooted oaks and pines. Other trees that associate well with these shrubs are flowering dogwood, birch, spruce, holly, shadblow, sassafras, sour gum, and sour wood. Planting woodlands with rhododendrons and other shrubs as well as wild flowers (see lists at end of chapter) can become a pleasurable experience.

Rhododendron and the azalea belong to the genus *Rhododendron,* and there are many, many species, as well as varieties and hybrids, of great interest to the specialist. Some are of ironclad hardiness, while others are borderline subjects most suited to the benign climate of sections of the Pacific Northwest, Northeast, and Washington, D.C. to Philadelphia regions. Yet rhododendrons are now growing in Michigan, Wisconsin, Kansas, Georgia, Texas, Colorado, and probably many other areas previously considered to be out-of-bounds. Mail-order as well as local nurseries offer the best means of starting a rhododendron collection. (See variety suggestions at end of chapter.)

The best planting and transplanting time for rhododendrons is spring and early fall; but if it is done in the fall, plants must have time to get root growth started before cold weather.

Some rhododendrons are easily propagated in the home garden by layering. (See also chapter 17.) Cut a notch in a low branch and peg down firmly so that the branch is buried in the soil and does not sway in the wind. It takes about 12 months for roots to form. Do not be in a hurry to sever from the parent plant.

Overgrown rhododendron plants may be renewed by cutting one-half the branches halfway back in the spring. New growth will come from these. The following spring the other half may be cut. Do not hesitate to cut through thick branches.

Among the most hardy rhododendron varieties is the white 'Boule de Neige.'

Other Acid-Soil Plants

The rhododendron is often called an *ericaceous* shrub because it belongs to the plant family *Ericaceae.* There are many other plants, some evergreen, others leaf-losing (deciduous) in this family, and all share with the rhododendron a need for acid soil. In fact, most need generally the same treatment and culture – an acid soil full of humus-yielding material that does not readily dry out, partial shade, and shelter from wind and extreme cold. Ericaceous plants – and therefore relatives of the rhododendron – include the ground-hugging wild flower, trailing arbutus (*Epigaea repens*), beloved for its sweet-scented pink and white flowers in spring, as well as heath (*Erica*) and heather (*Calluna*), a varied group of flowering evergreen shrubs with needle-like leaves. Heaths and heathers prefer full sun and thrive in a sandy, peaty soil mixture. In fact most of them do well in as lean a mixture as one-quarter sand and three-quarters peat moss.

With foliage more like certain rhododendrons, the andromeda (both *Pieris floribunda* and *P. japonica*) is a favorite landscape plant, especially for foundations and shrub borders. In addition to lustrous, dark

The mountain andromeda (Pieris floribunda) *is a native broad-leaved evergreen with white flowers.*

Ground-hugging bearberry is an attractive evergreen for sandy, acid soil in full sun.

green foliage, in early spring andromeda produces clusters of white, bell-shaped flowers. Equally attractive but of a more arching growth habit is drooping leucothoë (*Leucothoë catesbaei*). It is native to woodlands from Virginia to Georgia and Tennessee and is an excellent companion for other ericaceous plants. Leucothoë is a most obliging plant for the home gardener. If its foliage winter burns, or if stems die back, they can be cut off in spring; and fresh new growth will come forth.

Mountain laurel (*Kalmia latifolia*) is one of the hardiest of broad-leaved evergreens and one of the most famous members of the ericaceous family. Its natural range is wide – from New England and the East Coast to northern Florida and west to Tennessee, Ohio, and Indiana. It thrives in various exposures and climate extremes but needs acid soil that remains reasonably moist. Its pink and white flower clusters appear in late May and early June in New England, earlier in warmer climates.

Ericaceous Plants for Acid-Soil Regions

(E indicates Evergreen)

Arctostaphylos uva-ursi (Bearberry) Ground cover for sandy soil and sun. (E)

Bruckenthalia spicata (Spike heath) Ground cover for sand-peat soil. (E)

Calluna vulgaris (Heather) Low shrubs for sand-peat soil and sun. (E)

Enkianthus campanulatus (Red-vein enkianthus) Shrub with spring blooms.

Epigaea repens (Trailing arbutus) Ground cover, fragrant blooms. (E)

Erica carnea (Winter heath) Ground cover; tolerates less acidity. (E)

Erica tetralix (Cross-leaved heath) Low shrub and ground cover. (E)

Erica vagans (Cornish heath) Low shrub and ground cover. (E)

Gaultheria procumbens (Wintergreen) Ground cover for woodland. (E)

Kalmia latifolia (Mountain laurel) Shrub with spring blooms. (E)

Leiophyllum buxifolium (Sand myrtle) Low shrub for sand-peat soil and sun. (E)

Leucothoë catesbaei (Drooping leucothoë) Shrub with late spring blooms. (E)
Oxydendrum arboreum (Sorrel-tree) Grows to 60 ft. with summer flowers.
Pernettya mucronata (Pernettia) Low Erica-like shrub for mild climates. (E)
Pieris floribunda (Mountain andromeda) Shrub with upright flower clusters. (E)
Pieris japonica (Japanese andromeda) Shrub with drooping flowers. (E)
Rhododendron calendulaceum (Flame azalea) Hardy native shrub.
Rhododendron carolinianum (Carolina rhododendron) Shrub with pink flowers. (E)
Rhododendron catawbiense (Mountain rose bay) Parent of hardy hybrids. (E)
Rhododendron gandavense (Ghent azalea) Has many named hybrids.
Rhododendron maximum (Rose bay) Very hardy, large shrub. (E)
Rhododendron nudiflorum (Pinxter-flower) Hardy woodland shrub, pink flowers.
Rhododendron obtusum (Kurume azalea) Parent of many evergreen azaleas. (E)
Rhododendron schlippenbachi (Royal azalea) Large shrub with pink blooms.
Rhododendron viscosum (Swamp azalea) Fragrant flowers in summer. (E)
Vaccinium corymbosum (Highbush blueberry) Decorative shrub with fruit.
Vaccinium vitis-idaea (Cowberry) Ground cover for humus-rich soil.

Trees to Plant with Rhododendrons and Other Broad-Leaved Evergreens

Abies (Various kinds. Fir)
Acer palmatum (Japanese maple)
Acer pensylvanicum (Striped maple)
Acer spicatum (Mountain maple)
Amelanchier (All kinds. Shadblow, Juneberry, Serviceberry)
Betula (Various white-bark kinds. Birch)
Cercis canadensis (Redbud, Judas tree)
Cercidiphyllum japonicum (Katsura tree)
Cornus alternifolius (Pagoda dogwood)
Cornus florida (Flowering dogwood)
Cornus kousa (Kousa dogwood)
Franklinia alatamaha (Franklin tree)
Halesia carolina (Silverbell tree)
Liquidambar styraciflua (Sweet gum)
Magnolia (Various kinds. Flowering magnolia)

The canopy-like foliage of May-apple is especially attractive in spring woods. It and other native plants and ferns are often the best solution for problem shade areas.

Malus (Various. Flowering crabapple)
Nyssa sylvatica (Sour gum)
Picea (Various kinds. Spruce)
Pinus (Various kinds. Pine)
Quercus (Various kinds. Oak)
Sophora japonica (Japanese pagoda tree)
Stewartia pseudo-camellia (Stewartia)
Styrax japonica (Snowbell tree)

Rhododendron Varieties of Proven Hardiness

(Recommended for trial in the Midwest and like areas where summers are hot and winters very cold.)

Album Elegans, white
America, red
Boule de Neige, white
Caroline, rose-pink, fragrant
Catawbiense Album, white
Charles Dickens, red
Dr. H. C. Dresselhuys, red
Everestianum, rosy lilac
Ignatius Sargent, rose
Lady Armstrong, pink
Mrs. C. S. Sargent, rose
Nova Zembla, red
Purple Splendor, purple
Roseum elegans, lavender-pink

Sweet pepperbush (Clethra alnifolia) *has fragrant white flowers in summer and is often found in damp, acid soil. It adapts to other situations.*

Shrubs to Plant with Rhododendrons and Other Broad-Leaved Evergreens

(E denotes evergreen foliage)

Chionanthus virginicus (Fringe tree) Odd white flowers in spring.

Clethra alnifolia (Sweet pepperbush) Large shrub with fragrant summer blooms.

Cornus mas (Cornelian-cherry) Large shrub with early yellow flowers.

Corylopsis spicata (Winter hazel) Graceful shrub with yellow flowers.

Enkianthus campanulatus (Red-vein enkianthus) Bright fall foliage.

Fothergilla (All kinds. Fothergilla) Needs rich, moist soil.

Hamamelis mollis (Witch hazel) Early yellow flowers.

Hydrangea quercifolia (Oak-leaf hydrangea) Shrub of informal habit.

Ilex glabra (Inkberry) Evergreen holly with nonprickly foliage. (E)

Ilex verticilliata (Winterberry) Deciduous holly with red berries.

Lindera benzoin (Spice bush) Large shrub with early yellow flowers.

Parrotia persica (Parrotia) Needs rich, moist soil.

Viburnum (Most kinds).

Mild climate regions abound with broad-leaved evergreens. This is fatshedera in a California garden. In the north, it is a house plant.

A Selection of Wild Flowers to Grow in Shade with Rhododendrons and Other Broad-Leaved Evergreens

Actaea (All kinds. Baneberry)
Anemonella thalictroides (Rue anemone)
Aquilegia canadensis (Columbine)
Arisaema triphyllum (Jack-in-the-pulpit)
Asarum canadense (Wild ginger)
Chimaphila maculata (Pipsissewa)
Chiogenes hispidula (Creeping snowberry)
Clintonia borealis (Bead-lily)
Cornus canadensis (Bunchberry)
Cypripedium acaule (Pink lady slipper)
Epigaea repens (Trailing arbutus)
Erythronium americanum (Trout-lily)
Ferns (Most kinds)
Galax aphylla (Galax)
Gaultheria procumbens (Wintergreen)
Goodyera pubescens (Rattlesnake plantain)
Houstonia caerulea (Bluets)
Iris cristata (Crested iris)
Lilium canadense (Canada lily)
Lilium philadelphicum (Wood lily)
Lilium superbum (American Turks-cap lily)
Linnaea borealis (Twin flower)
Lobelia cardinalis (Cardinal flower)
Lobelia siphilitica (Great blue lobelia)
Maianthemum canadense (Wild lily-of-the-valley)
Mitchella repens (Partridgeberry)
Mitella diphylla (Bishop's cap)
Phlox divaricata (Blue phlox)
Polemonium reptans (Jacob's ladder)
Polygonatum biflorum (Solomons-seal)
Pyrola elliptica (Shin leaf)
Sanguinaria canadensis (Bloodroot)
Shortia galacifolia (Oconee bells)
Smalacina racemosa (False Solomons-seal)
Tiarella cordifolia (Foam flower)
Trientalis borealis (American starflower)
Trillium (Most kinds. Trillium)
Viola (Many kinds. Violet)

Hedges and topiary are in the grand style in the gardens of Hidcote Manor in the Cotswold hills of England. Hedges are often composed of two or more kinds of plants – beech and yew are shown.

CHAPTER 7

Hedges

Row upon row
The hedges are robing in green.
– Griffith

Hedges are living fences and combine utility with beauty.

They are screens to promote privacy and to discourage intruders. They hide the objectionable, while permitting the passage of air. They can serve as windbreaks in exposed situations, and as a background for landscape features.

When the average home gardener thinks of a hedge, it is usually of privet or barberry, which are much used because of their adaptability. Of course there are many other good hedge plants, for both formal and informal effects. Many kinds of shrubs planted in a row will form a casual hedge of the more free-and-easy type. Some of these may be pruned or sheared to a fairly regular form, many are better left to grow naturally.

Evergreens make fine hedges because they retain their green appearance in winter. Consider how you want the hedge to look before you make a selection. The cost may be a factor, too. Generally, the number of most kinds of evergreens you will need for a hedge cost more than the same number of deciduous (leaf-losing) shrubs. (If you are patient, you can buy small or seedling evergreens, at great savings over large plants, from nurseries that grow these plants by the thousands. But it may be 5 years or so before you will have a hedge that is much higher than 4 or 5 feet.)

If evergreens are chosen for hedging, the best time to plant them is early fall. The roots will become established during the cool fall weeks which follow and will be prepared for winter by fall rains. In spring, evergreens make new growth and there is a great advantage in having had several months of growing weather in the fall first to establish the plant underground. Spring-planted evergreens face the hot, trying conditions of summer in a weakened state because of the demands of new growth and the root shock due to transplanting.

In planting hedges, a good start is essential for future vitality. If your soil is very good, it may suffice to dig holes large enough to receive each individual plant. The best way is to dig a trench, adding good soil if the soil is poor. The subsoil should be broken up to insure drainage if it is hardpan. Peat moss and compost and possibly a complete fertilizer such as 5-10-5 can be mixed in also. Remember that hedge plants need help as they are going to compete with each other for food and moisture. After the plants are placed, the ground should be graded so that water runs toward the plant when applied to it. When a hedge is planted on a hillside or

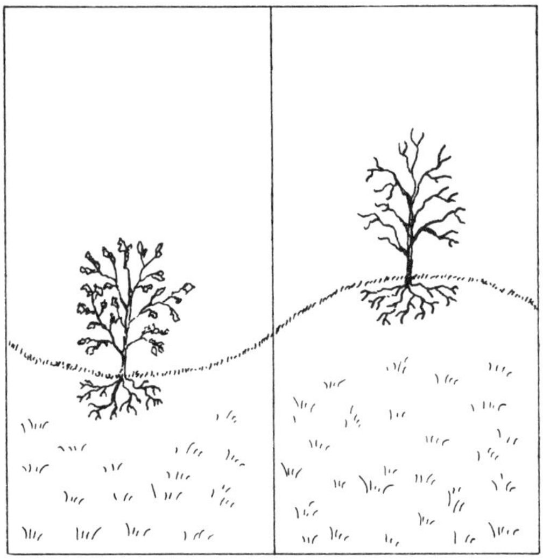

New planting (left) *is graded to hold water. In winter, mound soil* (right) *to prevent standing water.*

In damp, low places, set hedge on a ridge formed with earth from ditch. Sow grass on slopes.

bank, it may be necessary to cart soil to act as a waterbreak to prevent washing away of the soil about the plant roots and also to hold some of the water for deep penetration. Be sure to set the plants deep enough.

In most instances a single row of plants will be sufficient, but where a very heavy screen is desired it may be necessary to use a double row. Stagger the plants in two straight lines a suitable distance apart according to the material used. In all cases, a line should be used to get a straight row.

Planting distances vary according to the kind and size of plant. It is safe to say the younger the plants, the farther apart they should be spaced. Older plants, especially in the case of some evergreens like hemlock, should be spaced closely, with branches touching each other. Young privet can be planted a foot apart. Large hemlocks under 8 feet tall can be set 4 to 5 feet apart with their branches touching.

Suggestions for Pruning and Shearing

For all but the most informal of hedges and for some evergreens, like those of majestic old boxwood where their natural, billowing forms should be left alone, some pruning or shearing is required. Pruning is mostly done to keep the plants vigorous. Shearing gives them appearance.

No shrubbery can remain beautiful unless new growth is constantly replacing old worn-out branches. In deciduous hedges or flowering shrubbery, the first step in promoting this new growth is to cut off the oldest branches systematically at the ground to stimulate new shoots. If this process is carried on a little each year the shape or appearance of the plant need not be marred by drastic measures made necessary by accumulated neglect.

The best time to prune varies according to the type of plant. For shrubs which are grown for their foliage only, the best time is after the leaves drop in the fall or before they appear in the spring. While this is the ideal time, do not hesitate to prune moderately while they are in leaf. Take out a stick or two here and there, then wait for vacant spots to grow together before you prune it again.

In the case of flowering shrubbery the time of cutting must vary according to the time of bloom. To trim a shrub before it blooms means loss of the flower buds. The majority of flowering shrubbery blooms on

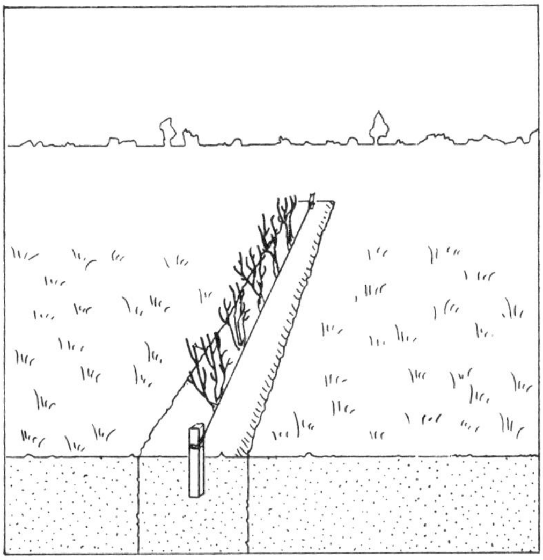

In planting, set hedge plants lower than their nursery depth. Stakes and cords keep row straight.

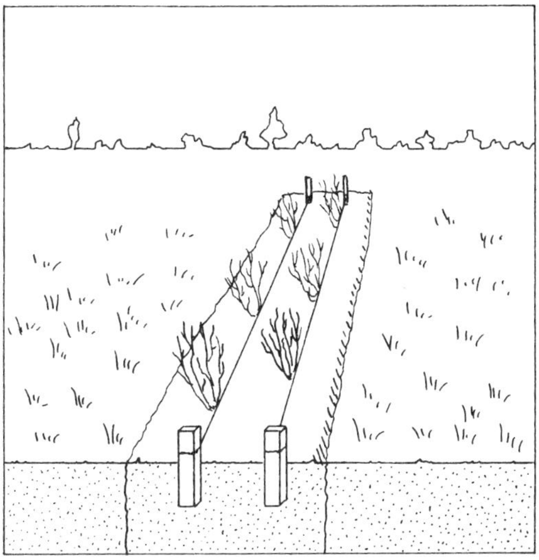

Double-row planting is set in wider trench than single hedge. Plants are spaced along two cords.

the new wood produced during the growing season of the previous year. It is wise to prune within a few weeks after flowers fade to give this new wood a chance to ripen for next year's flowering.

The best way to handle newly planted hedges, especially those that are deciduous and grown for their leaf effect only, like privet, barberry, buckthorn, or yew, is to keep them short until they branch freely at the ground. Allow the plant to increase in height as it shows increasing vigor.

The length of life or success of a formal hedge may be determined, to a large extent, by the way it is sheared. Remember that each leaf and branch demands its share of light, air, and rain. The number of times a yew, privet, or hemlock hedge is sheared each season depends, of course, on the rate of new growth, but usually at least two shearings will be required. Always shear new growth rather than cutting into old wood.

Shearing tools should be sharp, well-oiled, and clean. A pair of scissors-type shears is sufficient to care for the small planting, but for large jobs electric hedge trimmers are available. All hedges should be pruned and sheared so that they are wider at the base, to prevent the bottom

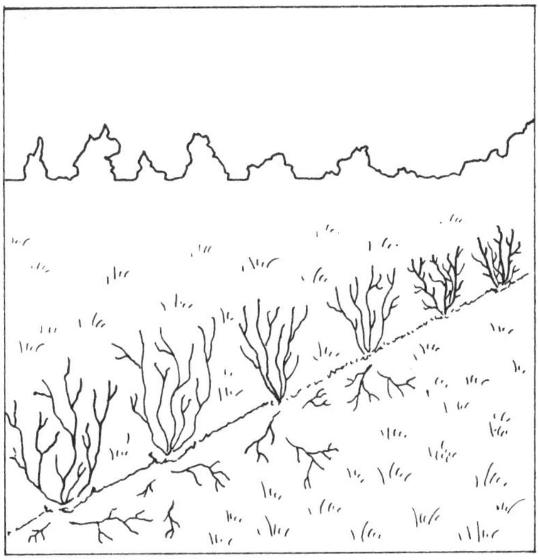

Flowering hedges (shown without foliage for clarity) should be pruned shortly after they have bloomed.

from being shaded by the top. While the tendency is often to shear a hedge flat at the top, in cold climates a rounded or tapered shape is better for it helps shed snow and ice.

In addition to correct renewal and shearing, hedges need a regular system of watering and feeding of balanced plant food. In spring, scatter a large handful under the branches of each large shrub or one pound

New hedges should be kept low until they have branched freely near the ground.

Shear new growth at least twice a season to keep hedge dense. Maintain greater width at base.

to each 15 feet of hedge. Water it in well, and repeat monthly. Discontinue all feeding or heavy shearing by August, or you may stimulate new growth which will not have time to harden before frost. This kind of soft growth may winterkill and cause other wood to die with it.

A Selection of Hedge Plants

In wide, open spaces, there is often need of a hedge of trees, such as can be made by Lombardy poplar (*Populus nigra italica*). These trees make beautiful screens, if planted 5 or 6 feet apart, where no other plants conflict and where they do not have to compete with paving. They are gross feeders, fast growers, and will send their roots 40 feet to find an opening in a drain which they proceed to clog up. If placed near a flower bed, their surface-feeding roots will rob it of every vestige of food and moisture. If the roots are cut yearly to avoid this, the trees will suffer and soon dry up. So if you want to make a hedge of poplars give them a well-cultivated space 15 to 20 feet on either side and feed well. Grass grows fairly well with them.

Another rampant grower for large grounds is the osage-orange tree (*Maclura pomifera*). If properly pruned, it becomes a thick, tangled thorny hedge that makes passage impossible. Although native to Arkansas and Texas, it is hardy in the North. It has the drawback of unkempt appearance, and its rampant feeding roots throttle all shrubbery near it. For an extensive

Russian-olive, a small tree, is excellent for a windbreak in cold or windswept locations.

Profile of correctly shaped hedge (left), *at right are two examples of incorrect shaping.*

hedge of osage-orange, plant rooted whips about 1 foot apart and then cut them back. Or plant 2 feet apart, and cut back the stems to the ground when they are 1 inch thick. Either way promotes a rank, thick fence, hardly suitable for the suburbs but fine for farms and large places.

The fruits of the osage-orange (it belongs to the mulberry family), though of no value, are decorative and always a novelty to people who see them for the first time. They are green, then turn to orange.

Equally thorny and a true citrus relative is the trifoliate orange (*Poncirus trifoliata*) that makes a formidable barrier in mild climates. In colder areas, it is not hardy enough to make a hedge but can be grown as far north as New York City as an accent in protected corners.

There are many other large trees and shrubs suitable for windbreaks and high hedges. Among them are the fast-growing Chinese or Asiatic elm (*Ulmus pumila*), several species of the rugged buckthorn (*Rhamnus*), including the patented form known as "Tallhedge," several maples, especially the Amur maple (*Acer ginnala*), several bush honeysuckles (*Lonicera tatarica* has red berries for birds), lilac (*Syringa vulgaris*), and many shrub roses.

Multiflora roses, advertised as the "living fence," are used extensively for hedges. This rose is very hardy, grows in any soil, and tolerates poor drainage.

It is recommended for farms and large estates. Annual cutting back and occasional pruning keep it to 5 feet and a 3-foot spread. Plants should be set from 3 to 4 feet apart and kept trimmed back the first year until they settle down to grow. By the second year they will make a 4-foot fence, perhaps taller, but it is wise to keep the plants low, at least until the bottom branches fill out.

Most types of flowering shrubs make good hedges, but they occupy considerable space, and some require careful pruning.

Privet is the most-used plant for hedging in the United States because of its quick growth. There are several kinds, some semi-evergreen or evergreen (not all are reliably hardy in the coldest areas) and others deciduous, often with variegated or colored foliage. Carefully planted and fertilized it will give excellent results. Plants should be set rather deep and cut back to 6 inches as soon as planted to stimulate the growth of side branches. When the new shoots are a foot tall, cut them back half way; repeat as growth is made so as to

Where space permits, fairly large, flowering shrubs (this is spirea) make lovely hedges.

Sheared privet hedge in rear is sparse at base, possibly because of too-rapid top growth after planting.

develop a thick, bushy base. After the desired height is reached shear once in June and again in late July, if necessary, to keep the hedge in form. Plants can be set from 8 to 10 or 12 inches apart depending on the size of the hedge desired. For an extra thick, tight one, set 1 foot apart in two rows about 10 inches apart, "staggering" the plants in the rows.

Prune so that the lower branches get plenty of light as well as the upper ones and are not shaded by them. When privet dies at the bottom from bad pruning or lack of other care, it is best to cut it to the ground and thin it out. It will grow back surprisingly fast if given water and food. Before doing this try watering, fertilizing, and spraying.

Apply chemical fertilizer in spring and again in July, 1 pound to every 15 feet of hedge. Do not fertilize privet later than midsummer.

Many varieties of privet are offered but for taller hedges in sun or shade, regel privet (*Ligustrum obtusifolium regelianum*) is one of the best. It will grow 7 feet or more tall, is of compact habit and if not pruned will develop a profusion of white, fragrant blooms. It is exceptionally hardy.

The winged euonymous (*Euonymus alatus*), with its beautiful cerise autumn foliage, is one of the most desirable hedge plants. It is not demanding as to soil and will tolerate shade. It is more informal than privet and generally is not sheared.

Of the low-growing hedge plants, certainly Japanese barberry (*Berberis thunbergi*) is one of the best for semiformal effect, growing to 4 feet high in a great variety of soils and standing some shade. It is hardy almost anywhere and, if clipped, makes a dense wall. It has bright berries in winter. Plants to be sheared are set 18 inches apart and for natural growth, 24 to 30 inches. There are many other kinds of barberry suitable for home property hedging, including other forms of the Japanese. They include the Mentor barberry (*B. mentorensis*), evergreen in all but the coldest areas, and dense and compact enough not to require shearing or pruning; the wintergreen barberry (*B. julianae*), a beautiful, evergreen barberry known for its hardiness that can make an informal (unsheared) hedge about 4 to 5 feet high.

The use of low-growing hedges is becoming increasingly popular and mail-order nursery catalogs list many kinds. Besides the evergreens like the elegant, low boxwood (*Buxus sempervirens nana*), the many forms of the Japanese holly (*Ilex crenata*), and low-growing yew (*Taxus*), there are dwarf varieties of privet and red barberry. The dwarf arctic willow (*Salix purpurea nana*) has blue-green leaves and will grow in poorly drained or wet soil. An attractive little flowering shrub for low hedges is *Deutzia gracilis*. It does well in full sun or part shade and during the spring comes alive with a mass of bell-shaped, white blooms. It can grow informally without pruning or can be kept low by cutting back after the flowering season.

Germander (*Teucrium chamaedrys*) is famous as a formal edging in herb gardens. The glossy leaves resemble the boxwood, and it can be clipped to suit any height.

There are several admirable hedge plants among the evergreens. They serve the same purpose in winter as in summer and always present a uniform appearance.

Norway spruce (*Picea abies*) comes in several varieties which vary in height, shape, and color. All make good hedges if they are well clipped, or rather, pruned. If they are allowed to grow too high they get a coarse appearance. Plant 4 or 5 feet apart and in a fairly short time the branches will intertwine.

Arborvitae (*Thuja occidentalis*) is as basic a hedge plant as privet but is more of an aristocrat. It is more expensive and slower growing, but its ultimate effect is superb. It is a good shearing evergreen and makes a dense, close hedge. Its chief enemy is red spider mite, mostly a nuisance when air circulation is poor. Plant 4 to 6 feet apart, according to effect desired.

Junipers are beautiful and reliable. The genus is large and well known, and every region of the United States has its favorites. Get the type which fits the hedge height that you need.

Japanese yew (*Taxus cuspidata*) is hardy in most of the United States and makes an excellent broad, dark green hedge in various heights, according to variety. It is good for city use as it will bear

Lavender-cotton is attractive low hedge for sunny beds. Cutting back in spring forces strong growth.

Arborvitae is an excellent choice for a tall tapered hedge of elegant form and good density.

A young hedge shows yew's natural denseness and pleasing form. Little clipping is needed.

Sheared for formality, a low hedge defines an entrance from the driveway or turnaround.

smoke and dust. It can be clipped formally or trimmed to bushiness at natural height. There are some excellent hybrids: *T. media hicksi* and *hatfieldi* are two of them. Properly planted, when 2 feet high at 2½ feet apart, they will touch in two years and grow about 6 inches per year thereafter.

Actually the yews hold their shapes and require so much less pruning than privet that when this is added to the factor of evergreen foliage, their larger first cost is really economy. Dwarf Japanese yew (*T. cuspidata nana*) makes a good dwarf hedge but grows more slowly than others.

There are many other good plants suitable for hedges. Some are found in the lists on the next page. Others are described in nursery catalogs.

Plants Suitable for Hedges

(s indicates suitability for shearing.)

PLANTS FOR LOW HEDGES

Deciduous

Berberis thunbergi (Dwarf forms) (Japanese barberry) (s)
Deutzia gracilis (Deutzia)
Ligustrum (Dwarf forms) (Privet) (s)
Lavendula officinalis (Lavender)
Rosa polyantha (The Fairy)
Salix purpurea nana (Arctic willow) (s)
Santolina chamaecyparissus (Lavender cotton) (s)
Spiraea bumalda ('Anthony Waterer')
Teucrium chamaedrys (Germander) (s)
Viburnum opulus nana (Dwarf cranberry bush)

Evergreen

Buxus microphylla koreana (Korean boxwood) (s)
Buxus sempervirens nana (Dwarf boxwood) (s)
Euonymus fortunei (Dwarf forms) (Wintercreeper) (s)
Hedera helix baltica (English ivy) (s)
Ilex crenata convexa (And other forms) (Japanese holly) (s)
Pachistima canbyi (Pachistima) (s)
Taxus cuspidata nana (Dwarf Japanese yew) (s)
Taxus media hicksi (Hick's yew) (s)
Thuya occidentalis (Dwarf forms) (Arborvitae) (s)

PLANTS FOR MEDIUM TO TALL HEDGES

Deciduous

Abelia grandiflora (semi-evergreen) (Glossy abelia)
Acer ginnala (Amur maple)
Berberis mentorensis (Mentor barberry) (s)
Berberis thunbergi (many forms) (Japanese barberry) (s)
Caragana arborescens (Siberian pea tree)
Cotoneaster acutifolia (Peking cotoneaster)

Euonymus 'Emerald Pride' makes a handsome formal edging for a shrub and flower border.

Cotoneaster divaricata
Cotoneaster racemiflora
Cotoneaster wardi
Crataegus cordata (Washington hawthorn)
Crataegus crusgalli (Cockspur thorn)
Euonymus alatus (Several forms) (Winged Euonymus)
Forsythia intermedia spectabilis (s)
Forsythia suspensa
Hibiscus syriacus (Rose of Sharon)
Ligustrum amurense (Amur privet) (s)
Ligustrum ibolium (Ibolium privet) (s)
Ligustrum obtusifolium regelianum (Regel privet) (s)
Lonicera fragrantissima (Winter honeysuckle) (s)
Lonicera maacki (Amur honeysuckle) (s)
Lonicera tatarica (Tatarian honeysuckle) (s)
Maclura pomifera (Osage-orange)
Malus sargenti (Sargent crabapple)
Populus nigra italica (Lombardy poplar)
Rhamnus columnaris (Tallhedge buckthorn) (s)
Ribes alpinum (Alpine currant) (s)
Rosa floribunda (Many kinds) (Floribunda rose)
Rosa multiflora (Multiflora rose)
Spiraea prunifolia (Bridal wreath)
Spiraea vanhouttei (Van Houtte spirea)
Syringa vulgaris hybrids (lilac)
Ulmus pumila (Chinese elm) (s)

Evergreen
Buxus sempervirens (Boxwood) (s)
Juniperus virginiana (Many forms) (Red cedar) (s)

Canada hemlock (Tsuga canadensis) *is unrivalled where a tall informal hedge is needed.*

Kalmia latifolia (Mountain laurel)
Picea excelsa (Norway spruce) (s)
Pinus strobus (White pine)
Rhododendron carolinianum (Carolina rhododendron)
Rhododendron catawbiense (Mountain rose bay)
Rhododendron maximum (Rose bay)
Taxus cuspidata (Several forms) (Japanese yew) (s)
Taxus media hicksi (Hick's yew) (s)
Thuya occidentalis (American arborvitae) (s)
Tsuga canadensis (Canadian hemlock) (s)
Tsuga caroliniana (Carolina hemlock) (s)

PLANTS FOR HEDGES OR SCREENS IN DAMP SOIL

Aronia arbutifolia (Red chokeberry)
Cephalanthus occidentalis (Button-bush)
Clethra alnifolia (Summersweet)
Ilex glabra (Inkberry)
Rhododendron viscosum (Swamp azalea)
Rosa multiflora (Multiflora rose)
Salix (Many kinds) (Willow)
Sambucus canadensis (Elderberry)
Vaccinium corymbosum (Highbush or Swamp blueberry)

PLANTS FOR HEDGES IN SANDY SOIL

Elaeagnus angustifolia (Russian-olive)
Hippophaë rhamnoides (Sea-buckthorn)
Juniperus virginiana (Red cedar) (s)
Myrica pensylvanica (Bayberry)
Pinus thunbergi (Japanese black pine)
Rosa rugosa (Japanese brier)

PLANTS FOR HEDGES IN MILD CLIMATES

Abelia grandiflora (Glossy abelia)
Buxus sempervirens (Boxwood)
Camellia japonica (Common camellia)
Chamaecyparis lawsoniana (Lawson false-cypress)
Eugenia paniculata australis (Eugenia)
Euonymus japonicus (Japanese euonymus)
Ilex aquifolium (English holly)
Ilex vomitoria (Yaupon)
Myrica cerifera (Wax myrtle)
Pittosporum tobira (Japanese pittosporum)
Poncirus trifoliata (Trifoliate orange)
Prunus laurocerasus (Cherry laurel)
Viburnum tinus (Laurestinus)

Wisteria has only one rival, clematis, for the title of queen of flowering vines. Once established, a plant will cover many square feet of pergola, wall, or fence. The scented blossoms, white to purple, appear in May.

CHAPTER 8

Vines and Ground Covers

I speak for all-shaped blooms and leaves,
For every long-armed woman-vine
That round a piteous tree doth twine.

– *Sidney Lanier*

Vines have a place in garden decoration that cannot be taken by any other plant. Some, like wisteria and clematis, produce a large quantity of flowers in a minimum of space. Others, like the evergreen ivy and euonymus, hide or soften ugly materials or outlines.

Certain vines grow well on masonry; others make good ground cover in sun or shade, whereas some must have artificial support or help in their climbing.

The hole for a vigorous perennial vine should be at least 2 feet square and 2 feet deep, or better, 3 feet each way. The soil in the bottom should be broken up and made to drain if it is hard. The excavation should then be filled with good soil mixed with compost or peat moss and two or three handfuls of superphosphate.

No vine should be planted where water drips on it every time it rains. This is bad for the foliage but worse still for the plant in winter. Much loss over winter is caused by the drip of water on warm days which coats the plant with ice at sundown. The ice-coated vine swaying in the wind may then suffer many cracks and wounds.

Large plants should be dormant if possible when planted. Spread the roots to the fullest extent, cutting off all broken or injured ones. See that wooden supports are made of substantial, long-lasting material. Plants grown against a sunny wall should receive special watering. They get heat not only from the sun but also that reflected from the wall. At night the wall will release heat long after sundown.

Use vines for screening, for softening architectural lines, for flowering beauty; but do not cover and blot out good architectural detail. Most vines, after a few years, will need annual pruning to prevent them from growing out of bounds.

Vines for Foliage Effect

Virginia creeper (*Parthenocissus quinquefolia*), sometimes called woodbine or American ivy, is a native vine common in woodlands. It clings to trees and tumbles over old stone walls. Its fall coloring is especially brilliant. It has five distinct dark green leaves in a group, which distinguishes it from the three-leaved poison ivy. For covering slopes, rough ground, or large tree trunks, it is excellent, but may need thinning out from time to time.

The Engelmann creeper is a variety of woodbine with smaller foliage and a more restrained growth habit.

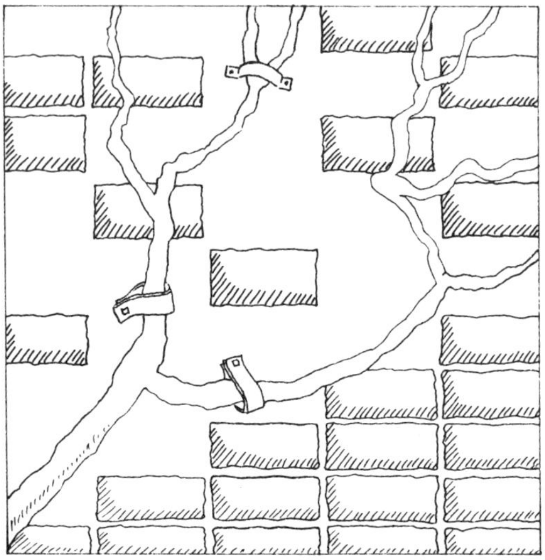

Loops of sheet lead are used correctly (below) *to support vine on wall; example at top is wrong.*

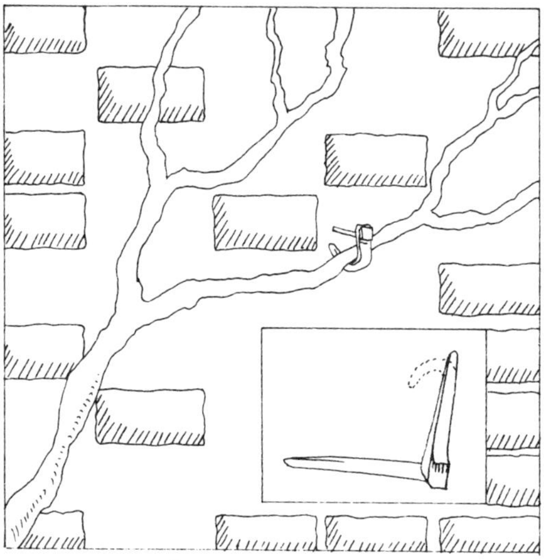

One type of hanging nail that holds fast in masonry. Flexible "arm" bends to form loop.

Boston ivy (*Parthenocissus tricuspidata*) is fine for growing, without fastening, over masonry walls. It also grows well on frame structures (but avoid those with shingles or tiles). It does not do well on south walls in the North. There are a few varieties of Boston ivy that are less rampant. The variety "Lowi" has small leaves; "Veitchi" has small leaves that are purple in the spring. Both give a delicate tracery on limited surfaces where pattern, not coverage, is wanted.

Virginia creeper, a rampant and informal vine, can also be trained to formal uses, as here.

English ivy (*Hedera helix*), one of our most useful evergreen vines, is slower in growth than Boston ivy. It is also self-clinging and fastens itself by rootlets along the stems. In cold-winter sections it must be sheltered from direct winter sun and does best on northern exposures. It can be easily propagated by layering or by cuttings inserted in sandy loam. Whole branches will also root in water.

English ivy becomes a low-growing shrub, used for hedges to about 5 or 6 feet without support when cuttings are taken from the flowering portion of the mature plant. It then becomes bush or tree English ivy (*Hedera helix arborescens*). Even the leaf shape changes, usually to a more triangular form.

If you wish a good evergreen hedge-effect background fairly quickly, using little space, train the vine form of English ivy over a wire netting, being careful to clip the trailing sprays at the ground to keep them from rooting. It is an excellent ground cover, even under trees if the soil is supplied with humus, water when needed, and an annual supply of plant food.

There are many forms of English ivy, some with variegated leaves. Baltic ivy (*Hedera helix baltica*) has much smaller foliage, is hardier, and makes a most satisfactory bank and ground cover.

All ivies thrive in rich, moist soil. They will not perform in poor soil that constantly dries out.

Wintercreeper (*Euonymus fortunei*) is an evergreen vine or trailing shrub that comes in several excellent varieties. Some make good ground cover as well as wall plants, rarely growing over 10 feet high. They thrive on north sides of buildings as well as in exposed locations, will grow readily in semishade, and reasonably well in dense shade.

The variety *Euonymus radicans vegetus* (Scarlet-fruited big-leaf winter creeper) is an excellent form, half shrub, half vine. For low-growing hedges or rounding out corners in foundation planting, it has the advantage of growing under broad eaves, clinging closely to the building by aerial rootlets, but having the appearance of an evergreen shrub. Its glossy, rich green foliage attracts much attention, as do its red berries. Once established, it grows and spreads rapidly but is easily confined to the space desired. Give it good soil and it is an economical evergreen in your planting. Pinching out the tops during the first year will produce healthy bottom growth.

Flowering Vines

American bittersweet (*Celastrus scandens*) is valued for its heavy foliage as well

Ivy in the East: A sloping ivy "lawn" is in harmony with flowering bulbs, evergreens, birches.

as for its orange and crimson berries used for winter bouquets. It is easily cultivated and especially good in semishade. It is scarcely ever troubled by disease and sometimes reaches a height of 30 feet. There are a few other species of bittersweet, but they, as well as the native American type, are too coarse and rampant for most suburban properties.

Clematis has many varieties, all with beautiful flowers, and most with growing habits tailored to the needs of suburban gardens. Its requirements are quite simple: rich, well-drained soil with plenty of lime. Bone meal or superphosphate in generous quantities are needed, as is a thick layer of compost as a mulch to shade their roots. They will grow in partial shade.

Plant on trellises, fences, walls, or lamp posts and provide support early. (They climb by tendrils.) When planting, cut the top back to the lowest large eye and cover entire plant with 4 inches of soil.

Clematis foliage is thick and handsome, but the plants are grown mostly for their flowers which, on the larger plants, come in June and July and repeat to some extent during the summer, depending on water, food, and weather conditions. The smaller flowering plants bloom later but have a fragrance lacking in the larger types.

The most popular small-flowering type is known as virgins-bower and can be either the Japanese *C. paniculata,* or the less-used native *C. virginiana.* This plant with bright cheerful foliage and numerous clusters of small, cream-white, hawthorn-scented flowers grows rampantly and blooms from August to October. It forms a good foliage vine all summer, and flowers are followed by attractive feathery seed pods. Cut back to the ground each spring, unless great masses of foliage are desired; then prune to keep in shape, and cut back every three years to strengthen. It requires practically no other care.

A hardy, strong-growing, disease-proof plant is *Clematis montana.* It has pinkish-white flowers like a windflower, 1 to 2 inches in diameter. They frequently open about May first. It should be pruned after flowering by shortening or cutting out old shoots. There are varieties almost identical with the above, but with rose and blue flowers.

Among some of the more glamorous large-flowered clematis varieties are mauve "Belle of Woking" and white "Duchess of Edinburgh." They bloom on old wood rather than new growth. Cut out or thin weak or crowded growth after flowering.

Henryi (white) and "Crimson King" are popular large-flowered varieties of *Clematis lanuginosa* that also flower on old growth.

The purple Jackmani clematis is still the best known of all clematis types. It and its many varieties bloom in late summer and fall on new growth so pruning can be carried out in spring without fear of losing flowers. Popular Jackmani varieties are "Comtesse de Bouchaud," deep rose; "Madame Edouard Andre," deep red; and "Star of India," plum red. The usual prac-

Sweet-scented Clematis paniculata blooms prodigally in autumn, when other flowers are scarce.

Trained to pillar form by a doorway, this vine shows typical form of large-flowered hybrid clematis.

tice for pruning this group is to cut their vines back to 2 or 3 feet in early spring to stimulate new growth.

The climbing hydrangea (*Hydrangea petiolaris*) is a handsome vine with white, fragrant flowers in summer. It grows in sun or shade, eventually to 50 feet, but can be confined by pruning to lesser areas. It is self-supporting and will cling to walls by stem rootlets.

Dutchman's pipe (*Aristolochia durior*) is an excellent, quick-growing foliage plant with an odd, pipe-shaped, greenish-brown flower. It used to be very popular as a screen for summer porches, a use that has been eliminated by modern architecture.

The best of the old-fashioned honeysuckles is Hall's evergreen honeysuckle (*Lonicera japonica halliana*) with its exquisitely perfumed white flowers which turn yellow before they fade. It holds its foliage almost all winter and is good for banks, arbor or trellis alike. It is too rampant for restricted areas and needs constant heading back.

Goldflame honeysuckle (*Lonicera heckrotti*) is a recent introduction combining flame and gold heavily fragrant flower clusters with dark, glossy, semi-evergreen

Shorten tips, remove old shoots of most large-flowered clematis after flowering ends.

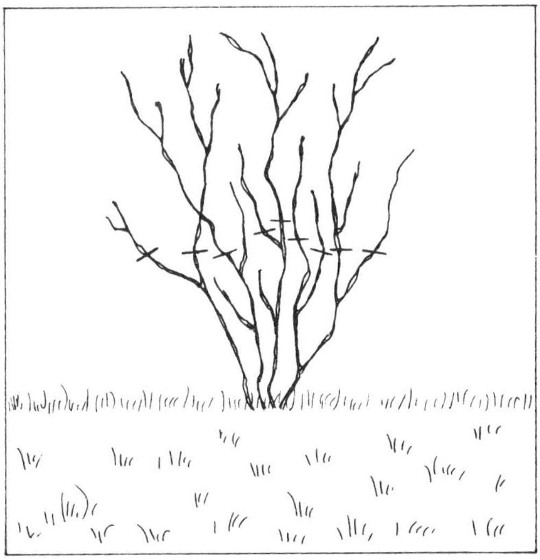

Jackmani *clematis and some other summer-blooming types should be pruned back sharply in early spring, as shown above.*

Dutchman's pipe, an old-fashioned favorite, is a fast-growing screening vine.

Strong support, such as this rustic board fence, is needed by wisteria, one of the most elegant vines.

foliage. It is a continuous bloomer with a restrained habit of growth.

Silver lace vine (*Polygonum auberti*) is a rapid grower, covered with a foam of white flowers in the fall. It is easily trained around downspouts which adds to its value.

The perennial sweet pea (*Lathyrus latifolius*) grows 6 to 8 feet tall, climbing by tendrils. Its pink or white blossoms are not fragrant.

The trumpet creeper (*Campsis radicans*) is useful for covering stumps and fences. It grows 10 feet high with bright orange-red flowers in late summer. A variety of this vine, "Madame Galen," with wide-open orange flowers, is highly recommended. The trumpet creeper can be pruned in the fall by cutting back lateral growth to two or three buds.

Wisteria (*Wisteria floribunda* and *W. sinensis*) ranks with clematis for sheer beauty of flower display. Its pendulous clusters of scented white or purple flowers in midspring are handsome enough to warrant special construction of a sturdy fence just so the vine can be planted. (Wisteria produces heavy growth that needs stout support.) It is unequaled for trellis or pergola and is especially suitable trained over an arbor or open shelter for terrace or patio so that its beautiful flower racemes can be enjoyed at leisure. Don't let a wisteria scramble at will over your house – it is not good for gutters or shingles. Wisteria vines must be pruned annually, often two or three times a year if growth is especially rampant.

Prune to 2 main stems, or not over 3 or 4, and administer hard top pruning after the first year, monthly in July and August. On young plants remove one-third of the top to develop side growth. Then cut back the side growth once or twice, or as needed, on young plants to 2 or 3 buds.

Prune older plants in August by cutting back all growth to within 4 feet of last year's wood to encourage blooming and to make a dense plant.

Seedlings of wisteria may not bloom at all or not for many years; so buy grafted plants from reliable nurseries that are guaranteed to flower. Newly planted vines are often slow to break out of their dormancy. Be sure to supply plenty of water during this critical period. Plant in full sun

Summer

Summer's favorite flower, the rose. 'Comanche' has orange-red flowers and bronze foliage.

White flowers – shasta daisy and petunias – add cool touch to a summer garden.

Flame-colored lupines point to a superb rock and water garden, constructed on a slight slope.

A semi-formal sundial garden features rose borders which alternate with borders of sweet William and snapdragons.

Single-flowered roses, like the pink, nearly everblooming 'Betty Prior,' have special appeal.

Multicolored floribunda rose 'Circus' grows in tree form.

Tuberous begonias need partial shade. Or grow them under protection of a lath house, a decorative yet practical garden feature.

Plants to grow in rooftop gardens include geranium, rose, chrysanthemum, yew, privet, tomato, petunia, and most kinds of annuals.

White-flowered vine (Clerodendron thomsonae) *is featured in a mild-climate rooftop garden.*

A half-moon pool and trickling waterfall in a city garden.

A unique display of pots of white petunias, which are very fragrant in the evening, decorates the terrace of a Colorado garden.

A yew, pruned in espalier fashion, is an accent among various kinds of midseason lilies.

Bright-colored African-daisies contrast with blue spires of perennial delphinium, which are excellent background plants. The massive spikes always need support.

Silver lace vine, once popular as screen for porches, tumbles over a modern brick wall.

Goutweed, a ground cover with silver-edged leaves, and the flame honeysuckle.

The beautiful large-flowered clematis, shown here with a double form, is a non-rampant vine for posts and trellises.

For quick and temporary beauty, the morning glory, an annual vine, is easily grown from seed.

An attractive outdoor planter has been filled with geraniums and the trailing vinca.

The typical form and color of Mid-century Hybrid lilies, which flower in early summer.

Much of the magic in the early summer garden is in the ethereal beauty of bearded iris.

in average garden soil, mixing several handfuls of superphosphate in the planting hole.

If after proper planting and pruning, a wisteria does not bloom or stops flowering, it is time to root prune to keep it from going to stem and leaves. Dig a narrow trench one spade length deep completely

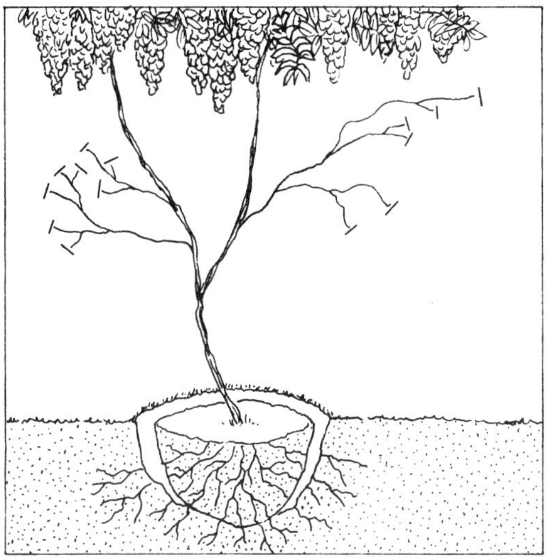

Remedy for non-blooming in wisteria is root pruning and the addition of rich soil to trench.

around the plant. Loosen the soil in the bottom and drive a spade down full length, cutting all roots in the circle. The trench may then be filled with good composted soil. On young plants the circle should be about 3 feet from the stem; from that it ranges up to 6 feet for very large ones.

Vines to Grow from Seed

There are a number of tropical vines, many with exotic flowers, suitable for regions with warm climates. Some of these can be grown from seed and treated as annuals in the North. In most cases, the seeds need warmth to germinate. They can be started indoors in peat pots and planted outdoors after frost danger is over and the soil has warmed. The ones listed below are available from the major seed houses:

Balsam-apple (*Momordica balsamina*): Height 15-20 ft. A handsome vine with good foliage and warty, apple-shaped fruits which expose a brilliant carmine interior when ripe. Balsam-pear (*M. charantia*) has pear-shaped fruit. Plant seeds 12 inches apart.

Canary-bird flower (*Tropaeolum peregrinum*): Height 15 ft. A dainty vine with finely cut leaves and sprays of small yellow flowers. Resembles its relative, the common garden nasturtium, except that it is much daintier. Plant seeds 8-12 inches apart.

Cardinal climber (*Quamoclit coccinea*): Height 10-20 ft. A striking vine with bright red flowers, resembling miniature morning glories. Blossoms all summer. Plant seeds 12 inches apart.

Cup-and-saucer vine (*Cobaea scandens*): Height 30 ft. One of the most rapid-growing vines and a perennial in the South. Large bell-shaped violet or greenish-purple flowers, plum-shaped fruits. Plant seeds 3-4 ft. apart. Seeds germinate best if planted edgewise rather than flat. Start seeds early indoors, five weeks before safe outdoor planting time.

Cypress-vine (*Quamoclit pennata*): Height 15-20 ft. A delightful vine with very finely cut leaves and numbers of small starry flowers, either scarlet or white. Prefers sun. Use for small trellis, posts, or other places where a small vine is desired. Plant seeds 1 foot apart.

Gourd (*Cucurbita*): Height 8-20 feet. The gourds are grown for their curiously shaped fruits, which may be dried, rather than for beauty of vine. Plant 24 inches apart.

Moonflower (*Calonyction aculeatum*): Height 10-20 feet. Fragrant, 6-inch white flowers open late in day to give evening charm to the garden. Notch seed or soak overnight in water. Seeds need heat to germinate; sow indoors in peat pots, at 70-75 degrees, a month before planting outdoors in North. Set plants 1 foot apart.

Morning glory (*Ipomoea*): Height 15-25 feet. Finest of all is the 'Heavenly Blue' morning glory, with its huge, pale blue flowers. 'Cheerio,' scarlet; 'Flying Saucers,' striped patterns; and 'Pearly Gates,' white, are fine varieties effective with 'Heavenly Blue,' but not as vigorous in growth. Soak all seed overnight or better still, notch with a file or chip the end off with a knife. Plant 12 inches apart.

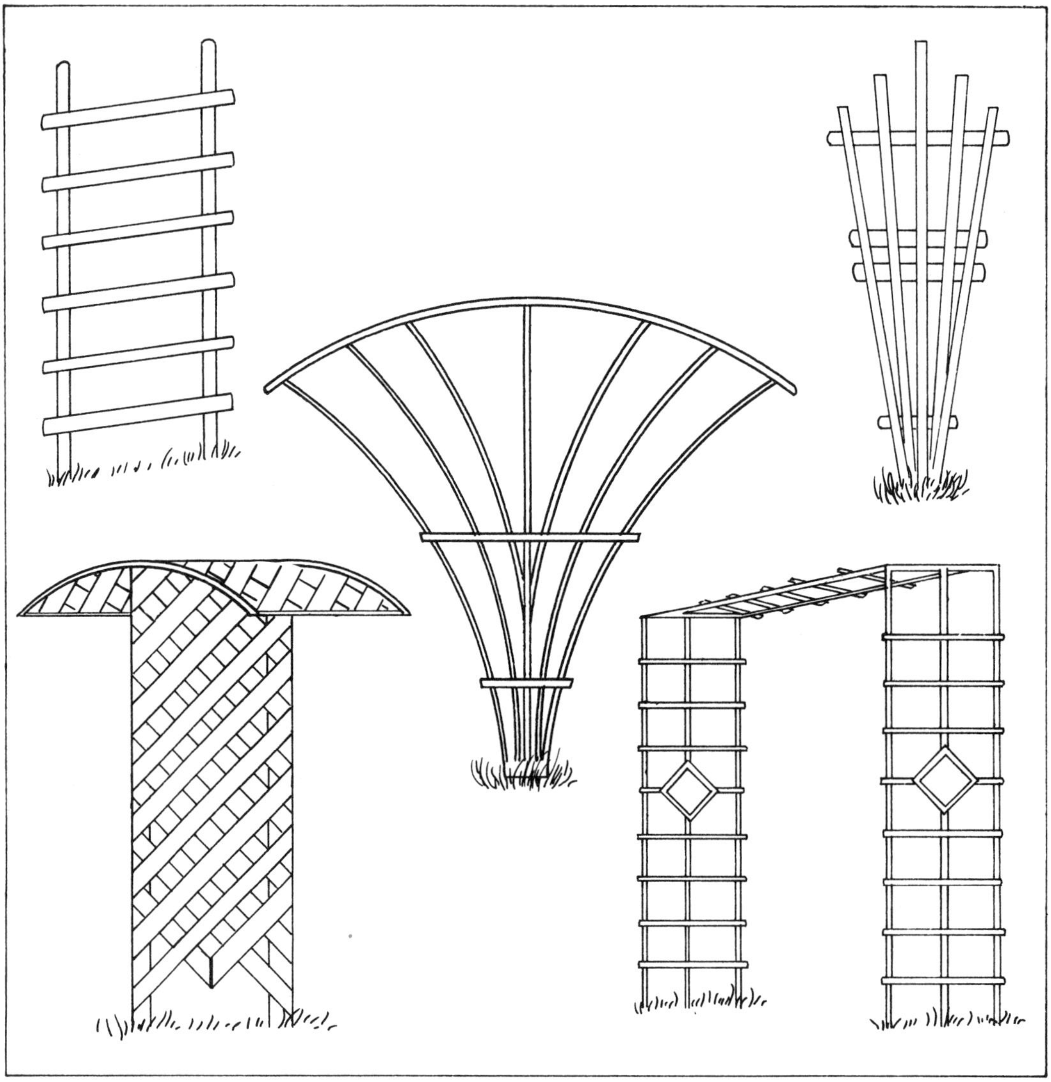

These five easily built trellises can be made from stock lumber by anyone who is handy with tools.

Nasturtium (*Tropaeolum majus* in many varieties): Height 8-15 feet. The climbing forms, although gaudy, are useful, easily grown, and popular for sunny locations. Plant 1 foot apart. Aphids, which often infest plants, can be controlled by contact sprays.

Scarlet runner bean (*Phaseolus coccineus*): Height 8-15 feet. A mass of brilliant scarlet flowers. Showy, attractive, easily grown. Blooms all summer. Pods are eatable. Plant 1 foot apart.

Black-eyed Susan (*Thunbergia alata*): Height 3-5 feet. A really charming little vine for rock gardens, porch boxes, or hanging baskets. Covered with numerous creamy-white flowers that always attract attention. Sow seed early in a cold frame or indoors in peat pots. Set plants 1 foot apart.

The Best of the Ground Covers

While ground cover plants have long been used on steep banks and in shade too dense for grass, today we seek space for these special plants because they have become integral parts of the landscape scheme, desirable for their own characteristics. Not all of them are vines; nor are they necessarily fast-spreading plants. But most plants that we think of as being suitable for ground cover in lieu of grass (or concrete) are fairly low-growing and sooner or later form a dense enough cover to prevent weed growth. Every region has special requirements in ground cover plants due to climate and soil, so visit local nurseries, public plantings (notice especially the better landscaped shopping malls and industrial buildings), and parks for ideas to incorporate in your home grounds.

Modern uses for ground cover plants are infinite: they are planted around and under trees, in the foreground of shrub groupings, in shade or in sun to hide unsightly soil areas, and some are tough enough to surface patios or terraces or at least be set between paving stones.

Bearberry (*Arctostaphylos uva-ursi*): Creeping ground-hugging evergreen for sunny, dry areas with sandy, acid soil. Difficult to transplant. Buy rooted cuttings.

Blue fescue (*Festuca glauca*): Spiky clumps of blue grass 12 inches high for interesting textural effect in sun or light shade.

Bugleweed (*Ajuga reptans*): Low-growing plants with good textural qualities. During the spring, small spikes of blue flowers cover the plant. There are several varieties, some with green leaves, others with copper leaves. Grows in average soil in sun or shade and spreads rapidly.

Christmas fern (*Polystichum acrostichoides*): Handsome evergreen fern, 15 inches high, for shade and good soil. Needs woodsy soil. Add peat moss to average garden soil when planting. Water during drought. There are many other good ferns for ground cover.

Creeping thyme (*Thymus serpyllum*): These plants need full sun and a well-drained location. Grow between flagstones on walks and terraces as their woody stems can take some abuse. Besides their fine foliage and neat habit of growth, the thymes are pungently fragrant. Use on banks adjacent to steps where they grow gracefully over the sides.

Epimedium (*Epimedium macranthum*): Heart-shaped foliage and delicate flowers present a beautiful picture in woodlands or in a part-shade location. Epimediums are slow to spread. Give them rich, moist soil.

The readiness of ajuga *to "cover ground" is shown in the way it has climbed over the log.*

A thriving cover of summer-flowering heathers (calluna) *is supported by sandy, acid soil.*

Ivy ground cover softens edges of geometrically patterned pavement. They can be cut back for more formality.

Pachysandra is easily kept within bounds of small beds, but it also can spread readily when desired.

Ground-hemlock (*Taxus canadensis*): Semi-prostrate, evergreen yew 2 feet or more tall for North and mountainous regions. Very hardy. Grow in shade.

Heath (*Erica carnea*): Low evergreen shrub that forms solid mats up to 2 feet high. White or rose flowers in late winter or early spring. There are several varieties. These heaths grow in sun or part shade in acid or slightly acid soil that is well drained.

Honeysuckle (*Lonicera*): See Vines.

Hosta (*Hosta*): Also known as funkia or plantain-lily. There are many varieties, some with variegated leaves with green and white or yellow patterns, others with crinkled blue-green leaves. All have stalks of lily-like blue or white flowers, a few with delightful fragrance. The hosta is an old-fashioned plant, popular again because it is easy to grow in shade and because its leaves offer such valuable patterns and textural variation. Unfortunately mice will eat the thick roots.

Houseleek (*Sempervivum*): Many species and varieties for dry or rocky situations in full sun. Most spread slowly.

Ivy (*Hedera*): See Vines.

Japanese spurge (*Pachysandra terminalis*): Has turned many an eyesore into beauty. It is 6 inches tall, about the easiest grown evergreen, enduring shade and drought as well as sun. Succeeds where other plants fail. Its cuttings root easily. Spreads quickly if the tops are pinched back occasionally. Used as a border for walks, it is easily kept within bounds. Try it where everything else has failed.

Juniper (*Juniperus horizontalis procumbens*): Blue-green evergreen foliage in low mat 6 inches high for sun or light shade. All the creeping junipers in many other species and varieties are unexcelled ground covers among rocks, on slopes, or flat land. Consult local nurserymen and catalogs for others.

Lily-of-the-valley (*Convallaria majalis*): The original ground cover, especially under li-

Periwinkle (vinca), *here interplanted with crocuses, produces abundant blue flowers in early summer.*

On the West Coast and in other mild climates, ivy-geranium (background) *can be used as flowering cover for steep banks. In foreground, English ivy.*

lacs. It thrives in sun or shade, but is a heavy feeder. An application of commercial fertilizer in the early spring will keep the plants in good condition. After a few years, the bed should be thinned and the soil fertilized, or they will become too thick to thrive.

Memorial rose (*Rosa wichuraiana*): The variety offered is "Max Graf," and it has large pink flowers. Fine for steep banks in full sun.

Pachistima (*Pachistima canbyi*): A delightful miniature evergreen shrub that is finally gaining recognition. It spreads by underground runners. Very hardy and once established in good soil is drought resistant. Grow in partial or full shade.

Periwinkle (*Vinca minor*): Also called running myrtle. Another low evergreen making excellent ground cover in shade or sun. Vigorous in habit. Lilac-blue flowers in early summer. The "Bowles" variety is superior to the type, with stronger foliage and more profuse flowers of deeper blue. There are also white-flowering varieties that are less vigorous.

Plumbago (*Ceratostigma plumbaginoides*): Though difficult to transplant, it will endure adverse conditions with no care or attention. In the fall when least expected, the peacock-blue flowers open – a sight to behold. An excellent plant to use along rock walls where it can bury its long roots into cracks and crannies.

Polygonum (*Polygonum reynoutria*): A knotweed for full sun and dry situations. It grows about a foot high and is too rampant for most locations but is ideal in places where it can spread. The foliage is excellent and in the fall the low-growing plants are covered with pink or reddish sprays of flowers.

Sedum (*Sedum acre*): Bright yellow flowers on succulent mats of foliage 4 inches high. For full sun and average or dry soil. Variety S. *aureum* has yellow leaves in the spring.

A flower garden of annuals, perennials, and roses in early summer. It has a border of pansies.

CHAPTER 9

The Flower Garden

The daisy, primrose, violet darkly blue,
And polyanthus of unnumbered dyes;
The yellow wall-flower, stained with iron brown,
And lavish stock, that scents the garden round.

– J. Thomson the Elder

The picture that first comes to many people when the word "garden" is mentioned is an arrangement of brilliantly colorful flowers, varying in types, textures, sizes, and habits of growth, but so placed and cared for as to give maximum pleasure to all the senses that a garden delights.

But garden effects can be created in many ways. There are formal and informal gardens in which additional effects are contributed by flowering shrubs, evergreens, trees, or vines. Such gardens can be extensive or limited, close to one's house, or at a distance. A flower garden can be a small, intimate grouping of flowering plants, perhaps planned to enhance a special piece of sculpture. It can be open so that neighbors and passersby can enjoy its beauty, or it can be a private retreat screened from the public by fences, walls or shrubs.

In the main, flower gardens are made up of 3 groups of flowering plants: perennials, annuals, and bulbs and tubers. (Bulbs and tubers are discussed in Chapter 10.)

A perennial has roots that live over from year to year, usually sending forth new growth above ground in the spring. Some perennials live longer than others: the peony is an example of a perennial that will outlast generations. Others, like the temperamental delphinium, have short lives.

An annual plant – the petunia is a popular example – lasts only for a season, growing from seed in the spring, flowering in the summer, and dying in the fall. In mild climates, and over mild winters in colder areas, some annuals, like the snapdragon, behave in perennial fashion, their roots surviving, with the result that the second year, plants are even bushier and more bountiful in their flower production.

In between perennials and annuals is a lesser group of plants called biennials that are grown from seed. They last for two years, making roots and above-ground leafy growth the first season. The second year they produce flowers, then gradually die. Common favorites among the biennials are pansies and hollyhocks. Again, though, one can't be too rigid in classifying their growth patterns for, like the snapdragon, they may be more perennial in habit under certain circumstances: some biennials may live a year or so beyond their expected two-year growth cycle.

Once you have an understanding of the various classes of plants that make up a flower garden, you can logically proceed to

The chrysanthemum is a typical perennial, a long-lived plant which should come up year after year.

Sweet William is a biennial, short-lived plant that is grown from seed one year, blooms the second year, and then dies. Another biennial is the hollyhock.

The petunia is a popular annual. Plants are killed by frost and must be grown each spring from seed.

Spring bulbs like these bluebells, hyacinths, tulips and daffodils, are often planted with perennials.

the next step—deciding what kind of a flower garden you want.

The Perennial Border

When we think of a garden, our visual image is fairly certain to center around an English flower border composed of perennial plants laid out in great drifts of glowing color, relieved by masses of white lilies and accented with towering spires of blue. It expresses the beauty of form and color that every real lover of flowers tries to create to the best of his ability and resources.

Other Kinds of Gardens

A variation of the all-perennial border or garden is the mixed border. This type of garden includes many basic perennials such as day-lily and phlox, but in addition utilizes groups of annuals and biennials, and perhaps some of the spring-flowering bulbs like tulips and hyacinths. Its advantages over the all-perennial garden are flexibility of design, greater masses of color over a longer season, and often lower cost and easier maintenance.

A third type of flower garden may be one composed entirely of annual plants. These can be arranged in artistic groups to make the best visual impact possible, or they can be grown in practical rows, to serve mostly as a source of cut flowers.

Of course styles of gardens change as do fashions in the architecture of the houses they surround. And cultural patterns and economic factors affect the types of gardens in vogue. Smaller properties and the demand for low maintenance (proper maintenance is the great lack of most American gardens when they are compared with their foreign counterparts) have resulted in a fourth type of flower garden. It involves the use of a few plants or as many as you wish, annuals or perennials or both, in a variety of ways and situations, depending on where you think your property can be enhanced by their addition. This kind of garden so prevalent over the entire nation today might be described as an accent garden.

Wherever and however flowers are used, they stand out as color accents in the overall landscape. You are aware of this kind of a garden everywhere: it may be a small bed of petunia plants nestled against shrubbery in a shopping mall. It may be one or three day-lily plants that a friend has set against an ancient boulder that existed long before her ranch-type house was built. Or it may be a narrow border of sweet alyssum along your neighbor's front walk or around her flagstone terrace. Its great merits are flexibility and simplicity, and such a kind of flower gardening is suitable to any property.

But in all these gardens, the basic principles of growing the flowers, and the kinds that can be used, are much the same.

A typical English border, this one at Chartwell, Winston Churchill's home. In bloom are delphinium and yellow dusty meadow-rue.

A flower border in grand style at Old Westbury Gardens on Long Island, N.Y. Although not all plants are in bloom at once, each plant contributes value to the overall effect of the garden.

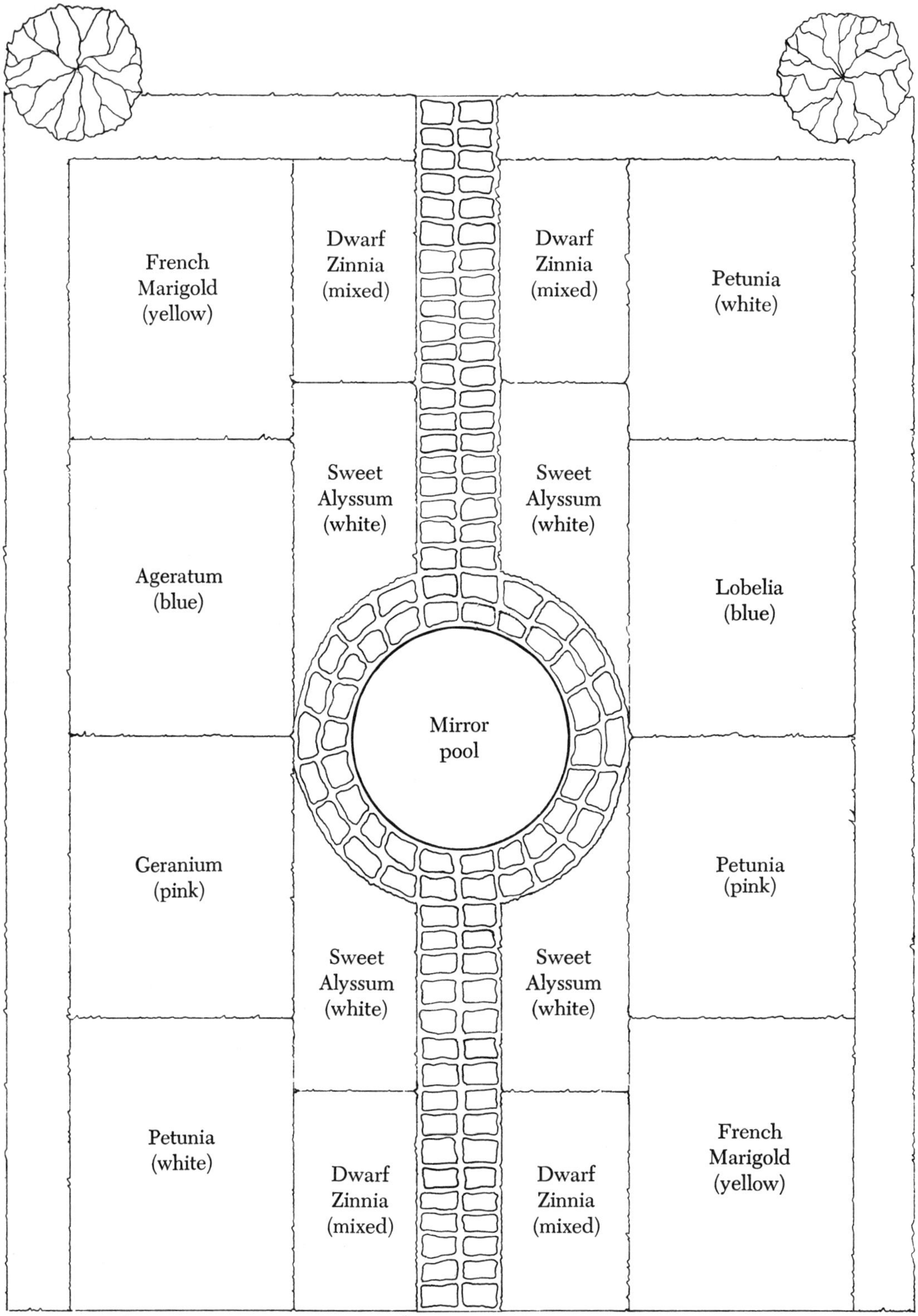

Pattern Garden of Low Annuals. A versatile pattern garden (about 12 by 18 feet or whatever size you wish) using annuals so its plant and color combinations can be varied every year. It can be surrounded by a low hedge (boxwood, teucrium, yew or the annual kochia *or summer-cypress). The path can be of brick, flagstone, sand, grass or bare soil. Optional are two trees; suggestions are the "Strathmore" crab or rose-of-Sharon. The small mirror pool in center is pleasant accent.*

Planning a Border

Now let's return to that first grand picture of a flower garden – the all-perennial or mixed border, the epitome of the flower garden today, yesterday, and tomorrow.

Start with a plan on paper drawn to a large scale so notes may be made directly on the plan. Ideally the border should be at least 5 or 8 feet deep.

Site: The ideal site is close to the house; preferably it should face south or southwest, but this is not of great consequence if it has sun and is several feet from the robbing roots of trees or shrubbery. Keep the border at least 2 to 3 feet away from any hedge.

In addition to a hedge, a good background may be a rough-textured wall, a view of distant trees or shrubbery, or a low fence covered with climbing roses. Above all there should be surrounding relief, and nothing sets off the border better than a stretch of lawn. It is better to have a smaller border than to deprive it of the grass setting. Free-form, "island" beds (roughly kidney or crescent shaped) may fit into the landscape scheme. They are most often planted with shrubs, but there is no reason why perennials and annuals can't be used. If such beds are used, plant the high-growing plants toward the center, then the medium-sized ones and the edging plants on the sides.

Selection of plants: Selection of plants for the flower border may seem like a weighty problem, but it is really one of the most pleasant aspects of garden planning. Studying the plant lists and looking up the descriptions of plants at the end of this chapter will help you. Use nursery catalogs and reference books found in garden cen-

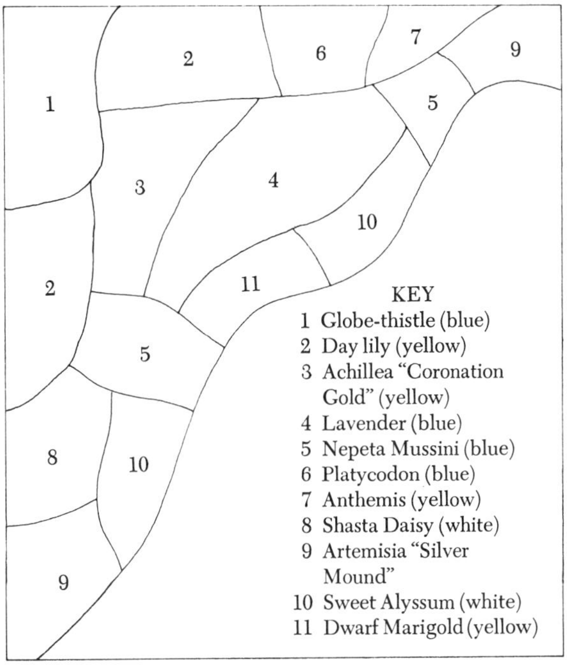

Early Summer Blue-Yellow Garden for Sunny Corner. Flower gardens often conveniently fit into corners, especially where hedges, fences or shrubs meet and form a background. The garden above is planned for early midsummer color but the few annuals massed in front will provide color all summer. After flowers fade, remove them and leave foliage to present neat, green effect. With the exception of globe thistle which makes a huge plant in a few seasons, use from three to five plants in each group.

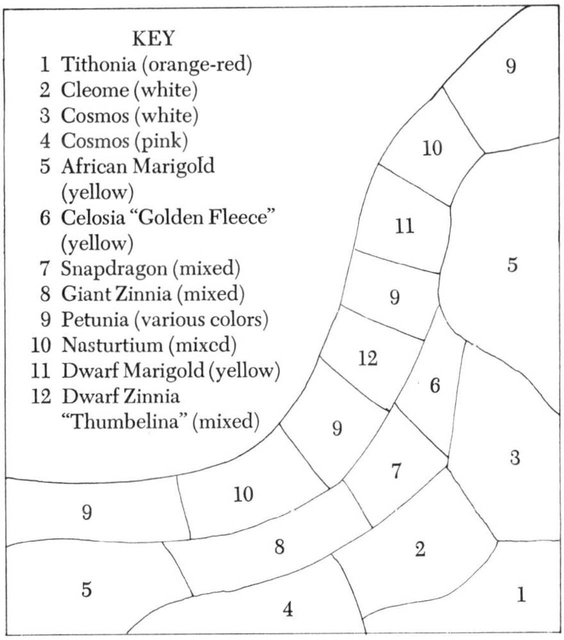

Corner Garden of Annuals for Display and Cutting. This garden, about 18 by 16 feet, is arranged with the tallest annual (tithonia) *in rear and low to medium annuals from front to middle.*

ters, horticultural societies, and your public libraries.

The following 10 points can guide you in an effective selection of plant material.

1. Length of life of the plant. Is it annual, biennial, or perennial?

2. Height and lateral spread or breadth.

3. Growing habit: prostrate, erect or climbing.

4. Time and length of flowering period.

5. Color of flowers and foliage; persistence of foliage and decorative effect.

6. Moisture, soil, and plant food requirements.

7. Sun or shade loving?

8. Hardiness in a given region.

9. Does the plant spread freely?

10. Susceptibility to disease and insects.

In planning the material for an all-season, mixed border, select key plants for line, mass, color and dependability. Try to avoid stiffness caused by too regular an arrangement. Do not place the plant groups in regular lines, like rows of cabbages, but in sections which are wider than they are deep. This gives each group a chance to be seen to good advantage from the front of the border.

Of course taller plants (tie them to stakes early) should be at the rear, then those of medium height, with the dwarfs in the front. This does not mean that some of the taller plants should not come out into middle ground or the medium-tall toward the front. For the charm of irregularity, break up height lines as well as planting lines. The aim is to imitate the irregular way in which nature grows her plants and still place them in order for display, within the limits of space. Also, strive for proportion; if the border is very narrow, tall plants should be avoided except for occasional accent. The border will appear top-heavy if it is too tall and narrow. Groups should be of sufficient size for display. Large masses of one-of-a-kind plants in a border are seldom successful. Borders which are more than 8 feet wide should have a 2-foot service path behind them.

Is it possible to have continuous bloom in a flower garden? The answer is certainly "yes" if you will settle for groups of color in sections of the garden – rather than for a complete blanket of color from spring to fall. To achieve the latter condition, you would need at your beck and call an array of greenhouses, cold frames, nursery rows, and an army of gardeners who would add and remove plants as they come in and out of bloom. There are very few ever-blooming flowers, despite the claims of over-zealous nurserymen! Yet very colorful gardens can be achieved with annuals, bulbs, and perennials that have especially long flowering seasons.

In planning a border, it is also wise to consider *when* the garden should be at its color peak. If August is vacation time, then common sense dictates that you choose

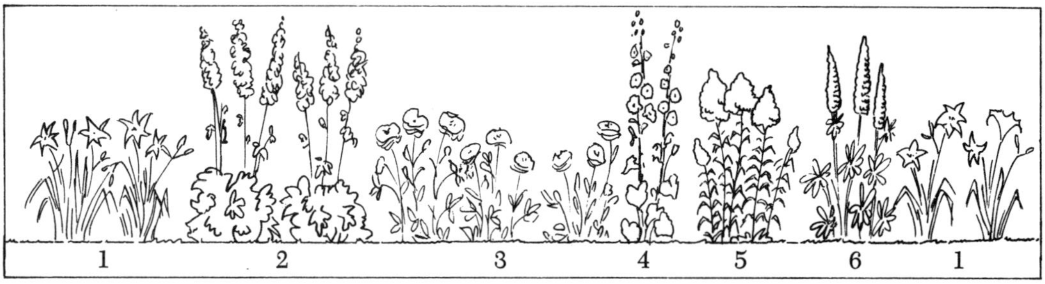

Flower and Plant Forms in Hardy Border. *The skyline of a flower border is varied by contrasting flower forms and heights and textural effects and patterns of foliage. Some groups of plants should be repeated while a few kinds of dominant plants should be used as single accents. Usually three to five plants of one kind are used in each group.* 1) *Day-lily* 2) *Delphinium* 3) *Peony* 4) *Hollyhock* 5) *Phlox* 6) *Lupine*

plants that reach their perfection in spring and early summer. If you start your borders with simple plants, hardy in your locality, they will need little coddling.

Hemerocallis (day-lily), phlox, and chrysanthemum are basic perennials. Add iris, peonies, and a few edging, filler, and background plants, and your border will be on its way.

Three forms of iris are useful: dwarf, bearded, and Siberian. Use the dwarf for spring color accent in the edging strip, spacing the clumps 2 to 3 feet apart to allow groups of other perennial edging plants between them. Arabis, candytuft, creeping phlox, the sedums, plumbago, and dwarf asters are suitable. Plants of such annuals as dwarf ageratum, petunia, and sweet alyssum can be worked in behind them for later color. To avoid a spotty effect use only a few varieties of each kind of plant.

Edging the Flower Border

Stone and brick edgings are effective, but it is difficult for a mower to get close enough to do a good job of cutting. The grass will grow tall and scraggly against them and must be trimmed with shears.

Rust-resisting metal strips are available that can be bent to fit curves and placed less than an inch above the ground to permit the mower to pass without interference.

Concerning the use of small plants for edgings, be sure they are compact and full as to foliage and have a long season of bloom. The dwarf compact petunia, *Nierembergia* (or blue cup-flower), dwarf ageratum, and the old standby sweet alyssum, can all be kept under control and give good service.

Hardy candytuft (*Iberis sempervirens*) is the ideal perennial edging in sections where it will not burn in the winter sun. It has white flowers in masses and evergreen foliage. Other dwarf perennials, selected for succession of bloom are: *Arabis alpina, Alyssum saxatile,* dwarf asters, *Campanula carpatica,* dianthus, *Nepeta mussini,* pulmonaria, sweet William, *Veronica incana.*

A famous edging plant is sweet alyssum. It is easily sown from seed and starts to flower when an inch or so high.

An informal summer flower garden with an inviting grass path.

These, planted in bands which overlap slightly, and interplanted with small bulbs, will give a good effect, and form a transition from the low edge to the higher plants in the beds.

Midsection and Background

The middle section of a mixed border uses taller plants than the front or edging strip but by no means should they all be of the same height. The aim is to create an undulating effect of blending and contrast-

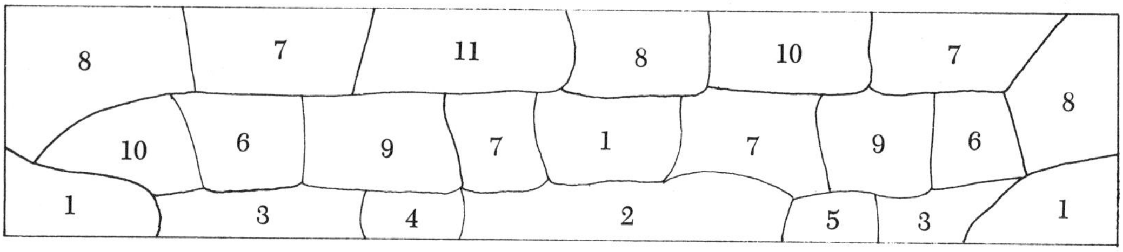

Summer Flower Border (about 22 x 1½ feet)
1) *Nepeta mussini*
2) *Dwarf marigold*
3) *Sweet alyssum*
4) *Artemisia 'Silver Mound'*
5) *Santolina*
6) *Shasta daisy*
7) *Phlox*
8) *Day-lily*
9) *Monarda*
10) *Siberian iris*
11) *Globe thistle*

ing colors, forms and textures. Some groups of low-growing plants from the foreground must dip into this section, and some taller plants from the background should be brought forward.

No matter whether your border is 10 feet wide or 5 feet wide, or whether it is 60 feet long or only 20, this middle section between foreground and background plant material is most important. Here the skill of the gardener is tested. He must contrast rounded flower shapes with spiky forms, utilize assets provided by varying foliage colors and textures, and, finally, think like an artist in planning his color effects.

Most of the major perennials can be classified as middle-of-the-border subjects as their heights fall between 18 and 36 inches. There are many varieties of annuals, notably zinnia, marigold, and snapdragon, of neat growth that are also suitable. A random list of medium-height, reliable perennials includes the following: astilbe, many day-lilies, bearded iris, blue salvia (*Salvia farinacea*), babys-breath, sweet William, peony, shasta daisy, Canterbury bells, veronica, nepeta, yarrow, summer phlox, bee balm, chrysanthemum, peach bell, columbine, bleeding-heart, gas-plant, and lupine.

Background plants are important, too, and while the list of reliable ones may not be as varied or extensive as the list of medium-height plants, there are plenty to select from. Some are bushy enough to be planted as individual accents, especially in the case of narrow or short gardens, but most plants – as elsewhere in the border – are most effective in groups of three, four, or five.

Good background plants include the following: delphinium, tall varieties of summer phlox, dusty meadow-rue (*Thalictrum glaucum*), false-indigo, hollyhock, foxglove, thermopsis, monkshood, globe thistle, lythrum, boltonia, and plume-poppy (*Macleaya cordata*). A few of these, like plume-poppy which grows up to 8 feet, are much too tall for borders restricted in length and width.

Beginning as well as more advanced garden makers tend to be impatient and often expect too much the first year from their new flower garden. Great borders are not usually made in one season. Many perennials, peony and gas-plant for instance, need a few years to become established before giving their best performance. Also, inevitably, mistakes will be made. Yet the failure of one planting does not spoil the season. Some continuous bloom from spring to fall is feasible by selection. The garden need not go dead in midsummer, especially when annuals are used.

Annuals are thc answer to the vacant space problem. The little effort needed to raise them coupled with their low cost and easy maintenance make them very popular.

They make the finest of cut flowers, and used in a border of their own or among the dominating perennials, they have many

Midsummer plant grouping; physotegia's *white spires contrast with rounded phlox flower heads.*

Early summer effect: blue flower balls of globe thistle and white form of Chinese balloon-flower.

Heat-and-drought-resistant daisies: anthemis *flowers remain effective for several weeks in summer.*

Border for early fall: fluffy chrysanthemums and exotic creamy yellow spikes of tritoma.

points of value. In rented property or for a short season at a summer home they have no equal.

Preparation of the Bed

The digging and preparation of a flower garden is very important. The bottom soil need not be as well tilled as the top but once prepared it will last for many years, making it necessary to renew only the fertility of the topsoil from time to time.

If the bottom soil is heavy, incorporate in it some sand, cinders or a large quantity of ashes to break it up. Lime is one of the best soil looseners; and strange as it may seem, it will also compact sandy soil. Use it generously in the bottom. Work in here also a lot of partially decayed leaves, grass clippings, manure, peat moss, or humus. If the soil is sandy you may add clay or a large amount of vegetable matter. Do not firm it down but let it settle naturally.

Topsoil, if heavy, can be made into good loam by the addition of sand and well-rotted manure, humus, peat moss or leaf mold. An application of bone meal or superphosphate, limestone, and possibly a general purpose fertilizer like 5-10-5, should be used generously when making new gardens. (See Chapter 2 for rate of application.) Wood ashes from the fireplace in the spring are excellent.

General Maintenance

With few exceptions, perennials must be divided every 3 or 4 years. The plant starts from the original clump and grows in all directions. After a while the center exhausts the food within reach and dies, leaving a ring of live growth with a dead center. The best portions of this ring must be lifted and divided, cutting away all dead roots and stalk, starting a number of new plants. Make the holes wide enough to spread out the roots. If your bed has been properly prepared they need not be deep. In case of deep-rooted varieties, such as lupine, the holes must be as deep as the root, which should be dug without breaking.

The border must also be overhauled to correct the encroachments of rampant-growing plants which try to smother their less hardy neighbors, and to replace the wayward seedlings which have a habit of growing in the wrong place. The seedlings can usually be turned to good account in regrouping, but it is best to discard seedling phlox as it never runs true to original color and invariably disappoints.

Some authorities recommend spring as the time to make over the border, but many factors seem to favor autumn. First there is the weather, which is more stable in the fall, and then the fact that any desired changes are fresher in the mind, just at the close of the season. Add to these the freedom from the rush of spring tasks, the more easy identification of plant groups and their limits, and the chance that winter freezing has to pulverize the newly turned soil – and it seems that the weight is largely in favor of September or October. This time allows the plants to get a new root start before becoming dormant at freezing time. Be sure to give them a good soaking.

Of course some perennials transplant better in the spring. Plants such as chrysanthemums do not divide well so soon after their blooming period. Move these with as large a clump of earth and as little root disturbance as possible. If division is desired this may be done in the spring when they are more nearly dormant. Divide spring and early summer perennials in the fall, and late summer bloomers in the spring. Remember this is a general rule, and general rules must be used flexibly.

Some perennial seeds are planted in spring and bloom the first year. Some are planted in fall just before frost in a sheltered spot under shrubbery, convenient for winter inspection. They seem to need freezing to germinate. The majority, however, do best sown in spring. Directions for raising plants from seed are given in Chapter 17.

Fertilizing a newly planted perennial in spring with a handful of complete fertilizer.

Apparent change of color of some perennials is due to the fact that the parent plant has perished from disease, or lack of division or other attention, and its place has been taken by seedlings which differ from the parents.

Perennials will respond to an application of a complete plant food in the early spring. The fertilizer should be cultivated into the soil and kept away from the stems of the plants. Annuals, planted in good soil, will not need additional food, though a starter solution of liquid plant food will help them to overcome the shock of transplanting when they are set out in the beds.

Plants subject to disease and insect pests such as peony, phlox, delphinium, and hollyhock should be sprayed or dusted once a week with an all-purpose chemical. (See Chapter 16.)

If you wish to prevent most weed growth and save some watering, mulch with a few inches of compost, peat moss, or whatever is handy. The mulch can gradually be cultivated into the soil in the spring. The material must remain loose enough to permit the entrance of water. Peat moss tends to pack; other materials are better for mulching.

Pinch back tops to produce compact plants. In dry spells water thoroughly rather than often. Stake such tall plants as delphinium at once. Tie a raffia strip to the stake first and then to the plant. Remove all blossoms as soon as they fade to induce a prolonged flowering season. A second flowering can be secured from such plants as Canterbury bells by this method. Cut delphinium stalks off after flowering to get new bloom stalks. Pansies bloom continuously if not allowed to seed.

Winter Protection

Winter protection is something that is generally misunderstood. We do not use a mulch to keep plants warm but to keep them cold. Sudden changes in temperature cause the ground to heave and break tiny roots. Warm days followed by cold nights do much damage, and most winter-killing is from this cause rather than from extreme cold.

If we place a layer of hardwood leaves, which take a long time to decay, over the bed, it lies loose during the whole season if lightly held in place with brush or wire. It must be light and airy and stay dry. If we use ordinary leaves they soon pack into a

Cultivate lightly around plant to mix fertilizer with soil. Water well.

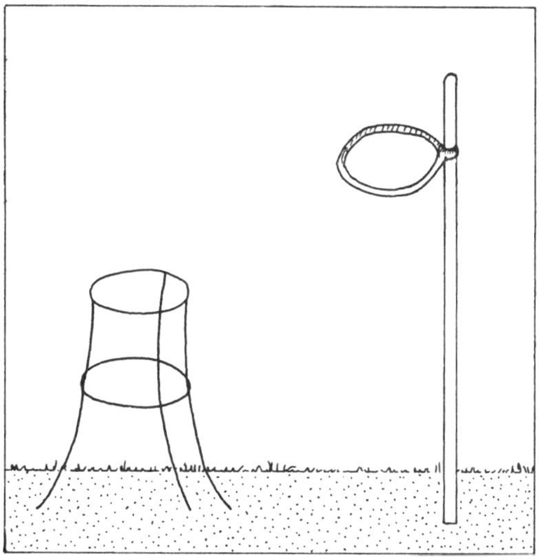

Two practical plant supports: (left) welded wire rack for peony, tomato, babys-breath and (right) adjustable hoop support for many large plants.

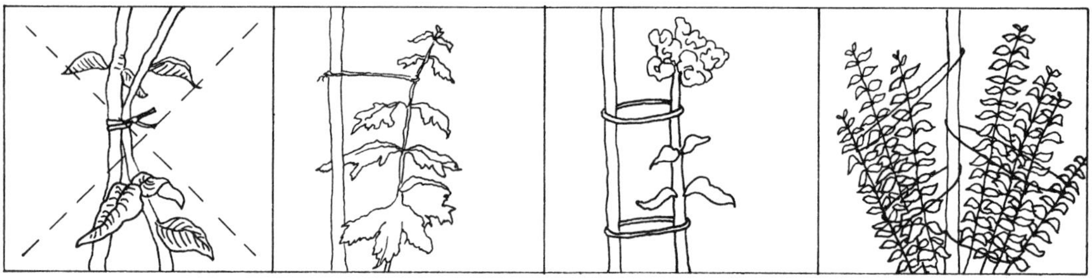

Rights and wrongs of fastening plants to supports: left, *wrong – too restrictive and unnatural; other three methods are all correct. Object is to support stems without strangling them. Heavier ones may need several ties along stems.*

heavy wet mass, which excludes air, smothers the plants, and induces decay. In the spring this type of leaf ferments and produces heat which helps the dormant plants to awaken too soon and defeats the very purpose for which it was placed over them.

One solution is to place an open layer of brush or other rough material to hold the leaves away from the soil. Additional brush or chicken wire should be placed upon the leaves to hold them in place. Do not cover too early. Let the mice find a winter home first. If they nest in the mulch, they will feed upon roots and bulbs.

Sometimes it is necessary to further protect plants which come from warmer climates (tritoma and the like). Use boxes of leaves or baskets loosely filled with leaves.

Notes on Important Garden Flowers

1. Chrysanthemums

Several factors have contributed to the increased popularity of the chrysanthemum, as a commercial greenhouse flower as well as for the home garden. When it was discovered that chrysanthemums could be made to bloom at any season of the year by giving them just the right amount of light, it became one of the most useful flowers for florists. The many different forms, as well as the wide range of colors, were additional values. Not to be overlooked is the long-lasting quality of the cut flower.

Chrysanthemums are sun-loving plants, and for this reason should be planted where they have the sun the majority of the day. The south side of a wall or building is ideal to hold the heat and protect from frost. The single Koreans are especially adapted to use on sunny terraces and in courtyards, as the heat of stones or brick forces their growth. They like a circulation of air as well as sunlight and well-drained ground, and respond to manure, superphosphate, or a good commercial fertilizer.

Plants should be divided in the spring every year; the divisions should consist of only 1 or 2 shoots taken from the outside of the clump. They should be spaced 15 to 18 inches apart and dusted regularly; most kinds should be pinched back.

Growing Exhibition Chrysanthemums

The light factor is a simple one. The chrysanthemum is a short-day plant; that is, it will not set buds if there is too much daylight. Hence the grower merely covers the plants with black cloth or black plastic to shorten their day. The plants must be completely covered; even a ray of light will cause uneven blooming. Growers can in turn increase the light artificially to delay bloom.

Home gardeners can use this idea to bring late-blooming varieties into flower before the season of killing frosts arrives. This method is often used with the tall standards – plants that produce one large globular flower on a single stem.

There are special varieties available for this purpose. When the plants or rooted cuttings arrive, they should be potted in good fertile soil, in small (about 4-inch)

There are many flower forms among chrysanthemums. These are known as "spoon" types.

pots. Sink the pots in a bed or cold frame; water, and feed with liquid fertilizer until the roots fill the pot.

They are now ready to be planted in the open ground or transferred to larger pots. Use 8-inch pots and sink them in the ground in a sunny location, not more than an inch apart. Staking should be done at this time; 7-foot galvanized iron stakes are ideal for this purpose. As an added support, stretch wires between the stakes as the plants grow upward. Remove side laterals on the stem as soon as they appear and disbud when the time comes so that only one flower opens at the top.

Plants must be fed at two-week intervals and a spraying program followed to control both leaf-eating and sucking insects. If shading is necessary to induce bud formation, a framework must be constructed. The covering should be easy to remove. The shade must be put on and removed at a definite time each day.

Generally ten hours of darkness are required starting in mid-August for buds to form in late September but one should consult local authorities (commercial growers) as to the timing. A clear plastic cover can be substituted for the black cloth to protect the plants from frost.

If there is any doubt as to the hardiness of some varieties, the entire clump should be wintered over in the cold frame. It can be divided in the spring. Chrysanthemum cuttings root quickly in the spring. Keep a pot or box of sand or vermiculite handy to the water faucet (the medium must be kept moist); then as you nip back plants to induce bushiness, stick the cuttings in the medium.

While many chrysanthemum varieties remain standard for years, there are changes as some drop from favor and new ones take their places. Consult catalogs of mail-order nurseries for descriptions of current and choice varieties. Most catalogs give the

Growing chrysanthemums from cuttings in spring. Flat contains soil, sand and peat moss. Soak mixture with water before adding cuttings.

Each cutting is dipped into hormone powder to speed up rooting process.

Rows are marked with a knife and cuttings are inserted into sections separated according to variety. Cuttings are then watered and flat is placed in shaded location during rooting period.

After three weeks, all cuttings are rooted and ready for transplanting into pots or open ground.

blooming date, so keep this in mind when you order new plants.

2. Delphiniums

Almost every home garden has a few delphinium plants, which speaks eloquently for the value and popularity of the flower. A native of Siberia, it originated in shades of blue and purple, but hybrids have been developed in a range of colors including crystalline white and pink. As to sizes and shapes, the development has also been wide. Unfortunately, the strain that will persist a reasonable length of time in all parts of the country still seems to be a dream of the future. Perhaps the best way to keep delphinium plants in the garden is to treat them as biennials: have young plants growing to replace those that are lost. One-year plants, of the fine strains now being offered, make a good showing in the flower border in August when planted in among the older clumps.

Start with good seed sown as soon as

obtainable, in August or late July. (Spring-sown seed germinates better if first refrigerated for a few weeks.)

Delphiniums must be planted so that their crowns are level with the soil surface to prevent rot and discourage the numerous diseases these beauties are susceptible to. Their soil must be rich, neutral or slightly alkaline (apply ground limestone if your soil is acid), and well drained. The plants must be sprayed weekly with a miticide such as Dimite during the growing season (starting in spring as new growth begins) to control the cyclamen mite, a pest of microscopic size that causes distorted, blackened growth. The large-flowered hybrids respond to heavy feeding, first in spring and again after flowering. The spikes must be staked. There is no doubt of the temperamental character of delphinium hybrids. One grower suggests if you cannot grow hybrids, revel in the Belladonna types, and he might add the Chinese, which are lovely and should be treated as annuals. Both types are easy to grow from seed.

Delphinium are among easiest of perennials to grow from seed. Young plant is being set out in enriched soil.

The massive but beautiful spikes of delphinium always require staking.

Firm soil around crown. Be sure crown of plant is level with soil surface. Water. Spray weekly.

3. Summer Phlox

The glory of the summer garden is a display of brilliantly colored phlox – a flower of pink, white, red, purple, blue, and violet. Neglect and lack of knowledge of its requirements are the most frequent causes of failure, as gardens full of dried-up magenta phlox will attest. The reason for this apparent reversion is that phlox (*Phlox paniculata*) reseeds easily, and few if any seedlings will come true to their parents' color, as is the case with seeds of most hybrids. For this reason seedlings must be treated as weeds to keep them from stealing the show and crowding out the original plant.

The major requirement of perennial phlox is a rich soil. Apply a handful of complete fertilizer around each plant in the spring. An additional application of potash – wood ashes – gives good results. Phlox requires more water than the average perennial. Use an all-purpose dust or spray containing a fungicide and an insecticide at frequent intervals during the growing season. The clumps should be divided and reset about every third or fourth year in the fall or early spring.

A great deal can be done to keep bloom nearly continuous. Watering will encourage new flower formation as will removing faded flowers. In some, the very tip of the head can be pinched out to encourage the growth of the laterals. On more compact varieties, the buds will develop in the tops beside the fading flowers which should be removed. Unless wanted for cut flowers, the whole stalk should not be cut down.

The phlox varieties introduced by the late Captain Symons-Jeune of England are superb and are now available from most American nurseries. They are especially fragrant. A few outstanding Symons-Jeune varieties are: 'Cecil Hanbury' (salmon orange, 36 inches); 'Dod Hanbury Forbes' (pink, 30 inches); 'Russian Violet' (violet purple, 40 inches); 'Prince Charming' (flame red, 36 to 40 inches); 'Lilac Time' (lilac blue, 42 inches). Standard phlox varieties that retain their popularity year after year include 'White Admiral,' 30 inches; 'Mary Louise,' 30 inches and also white, 'Leo Schlageter,' scarlet, 36 inches. The variety 'Miss Lingard' (derived from another species *Phlox suffruticosa*) is prized for its pure white flowers in early summer.

Bold color effects can be expected from present-day varieties of the day-lily.

4. Hemerocallis – Day-lily

One of the horticultural triumphs of recent years has been the development of a class of hemerocallis hybrids from the "lemon-lilies" of our grandmothers' gardens. Among these species were *Hemerocallis flava,* with fragrant, yellow lily-like flowers in May or June; *Hemerocallis dumortieri,* a clear orange that bloomed at about the same time; *Hemerocallis fulva,* the tawny lily of our roadsides, and *Hemerocallis thunbergi,* the late yellow day-lily of July.

From these have sprung a world of beauty and satisfaction. More than 200 hybrids are listed in variations of apricot, yellow, orange, and buff, with shadings of brown, red, and pink. Besides having charm of color, foliage, and habit of growth, this is a plant without a serious pest, requiring a minimum of care.

There are few cultural directions for the plant. Like any other perennial, it produces better results from soil supplied with plenty of humus. The removal of faded flowers adds to neatness. The day-lily supplies its own winter mulch, so leave the dead tops (some varieties have evergreen foliage) for protection. It grows very well in part shade and in such locations needs less water than in full sun. However, it should always have the full requirement of all perennials, a good thorough soaking when rain fails.

Variation in height and blooming times of the day-lilies make them adaptable to many purposes. Unlike many perennials, they do not look out of place grouped in front of shrubs. They are ideal for naturalizing, either in light shade in open woodlands or in full sun. Use them freely around water – garden pools or near swimming pools. Day-lilies can be grown in number or as single accents. Some of the taller kinds which can be used for background are: 'Hyperion' (lemon); 'Mabel Fuller' (ruby red); 'J. A. Crawford' (apricot); and 'Gay Troubador' (bright red, yellow stripe).

Medium-height varieties which are useful in the border are: 'Painted Lady' (terra cotta); 'Golden Beacon' (orange); 'Pink Prelude' (pale pink); 'Colonial Dame' (apricot); 'Evelyn Claar' (pink).

Low-growing (15-20 inches) varieties which may be used in the foreground or near the terrace are: 'Duchess of Windsor' (cream yellow); 'Rhodora' (bright pink); 'Bonanza' (yellow bicolor).

5. Oriental Poppy

The colors of the Oriental poppy (*Papaver orientale*) were originally orange and scarlet but today range from white through many shades of pink, rose, red, to lavender, with great variation in height and in size of bloom. Poppy stems attain heights of up to 4 feet, which lift the flowers far above their surroundings.

Oriental poppies thrive in average garden soil, their essential requirement being good drainage. They also prefer full sun, but will stand a small amount of shade. They require ample room for development of their roots.

Transplanting is most successfully done when the plant is dormant, in August or September. The plants can be raised from seed, but seedlings will not come true to parental color, so root propagation is best. This is very easy as a 2-inch root cutting as thick as a lead pencil soon grows into a blooming plant. Cuttings should be taken from mature dormant plants about 2 or 3 years old. Root growth starts in about 3 weeks, so keep the cuttings well watered and shaded after growth starts.

The bearded iris is a most adaptable plant for many landscape situations, needing only sun and well-drained soil which is not especially rich.

Care must be exercised to avoid disturbing the plant or its roots by cultivation, especially during the period when no foliage is showing. Too deep planting is often the cause of lack of bloom, as the crowns seldom bloom well if set more than 2 or 3 inches deep. They also resent transplanting, preferring to remain in one place.

A recommended list of varieties includes: (pink) 'Helen Elizabeth,' 'Adorable,' 'Betty Ann,' and 'Lighthouse'; (deep pink and coral) 'Watermelon,' 'Salome,' and 'Master Richard'; (red) 'Empress of India,' and 'Royal Robe'; (lavender-purple) 'Raspberry Queen' and 'Lavender Giant'; (white) 'Barr's White' and 'White Queen'; (bicolor) 'Show Girl,' 'Carousel.'

6. The Many Kinds of Iris

Perhaps the ultimate of garden magic is the unfolding of a bearded iris bud. The wonder is that a mere bud could hold such a spectacular flower. This magic, in varying degree, is common to all the kinds of iris, from the magnificent bearded iris and early summer-blooming Japanese iris to the less flamboyant but still undeniably lovely Siberian iris. Earlier, spring offers minia-

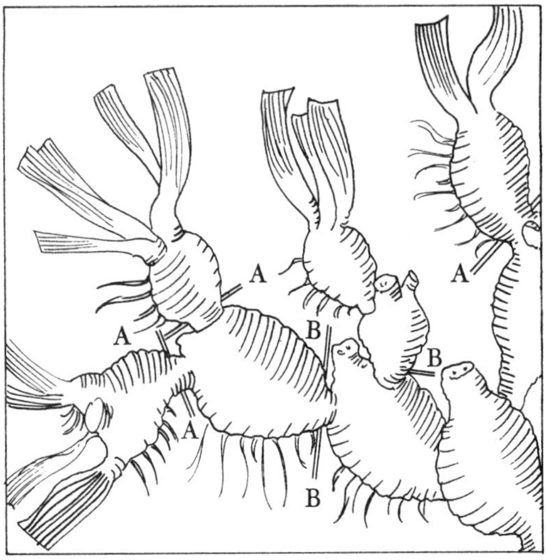

An iris clump ready for division: cuts made at point marked "A" give fewer blooms the year after dividing than larger divisions marked "B".

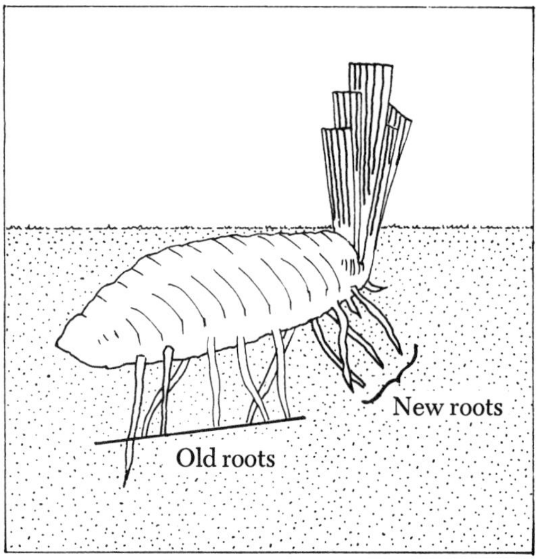

Planting iris rhizome: it should be barely below surface.

tures of the bearded iris, the low-growing *Iris pumila* varieties that flower with tulips.

The June-flowering bearded iris has few requirements – full sun, or nearly full, and well-drained soil of reasonable fertility. Iris specialists ship the rhizomes, as the roots are called, in summer and early fall. Before planting each rhizome (in clumps about 6 or 8 inches apart) ground limestone should be mixed with the soil, about a good handful per group. The rhizomes should be barely covered with soil and then thoroughly soaked.

Newly purchased rhizomes usually are shipped with their leaves trimmed. After transplanting (or planting) is the only time that leaf removal is justified. Although many gardeners practice it every year, for appearance, it cannot help but affect the energy of the plants needed for next season's flowers.

The foliage of iris is handsome unless some of the fans have been mutilated by borers, the main bearded iris pest. Borers seem to resent sunshine and seldom attack in locations where the rhizomes have a chance to bake. Once borers are found, lift the clumps, separate, and discard the decayed parts, including the borer. Replant only healthy rhizomes, each with a shoot attached.

The Siberian iris have beardless flowers a little later than the bearded types and grassy foliage in definite clumps, growing from fibrous roots. They are very effective in groups of three varieties in the middle of the border or toward the rear. The color range hardly rivals the rainbow, as does that of the bearded iris, but the flowers are effective in blue, purple, maroon, and white. Siberian iris have no special requirements, but the roots will tolerate more moisture than the bearded kinds, as will the Japanese iris.

The Japanese iris, another beardless sort, extends the season well into summer and is a spectacular finale to the major iris season. This iris does demand rich, moist soil, especially necessary during the flowering season. The rest of the time the soil should be well drained. This need makes the Japanese iris more difficult to please, but it is such a spectacular flower that any extra effort with the hose is worthwhile.

There are many other kinds of iris – some hard to grow, others lacking any quirks at all. A few, like the common blue flag of American prairies, *Iris versicolor,*

When possible, divide and reset only part of an iris border or grouping each year to avoid poor appearance and lack of bloom that must be expected first year after dividing. Most iris clumps need division after three or four years.

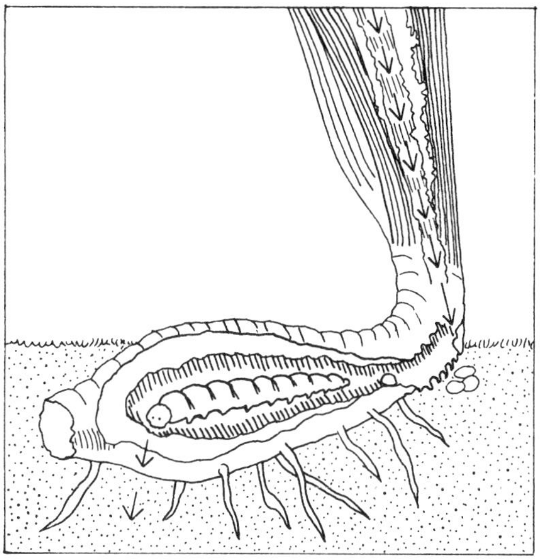

Life cycle of iris borer: ragged edges and blotches in foliage indicate iris borer's presence – out of reach of sprays. If not destroyed by pinching, it enters rhizome and finally the soil for pupation.

and the European yellow flag, *Iris pseudacorus,* are true water plants that grow best in boggy situations. Especially charming for woodland plantings is the low-growing American native, *Iris cristata.* It is a choice wildflower readily naturalized in humus-rich soil.

7. The Peony

When was the peony not a favorite? This remarkable perennial will survive for years, for generations, and flower quite well without special care. When properly planted and loved, it rewards such extra attention by being one of the handsomest of all perennials.

Peonies will do fairly well in some shade (but will not bloom in full shade); a fully sunny exposure is preferred. Peonies are amazingly tolerant of many soil types, but they should be given soil that is close to neutral or at the most only slightly acid. Good drainage is important but so is organic material to retain some soil moisture – before planting, add a quantity of peat moss, rich, partially decomposed compost, or rotted, strawy manure – the last if you can get it. Each root should show about three to five buds or "eyes" at planting time in early fall. The buds should be set about 2 inches deep. Too deep planting is said to be a cause of bloom failure.

Peonies are especially partial to potash in any form, applied in early spring. Two or three handfuls of wood ashes from the fireplace can be lightly cultivated into the soil around clumps in the spring. Most peony stems require support – wire hoops, either purchased or homemade, are the best. When quality flowers are desired, remove all but one bud from each stalk.

In the fall after frost has killed the foliage, all above-ground parts of the peony should be cut off at ground level, and burned. This type of sanitation is the best way to control botrytis blight, a common disease that "nips peonies in the bud," causing them to mummify when they are about the size of a marble. Ants swarming over peony blooms do no direct damage, but they may spread diseases.

While herbaceous peonies can be grouped effectively in the foreground of shrub colonies (but even better for such

Digging an established peony clump in early fall for division. Roots may be 15 inches long.

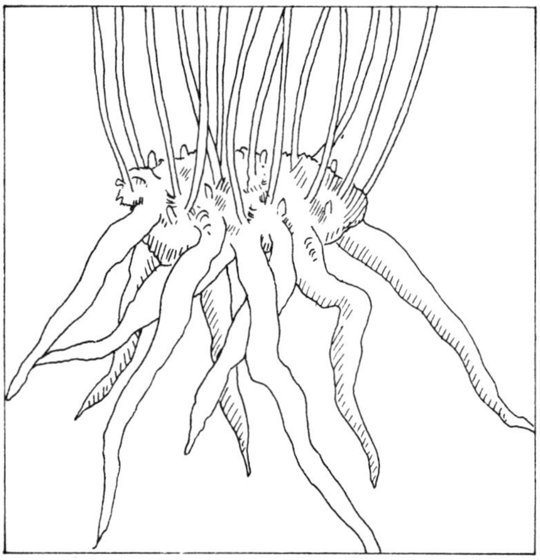

Clump after lifting. Soil may be washed off with a hose to make division easier.

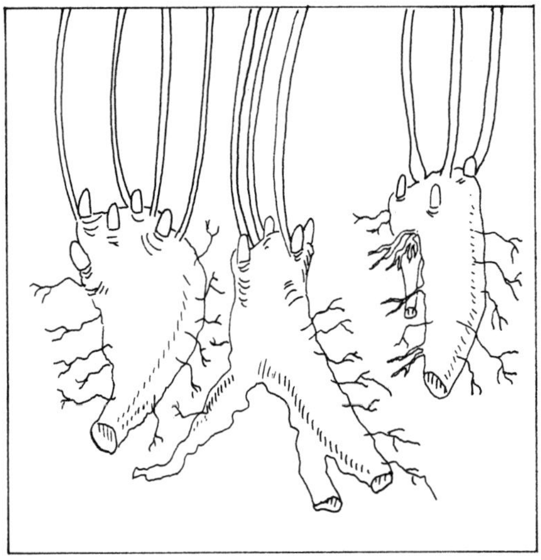

Several healthy divisions, all containing from three to five "eyes," ready for planting.

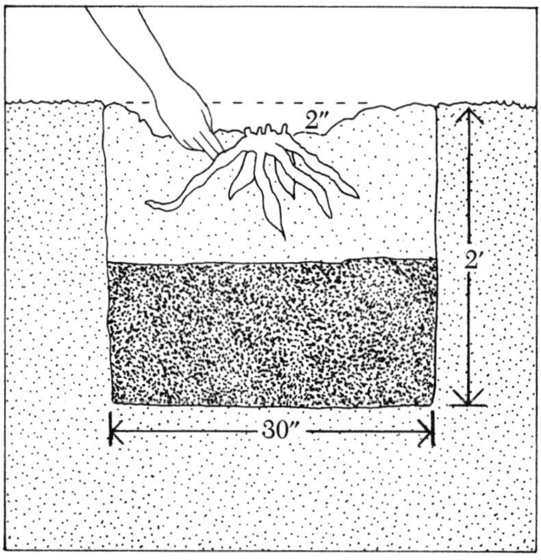

Planting new peony: make generous hole and enrich soil with compost or rotted manure, and one handful of lime and one of superphosphate. Apply wood ashes every spring. Crown should be two inches below soil surface.

use is the tree peony), they are best in large flower gardens as important accents. Whatever the temptation, don't plant peonies as lonesome specimens in lawns or other unsuitable areas.

The early Decoration Day peonies are varieties of *Paeonia officinalis.* Other herbaceous types are hybrids or varieties of various species. Consult catalogs for names and descriptions. The tree peony varieties and hybrids are derived from several species including *P. suffruticosa,* and the beauty of their flowers is truly breathtaking. They are true shrubs, as their main stem remains woody and does not die down in fall.

THE MORE EASILY GROWN, HARDY PERENNIALS

Varieties marked R are suitable for the rock garden

	Color	*Blooming Season*	*Height*	*Location*
Achillea (Milfoil) Boule de Neige	White	July–Oct.	2 ft.	Sun, average soil
Achillea (Golden plate)	Yellow	July–Aug.	3 ft.	Sun, average soil
R *Alyssum saxatile* (Gold dust)	Yellow	April–May	6 in.	Sun, average soil
R *Aquilegia alpina* (Columbine)	Blue	May–June	1–2 ft.	Sunny or semi-shade Moist loam soil
R *Aquilegia coerulea*	Blue and white	May–June	1½–2½ ft.	
Aquilegia chrysantha	Yellow	May–June	2–3 ft.	
Aquilegia McKana hybrids	Various	May–June	2–3 ft.	
R *Armeria maritima* (Sea thrift)	Pink	May–July	12 in.	Sandy, sunny
Aster frikarti	Bluish lilac	June–Sept.	2½ ft.	Average garden soil, sun or partial shade
Aster hybrids	Various	Sept.–Oct.	3–4 ft.	
R *Aster*, dwarf	Various	Oct.–Nov.	9 in.	
Baptisia australis (False indigo)	Dark blue	May–July	2–3 ft.	Sunny, rich soil
Centaurea montana	Blue	June–Sept.	15 in.	Sunny border
R *Cerastium tomentosum*	White	May–July	6 in.	Sunny border
Chrysanthemum, garden	Various	Aug.–Oct.	1–3 ft.	Sun, average soil
Chrysanthemum maximum (Shasta daisy)	White	July–Aug.	1–3 ft.	Sun, average soil
Coreopsis grandiflora (Tickseed)	Yellow	June–Aug.	2½ ft.	Sun, average soil
R *Dianthus deltoides* (Maiden pink)	Pink	June–July	9 in.	Sun, dry soil
R *Dianthus plumarius* (Grass pink)	White and crimson	May	6–8 in.	Sun, dry soil
Euphorbia pithymoides (Spurge)	Yellow	May–June	18 in.	Sun, dry soil
Gypsophila paniculata (Babys-breath)	White	June–Aug.	3 ft.	Sun, average soil
Heliopsis scabra	Yellow	July–Aug.	2–3 ft.	Sun, average soil
Hemerocallis (Day-lily)	Orange-yellow, red	June–Sept.	3–4 ft.	Sun or shade
Hesperis matronalis (Sweet rocket)	Purple, white	June–July	2–3 ft.	Moist, sun
Iris, bearded	Various	June	2–4 ft.	Sun, average soil
Iris, Siberian	Blue, white	June	3–4 ft.	Sun, rich soil
R *Linum perenne* (Blue perennial flax)	Blue, white	June–Aug.	2 ft.	Sun, average soil
Lobelia cardinalis (Cardinal flower)	Red, white	Aug.–Oct.	2–3 ft.	Moist, rich soil
Lobelia syphilitica (Great blue lobelia)	Blue, white	July–Sept.	2½–3 ft.	
Lythrum (Loosestrife)	Rose	July–Aug.	3–4 ft.	Moist, rich soil Sun or part shade
Monarda (Bee balm, Bergamot)	Scarlet, pink, white	June–July	3 ft.	Sun or semi-shade Rich soil
R *Myosotis* (Forget-me-not)	Blue	June–Oct.	1 ft.	Moist, shade
Nepeta mussini (Catmint)	Blue	June–Oct.	2 ft.	Sun, average soil
R *Phlox subulata*	Rose, pink, white	April–May	6 in.	Sun, dry soil
Polemonium coeruleum (Jacob's ladder)	Sky-blue	April–Sept.	1–1½ ft.	Semishade
Salvia azurea	Light blue	June–Aug.	2–3 ft.	Sun
R *Sedum acre*	Yellow	June–Aug.	3 in.	Sun or semi-shade, dry soil
R *Sedum kamtschaticum* (Evergreen)	Yellow	June–July	6 in.	
Sedum spectabile	Deep red	Aug.–Sept.	16 in.	Sun or shade
Thermopsis caroliniana	Yellow	June–July	3–4 ft.	Sun, average soil
Veronica amethystina (Speedwell)	Deep blue	May–July	2 ft.	Rich soil, sun

Perennials

Perennials for Borders of Ponds and Streams (Well-drained Soil)

Sunny Locations

Anchusa myosotidiflora (Siberian bugloss)
Astilbe japonica (Astilbe)
Chrysanthemum uliginosum (Giant daisy)
Cimicifuga racemosa (Cohosh bugbane)
Grasses (Ornamental grasses)
Hemerocallis (Day-lily)
Iris various (Iris)
Lythrum salicaria (Loosestrife)
Myosotis palustris semperflorens (Dwarf forget-me-not)
Tradescantia virginiana (Spiderwort)
Trollius europaeus (Globe flower)

Semishady Locations

Anemone japonica (Japanese anemone)
Cimicifuga racemosa (Cohosh bugbane)
Epimedium macranthum (Longspur epimedium)
Eupatorium purpureum (Joe-pye-weed)
Ferns
Hemerocallis various (Day-lily)
Iris cristata (Crested iris)
Lythrum salicaria (Loosestrife)
Primula japonica (Primrose)
Tradescantia virginiana (Spiderwort)

Perennials for Naturalizing

Asclepias tuberosa (Butterflyweed)
Aster various (Aster)
Cimicifuga racemosa (Cohosh bugbane)
Convallaria majalis (Lily-of-the-valley)
Coreopsis grandiflora (Tickseed)
Geranium maculatum (Spotted geranium)
Helianthus various (Sunflower)
Hemerocallis various (Day-lily)
Hepatica americana (Hepatica)
Lythrum salicaria (Loosestrife)
Mertensia virginica (Virginia bluebells)
Monarda didyma (Bee balm)
Physostegia virginica (False dragonhead)
Polemonium reptans (Creeping polemonium)
Sanguinaria canadensis (Bloodroot)
Smilacina racemosa (False Solomons-seal)

Perennials for Ground Cover

Sunny Locations

Aegopodium podograria (Goatweed)
Ajuga various (Bugle-weed)
Cerastium tomentosum (Snow-in-summer)

Day-lilies will grow in part shade but then usually lean toward light.

Ceratostigma plumbaginoides (Plumbago)
Coronilla varia (Crown vetch)
Dianthus plumarius (Grass pink)
Helianthemum mutabile (Fickle sunrose)
Iberis sempervirens (Evergreen candytuft)
Nepeta mussini (Mussin catmint)
Phlox subulata (Moss phlox)
Sedum sarmentosum (Stringy stonecrop)
Thymus serphyllum (Mother-of-thyme)
Veronica teucrium rupestris (Rock speedwell)
Vinca minor (Periwinkle)

Perennials for Edging

Alyssum saxatile compactum (Dwarf goldentuft)
Arabis alpina (Alpine rock-cress)
Bellis perennis (English daisy)
Campanula carpatica (Carpathian bellflower)
Cerastium tomentosum (Snow-in-summer)
Dianthus plumarius (Grass pink)
Festuca glauca (Blue fescue)
Heuchera sanguinea (Coral-bells)
Iberis sempervirens (Evergreen candytuft)
Nepeta mussini (Mussin catmint)
Primula veris (Cowslip primrose)
Sedum album (White stonecrop)
Sedum reflexum (Jenny stonecrop)
Tunica saxifraga (Tunic-flower)
Veronica teucrium (Rock speedwell)
Viola cornuta (Tufted pansy)

Perennials for Background Planting

Althaea rosea (Hollyhock)
Aster novae-angliae and hybrids (New England aster)
Bocconia cordata (Plume-poppy)
Boltonia asteroides (White boltonia)
Campanula pyramidalis (Chimney bellflower)
Cimicifuga racemosa (Cohosh bugbane)
Delphinium hybrids (Delphinium)
Echinops ritro (Globe thistle)
Helenium autumnale (Sneezeweed)
Hemerocallis (Day-lily)
Hibiscus grandiflorus (Great rosemallow)
Solidago altissima (Tall goldenrod)
Thalictrum glaucum (Dusty meadow-rue)
Thermopsis caroliniana
Valeriana officinalis (Common valerian)
Yucca filamentosa (Common yucca)

Perennials for Foliage Effects

Achillea filipendulina (Yarrow)
Achillea tomentosa (Woolly yarrow)
Artemisia various (Wormwood)
Hosta sieboldiana (Short-cluster plantain-lily)
Lamium maculatum (Dead nettle)
Lavendula officinalis (Lavender)
Nepeta mussini (Mussin catmint)
Ruta graveolens (Rue)
Santolina chamaecyparissus (Lavender-cotton)
Thalictrum glaucum (Dusty meadow-rue)

Perennials Suitable for Cut Flowers

Achillea various (Milfoil, Yarrow)
Anemone japonica (Japanese anemone)
Aster various (Aster)
Astilbe various (Astilbe)
Chrysanthemum hortorum (Garden chrysanthemum)
Chrysanthemum maximum (Shasta daisy)
Coreopsis grandiflora (Tickseed)
Delphinium hybrids (Delphinium)
Dianthus barbatus (Sweet William)
Gaillardia aristata (Blanket flower)
Gypsophila paniculata (Babys-breath)
Helenium autumnale (Sneezeweed)
Iris various (Iris)
Paeonia various (Peony)
Pyrethrum roseum (Painted daisy)
Rudbeckia various (Coneflower)
Salvia various (Sage)
Veronica longifolia subsessilis (Clump speedwell)

Garden in the shade: it contains ajuga, *ivy,* Vinca minor, *day-lily and hosta as an accent.*

Fragrant Perennials

Centranthus ruber (Jupiter's beard)
Convallaria majalis (Lily-of-the-valley)
Dianthus plumarius (Grass pink)
Hemerocallis various (Day-lily)
Hesperis matronalis (Sweet rocket)
Hosta plantaginea grandiflora (Big plantain-lily)
Phlox paniculata (Garden phlox)
Valeriana officinalis (Common valerian)
Viola cornuta (Tufted pansy)

Plants To Be Handled as Biennials

Althaea rosea (Hollyhock)
Anchusa azurea (Alkanet)
Bellis perennis (English daisy)
Campanula medium (Canterbury bells)
Campanula pyramidalis (Chimney bellflower)
Cheiranthus (Wallflower)
Delphinium (Most hybrids)
Dianthus barbatus (Sweet William)

Digitalis purpurea (Foxglove)
Lunaria biennis (Honesty, Money plant)
Viola tricolor (Pansy)

Perennials Enduring Shade
Aconitum fischeri (Azure monkshood)
Ajuga genevensis (Geneva bugle)
Amsonia tabernaemontana (Willow amsonia)
Anemonella thalictroides (Rue anemone)
Convallaria majalis (Lily-of-the-valley)
Cornus canadensis (Bunchberry)
Dicentra eximia (Fringed bleeding-heart)
Dodecatheon meadia (Shooting-star)
Ferns
Helleborus niger (Christmas-rose)
Hosta caerulea (Blue plantain-lily)
Hosta plantaginea grandiflora (Big plantain-lily)
Lobelia cardinalis (Cardinal flower)
Mertensia virginica (Virginia blue bells)
Myosotis palustris semperflorens (Dwarf forget-me-not)
Polygonatum biflorum (Small Solomons-seal)
Thalictrum adiantifolium (Low meadow-rue)
Trillium grandiflorum (Snow trillium)

Perennials Enduring Semishady Conditions
Anchusa italica (Dropmore bugloss)
Anemone japonica (Japanese anemone)
Aquilegia hybrids (Columbine)
Asperula odorata (Woodruff)
Belamcanda chinensis (Blackberry lily)
Campanula rotundifolia (Hare bell)
Chelone lyoni (Pink turtlehead)
Cimicifuga racemosa (Cohosh bugbane)
Digitalis purpurea (Common foxglove)
Doronicum plantagineum (Leopardbane)
Hemerocallis (Day-lily)
Heracleum villosum (Cow parsnip)
Heuchera sanguinea (Coral-bells)
Monarda didyma (Bee balm)
Primula various (Primrose)
Pulmonaria saccharata (Bethlehem lungwort)
Silene caroliniana (Catchfly)
Trollius europaeus (Globe flower)

Perennials for Dry, Sandy Soils
Achillea various (Yarrow)
Anthemis tinctoria (Yellow camomile)
Asclepias tuberosa (Butterflyweed)
Callirhoë involucrata (Poppymallow)
Cassia marilandica (Wild senna)
Coreopsis grandiflora (Tickseed)
Dianthus deltoides (Maiden pink)

The majority of primroses prefer sunshine in the spring when they flower, but during warm summer weather, filtered sun or part shade are better.

Dianthus plumarius (Grass pink)
Echinops ritro (Steel globe thistle)
Euphorbia epithymoides (Milkwort)
Gypsophila paniculata (Babys-breath)
Helianthus various (Sunflower)
Limonium latifolium (Sea-lavender)
Lychnis chalcedonica (Maltese cross)
Papaver nudicaule (Iceland poppy)
Phlox subulata (Moss phlox)
Rudbeckia laciniata (Goldenglow)
Sedum spectabile (Showy stonecrop)
Yucca filamentosa (Common yucca)

Perennials for Wet Situations
Arundo donax (Giant reed)
Asclepias incarnata (Swamp milkweed)
Caltha palustris (Marsh marigold)
Eupatorium purpureum (Joe-pye-weed)
Filipendula hexapetala floreplena (Dropwort)
Gentiana Andrewsi (Closed gentian)
Helenium autumnale (Sneezeweed)
Hibiscus moscheutos (Rosemallow)
Iris pseudacorus (Yellow flag)
Iris versicolor (Blue flag)
Lobelia cardinalis (Cardinal-flower)
Lysimachia clethroides (Clethra loosestrife)
Lythrum salicaria (Loosestrife)
Monarda didyma (Bee balm)
Myosotis palustris (True forget-me-not)
Onoclea sensibilis (Sensitive fern)
Osmunda cinnamonea (Cinnamon fern)
Osmunda regalis (Royal fern)
Primula japonica (Primrose)
Sarracenia purpurea (Pitcherplant)

SEQUENCE OF BLOOM CALENDAR

(Dates are approximate and vary according to region and weather)

Perennials and Bulbs for March Bloom

Scientific Name	*Common Name*	*Height, in Inches*	*Color*
Helleborus niger	Christmas-rose	12	White
Sanguinaria canadensis	Bloodroot	8	White
Galanthus nivalis	Common snowdrop	6	White
Scilla siberica	Siberian squill	6	Blue
Chionodoxa luciliae	Glory-of-the-snow	4	Blue
Crocus vernus	Common crocus	4	Various
Eranthis hyemalis	Winter aconite	3	Yellow
	Perennials for April Bloom		
Claytonia virginica	Spring beauty	4	Pink
Cheiranthus cheiri	Common wallflower	24	Yellow
Iberis sempervirens	Evergreen candytuft	12	White
Aquilegia canadensis	American columbine	18	Red-yellow
Dodecatheon meadia	Common shooting-star	15	Lilac
Bergenia cordifolia	Heartleaf saxifrage	12	Rose
Pulmonaria angustifolia	Cowslip lungwort	12	Blue
Mitella diphylla	Bishop's cap	12	White
Arabis alpina	Alpine rock-cress	12	White
Adonis amurensis	Amur Adonis	12	Yellow
Tulipa (early)	Tulip	12	Various
Iris pumila	Dwarf bearded iris	8	Various
Narcissus (various)	Daffodil	12	Yellow, white
Leucojum vernum	Spring snowflake	12	White
Dicentra cucullaria	Dutchman's breeches	10	White
Primula (various)	Primrose	9	Various
Anemone pulsatilla	European pasqueflower	9	Purple
Viola cornuta	Tufted pansy	8	Various
Viola odorata	Sweet violet	8	Violet
Muscari botryoides	Grape hyacinth	8	Blue
Aubrieta deltoides	Common aubrieta	6	Purple
	Perennials for May Bloom		
Dicentra spectabilis	Bleeding-heart	36	Pink
Iris germanica	Bearded iris	18–36	Various
Thalictrum aquilegifolium	Meadow-rue	36	Purple
Hemerocallis flava	Lemon day-lily	36	Yellow
Paeonia officinalis	Common peony	30	Various
Aquilegia chrysantha	Golden columbine	24	Yellow
Doronicum caucasicum	Caucasian leopardbane	24	Yellow
Euphorbia epithymoides	Cushion spurge	24	Yellow
Chrysanthemum coccineum	Painted daisy	24	Various
Trollius europaeus	Common globe flower	24	Yellow
Alyssum saxatile	Goldentuft	18	Yellow
Tulipa (various)	Tulip	12–24	Various
Gaillardia aristata	Gaillardia	15	Red-orange
Anchusa myosotidiflora	Siberian bugloss	12	Blue
Convallaria majalis	Lily-of-the-valley	12	White
Phlox divaricata	Blue phlox	12	Lavender
Asperula odorata	Sweet woodruff	8	Yellow
Ajuga reptans	Carpet bugle	6	Purple
Phlox subulata	Moss phlox	6	Pink
Polemonium reptans	Creeping polemonium	6	Blue
Ranunculus repens	Creeping buttercup	6	Yellow
Silene alpestris	Alpine catchfly	6	White
Cerastium tomentosum	Snow-in-summer	6	White
Veronica teucrium	Rock speedwell	4	Blue

Scientific Name	*Common Name*	*Height, in Inches*	*Color*
	Perennials for June Bloom		
Nepeta mussini	Mussin catmint	12	Blue
Althaea rosea	Hollyhock	72	Various
Delphinium hybrids	Larkspur	24–60	Various
Digitalis purpurea	Common foxglove	48	Purple
Lilium regale	Royal lily	48	White
Anchusa italica	Italian bugloss	36	Blue
Gypsophila (Bristol Fairy)	Babys-breath	36	White
Lupinus polyphyllus	Lupine	36	Various
Penstemon (various)	Penstemon	36	Various
Papaver orientale	Oriental poppy	36	Red-pink
Lilium candidum	Madonna lily	36	White
Baptisia australis	Blue wild indigo	24	Blue
Baptisia tinctoria	False indigo	48	Yellow
Campanula medium	Canterbury bells	24	Blue
Chrysanthemum maximum	Shasta daisy	24	White
Achillea ptarmica	Sneezewort	24	White
Lilium tenuifolium	Coral lily	24	Red
Achillea millefolium rosea	Common yarrow	18	Rose
Centranthus ruber	Jupiter's beard	18	Crimson
Dianthus barbatus	Sweet William	18	Various
Linum perenne	Perennial flax	18	Blue
Oenothera fruticosa	Common sundrops	18	Yellow
Dianthus plumarius	Grass pink	12	Various
Lychnis viscaria	Clammy campion	12	Purple
Papaver nudicaule	Iceland poppy	12	Various
Thalictrum minus adiantifolium	Maidenhair meadow-rue	12	Yellow
Veronica spicata	Spike speedwell	12	Purple
Astilbe japonica	Japanese astilbe	12	White, pink, red
Dianthus deltoides	Maiden pink	9	Pink
Campanula carpatica	Carpathian bellflower	8	Blue
Iris siberica	Siberian iris	24–36	Blue, white
Thalictrum glaucum	Dusty meadow-rue	48	Yellow
Thermopsis carolinia	Carolina lupine	48	Yellow
	Perennials for July Bloom		
Bocconia cordata	Pink plume-poppy	72–96	Cream
Lilium tigrinum	Tiger lily	24–60	Orange
Cimicifuga racemosa	Cohosh bugbane	48	White
Lavendula vera	Lavender	24	Lilac
Achillea filipendulina	Yarrow	36	Yellow
Hemerocallis (various)	Day-lily	24–48	Yellow, orange
Lythrum salicaria	Purple loosestrife	48	Rose-purple
Heliopsis scabra	Orange sunflower	36	Orange
Physostegia virginiana	Virginia false-dragonhead	36	Pink
Monarda didyma	Oswego bee balm	36	Scarlet
Platycodon grandiflorum	Balloon-flower	24	Blue-white
Echinops ritro	Steel globe thistle	36	Blue
Phlox paniculata	Garden phlox	24–36	Various
Asclepias tuberosa	Butterflyweed	24	Orange
Lychnis chalcedonica	Maltese cross	24	Scarlet
Eryngium amethystinum	Sea-holly	24	Amethyst
Heuchera sanguinea	Coral-bells	18	Crimson
Veronica incana	Woolly speedwell	12	Rosy purple
Tunica saxifraga	Tunic-flower	8	White
Iris kaempferi	Japanese iris	30–36	Various
Stokesia laevis	Stokes aster	12–24	Lavender-white
Kniphofia uvaria	Red hot poker	36	Orange-red

Scientific Name	Common Name	Height, in Inches	Color
	Perennials for August Bloom		
Eupatorium purpureum	Joe-pye-weed	48	Purple
Campanula pyramidalis	Chimney bellflower	48	Blue
Lilium henryi	Henry lily	60–72	Orange
Artemisia vulgaris lactiflora	White mugwort	48	White
Liatris pycnostachya	Cattail gayfeather	60	Purple
Lilium speciosum	Speciosum lily	24–48	Pink
Solidago canadensis	Canada goldenrod	36	Yellow
Rudbeckia speciosa	Showy coneflower	36	Golden
Lilium superbum	American Turks cap lily	24–36	Orange-red
Veronica longifolia subsessilis	Clump speedwell	36	Blue-purple
Aster spectabilis	Seaside aster	24	Purple
Liatris spicata	Spike gayfeather	24	Purple
Limonium latifolium	Bigleaf sea-lavender	20	Lavender
Hosta plantaginea	White plantain-lily	24	White
Colchicum autumnale	Common autumn crocus	3–4	Purple
Ceratostigma plumbaginoides	Plumbago	6	Blue
Lobelia cardinalis	Cardinal flower	24–30	Red
Kniphofia uvaria	Red hot poker	36	Orange-red
	Perennials for September and October		
Boltonia asteroides	White boltonia	60–72	Creamy
Boltonia latisquama	Violet boltonia	48–72	Pink
Chrysanthemum hortorum	Chrysanthemum	12–36	Various
Aster novi-belgi	New York aster	36–60	Blue
Aster novae-angliae	New England aster	36–48	Various
Helenium autumnale	Common sneezeweed	36–48	Yellow
Echinacea purpurea	Purple coneflower	36	Purple-rose
Anemone japonica	Japanese anemone	24–36	Various
Chelone lyoni	Pink turtlehead	24–36	Pink
Aconitum fischeri	Azure monkshood	24–36	Blue
Salvia patens	Gentian sage	12–24	Blue
Sedum spectabile	Showy stonecrop	18	Crimson
Eupatorium coelestinum	Mistflower	18	Blue
Chrysanthemum arcticum	Arctic chrysanthemum	6	White
Gentiana Andrewsi	Closed gentian	24	Blue

Annuals

Slow-growing Tender Annuals

Many tender and half-hardy annuals require a long growing season before blooming and in the North should be sown indoors or in a cold frame or hotbed in March.

Ageratum houstonianum (Floss flower)
Antirrhinum majus (Snapdragon)
Begonia semperflorens (Wax begonia)
Browallia speciosa (Browallia)
Callistephus chinesis (China-aster)
Centaurea cineraria (Dusty miller)
Helichrysum bracteatum (Strawflower)
Lobelia erinus (Lobelia)
Nemesia strumosa (Nemesia)
Nicotiana sylvestris (Flowering tobacco)
Petunia hybrida (Petunia)
Reseda odorata (Mignonette)
Salpiglossis sinuata (Painted tongue)
Salvia farinacea (Mealycup sage)
Salvia splendens (Scarlet sage)
Scabiosa atropurpurea (Sweet scabiosa)
Verbena hybrida (Verbena)
Vinca rosea (Periwinkle)

Annuals Difficult To Transplant

Sow seeds where the plants are to bloom. Or sow in peat pots; then set out pot and plant, which will not disturb roots.

Argemone grandiflora (Showy prickly-poppy)
Eschscholzia californica (California poppy)
Delphinium ajacis (Larkspur)

Black-eyed Susan daisies have a new look and a new name as a result: gloriosa-daisy.

Monkshood (Aconitum) is a tall perennial with blue or purple flowers in late summer.

Godetia grandiflora (Godetia)
Gypsophila elegans (Annual Babys-breath)
Helianthus annuus (Sunflower)
Lathyrus odoratus (Sweet pea)
Lavatera trimestris (Treemallow)
Lupinus Hartwegi (Lupine)
Nigella damascena (Love-in-a-mist)
Papaver rhoeas (Corn poppy)
Phaseolus coccineus (Scarlet runner)
Portulaca grandiflora (Rose moss)
Trachymene caerulea (Blue laceflower)
Tropaeolum majus (Nasturtium)

Annuals That May Be Sown in Late Fall for Spring Germination
Alyssum maritimum (Sweet alyssum)
Antirrhinum majus (Snapdragon)
Calendula officinalis (Pot-marigold)
Centaurea cyanus (Cornflower)
Clarkia elegans (Clarkia)
Coreopsis tinctoria (Calliopsis)
Cosmos bipinnatus (Cosmos)
Delphinium ajacis (Rocket larkspur)
Dianthus chinensis (Chinese pink)
Eschscholzia californica (California poppy)
Gypsophila elegans (Annual babys-breath)
Lathyrus odoratus (Sweet pea)
Lavatera trimestris (Treemallow)
Nigella damascena (Love-in-a-mist)
Papaver rhoeas (Corn poppy)
Saponaria vaccaria (Cow soapwort)
Viola tricolor (Pansy)

Edging Annuals

Edging plants should be short and compact and continue to flower the entire season. The following are the best for this purpose:

Ageratum various (Floss flower)
Alyssum maritimum (Sweet alyssum)
Celosia lilliput varieties (Feather cockscomb)
Centaurea cineraria (Dusty miller)
Lobelia erinus Crystal Palace (Edging lobelia)
Petunia hybrida (Common petunia)
Sanvitalia procumbens (Creeping zinnia)
Tagetes various (Dwarf marigold)
Tropaeolum majus (Nasturtium)
Verbena hybrida (Garden verbena)

Annuals for Shady Locations

Annuals are not lovers of shade, but a few succeed under partial shade. The following sorts may be recommended:

Alyssum maritimum (Sweet alyssum)
Antirrhinum majus (Snapdragon)

Begonia semperflorens (Wax begonia)
Centaurea americana (Basketflower)
Centaurea imperialis (Royal sweet sultan)
Centaurea suaveolens (Sweet sultan)
Clarkia elegans (Clarkia)
Coleus various (Coleus)
Cynoglossum amabile (Chinese forget-me-not)
Godetia amoena (Farewell-to-spring)
Impatiens various (Balsam)
Myosotis palustris (True forget-me-not)
Nicotiana various (Flowering tobacco)
Torenia fournieri (Bluewings)
Vinca rosea (Periwinkle)
Viola tricolor (Common pansy)

Annuals for Window Boxes and Planters
Ageratum houstonianum (Floss flower)
Alyssum maritimum (Sweet alyssum)
Browallia speciosa (Browallia)
Centaurea cineraria (Dusty miller)
Pelargonium various (Geranium)
Lobelia erinus (Edging lobelia)
Petunia hybrida (Petunia)
Tagetes various (Dwarf marigold)
Thunbergia alata (Black-eyed clockvine)
Verbena hybrida (Garden verbena)
Vinca rosea (Periwinkle)

Annuals That Will Grow in Poor Soil
Alyssum maritimum (Sweet alyssum)
Amaranthus caudatus (Love-lies-bleeding)
Browallia speciosa (Browallia)
Calendula officinalis (Pot-marigold)
Celosia plumosa (Feather cockscomb)
Centaurea moschata (Sweet sultan)
Cleome spinosa (Spiderflower)
Coreopsis tinctoria (Calliopsis)
Eschscholzia californica (California poppy)
Gaillardia lorenziana (Gaillardia)
Godetia grandiflora (Godetia)
Impatiens balsamina (Garden balsam)
Mirabilis jalapa (Common four-o'clock)
Papaver rhoeas (Corn poppy)
Portulaca grandiflora (Rose moss)
Sanvitalia procumbens (Creeping zinnia)
Tropaeolum majus (Nasturtium)

Fragrant Annuals
Alyssum maritimum (Sweet alyssum)
Antirrhinum majus (Snapdragon)
Centaurea moschata (Sweet sultan)
Delphinium ajacis (Rocket larkspur)
Dianthus chinensis (Chinese pink)
Heliotropium peruvianum (Common heliotrope)
Iberis umbellata (Purple candytuft)
Lathyrus odoratus (Sweet pea)
Mathiola bicornis (Evening-scented stock)
Mathiola incana (Common stock)
Nicotiana affinis (Jasmine tobacco)
Phlox drummondi (Drummond phlox)
Reseda odorata (Mignonette)
Scabiosa atropurpurea (Sweet scabiosa)
Tropaeolum majus (Nasturtium)
Verbena hybrida (Garden verbena)
Viola tricolor (Common pansy)

Annuals for Foliage Effects
Amaranthus caudatus (Love-lies-bleeding)
Argemone grandiflora (Showy prickly-poppy)
Briza maxima (Big quaking grass)
Coix lacryma-Jobi (Job's tears)
Coleus blumei (Common coleus)
Euphorbia marginata (Snow-on-the-mountain)
Kochia scoparia (Summer-cypress)
Lagurus ovatus (Rabbittail grass)
Perilla frutescens (Green perilla)
Ricinus communis (Castor-bean)
Tagetes Irish Lace (Marigold)

Tall Annuals for Background
Amaranthus caudatus (Love-lies-bleeding)
Celosia argentea (Feather cockscomb)
Cleome spinosa (Spiderflower)
Coreopsis tinctoria (Calliopsis)
Cosmos bipinnatus (Cosmos)
Datura various (Trumpet flower)
Delphinium ajacis (Larkspur)
Helianthus annuus (Sunflower)
Kochia scoparia (Summer-cypress)
Nicotiana various (Flowering tobacco)
Salvia farinacea (Mealycup sage)
Salvia splendens (Scarlet sage)
Tithonia rotundifolia (Mexican sunflower)
Tagetes various (African marigold)
Zinnia various (Zinnia)

Interesting Groupings of Annuals
Sweet Alyssum, Ageratum, and Petunia
Ageratum and Calendula
Tasselflower and Browallia
Spiderflower and Tobacco
Gaillardia, Petunia, and Verbena
Mexican zinnia and Ageratum
Prickly-poppy, French marigolds, and Cape bugloss

Marigold and Mealycup sage
Cape bugloss and French marigold
California poppy, Cornflower, and French marigolds
Nemesia, Stocks, and Ageratum
Gypsophila, Cape-marigold, and Browallia
Snapdragon, Phlox, and Spiderflower
Cosmos, Spiderflower, and Giant zinnia
Prickly-poppy, Coleus, and Tobacco
Clarkia, Browallia, and Mignonette
Perilla, Snow-on-the-mountain, and Summer-cypress
Petunia and Ageratum
French Marigold and Chinese forget-me-not
Chinese forget-me-not and Calendula
Forget-me-nots and Gypsophila annual
Dwarf marigolds and Ageratum
Salpiglossis and French marigolds
Ageratum, Oriental woodruff and Calliopsis

Annuals for Hot, Dry Places (Drought Resistant)

Arctotis grandis (African daisy)
Argemone grandiflora (Showy prickly-poppy)
Convolvulus tricolor (Dwarf convolvulus)
Coreopsis tinctoria (Calliopsis)
Dimorphotheca aurantiaca (Winter cape-marigold)
Euphorbia marginata (Snow-on-the-mountain)
Helianthus annuus (Common sunflower)
Ipomoea purpurea (Morning glory)
Kochia scoparia (Summer-cypress)
Mesembryanthemum crystallinum (Ice plant)
Mirabilis jalapa (Common four-o'clock)
Perilla frutescens (Green perilla)
Phlox drummondi (Drummond phlox)
Portulaca grandiflora (Rose moss)
Salvia splendens (Scarlet sage)
Sanvitalia procumbens (Creeping-zinnia)
Zinnia elegans (Common zinnia)

Annuals for Dried Arrangements

Ammobium alatum (Winged everlasting)
Celosia cristata (Common cockscomb)
Gomphrena globosa (Common globe-amaranth)
Gypsophila elegans (Annual babys-breath)
Helichrysum bracteatum (Strawflower)
Helipterum manglesi (Mangles, everlasting)
Helipterum roseum (Rose everlasting)
Lunaria biennis (Honesty)
Limonium suworowi (Sea-lavender)
Xeranthemum annuum (Common immortelle)

Notes on Annual Flowers

(Symbols: H. – height of plant.
P.D. – planting distance.)

Ageratum. *Ageratum houstonianum.* H. – 6 to 24″ P.D. – 8 to 12″ A charming, constant bloomer, essential in every garden. The blue-violet color combines with practically any other garden color, but the white varieties are not as decorative. The dwarf and compact forms are generally preferred to the tall ones, which are useful for cutting. 'Blue Mink' is a favorite. 'Summer Skies' has pale blue flowers. All self-sow under certain conditions. For early bloom, start seed indoors.

Arctotis (African daisy). *Arctotis grandis.* H. – 24″ P.D. – 8 to 12″ A daytime bloomer, closing at night; white flowers, lilac-blue outside, effective gray-green foliage. Easily grown.

Balsam. *Impatiens balsamina.* H. – 18″ P.D. – 12″ An old-fashioned favorite obtainable in double, camellia-flowered hybrids in separate colors. Effective for garden or cutting, the individual blooms can be floated, or the whole flower stalk used. Take off part of the leaves to show off the flowers.

Bartonia. *Mentzelia aurea.* H. – 12″ P.D. – 8 to 12″ An interesting but little-grown plant with grayish foliage and handsome golden flowers. Sow the seed where it is to bloom.

Browallia. *Browallia speciosa.* H. – 12″ P.D. – 12″ Effective and free blooming, it makes an excellent filler among tulips, where, if the bed is winter mulched, it will often self-sow. The flowers are good for cutting as well as garden effect. Pot up in fall for bloom during winter.

Calendula. *Calendula officinalis.* H. – 12″ P.D. – 6 to 8″ Calendulas are hardy, free-blooming, decorative, making excellent combinations with blue flowers.

California poppy. *Eschscholzia californica.* H. – 8″ P.D. – 8 to 12″ A favorite with its colors of brilliant yellow, white, pink, and red above fine-cut, grayish-green foliage. It gives constant bloom from June until frost. Difficult to transplant; should be sown in place in early spring.

Calliopsis. *Coreopsis tinctoria.* H. – 16 to 36″ P.D. – 8 to 12″ The calliopsis in its several forms is an asset to any garden. Its one handicap is its profuse blooming and abundance of seed; unless the old flowers are removed it will soon spend its energy and cease blooming. This is especially true during hot weather.

Candytuft. *Iberis*. H. – 6 to 12″ P.D. – 8″ An old favorite, still worth growing. *Iberis umbellata*, with its rather flat heads of flowers, comes in beautiful colors, but *I. amara*, the rocket and hyacinth-flowered candytuft, with its long spikes of flowers, is more showy. They are all fragrant and bloom profusely. Several sowings should be made for continuous bloom.

Cape Bugloss. *Anchusa capensis*. H. – 12″ P.D. – 6 to 8″ It is surprising that this lovely blue flower is not grown more extensively. A constant bloomer under all conditions, it supplies the clear blue given only by the forget-me-not and Chinese forget-me-not. It will often self-sow. Variety 'Blue Bird' is dwarf and compact.

Cape-marigold. *Dimorphotheca aurantiaca*. H. – 8 to 12″ P.D. – 8″ Often listed as African daisy. Although available in colors from white to salmon, the orange is most interesting. Excellent for cutting and garden effects. Several sowings should be made.

Castor-bean. *Ricinus communis*. H. – 4 to 8′ P.D. – 3 to 5′ This is the most vigorous of all annuals, giving a coarse, luxuriant, even rank growth, which soon crowds out all other flowers. It is best used as a shrub. Caution is necessary in regard to the seeds, since they contain a very active poison. When dropped in mice-runs, they are an old-fashioned remedy for ridding the garden of these pests.

China-aster. *Callistephus chinensis*. H. – 12 to 36″ P.D. – 8 to 12″ The China-aster is one of our most important annual flowers. Asters do best in good rich soil, where they may be given liberal cultivation and plenty of space to grow. Consult seed catalogs for varieties.

Chinese forget-me-not. *Cynoglossum amabile*. H. – 2′ P.D. – 15″ A glorified blue forget-me-not which should be in every garden. Keep the old flowers removed. Plants will self-seed.

Clarkia. *Clarkia elegans* and *C. pulchella*. H. – 2′ P.D. – 8″ An old-fashioned annual with colors from white through pink to deep rose, in single and double form. It is free blooming and makes an excellent cut flower. Seed may be sown in fall or spring.

Cockscomb. *Celosia*. H. – 10 to 36″ P.D. – 6 to 12″ The crested varieties come in dwarfs and separate colors of crimson and yellow; Chinese woolflower in crimson, pink and yellow. If the latter is allowed to self-sow, interesting forms and colors are created. This type dries successfully.

Collinsia. *Collinsia*. H. – 6 to 8″ P.D. – 6″ A native Western plant, preferring cool weather and a well-drained soil. It will generally require special care to last through hot, dry summers, but it is charming when well grown.

Cornflower. *Centaurea cyanus*. H. – 18 to 24″ P.D. – 6 to 8″ Easily grown, absolutely hardy, always self-sowing, cornflowers produce a wealth of flowers which are enjoyed by ourselves as well as by the goldfinches. Use named varieties of the double strains. 'Jubilee Gem' is a blue dwarf. Always fall-sow a few for early bloom.

Cosmos. *Cosmos bipinnatus*. H. – 4 to 6′ P.D. – 2′ As a cut flower, cosmos is unexcelled. The early strains come in single, double-crested and mammoth-flowering ('Sensation' strain), and disbudding is suggested for still larger flowers. Seed may be sown in the fall for earlier blooming. The 'Klondyke' varieties, though smaller and more delicate in appearance, supply attractive flowers of a rich orange and scarlet.

Cup-flower. *Nierembergia rivularis*. H. – 6″ P.D. – 6″ A compact plant covered with a mass of lavender-tinted white flowers. Useful as rock plant or in front of borders, alone or with dwarf pink or white petunias, or pansies. As seed is sometimes hard to start, buy plants. It likes abundant water.

Dahlia. *Compositae*. H. – 12 to 24″ P.D. – 12″ The small-flowered varieties may be classed as annuals since they flower from seed as soon as zinnias. They come in mixtures such as 'Unwin's Dwarf Hybrids' and 'Coltness Hybrids.' Winter the tubers in peat moss.

Datura (Angel's trumpet). *Datura*. H. – 36″ P.D. – 24″ This is a large plant adapted to unrestricted areas, and grown for the fragrance and beauty of its large trumpet-shaped flowers, which can be used in decoration. *D. metel* is the commonly grown annual kind. *D. arborea* is tree-form; tender.

Everlasting. *Helipterum*. H. – 12″ P.D. – 6″ Although this name is often applied to any type of flower which may be dried, it is properly applied to Helipterum. Rather small, delicate plants, they are really grown more for their dried flowers than for their garden effect. The best place for them is in rows in the cutting garden, where they may be cut when in bud and hung up to dry.

Many people consider it best to strip the leaves off all forms of everlastings and strawflowers before drying. Others prefer to leave them on for their decorative effect. See Strawflower, Winged everlasting, Honesty, Immortelle, Cockscomb and Gomphrena.

Feverfew (Camomile). *Matricaria parthenoides.* H. – 2 to 3′ P.D. – 18″ A sturdy, dependable plant bearing a profusion of white flowers. Not especially beautiful but always reliable. It will often live over in protected situations. There is also a dwarf form, with yellow or white flowers.

Forget-me-not. *Myosotis.* H. – 6″ P.D. – 6″ If not allowed to seed, the plants will bloom all summer. Partial shade will help during hot, dry weather. Grow in masses. Forget-me-nots will often self-sow.

Four-o'clock. *Mirabilis jalapa.* H. – 24″ P.D. – 15″ Although most of us know the four-o'clocks as annual hedge plants, they may be used in other ways. They can be grown by themselves or as a group in front of shrubs. The plants self-sow, or the heavy roots may be dug in the fall and stored in the cellar over winter.

Gaillardia. *Gaillardia.* H. – 12 to 24″ P.D. – 15″ Easily grown, vigorous, and free blooming, the annual blanket flower is highly desirable for cutting or garden effect. Its globular heads of yellow, pink, red, and maroon go well with French marigolds.

Godetia. *Godetia grandiflora.* H. – 12″ P.D. – 12″ This relative of the evening primrose forms a dwarf, compact plant bearing a mass of large flowers. Adapted to poor, sandy soil. Sow in early spring.

Gomphrena. *Gomphrena globosa.* H. – 18″ P.D. – 12″ Another of our everlastings of easy culture, with white, rose, purple and salmon flowers. It is decorative as a garden plant.

Gypsophila (Babys-breath). *Gypsophila elegans.* H. – 12″ P.D. – 6″ The annual babysbreath is useful as a cut flower and for temporary garden effect. Its short blooming period of a few weeks necessitates resowing every three weeks, but it will bloom 6 weeks from sowing.

Honesty. *Lunaria annua* (or *L. biennis*) H. – 2 to 3′ P.D. – 15″ Although uninteresting as a garden subject, it is useful for its seed pods which may have the outer layer removed after they are dried, leaving a thin transparent disk for decorative use in winter bouquets. Plants, unless seed is started very early indoors, will not produce seed pods until the second year.

Immortelle. *Xeranthemum annuum.* H. – 3′ P.D. – 12″ A good garden plant and a source of flowers for winter bouquets. Its foliage is silver-gray. It flowers in clusters of purple, lavender, pink, and white. Sow seed in April.

Job's tears. *Coix lachryma-Jobi.* H. – 2 to 3′ P.D. – 18″ A coarse grass with large pearly seeds often strung for children's necklaces. Not especially decorative in the garden.

Laceflower. *Trachymene* (*Didiscus*) H. – 24″ P.D. – 12″ It is not particularly ornamental as a garden plant but excellent as a cut flower. Difficult to transplant. Sow in pots or where it is to bloom, in early spring.

Larkspur. *Delphinium ajacis.* H. – 24 to 36″ P.D. – 12″ One of the most widely grown annuals. The 'Giant Imperial' strain with wide color range, compact growth, and long stems for cutting is supplanting all others for garden and cut flower use. Seed may be sown outdoors in the fall or in very early spring. Difficult to transplant.

Lobelia. *Lobelia erinus.* H. – 6″ P.D. – 6″ A low, compact plant with brilliant blue flowers. Unfortunately it is often associated only with straight-line flower bed edging, but it is really charming in mass plantings. The trailing varieties are fine for planters or hanging baskets. Sow seed early.

Love-in-a-mist. *Nigella damascena.* H. – 8 to 12″ P.D. – 8″ A delightful hardy annual flower with finely cut leaves and lacy blue and white flowers. It blooms when very small. Sow seed in fall or spring.

Lupine. *Lupinus hartwegi.* H. – 24 to 36″ P.D. – 12″ Interesting as border plants, exquisite as cut flowers. Sow in pots or where they are to bloom as plants do not transplant well. Partial shade will give better results. Removal of old flowers will increase bloom.

Madagascar periwinkle. *Vinca rosea.* H. – 18″ P.D. – 12″ One of the best annuals for all conditions. It forms bushy, compact plants. Sow seeds very early indoors or purchase plants from a florist. Its dark shiny foliage and star-shaped flowers in light pink, blush, rose, white, and white with red eye, add brilliance to any planting. It is a satisfactory plant for general use, for cutting, for growing in the shade, and in many types of soil, and has no enemies.

Marigold. *Tagetes.* Marigolds need no introduction. For tall plants use African marigold (H. – 3′; P.D. – 18″) with large, heavy flowers, rather stiff and formal. More graceful are the French marigolds (H. – 12 to 18″; P.D. – 15″) of compact, free-flowering habit. There are fine varieties of both groups.

For a dainty plant, use the Mexican marigold, *Tagetes signata pumila* (H. – 15″; P.D. – 12″) with small, starry, orange flowers. Hardy, free blooming, easily grown, there are few other annuals so universally satisfying.

Mignonette. *Reseda odorata.* H. – 12″ P.D. – 8 to 12″ Known for its fragrance. Although blooming best during cool weather in May, sowings in partial shade will give midsummer bloom. Difficult to transplant. Seed should be sown in pots or where it is to bloom. Liberal fertilization will increase size of flowers.

Morning glory, dwarf. *Ipomoea.* H. – 12″ P.D. – 12″ A very low, compact, free-blooming plant, inclined to trail a little. Prefers full sun. Does not transplant easily; should be sown in early spring, where it is to bloom.

Nasturtium. *Tropaeolum majus.* H. – 12″ P.D. – 12″ Nasturtiums may be sown where they are to bloom as early as ground can be worked. The plants are sometimes bothered with lice, which can be controlled by spraying or dusting.

Nemesia. *Nemesia strumosa, N. versicolor.* H. – 12″ P.D. – 8″ A worthy plant, all too-little known. The "saucy little faces" of the various colored flowers appear from June until frost. Sow seed in early spring. The large-flowered hybrids are most showy.

Nemophila. *Nemophila mengiesi.* H. – 8 to 12″ P.D. – 6 to 8″ Small, dainty flowers, preferring partial shade and fairly moist soil, blooms throughout the summer in cool climates. May be used in rock gardens or on shady side of house. Seed must be sown in early spring.

Nicotiana. *Nicotiana.* H. – 2 to 4′ P.D. – 8 to 12″ The fragrant, evening-blooming white flowered *Nicotiana affinis* is by far the commonest flowering tobacco, due possibly to

An unusual marigold with fine-cut foliage is called 'Irish Lace'. Its tiny flowers are white.

An attractive display of petunia plants. The edging plant is the dwarf evergreen pachistima.

its ability to self-sow. Even more decorative, however, is *N. sanderae* with pink, red, and lavender flowers. *N. sylvestris* is a day-blooming, white-flowered variety.

The nicotianas are desirable for use among round flowers, such as zinnia or marigold, to give contrast in form.

Pansy. *Viola tricolor.* H. – 6″ P.D. – 6″ Home-grown pansies are much more satisfactory than those you buy. The pansy is really a biennial, best started in August and wintered with a light mulch of straw, in a shaded cold frame. (Seed may also be sown in early spring for summer bloom.) Buy only the very best fresh seed, even though it seems expensive; old pansy seed is unsatisfactory. Many of the best colors are slowest to germinate and develop. Partial shade and sufficient moisture will give best results, especially for summer bloom.

Perilla, purple. *Perilla frutescens nankinensis.* H. – 18″ P.D. – 12″ An old-fashioned plant with dark purple leaves resembling the coleus. Used only as a foliage plant, especially with flowers such as pink petunias. This annual usually self-sows, coming up year after year.

Petunia. *Petunia hybrida.* H. – 12 to 24″ P.D. – 8 to 12″ Perhaps the most beautiful and useful of modern annuals. Borders, banks, rock walls, planters, and hanging baskets are some of the possible places to use petunias. Seed should be sown early indoors or in a cold frame. The best seed, although costing considerably more, will give the finest flowers.

Phlox. *Phlox drummondi.* H. – 6 to 12″ P.D. – 8 to 12″ A continuous bloomer, producing a brilliant mosaic of color when planted in mixtures. Both the dwarf and tall forms are very fine for garden effects and cut flowers. Sow in open ground in early spring. Plant in full sun, and keep seed pods removed.

Pinks. *Dianthus chinensis.* H. – 8 to 12″ P.D. – 6 to 8″ As useful as their perennial sisters, the several forms of annual pinks come in single and double forms. They are constant bloomers and desire rich soil and sunlight. Plants may live over winter if mulched.

Poppy. *Papaver.* Showy flowers in a variety of colors and forms. The Shirley poppy, *P. rhoeas* (H. – 24 to 36″; P.D. – 12″), with long, slender, hairy stems and single or double flowers, is more graceful than the opium poppy, *P. somniferum* (H. – 18 to 24″; P.D. – 8″), with heavy leafy stems and larger flowers.

The very fine seed of poppies should be sown where the plants are to bloom, in either fall or very early spring. The plants do not grow well in warm weather, and the seeds need cool weather for germination. Poppies are excellent cut flowers if cut in the bud stage.

Portulaca. *Portulaca grandiflora.* H. – 6″ P.D. – 6″ Since it has an ability to grow in hot, dry, almost impossible places, we must respect this brilliant flower, even if we hesitate to grow it in our borders. Try the double varieties in hot, dry spots where nothing else will grow.

Prickly-poppy. *Argemone mexicana.* H. – 3′ P.D. – 18″ Interesting as a foliage plant, with its spiny white-veined leaves; also as a flowering plant. It is a vigorous, hardy plant with yellow flowers, often self-sowing. It is a good filler in any border. Difficult to transplant, it should be sown in its permanent position.

Salpiglossis. *Salpiglossis sinuata.* H. – 2 to 3′ P.D. – 12″ Highly decorative in the garden or as cut flower. Resembles a refined petunia, but with more delicate effects, and more intricate color patterns. Sow seed early, preferably indoors. Pinch seedling tops to produce bushy plants. It will grow in the sun or in partial shade and prefers a sandy soil.

Salvia. *Salvia.* H. – 2 to 3′ P.D. – 18″ Commonest of all is the scarlet sage, *Salvia splendens,* available in salmon, maroon, and white as well as fiery red. Sow seed early indoors or in cold frame and plant out after last frost.

Mealycup sage, *S. farinacea,* also usually listed as a perennial, is a free blooming, attractive plant worthy of wider use. Its blue flowers and gray leaves make it useful as a cut flower or as garden subject. Often self-sows profusely, and never fails to give satisfaction. Seeds must be started indoors for a long flowering season. (Height, 3 – 4′)

Sanvitalia. *Sanvitalia procumbens.* H. – 6″ P.D. – 8 to 12″ A very satisfactory ground cover and edging plant. The golden yellow flowers with dark centers resemble small zinnias, and bloom in profusion until frost. Sow seed in early spring. Try a few in the rock garden. (Also known as creeping-zinnia)

Scabiosa. *Scabiosa atropurpurea.* H. – 24″ P.D. – 12″ One of our best annual cut flowers. Sow seed indoors or out, give sufficient room and fertilizer, and they will bloom until frost if not allowed to go to seed.

Snapdragon. *Antirrhinum majus.* H. – 12 to 36″ P.D. – 8 to 12″ Elegant when well-grown as border plants or in rows for cutting. Seeds are slow to germinate. Therefore if early bloom is desired, they should be started indoors in the colder regions.

Snow-on-the-mountain. *Euphorbia marginata.* H. – 3′ P.D. – 12″ An old-fashioned flower which may become a pest. The upper leaves, margined with white, make a showy effect. Milky juice poisons some people.

Spiderflower. *Cleome spinosa.* H. – 3 to 4′ P.D. – 12″ A vigorous, rather coarse plant, well adapted to poor soil, and useful as background accent in an annual garden. Plants have a peculiar odor – objectionable near windows or terraces. Flowers are lavender, pink, or white. In a small garden a few plants will suffice. Sow seed in early spring. You may find it will self-sow.

Stock. *Mathiola incana.* H. – 12 to 18″ P.D. – 12″ Although stocks prefer a cool, moist climate with a rich soil, they often do well under other conditions. Sow seed early. The 'Trisomic Seven Weeks' stocks are especially reliable where summers are hot and dry.

Strawflower. *Helichrysum bracteatum.* H. – 3′ P.D. – 12″ This name is properly applied only to *Helichrysum,* although often loosely to any flower which may be successfully dried. This genus is the largest and most showy of the everlastings. Start the plants early indoors or in the cold frame, if possible, and give them plenty of space to grow. Cut the flowers before they are open – since small buds will open when dried. Tie in bunches and hang up until dry.

Summer-cypress. *Kochia scoparia.* H. – 24″ P.D. – 18 to 24″ The summer-cypress grows under most trying conditions, produces its formal light-green bushes, turns brilliant red in the fall and then self-sows most profusely. Once you grow it you will always have it. Use it as you would a small shrub.

Sunflower. *Helianthus.* H. – 3 to 7′ P.D. – 2 to 3′ The annual sunflowers are an interesting group of plants giving a variety of flowers in size, form, and color.

The larger plants are rather coarse, but the lower-growing varieties with small flowers harmonize with zinnias and cosmos. Useful as a background for other annuals. The seed makes excellent bird food.

Swan River daisy. *Brachycome iberidifolia.* H. – 6 to 12″ P.D. – 6 to 8″ A dainty dwarf plant with blue, white, or mauve daisy-like flowers. It prefers full sun but unless liberally watered does better in partial shade during hot weather. Sow seed in early spring.

Sweet alyssum. *Lobularia maritima.* H. – 8″ P.D. – 12″ This sweet-scented flower is effective in masses in informal beds or for edgings. Sown early, it will bloom in six weeks. There are many varieties, some compact, others trailing.

Sweet pea. *Lathyrus odoratus.* H. – 5 to 8′ P.D. – 4″ The sweet pea is distinctly a cool season crop and to be grown well requires care and attention. It prefers a cool deep soil. The ground should be thoroughly prepared in the autumn by digging a trench 2 feet deep. Place several inches of manure or rich compost in the bottom, and fill in with the best soil or compost available. Mound it up well as it will settle during the winter.

Sowing seed: If soil is well drained, seed (especially of dark-seeded varieties) can be sown in late November; otherwise sow in early spring. The old rule of Good Friday in cold climates is not as far off as most of the old garden myths, for it insures early

The pink-flowered tree-mallow is a little-known but pretty annual for summer display.

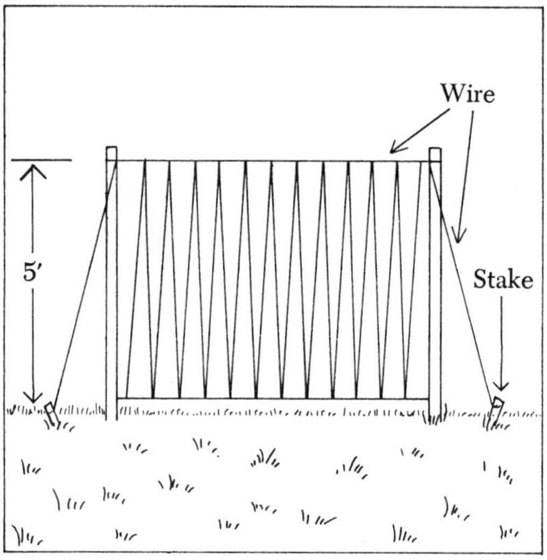

Sweet peas and other annual vines may be supported by strings strung between a wire rack.

sowing. Plant seed about 2 inches deep, 4 inches apart.

Support: A support of string or wire (string is less likely to burn stems) should be ready for the seedlings as soon as they start to climb. It is neater than brush. There are nonclimbing, bush varieties that don't need support.

Summer blooming will be obtained in most sections only by liberal watering, together with a mulch of straw, leaves or compost. Monthly applications of a complete chemical fertilizer (2 pounds to 100 square feet of soil) or other plant food are helpful.

Keep all old flowers picked. To control the red spider which so often ruins the vines, spray daily with a garden hose or dust with sulfur every two weeks.

Sweet sultan. *Centaurea moschata.* H. – 2′ P.D. – 12″ Showy flowers and decorative plants preferring nonacid soil. Flowers last well if cut when in bud.

There is also the royal sweet sultan, *Centaurea imperialis,* H. – 2′; P.D. – 12″; the flowers are sweet-scented, lasting well as a cut flower. It is an enlarged form of the sweet sultan, and preferred by many.

Tasselflower. *Emilia sagittata.* H. – 18″ P.D. – 6″ The tasselflower, although dainty and far from showy, always attracts attention. Its feathery tufts of orange or yellow give a charming and unique effect. Combine it with ageratum or browallia. It may be used in the border, or as a cut flower. It also can be dried.

Torenia. *Torenia fournieri.* H. – 9 to 12″ P.D. – 6″ A low, compact plant producing a constant mass of flowers until frost. The lavender flowers with intricate markings of white and yellow are interesting in themselves. It is suitable for use in the border or as a pot plant.

Sow seed indoors or in a cold frame in March. Do not set plants out until weather is warm.

Tree-mallow. *Lavatera trimestris.* H. – 2 to 3′ P.D. – 12″ Resembling a hollyhock, these rather coarse annuals are effective for accent in the border.

Sow seed where plants are to bloom. Abundant moisture and plenty of sun are their preference. The variety 'Loveliness' has bright pink flowers.

Verbena. *Verbena.* H. – 8 to 12″ P.D. – 12″ Verbena, with its brilliant flowers, is fine for border effects or cutting. Seed should be started indoors as the plants grow slowly. Then plant outside in full sun.

Virginia stock. *Malcomia maritima.* H. – 6 to 8″ P.D. – 8″ Not as showy as the common stock, and more delicate in appearance.

Giant-flowered zinnia plants are handsome enough to deserve a garden all to themselves.

Often used for rock gardens as well as borders. Seed may be fall or spring sown. It will often self-sow.

Winged everlasting. *Ammobium alatum.* H. – 18″ P.D. – 8″ A satisfactory everlasting having white flowers with yellow centers. More interesting as a cut flower than as a garden subject. Prefers a sandy soil.

Zinnia. *Zinnia.* Zinnias in their many forms and colors provide one of the most inexpensive, easy to grow, and reliable of materials for the annual garden.

The present forms have been developed from the Mexican species, Z. *elegans,* an erect, hairy annual about 3′ tall with mostly lilac or purple flowers. The varieties now offered fall into three classes – *Tall,* to 30″ or more; *Medium,* averaging about 20″; and *Dwarf,* from 12″ to 15″. Another 12″ species, Z. *linearis,* with yellow flowers, retains some popularity. Hybrids have been added to the long list of varieties. Sow seed in open ground and not too early. Buy only named kinds except for mixtures of note, and do not save seed for you will have reversion and your entire planting will be disappointing.

As a preventative of mildew do not sprinkle the foliage after sundown. Grow plants where there is good air circulation.

Public gardens and parks offer a wealth of ideas for using bulbs in the home landscape. This scene is in the Keukenhof Gardens in The Netherlands.

CHAPTER 10

Bulbs, Corms, & Tubers

Fair-handed Spring unbosoms every grace –
Throws out the snow-drop and the crocus first.
– J. Thomson The Elder

Spring starts with snowdrops and similar small bulbs, which come with the melting snow. Then follow daffodils, tulips, gladioli, lilies, tuberous begonias, and cannas until dahlias end the season. The winter months also may be filled with bloom from bulbs indoors.

A true *bulb* is really a bud containing within it the flower in miniature. It needs only warmth, moisture, and the means (roots) of absorbing the moisture to grow and flower. The true bulb is composed of layers of overlapping scales and increases chiefly by division. The scales divide from the parent plant to form new bulbs, actually parts of the old plant. Among these true bulbs are the lily, made up of loose scales, each one of which may become a new plant, and the tight-scaled bulbs which appear to be solid, such as the onion, hyacinth, and tulip.

The *corm* – the best known example is the gladiolus – is solid flesh. It blooms for a single season and an entirely new corm grows above it to take its place. In addition to this it forms cormels or bulblets around its base which are also new growths.

An example of the true *tuber* is the potato; it has buds or "eyes" scattered over its surface from which new sprouts start, whereas the dahlia, which is really a tuberous root, sprouts only from its crown or the neck of the root. Each of these plants forms a new bulbous growth every year, but the thickened root of the tuberous begonia lasts from season to season.

The Dependable Bulbs of Spring

Spring-blooming bulbs are the easiest grown of all bulb-type plants, and are almost free from pests. Someone has said: "All you do is plant them, cover them, and forget them until they remind you by blooming in the spring." No hoeing, no weeding, no pruning.

Fall planting for the spring-flowering bulbs is a "must." Narcissus, crocus, bulbous iris, snowdrops, snowflakes, and winter aconite should be planted in early fall. Tulips, hyacinths and scillas may be planted later – in fact throughout the fall season.

It used to be the custom to plant tulips and hyacinths in formal rows in beds, sometimes with an edging of pansies, English daisies, or forget-me-nots. This practice is largely out of fashion today except in parks and public gardens. However, a

Tulips on the terrace of this moderately formal garden have been grouped by varieties.

Daffodils thrive when naturalized in woodland such as this or in grassland that need not be mowed.

modest variation of this kind of planting is practical for the home garden, especially around paved terraces and along walks. (For a uniform effect, plant each bulb at the same depth. Use a notched stick to measure hole depth.)

Actually spring bulbs, by the dozen or in the hundreds, fit into any modest or vast garden setting. They are fine against the dark green foliage of both needle- and broad-leaved evergreens, in groups in front of shrubbery, under high-pruned trees, in rock gardens, and of course in any kind of flower garden. (See Chapter 9, The Flower Garden, for more suggestions.) Crocuses and daffodils can be naturalized – that is, planted in informal, seemingly haphazard fashion as though they were wild – in lawn and woodland. In such situations, as elsewhere, care must be taken to permit the foliage to ripen if you want blooms the next year.

It pays to plant only top-quality, number-one bulbs bought from reliable dealers. Bargain mixtures are rarely the "bargain" they first appear to be – especially when you consider that it takes the same effort to plant them as good quality bulbs.

Spring bulbs grow well in average soil – any soil that supports the growth of other plants – perennials, vegetables, shrubs. The deeper the soil has been initially prepared, the better. Bulbs will rot if put in soil that is not freely drained. In the case of questionable soil or in any that is known to remain wet the soil should be excavated to 2 feet and a 3-inch layer of cinders placed in the bottom. Or you can raise the level of the soil 6 to 12 inches above the existing level, holding the raised soil in place with stones arranged as naturally as possible. A third solution – and the only one in really wet soil – is the laying of tile to drain off any accumulated excess water. (See Chapter 2.)

Before planting bulbs in virgin soil, the soil should be forked over or tilled, after you have spread superphosphate (about 4 pounds per 100 square feet). Very acid soil will benefit from an application of ground limestone, from 5 to 15 pounds per 100 square feet, depending on the degree of acidity of the soil. (Some gardeners prefer to use bone meal in place of superphosphate, but it is more expensive and slower acting.) Special bulb fertilizers are often available and should be applied according to directions. (Potash, in the form of wood

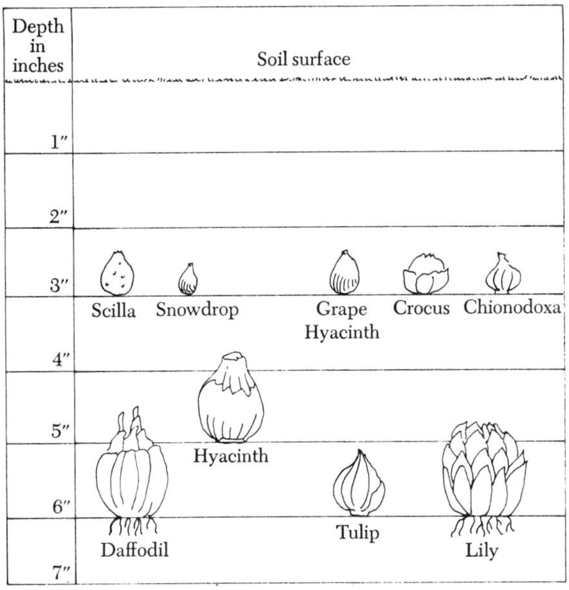

Correct planting depths for spring-flowering bulbs. Always make flat-based holes for bulbs.

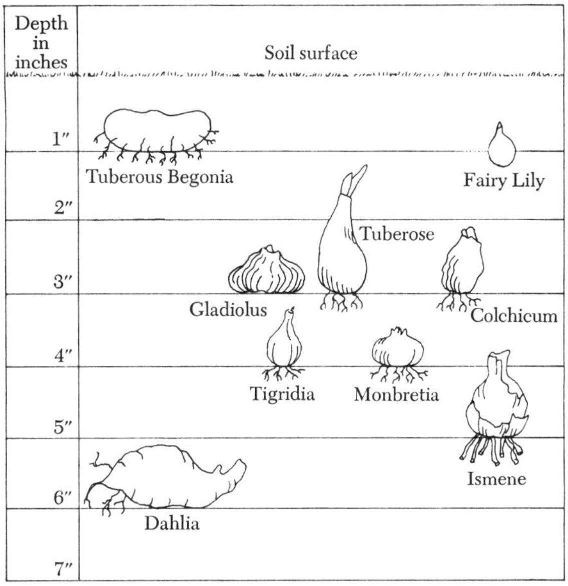

Correct planting depths for summer-flowering blubs, corms, and tubers.

ashes, muriate of potash or potassium sulphate, will also benefit bulb growth.) Fertilizers high in nitrogen should always be avoided.

Very sandy soils or their opposite, heavy clay or adobe, should receive organic matter before bulbs are planted. Peat moss is usually the most readily available humus material. Animal manures (in very short supply these days) are fine if well rotted, but fresh manure means death to bulbs.

Be sure the soil has settled sufficiently before planting bulbs, and then press the bulbs firmly into their holes. Air pockets underneath may cause the bulb to die before its roots reach the moist soil. It is important to plant with a trowel when naturalizing under trees or in the grass, to be sure that the bulb (no matter how small) sits firmly on the soil.

Some failure may be due to too shallow planting. Rather too deep than too shallow, but best of all is the right depth. This varies with soil conditions; in sandy soil, plant deeper. The general rule is to cover the top of the bulb with soil to 3 times its greatest diameter. (Specific planting directions for various bulbs will be given later.) Plant all bulbs of the same kind in each group at the same depth, regardless of variations in their size, or they will bloom unevenly. A thorough watering just after planting will start root growth at once.

Most spring bulbs are very hardy and don't need a winter mulch. However, in very cold regions, or if you planted the bulbs so late that they did not have a chance to make roots, a mulch is a good idea.

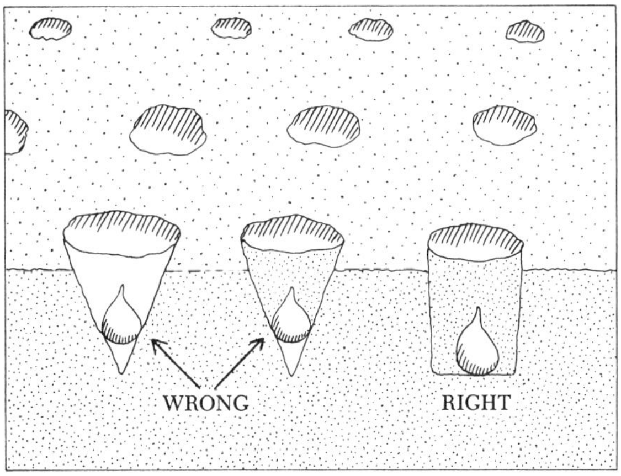

Wrong way (left) and correct way (right) to prepare planting holes for bulbs. If air space is left, bulb may die before rooting.

Zephyr-lily or Atamasca-lily is a southeastern native. Lift bulbs where winters are severe.

After the ground has frozen, cover the area with 4 to 6 inches of leaves (hardwood, if possible), evergreen boughs (cut up your Christmas tree), or pine needles. Don't mulch until the ground is frozen, when field mice will have gone into winter quarters. In the spring, take the mulch off carefully to avoid injury to any young sprouts that may have started through it. An early spring application of fertilizer may be scattered over bulb plantings, and is especially recommended for established colonies of bulbs and for those growing in sandy-type soils. A regular commercial fertilizer (5-10-5) or special bulb fertilizer may be used. Wood ashes from the fireplace or muriate of potash (1 to 2 pounds per 100 square feet) can also be applied in early spring.

After spring bulbs have bloomed, the top growth must mature for 3 to 5 weeks in order for the bulbs to develop for the following season. If it is necessary to lift them while their leaves are still green, do it with as little root disturbance as possible; and replant as soon as possible. Never lift them if it is possible to wait. When bulbs are lifted, after their tops dry, keep them in boxes of dry sand, sawdust, or peat until they are replanted.

Notes on Spring Bulbs

Cultural directions for spring-blooming bulbs follow. For full descriptions and varieties, consult plant catalogs.

Crocus: A good reliable bulb, but a favorite of mice. Plant 3 inches deep, 2 to 3 inches apart for mass effect. Best in sandy, well-drained soil; avoid very damp situations. Plant in sun or partial shade in September or as soon as received. Naturalize in grass or shrubbery. Disappears if top is mowed too soon. Excellent in rockery. Multiplies rapidly, so crowded clumps can be divided every few years after flowering.

Glory of the snow (*Chionodoxa*): Good for naturalizing. Plant in sun or light shade, 3 inches deep, 3 inches apart in September or October. Likes moist but not wet soil while growing. Leave undisturbed. Blooms with *Scilla siberica.*

Snowdrops (*Galanthus*): About the first to bloom in early March. Plant in mass by dozens or hundreds. Plant 2 to 3 inches deep and space same distance apart. Prefer cool, moist but well-drained soil. Dislike being disturbed.

Spring snowflake (*Leucojum*): Plant in groups; cover with 3 inches of soil. Prefers moist, rich, soil, in shaded corner or semi-shaded rock garden. Blooms early. Summer snowflake blooms April, May, or early June; same culture.

Grape hyacinth (*Muscari*): Not particular. Set 2 or 3 inches deep, 3 inches apart. Thrives if left undisturbed and leaves are allowed to fully ripen. New bulbs should be planted in early fall.

Squill (*Scilla*): Makes dense mat of foliage. Set 2 inches deep, 3 inches apart, in September or October. Thrives for years; will stand some shade.

Winter aconite (*Eranthis*): Odd yellow flowers, not showy, but early. Set 2 to 3 inches deep in semishady location in rich, moist but well-drained soil. Plant new bulbs as early as possible. Good among trees or shrubbery.

In a woodland garden, daffodil 'White Lion,' a double variety, is grouped with rhododendron.

The base of a clump of birches is a "natural" for a daffodil planting on the home grounds.

Daffodil, jonquil (*Narcissus*): The name daffodil can be used for all members of this genus but is commonly applied to those varieties with large trumpet flowers.

All daffodils (except the paper white kinds grown indoors in pebbles and water) are exceptionally hardy. This genus is a remarkably varied one, containing delicate varieties in scale for rock gardens as well as the bold, more familiar trumpets. Study catalog descriptions; purchase early, midseason and late varieties to prolong the bloom season.

Plant new bulbs 5 to 6 inches deep as early as possible in the fall. Mix superphosphate or bone meal in the soil as suggested earlier in this chapter. In the spring scatter a complete commercial fertilizer (4-12-4, 5-10-5 or the like) over the soil of newly planted, as well as established, plantings.

Daffodils can be left undisturbed for several years, but when the clumps show more foliage than flowers, it is time to lift and divide them. Wait until the foliage dies or if the foliage is still green, do the job as gently and quickly as possible. With old clumps, it is necessary to dig deep as the bulbs and roots may go farther than you realize. Reset the bulbs 6 to 10 inches apart according to size and from 5 to 6 inches deep. Water thoroughly as soon as planted. Mice never eat daffodil bulbs!

Tulip (*Tulipa*): Tulips, favorite flowers for centuries, can be planted until the ground freezes hard.

In formal beds new bulbs are used each year to maintain uniform height and size of flower. After blooming, lift and heel in in a trench until foliage ripens, then dig, clean, and store in dry place in flats and replant in borders in the fall. In perennial borders, deep planting, 10 to 12 inches, retards splitting into many small bulbs; also prevents injury in cultivation. When cutting flowers for indoors leave foliage untouched; otherwise flower stalks can be cut off as soon as the petals fall, and a third of the leaf area reduced. When all foliage is limp and yellow, it can be cut to the ground.

Avoid planting in open windswept places where the heavy blooms may be blown

A favorite spring combination: Mixed tulips edged with pansies and English daisies.

about. Tulips need especially good soil, and a sunny location, although Parrot types will stand some shade. Unfortunately, tulips are far less reliable than daffodils. The bulbs tend to split the second year, and the resulting small bulbs need rich soil and a couple of seasons before reaching the necessary size for good blooms. They are beloved by mice; if you live in an area where these pests abound, you must plant the bulbs in wire baskets. Perhaps the best way to handle tulips is to treat them as annuals. This means buying and planting new stock each fall.

Hyacinth (*Hyacinthus*): These bulbs prefer light, well-drained soils that contain some humus (use peat moss). Add superphosphate or bone meal.

Plant 6 inches apart and 6 to 8 inches deep (3 times their greatest diameter) in a sunny location. Protect them from strong winds. Mice will eat the bulbs.

Best results are obtained from early fall planting to produce good roots. Plant at a uniform depth to have them bloom at the same time. It is not necessary to buy the largest bulbs. Good 2- or 2¼-inch bulbs are satisfactory.

You don't have to lift hyacinths each year. They should perform well for several years before becoming crowded. Then lift after foliage ripens, and store in a cool dry place until ready to plant again. Discard all soft or small bulbs.

The Major Summer-Flowering Bulbs

Autumn crocus or Meadow saffron (*Colchicum*): The leaves appear in the spring and soon die. Then, like magic, in the fall white or lavender flowers spring from the ground. Plant 2 inches deep in late summer in gardens close to the house where flowers will be protected from the hot sun. Often sold as house plant novelty as it will bloom without water or soil in midwinter.

Hardy amaryllis (*Lycoris squamigera*): An interesting plant that blooms like the colchicum. The foliage dies down in early summer and is followed by fragrant rose-lilac flowers, 2 feet high, in August, rising directly from the ground. Plant in early fall 4 to 5 inches deep and 6 to 8 inches apart, in groups of three or more in perennial border or in very slight shade. The bulbs will multiply and must be divided after three or four years. For the true amaryllis, see Chapter 19.

Calla (*Zantedeschia*): Tender, South African plants with rhizomes. Plant outdoors in

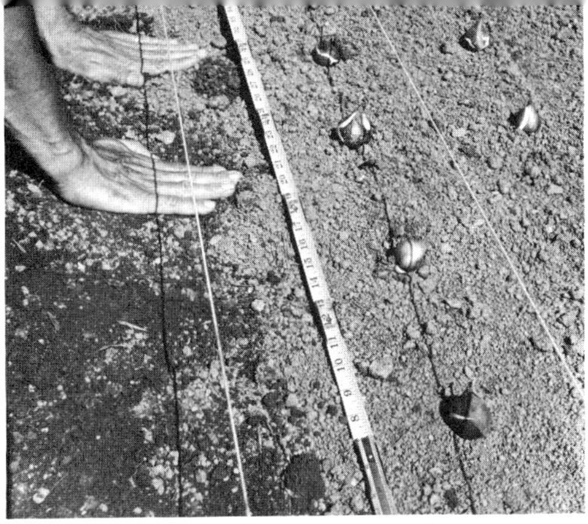

When a formal effect is wanted, use twine and ruler to space tulips and to plant at same depth.

Using a bulb-planting tool will make holes of uniform depth with a level bottom.

Use lines of lime or flour to mark bounds for each variety of tulip (background) or daffodils (foreground). Homemade gauge checks hole depth.

Another way to lay out groups of tulips. Trowel and ruler are used to plant at uniform depth.

spring, lift in fall, and winter in a cool, dry place. Use rich, heavy soil in a sunny spot with ample drainage. They bloom beautifully in August or September just when the garden slumps.

Canna (*Canna*): Same culture as dahlia, thriving in any well-drained soil, away from strong winds, where moisture is readily obtainable.

They are sensitive to frost. Do not plant outdoors until the weather becomes warm.

Divide last year's roots into fairly large sections with several buds on each, and plant in rich soil 2 inches below the surface and 1 to 3 feet apart. Use wide planting for specimen plants; close for mass effect.

They bloom by midsummer. Liquid manure or complete fertilizer at blooming time increases size. Lift after frost kills tops, and store in cool place in dry sand, soil, or peat moss to avoid shriveling.

Dahlia (*Dahlia*): Its chief needs are sun, drainage, and moisture. The ideal soil is one-half sand and one-half loam. A fair standard of fertility is required, but excessive richness must be avoided. An excess of nitrogen will make the plant run to stem and leaves at the expense of flowers. Lighten heavy soil with sand and peat moss. Superphosphate and manure or compost may be used in spring on light or sandy soil.

Dahlias are a favorite with hobbyists. Disbudding produces largest size blooms.

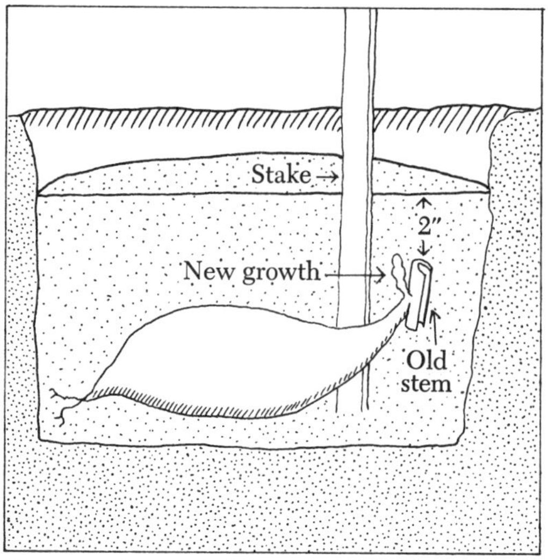

How to plant a dahlia tuber. Set stake when planting. Hole is filled gradually after shoots reach surface (two inches above top of sprout).

As dahlia stem grows, it is tied in several places to the stake.

To grow the large, exhibition dahlias, dig a generous-sized hole, 14 inches deep in heavy or clay soils; 16 inches in sandy soil. Condition the soil as previously instructed and replace 8 inches or more of it in the bottom, firming it well. Drive stakes before planting.

Plant the tuber horizontally with sprout end nearest to stake, covering the crown 2 inches. As soon as growth has risen above the soil, fill in around it; and repeat until the hole is level. This method keeps the tuber deep in the ground where it is cool and moist during hot weather.

After the plant has reached 1 foot in growth use a 2-10-6 or similar fertilizer at the rate of 2 to 3 ounces to the plant. Stir into upper few inches only; it will wash in.

The plants should be kept well watered. Mulch to conserve moisture. Remember that careful culture produces not only good flowers but also good roots for next year.

Dahlias are usually grown in masses by themselves rather than singly in garden beds of mixed flowers. There is no reason why they should not be grown in the border, except that they can be more easily handled in beds by themselves or in rows in the vegetable garden. They need abundant air and sunlight and protection from high winds.

Large-growing varieties need from 4 to 5 feet of space each way; smaller varieties, about 3 feet, varying according to size, down to 2 feet. The smaller varieties are admirably suited to borders and are more useful in suburban gardens. All dahlias need 4 to 5 hours of sunshine.

As soon as tops are killed by frost in the fall, cut off 4 inches above the crown, and in a few days dig up the roots. After a few

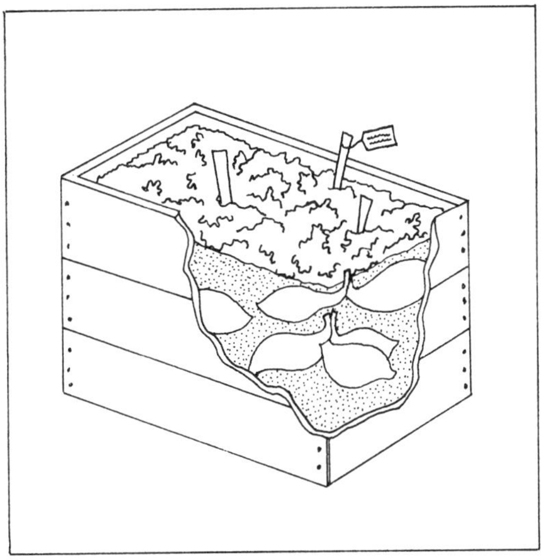

Storing dahlia tubers in box of peat moss or vermiculite. Labels on clumps indicate variety.

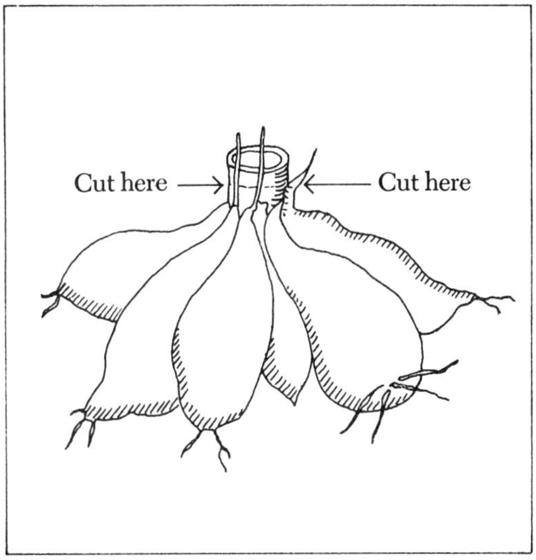

In dividing a clump of dahlia tubers, cut old stalk as indicated by arrows.

hours drying in the air, they may be stored in any of several materials (peat moss, vermiculite) in a cool cellar protected from freezing.

In spring do not be in too big a hurry to plant. Dahlias are very susceptible to injury from cold. Take from storage and divide, allowing one "eye" or "bud" to each root. Handle with care to avoid bruising, which will produce decay.

The practice of disbudding varies somewhat. On the dahlia shoot the top or terminal flower bud is the first to develop. If all the conditions of growth and weather are perfect it makes the finest flower. The other flowers are produced on the side shoots from the axils of the leaves, which are paired. Very good flowers can be raised when the three pairs of flower buds below each terminal bud are removed. Further disbudding will concentrate more strength in the terminal flower and give longer stems for cutting.

Elephants-ear (*Colocasia*): Plant outdoors late in spring 2 or 3 inches deep. Needs very rich, moist soil in shade. It will grow 6 feet high with immense leaves. Lift after frost. Too large for the average garden but effective in large tub on shady terrace or patio.

Fancy-leaved caladium (*Caladium*): Ideal for planters and patio boxes as well as for decorating shady locations. They do quite well in full sun if there is adequate moisture.

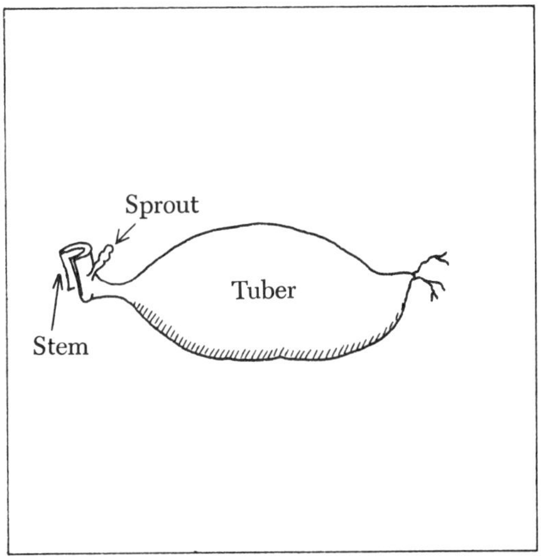

Dahlia tuber with section of old stem. Note sprout.

Tubers can be started indoors and set out in the garden after the danger of frost has passed. Or plant directly outdoors when weather warms. They respond to liquid fertilizers, especially if they are confined to pots and planters. Plant 4 inches deep and at least 6 inches apart. Lift in the fall and store at 60 degrees. Replant in the spring.

Gladiolus (*Gladiolus*): The gladiolus grows in all regions in any kind of soil that is well drained and sunny.

In clay soil, sand should be added to lighten it and in lighter soils an extra amount of decayed vegetable matter such

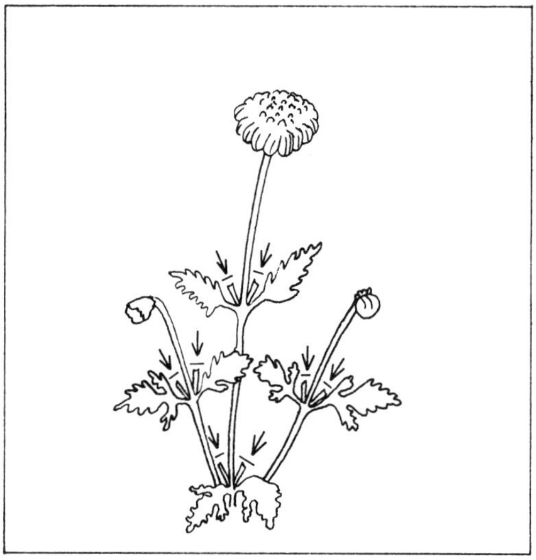

Disbudding dahlias when a large flower or long stem is desired. Remove three or more pairs of buds.

as compost and peat moss are necessary. Cultivating the soil 18 inches deep cannot be too highly recommended. The gladiolus corm is planted 4 to 6 inches deep, and its roots will go considerably farther to feed.

Plant 6 inches apart in the spring as soon as the ground can be worked. (Gladiolus corms are very hardy.) Make a series of succession plantings 10 days apart up to early summer to give a long season of bloom. Soak soil as needed during dry weather.

Good corms pay. Large old corms (usually flat and slightly hollowed on the bottom) are not as good as smaller high-crowned young corms. Number 2 size gives a good flower spike as it gives more support to the plant. If the purchased corms are healthy and the site of planting is changed often, few pests will affect them. Disease is best checked by treating the corms before planting. Immerse the peeled corms in a solution of calomel (3 ounces to 1 gallon of water) or dust the corms with Arasan. For thrips, by far the worst pest of gladiolus, spray as early as plants come up and repeat every 2 weeks until flowering time with nicotine-sulphate or Malathion, mixed according to directions on containers.

Stake only when necessary to keep plants from drooping or working loose at the roots. If you stake, first tie the cord or raffia to a small bamboo plant stake; then around the plant. Cutting the spike as soon as the first flower opens allows the plant strength to go into the corm.

Fine flowers come from fertilizing. Side dress the plant with a general-purpose fertilizer such as 5-10-5 (about 1 level teaspoon to each plant) when they are 6 to 8 inches high. Liquid manure or any liquid fertilizer can be applied as plants are ready to bloom. Liquid manure is made by suspending a sack containing a bushel or more of cow manure in an ash can. Tie a cord to the sack and to a handle of the can. The lid can then be applied to prevent unpleasant odors. Dilute the liquid until it resembles weak tea and apply with watering can nozzle removed, first wetting the ground.

The best time to lift the corms is when the tips of the leaves begin to turn brown. Cormels (baby corms) adhere to them better; the bulbs, too, are then fully matured. Store them in bunches for about eight weeks in open slatted trays in a cool cellar. Never remove stalks as long as any green shows – meaning that growth is still present. If they must be stored in a furnace-heated cellar, they may be placed in dry sand or dry peat moss. To control thrips add 1 oz. naphthalene flakes to 100 corms; close in paper bags for 2 weeks at 70°.

Cormels or bulblets may be planted in shallow trenches outdoors in early spring. They will grow into flowering bulbs in about two seasons.

Summer-hyacinth (*Galtonia*): For the back of the perennial border. It bears white, drooping, bell-shaped flowers on slender 1- to 4-foot stems in midsummer. Plant in early spring 6 inches deep and 6 inches apart in clumps of several bulbs. Lift in the fall, and store at 60 degrees until spring. For best results buy new bulbs each year.

Bulbous iris: Mostly popular florists' flowers for forcing for cut flowers but not suitable for landscape purposes. The Dutch iris are most tender; Spanish and English types are more generally used. Grow them where the foliage may ripen without becoming an eyesore. They like a gritty, deeply dug soil in a warm, sunny place. In warmer climates they are planted from August to October, 8 to 10 inches apart, twice as deep as the height of the bulb, and divided every three years.

In colder climates they need heavy winter protection or they may be dug each

Dig gladiolus when foliage tips turn brown. Store with leaves attached until all green is gone.

Cut off gladiolus stalks when well dried.

Sprinkle corms with naphthalene flakes, then keep in closed paper bags for 2 weeks.

Store corms in dry sawdust, sand, or peat moss.

Three generations of gladiolus corms. Note old shriveled corm at base of new one, left; cormels are attached to corm at right and on table.

year to be replanted in the spring. If lifted, transplant to a new location and reject all diseased or injured bulbs. The supply should be augmented by new purchases each year.

Lily (*Lilium*): The name "lily," as applied to some of our garden plants, can be confusing. Lily-of-the-valley, African-lily, day-lily, arum-lily, water-lily. Which are really lilies? None of these are true lilies in that they belong to the genus *Lilium* as does the madonna lily. They belong to different genera, but because their flowers bear a resemblance to those of the true lily, the term "lily" has become part of their common name.

The lily genus is divided into 2 main groups: stem-rooting and base-rooting. Each demands a different planting depth. A planting of 6 to 8 inches (to base of bulb) is recommended for stem-rooting varieties and 4 to 6 inches for bottom-rooting types. The modern hybrid lilies from the Pacific Northwest can be planted about 6 inches deep unless instructions to the contrary are sent with bulbs. Special instructions for the madonna lily are given later in the section.

Lily bulbs should be planted as soon as received, whether in fall or spring. The usual planting time for new bulbs is fall (transplanting and dividing of established bulbs should be done in fall, too), but early spring planting is also possible if growers offer to ship at that time.

The majority of lilies require a deeply prepared, rich soil that is well drained and slightly acid or near neutral in reaction. If your soil is excessively sandy or at the other extreme – of a stiff clay – peat moss, leaf mold, and/or compost should be added in generous quantity to improve texture and tilth. Superphosphate, about a handful per bulb, can be mixed with the soil before planting. Most lilies thrive in sun or partial shade. Plant from 3 to 6 bulbs in groups in the flower garden, the lower-growing varieties near the center of the border and the really tall ones toward the rear. Mark each bulb or group with a bamboo stake at planting time to prevent later disturbance. Lilies can also be planted among shrubs and seem to appreciate the light shade their bulbs and roots receive in such situations. Avoid windswept sites. Lilies especially thrive with ground cover of ferns and columbine.

Most lilies can remain undisturbed from 3 to 5 years; but when it is evident that the increase of bulbs is inhibiting free growth, the bulbs should be lifted for dividing about 4 weeks after blooming. Replant as soon as possible after they have been dug. They are never really dormant, and exposure naturally weakens them. After replanting, water as you would any other growing plant. Just before or during the blooming season, an application of a 5-10-5, 4-12-4, or similar commercial fertilizer is beneficial. During periods of drought, lily plantings should occasionally be thoroughly soaked.

While lilies may fall heir to more pests and diseases than many bulbous plants, it is rare that a gardener has to cope with all of them. A regular spraying or dusting program such as is followed for delphinium will benefit lilies, too. Many of the modern lily hybrids mentioned at the end of this section have proved to be most resistant to many lily pests.

A word of caution: lilies are especially attractive to mice, both field and pine types. If you live in a region where these creatures are numerous, you had better forget about trying to grow lilies, or plant the bulbs in baskets of hardware cloth.

There are several ways to increase lilies. Perhaps the easiest way is to divide established bulbs.

The scale method may be applied to

A stem-rooting lily. Roots emerge from the stalk above the bulb and from the bulb itself.

Easter lilies forced by florists, usually a form of Lilium longiflorum, *may be planted outdoors when weather warms.*

most lilies. It consists of removing four or five thick outside scales of the old bulb at replanting time. Merely plant the scales in a trench 4 inches deep surrounded by an inch of sand (above and below). Mulch during the winter. The bulbs are transplanted the following year when they have formed at the base of the scale.

Tiger lilies and several others may be increased by planting the tiny bulbs which form in the axils of the leaves. Plant as above in a shallow trench.

Many gardeners prefer to raise lilies from seed, as it is the surest way to raise healthy bulbs. It has the disadvantage that all hybrids do not come true from seed and that it takes 2 to 3 years to produce blooming plants. But to the person interested in propagation, it forms an interesting, economical, and simple way of obtaining a large number of plants.

Plant them in a cold frame or sheltered spot in the open. If planted in late August, they will germinate and get a start before cold weather. If planted late in the fall, they will not germinate until spring. Fall planting is best, but they can be raised by spring planting if protected by slat screens. Plant about 1 inch apart, and cover lightly with soil. Watch to see that the soil covering is replaced at once if washed off by rain. Mulch during the winter as for other lilies. Transplant them to nursery rows as soon as they become crowded.

Hybrid lilies are much easier to grow than their parents. They are vigorous, far less finicky as to environment, and the bulbs do not carry over diseases like the species. Hybrids are generally grown from seeds, whereas their parents were propagated from scales, or parts of the old bulb. Since lilies grown from seeds will not be exactly like the parent, the results of crossing are called strains.

The modern method of packing in moisture-retaining polyethylene bags means that the bulbs will be in good condition when you receive them. Since lilies are grown extensively in the Pacific Northwest, there is no delay in receiving them in time for fall planting.

Some of the well-known strains are: Olympic, Aurelian, Mid-century, Bellingham, Rainbow, and Fiesta hybrids. They are all magnificent in the border.

The Most Popular Lilies

Lilium auratum (Goldband lily): Stem-rooting; ivory spotted and striped; very fragrant; 4 to 5 feet tall. Blooms July, August.

L. canadense (Canadian lily): Medium-sized, orange-yellow flowers, spotted brown. June to August; 4 feet tall.

L. candidum (Madonna): Base-rooting. Fragrant white blooms. Blooms June and July; 3 to 4 feet tall. Plant in August about 4 inches deep (about 4 to 6 weeks after blooming season is over) in order that it may become established and develop leaves before cold weather. The evergreen leaves are carried over winter and must be protected along with the bulb by mulching after the ground is frozen with several inches of straw or leaves held in place by boughs or wire netting. This mulch is left until all danger of freezing is past. This lily requires full sun.

L. henryi (Yellow show lily): Apricot and yellow; few spots; stem-rooting; 3 to 5 feet tall. Blooms August.

L. regale (Regal or royal lily): Stem-rooting. White, yellow spots; 5 to 6 feet. Blooms July, August.

L. speciosum (Showy Japanese lily): Stem-rooting. White tinted with rose, rose pink, crimson spots. Very fragrant; 4 feet tall Blooms August and September. Many variations.

L. superbum (Swamp lily): Base-rooting. Brilliant orange, scarlet spotted; 5 to 6 feet tall. Blooms July to September.

L. tigrinum (Tiger lily): Stem-rooting. Bright orange with black spots; 4 to 5 feet high. Blooms in August and September.

Montbretia and Tiger-flower (*Tritonia and Tigridia*): Plant in early May when the trees are coming into leaf, 2 to 3 inches deep and 3 to 6 inches apart in large clumps or masses. Both require well-drained soil, a protected location, and much the same culture as gladiolus, although they may be wintered over with a heavy mulching. In colder locations lift and store with gladiolus.

Peruvian daffodil (*Hymenocallis calathina*): A member of the amaryllis family with large white flowers and broad strap foliage. In clumps of 6 or a dozen it is effective in front of dark shrubs and evergreens. Plant in May or June 6 inches deep in any good garden soil. It flowers quickly. Dig bulbs before a hard frost and store in a cool, dry place. The heavy roots must not be injured or removed until dry. Bulbs multiply rapidly. Effective cut flowers.

Tuberous begonia (*Begonia tuberhybrida*): A beautiful summer-blooming plant for partial shade. The tubers may be planted directly out-of-doors after all danger of frost is past, but the usual way is to start them indoors in trays, flats, or pots containing peat moss. First soak the peat, then place the flat (bottom) side of the tubers in depressions in the peat, 3 inches apart. Firm them down so that only a little of the tuber remains out of the soil. (The concave side of the tuber is the top.) After the pink sprouts begin to

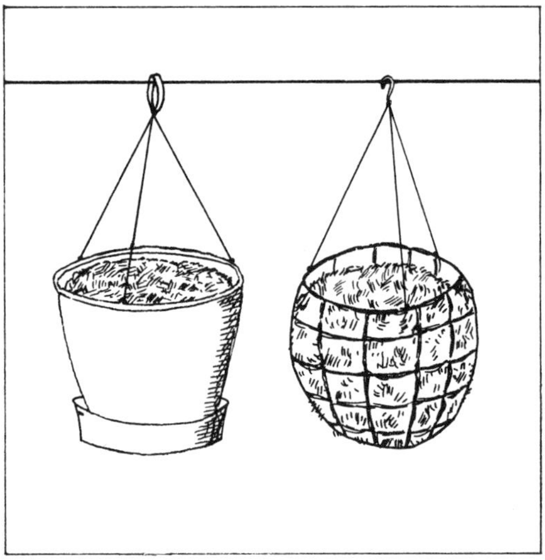

Two kinds of hanging baskets. Left, a ceramic pot with saucer attached to catch drip. Right, a wire or plastic basket, lined with sphagnum moss before soil filling is added.

Tuberous begonias are ideal for window boxes that receive a little sun and are sheltered from wind.

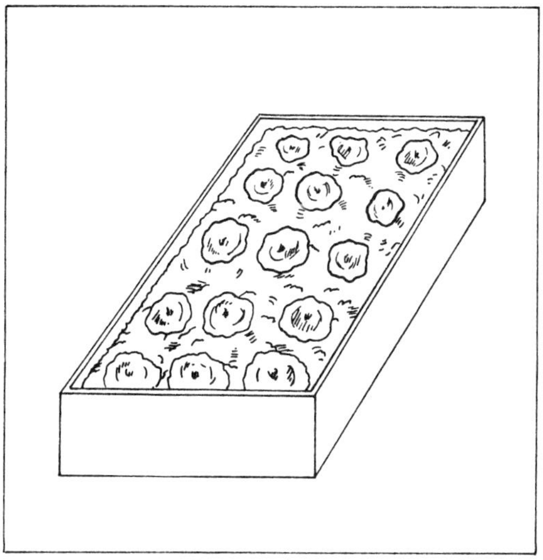

How to root tuberous begonias in a flat of damp peat moss. Concave side of tubers is upward.

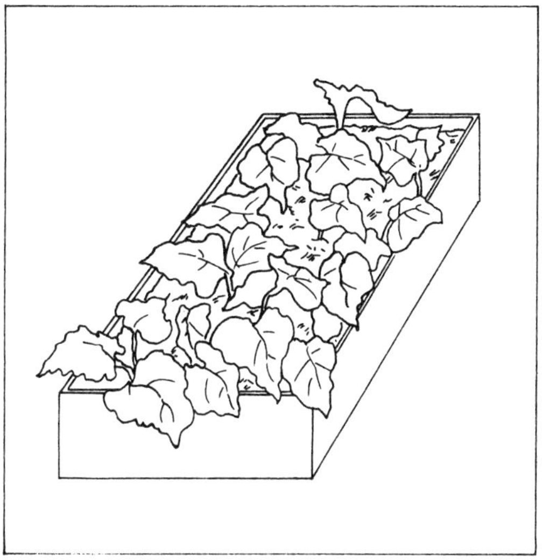

When top foliage is abundant (four or more leaves per tuber), begonias can be potted up or planted out.

show, the growing tubers need a sunny window and a uniform temperature of 50 to 65 degrees. After making good top growth, they can be planted directly outside after nights become frost-free. Or plant them into 4- or 5-inch pots when they have four leaves. Crowding of roots results in better top growth. April 1 is a good time to start the tubers indoors for most regions.

Soil for tuberous begonias should contain an abundance of organic matter in the form of peat moss, leaf mold, rich compost, or whatever is at hand. An occasional application of liquid fertilizer during the summer helps. Never let their soil become dry.

When planting the unrooted tubers in the open ground, plant them 2 inches deep and 10 to 12 inches apart in open beds on the north side of the house, or under trees whose roots are not too greedy and whose branches are cut off for a considerable distance above the ground. They are useful to fill out the semishaded end of the perennial border, and the trailing types are ideal in window boxes or hanging baskets. Consider them for planters and large pots on a terrace or patio.

About 2 weeks before frost is expected, take up the tubers with a little soil attached. When the tops have wilted, remove them, also cleaning off the soil. Cool, dry storage in slat-bottomed flats at about 45 degrees until the following spring will insure years of productiveness.

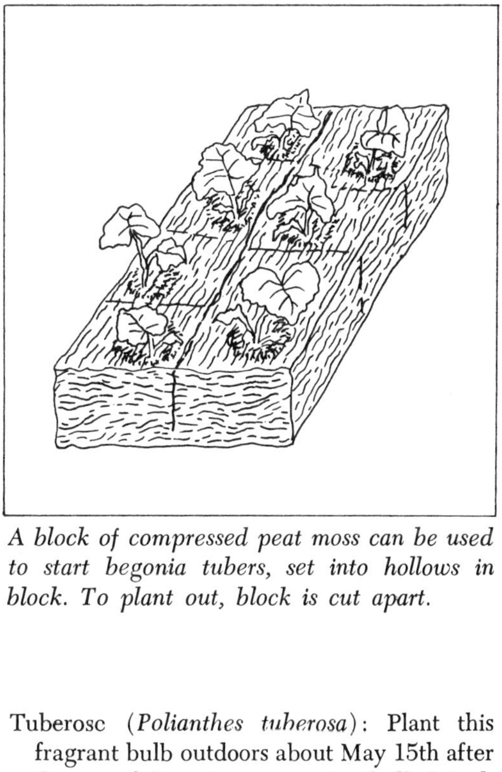

A block of compressed peat moss can be used to start begonia tubers, set into hollows in block. To plant out, block is cut apart.

Tuberose (*Polianthes tuberosa*): Plant this fragrant bulb outdoors about May 15th after danger of frost is past, setting bulb 1 inch deep; or bulbs may be started indoors in pots in April for early bloom. They need rich soil, moisture and warmth. Lift after frost and store in cool cellar with gladiolus. In digging, numerous bulblets will be found which, if dried and planted in spring (6 inches apart), will attain size enough to bloom the following year.

For centuries the rose has epitomized floral perfection. Today new forms and varieties give abundant bloom all summer and lend themselves to informal arrangements as well as classic mixed bouquets such as this one.

CHAPTER 11

The Rose Garden

Who knows not roses, knows not Beauty's smile;
Romance hath spurned him –
Poetry passed him by.

– *Anonymous*

In 1867 the firm of Guillot Fils introduced the 'La France' rose, the first hybrid tea variety. It resulted from crossing a hybrid perpetual variety with one of the tea roses which originated in China. Since then the rose has remained the favorite child of hybridizers. Each year sees an array of newcomers to a list already far more extensive than that of any other shrub. No one is immune to the pure beauty of roses. Nor are roses difficult to grow, and no plant is more adapted to so many uses. If you will follow these rules you can confidently achieve success.

1. Buy good plants.
2. Select a location where you have sun at least half of the day and away from the foraging roots of other plants.
3. Plant properly.
4. Prune early in the spring.
5. Start spraying or dusting early, and provide water during drought.
6. Protect in the winter in cold climates.

Most varieties of roses do not possess adequate vigor and are so grafted to a root stock, which is usually a hardy wild form. A good field-grown budded rose should endure for years.

Making a Rose Garden

The best site for a rose garden is an open space on a southerly slope, sheltered to the north and west by higher ground, walls or hedges. The beds should not be too close to the walls or hedge and should have some sunlight and plenty of air all year around them. Confined gardens are productive of disease. You cannot always select the ideal site, though. If you must place the plants close to a hedge or wall, use care to see that they have direct sunlight a little better than half the day. If the site must be close to other plants, cut down into the ground near the bed, the full length of a spade, several times each year, to see that the unwanted roots do not grow into the bed itself. Poplars and willows of all kinds are extremely dangerous to rose beds. Do not make the beds too wide. If the beds are more than 4 feet wide, it will be necessary to walk in them in pruning, picking the flowers, and spraying, which will compact the soil.

A medium heavy soil, well supplied with humus and well drained, is all that is necessary. Every kind of soil, capably handled,

Curving island rose bed edged with teucrium is narrow enough to be tended from the sides.

Roses for "portable gardening": Redwood tub holds a bush that will give weeks of bloom.

will support roses. Very stiff clay or adobe-type soils need heavy additions of organic matter such as peat moss. The secret of later success is deep cultivation at planting time. The top 4 to 6 inches are not so important; but the next 12 inches of soil in the bed should contain the plant food. Generous quantities of humus, well-decayed manure, if you have it, and plenty of bone meal or superphosphate (a good handful per hole) should be added. Do not force the plants too fast with chemical fertilizer, and above all do not fertilize late in the season. Chemical fertilizer should be applied around each plant after it has produced leaves.

Planting Techniques

The best time to plant is early in the spring, although in mild-climate regions fall and winter are satisfactory times. If you order roses by mail, you can count on the nurseryman to ship them at your correct planting time.

Take the rose from the package upon receipt from the grower. Cut off damaged or broken roots, and cut the thick ones back about 6 inches from their starting point. Preserve as much as possible the tiny fibrous roots, as these are the ones which feed the plants. Heavy roots may take up a little water, but the fibrous roots are the important ones. Soak the plants in a bucket of water for a few hours or overnight before planting.

Dig a hole from 12 to 18 inches deep and wide enough not to cramp the roots. Make a cone of soil on which to place the plant's crown, spreading the roots as naturally as possible on and around it. Then fill in soil, firming it to eliminate air pockets. Add water, and after it has soaked in, finish filling hole with soil. Water again.

The bud union, a swollen, knotty formation where the graft was made, should be just above the surface of the ground, *after it settles,* in mild climates. In the North (all areas where temperatures fall below freezing in winter), the bud union should be 1 inch *below* the ground's surface – after the soil has settled. It is well to mound the soil 4 to 6 inches around the plants to pre-

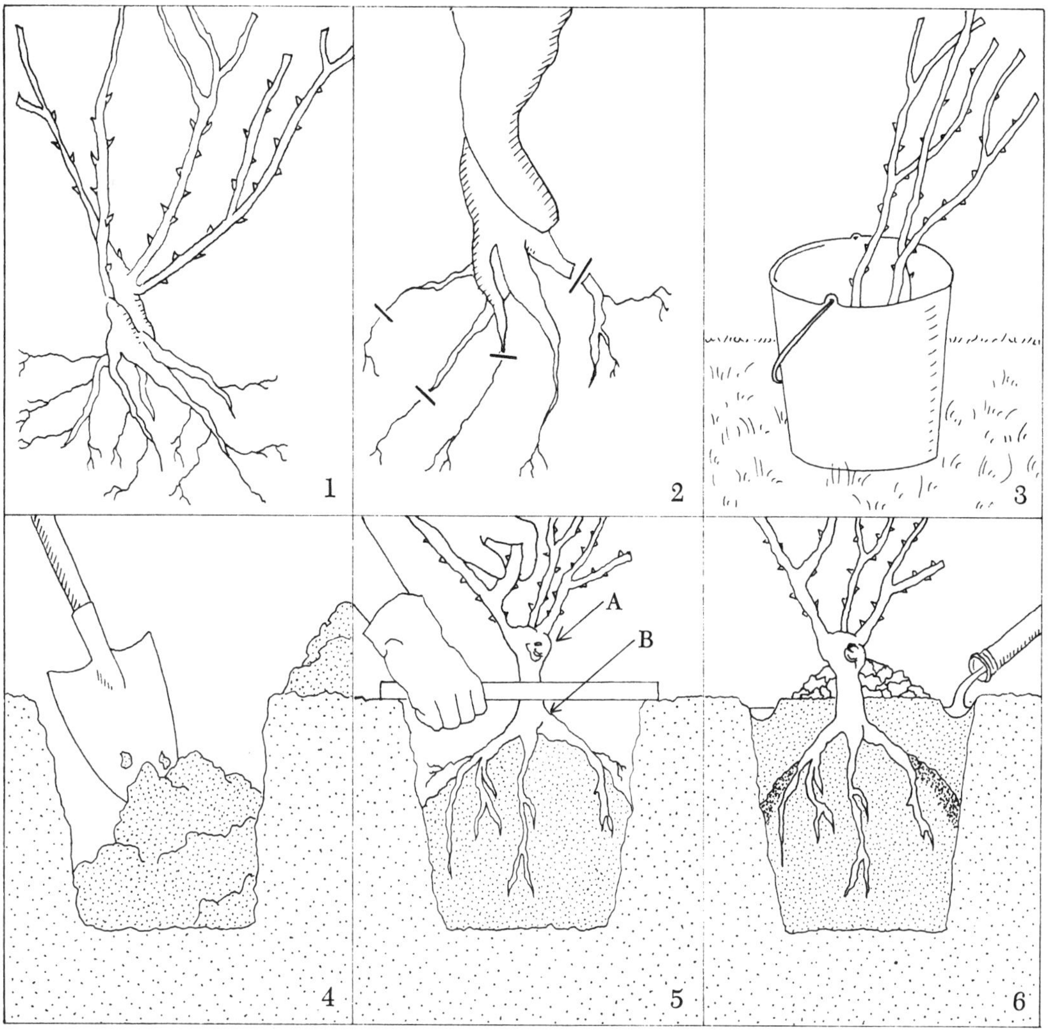

Planting a bare-root rose. 1) Bush as it arrives. 2) Shorten main roots. 3) Top has been pruned. Soak roots for a few hours. 4) Dig hole 12 to 18 inches deep, wide enough for all roots. 5) Set plant on cone of soil. Bud union should be above ground (as at A) in mild regions, one inch below surface (as at B) in cold climates. 6) Fill hole partially; firm soil; soak well. Complete filling, soak again, and mound loose soil around stem. Remove mound when growth begins.

vent excessive evaporation after planting for 2 or 3 weeks. Gradually remove soil as new growth is made.

It used to be a firm rule that plants should be set 2 to 3 feet apart, but most gardeners get excellent results and a better looking bed at 12 to 15 inches for hybrid teas and floribundas. Hybrid perpetuals and large shrub roses, of course, need more room. (Shrub roses, not surprisingly, should be handled just as any other shrub, and most eventually fill an area 6 feet or more wide.)

Pruning

The purpose of pruning roses is to produce strong roots and shoots. New shoots must come from the base to take the place of old woody branches. Pruning opens the plant to the sun and air by taking away the dense middle growth. It cuts away diseased and exhausted wood, prevents legginess, and restricts the plant to the proper dimensions. The number of shoots must be limited to encourage large blooms.

In general, it is best to prune the weaker plant severely and to allow the stronger

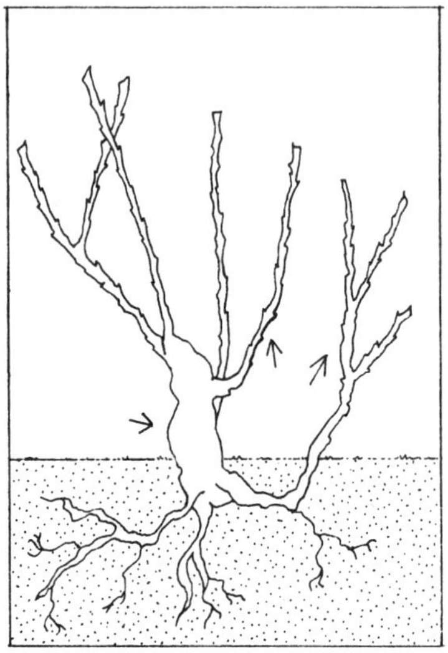

Sucker removal. Suckers – growth springing up below bud union (arrow at left) should be pulled or cut away from stem or root (arrows at right).

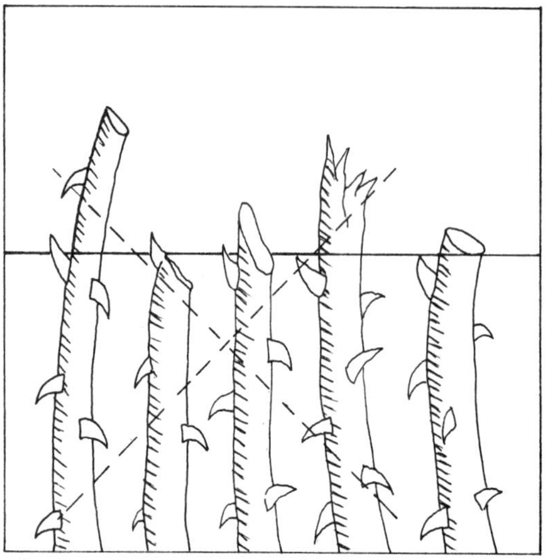

The four pruning cuts at the left are incorrect. Cut a 45-degree angle.

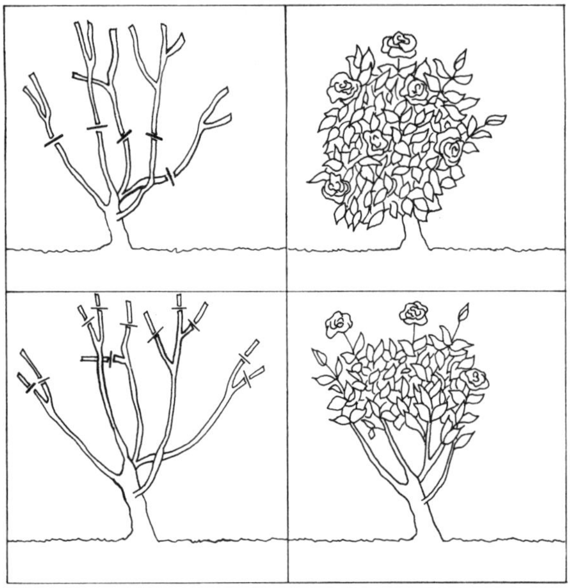

Pruning comparison. Top, correct pruning results in well-shaped bush. Below, too-high cuts result in lanky growth, few and small flowers.

There are 2 distinct types of climbers whose pruning needs are often misunderstood. The rambler type bears its best blooms on new canes which spring from the base of the plant. Therefore, remove all old canes, which are not needed, as soon as the flowering is over. This usually reduces the plant close to its supporting trellis and has the advantage of removing old wood and preventing disease spread. Train the plant more freedom. In spring, before leaves appear, prune just above a bud that points outward from the plant so that the branch from that bud will grow away from the center, leaving it open to the sun and the air. Leave from 3 to 5 buds on each stem. Cut in a slanting direction.

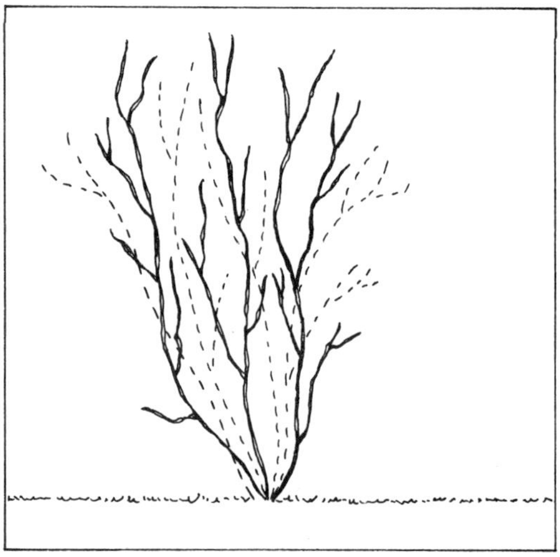

Prune large-flowered climbers lightly in early spring. Remove dead, weak or diseased canes, shorten side shoots. Prune again, if necessary for shaping, after first main bloom period.

Buy good pruners for the pleasure of clean cutting. Gloves protect hands during pruning.

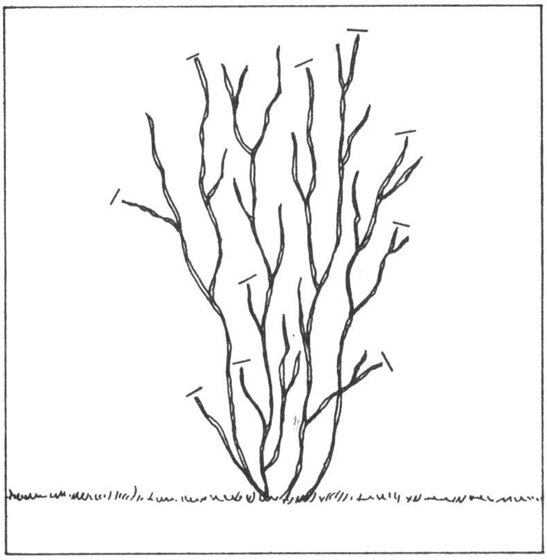

Prune rambler roses after flowering, as they bloom on last year's wood. Prune tips to shape plant; remove oldest (or diseased) canes at base.

new branches to replace the old. The idea is to renew the plant above ground each year.

Any pruning, of course, should be tempered to fit the needs of the plant. If a large cover or tall plant is desired, cut back side growth in the spring, close to the main stems to stimulate new growth, removing a part of the oldest canes each summer.

For the many larger-flowered climbing roses, which bloom abundantly on old canes, only light pruning is necessary and that in spring. Prune to remove dead or diseased canes and to thin rank growth. The rest of the vine is pruned only to shape it.

Pest Control

Roses must be sprayed or dusted at least once a week (and after rain) to control a variety of pests and diseases that find their flowers and leaves irresistible. Black spot and mildew are examples of disfiguring diseases, and the rose chafer and Japanese beetle are two hated pests that devour blooms and buds. There are all-purpose sprays or dusts that will control all rose pests if applied with regularity. To be effective the spray or dust must reach the underside of the leaves as well as their tops. Start spraying or dusting in spring before you see the pests – with luck you may never see them at all! (There is a hardy, nearly ever-blooming rose called 'The Fairy' that resists all pests. Many of the large, old-fashioned shrub roses are quite resistant, too.)

General Care

Roses are heavy feeders. Food should be provided when new growth appears and again after the first heavy bloom. A trowel heaped with complete plant food should be scattered around each bush, then scratched and watered into the soil. Some rose roots may be near the surface, so never dig deeply around the plants.

A mulch should be applied after the plants have been pruned, fed, and cultivated in the spring. Keep in mind that some mulches absorb nitrogen so it is important to give them a square meal before the mulch is applied. Good mulching materials include ground corncobs, buckwheat hulls, wood chips, sawdust, straw, sugar cane, compost, seaweed, rotted animal manures, and pine needles. Peat moss, once recommended for mulching, is best worked into the soil, especially in sandy soils defi-

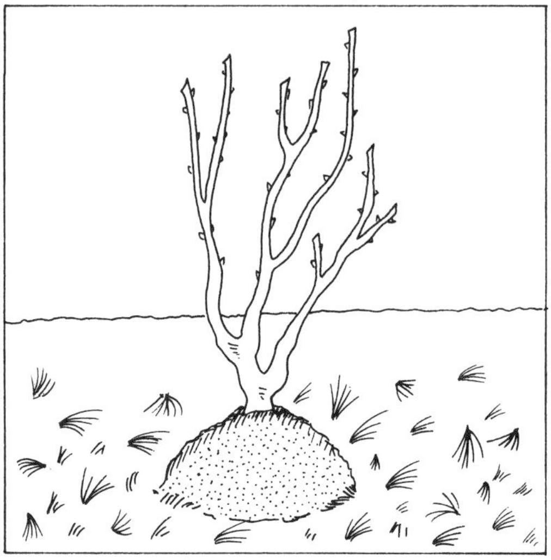

Hilling up for winter protection. Soil mound should cover fourth bud. After soil freezes, a mulch of straw or leaves may be added.

How to cut a rose: Leave at least two lowest sets of leaves; new stem grows from top axil.

cient in humus. As a mulch, it tends to draw moisture from the soil as well as to prevent its entry.

When Winter Comes

In northern parts of the country, plants should be hilled up around the base for the winter season. Do not draw the soil from around the bushes, thus making trenches where water would accumulate. Rather, bring soil or compost from other parts of the garden. The mounds should be from 8 to 12 inches high. If this is done properly, no further covering will be necessary. Heavy mats of leaves and debris around the canes may do more harm than good. Before hilling up, some of the long, loose canes should be cut back, so that the wind will not whip the roots loose from the soil. You may also find it easier to tie up the branches that are sprawling on the ground. Remove the soil gradually in the spring, starting when new growth appears. In mild climates, fall pruning is often practiced, but where some die-back from winter injury can be expected, pruning should be done in spring.

New roses appear so rapidly that it is impossible to keep up with all the good ones. To the rescue comes the American Rose Society, which keeps a running evaluation of roses in commerce through its membership of more than 17,000 avid growers all over the country. Another group, All-American Rose Selections, puts its seal of approval on a limited number of new varieties each year. By heeding the recommendations of both groups, no gardener need worry about acquiring a lemon of a rose!

The following roses have all been given a rating of "excellent" to "outstanding" by the American Rose Society. (Following this list are varieties honored by the All-American Rose Selections Committee.)

Hybrid Teas

Aida (red)
American Heritage (yellow blend)
Charlotte Armstrong (combination of red and pink)
Chicago Peace (pink blend)
Chrysler Imperial (dark red)
Dainty Bess (single flowers, light pink)
First Love (light pink)
Granada (pink blend)
Helen Traubel (pink blend)
Henry Ford (pink)
Imperial Queen (medium red)
Isabel de Ortiz (pink blend)
Manuel Pinto d'Azevedo (pink blend)
Mediterranea (pink blend)

Floribunda *roses bear clusters of bloom in abundance over a long season. Left, coral-pink 'Fashion.' Right, orange-red 'Sarabande.'*

Mexicana (red blend)
Miss Canada (pink blend)
Mister Lincoln (medium red)
Oriental Charm (medium red)
Pascali (white)
Peace (yellow blend)
Pink Favorite (light pink)
Royal Highness (light pink)
Rubaiyat (combination of light red and deep pink)
Swarthmore (pink blend)
Tiffany (pink blend)
Tropicana (orange)
Uncle Sam (light red and deep pink)

Floribunda Roses

Anna Wheatcroft (orange)
Aurora (pink blend)
Betty Prior (medium pink)
Border Gem (pink blend)
Celebration (red blend)
Circus (yellow blend)
Cocorico (orange)
Coup de Foudre (orange)
Crimson Rosette (dark red)
Cupid's Charm (pink blend)
Dearest (pink blend)
Fashion (pink blend)
Feurio (orange)
Florabelle (light pink)
Frensham (dark red)
Ginger (orange)
Iceberg or Schneewittchen (white)
Ivory Fashion (white)
Little Darling (yellow blend)
Orangeade (orange)
Pink Rosette (red)
Red Glory (red)
Sherry (red)
Showboat (yellow blend)
Skylark (medium pink)
Summer Song (orange blend)
Sweet and Low (pink blend)
Sweet Vivien (pink blend)
Tom Tom (light red and deep pink)
Vera Dalton (medium pink)
Vogue (pink blend)
Zorina (orange blend)

Shrub roses are handsome as lawn specimens. This is 'Nevada.' Also choice is yellow "Father Hugo."

Grandiflora Roses

Carrousel (dark red)
El Capitan (medium red)
Montezuma (orange)
Olé (orange)
Queen Elizabeth (medium pink)
Starfire (medium red)

Polyantha Roses

The Fairy (light pink)
Mrs. R. M. Finch (medium pink)
Starina (light red and deep pink)
Sweet Fairy (light pink)
Sweet Vivid (medium pink)
Tinker Bell (medium pink)
Wayside Garnet (dark red)
Yellow Doll (yellow blend)

Climbing Roses

Chevy Chase (dark red)
City of York (white)
Clair Matin (medium pink)
Climbing Cecile Brunner (light pink)
Climbing Mrs. Sam McGredy (orange blend)
Climbing Texas Centennial (light red and deep pink)
Don Juan (dark red)
Dr. W. Van Fleet (light pink)
Glenn Dale (white)
Heidelberg (medium red)
New Dawn (light pink)
Paul's Scarlet Climber (red)
Pink Cameo (apricot blend)
Royal Sunset (apricot blend)

(The above ratings are to 1969. To obtain a complete list of rose varieties each year evaluated from the top rating of "Outstanding," through "Excellent, Good, Fair" and down to "Questionable Value," send 10 cents for the booklet *Rose Buying Guide*, published yearly by the American Rose Society, Columbus, Ohio 43214.)

All American Rose Selections

1940 Dickson's Red (Hybrid tea)
World's Fair (Floribunda, deep red)
1941 Charlotte Armstrong (Hybrid tea, cerise red)
1942 Heart's Desire (Hybrid tea, rose red)
1943 Mary Margaret McBride (Hybrid tea, rose pink)
1944 Fred Edmunds (Hybrid tea, apricot)
Katharine T. Marshall (Hybrid tea, deep pink)
Lowell Thomas (Hybrid tea, yellow)
Mme. Marie Curie (Hybrid tea, yellow)
1945 Floradora (Floribunda, salmon rose)
Mirandy (Hybrid tea, red)
1946 Peace (Hybrid tea, yellow blend)
1947 Rubaiyat (Hybrid tea, cerise red)
1948 Diamond Jubilee (Hybrid tea, buff)
High Noon (Climber, yellow)
Nocturne (Hybrid tea, dark red)
Pinkie (Floribunda, light rose)
San Fernando (Hybrid tea, red)
1949 Forty-Niner (Hybrid tea, red and yellow)
1950 Capistrano (Hybrid tea, pink)
Fashion (Floribunda, coral pink)
Sutter's Gold (Hybrid tea, yellow)
1951 No selections
1952 Vogue (Floridunda, cherry coral)
Helen Traubel (Hybrid tea, apricot pink)

Miniature roses such as 'Pixie,' shown in both shrub and tree form, can be grown in garden beds or containers. Tree is less than one foot high.

1953 Chrysler Imperial (Hybrid tea, crimson)
Ma Perkins (Floribunda, coral-shell pink)
1954 Mojave (Hybrid tea, apricot orange)
1955 Jiminy Cricket (Floribunda, coral orange)
Tiffany (Hybrid tea, yellow-pink bicolor)
Queen Elizabeth (Grandiflora, pink)
1956 Circus (Floribunda, multicolor of yellow, pink, red)
1957 Golden Showers (Climber, yellow)
White Bouquet (Floribunda)
1958 Fusilier (Floribunda, red)
Gold Cup (Floribunda, yellow)
White Knight (Hybrid tea)
1959 Ivory Fashion (Floribunda, white)
Starfire (Grandiflora, red)
1960 Fire King (Floribunda, red)
Garden Party (Hybrid tea, ivory pink)
Sarabande (Floribunda, orange pink)
1961 Duet (Hybrid tea, salmon pink and orange red)
Pink Parfait (Grandiflora, pink)
1962 Christian Dior (Hybrid tea, scarlet)
Golden Slippers (Floribunda, orange-gold)
John S. Armstrong (Grandiflora, deep red)
King's Ransom (Hybrid tea, yellow)
1963 Royal Highness (Hybrid tea, pink)
Tropicana (Hybrid tea, orange red)
1964 Granada (Hybrid tea, pink blend)
Saratoga (Floribunda, white)
1965 Camelot (Grandiflora, shrimp pink)
Mister Lincoln (Hybrid tea, red)
1966 American Heritage (Hybrid tea, white-tinged carmine)
Apricot Nectar (Floribunda, apricot)
Matterhorn (Hybrid tea, white)
1967 Bewitched (Hybrid tea, pink)
Gay Princess (Floribunda, pink)
Lucky Lady (Grandiflora, cream pink)
Roman Holiday (Floribunda, orange red)
1968 Europeana (Floribunda, red)
Miss All-American Beauty (Hybrid tea, pink)
Scarlet Knight (Grandiflora, scarlet red)
1969 Angel Face (Floribunda, lavender)
Comanche (Grandiflora, pink)
Gene Boerner (Floribunda, pink)
Pascali (Hybrid Tea, white)

Most rock garden plants are native to alpine regions and the ideal rock garden begins with natural outcroppings similar to those found in the same regions as the plants.

CHAPTER 12

The Rock Garden

Flower in the crannied wall,
I pluck you out of the crannies;
Hold you here, root and all, in my hand . . .

– *Alfred, Lord Tennyson*

Rock gardens are unique in that they can hold our interest the year around. Some rock garden plants bloom as early as February and some as late as December. Because a rock garden takes so little space and is readily adapted to any contour, it can fit into most garden settings. When combined with a small pool, it is one of the most interesting of garden features. The foliage of many rock garden plants is as beautiful as the flowers. In order to be at its best a rock garden should be almost covered with plants; a mound with a few petunias is not a rock garden; it is more likely to be an eyesore!

The first essential to success is the careful selection of the site. This should be a hilly, sunny location since the most typical rock garden plants do not thrive in shade. However, a rock garden can be built in shade and planted with ferns and shade-loving wild flowers. Drainage is absolutely necessary for success. As rock gardens are supposed to mimic nature's own landscaping as much as possible (with the possible exception of some of the more studied effects achieved in Japanese gardening), the ideal rock garden is made when nature has already placed the basic stonework. The second best results come from moving in neighboring rocks and fitting them into naturally sloping land.

But don't forgo a rock garden if you have neither existing rocks nor slopes. Though you must avoid the mound effect mentioned earlier, it is still possible to achieve a natural-appearing rock garden working from flat land. Here, 2 approaches are possible. One is to make a gradual incline above the surrounding level (no mounds, please!), perhaps only a few feet high, by the clever, careful placement of rocks and the addition of soil. The back of such a rock garden can be shored up by any material handy – concrete blocks, broken cement, and the like – as it can be camouflaged by shrubs. (Or it can be an "island," in which case no special background is necessary.) The second approach to rock garden construction from flat land is the reverse procedure to the one just described. It is making a sunken rock garden by first making as deep and extensive a depression as you want, then working rocks into the sides to hold back the soil. Either way is a challenge, but then so is the making of a rock garden even under nearly ideal conditions.

The material for any type of rock garden, of course, depends upon what is readily obtainable. Limestone or well-worn rock of any kind is very good. However, it should not be so soft that it will crumble away in a few years. Boulders – any

Terrace and adjoining rock outcroppings make one rock garden when plantings are skillfully blended.

rounded stones – are harder to use, but properly handled can be successful. Avoid absolutely: broken concrete and building rubbish. The idea is to use as few stones as possible for the effect desired and to use these materials so that they look like a natural formation. For instance, a limestone rock garden in connection with a pool and waterfall should look like the natural outcropping of limestone in hills.

Fortunately, modern construction and gardening equipment can speed up as well as provide muscle for the arduous job of earth digging and moving necessary before work can start with laying stones. For small jobs, tillers or tractors can loosen soil; for more extensive work, you can probably hire an operator and small bulldozer. In the construction of really large rock gardens of very heavy rocks, equipment with mechanized lifts can be used.

Generally, though, the placement of rocks must be done by the gardener himself – with the aid of a crowbar plus his own muscle and sweat! See that the stones extend back into the soil and are tilted back so that any rain falling on them will run back into the ground.

Place the stones irregularly with good sized pockets of soil between. Leave out a stone once in a while to make larger pockets. Irregularity is essential. A rock garden must not look like a masonry wall, unless

A low retaining wall, often built around a patio, offers opportunity for growing rock plants when no site for a regular rock garden exists.

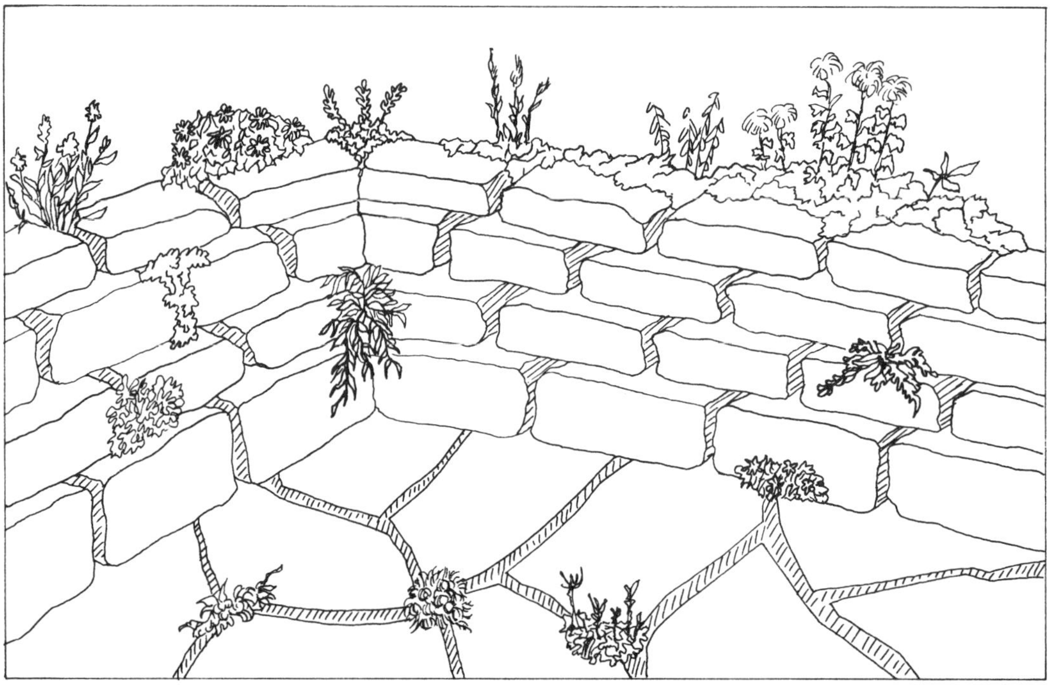

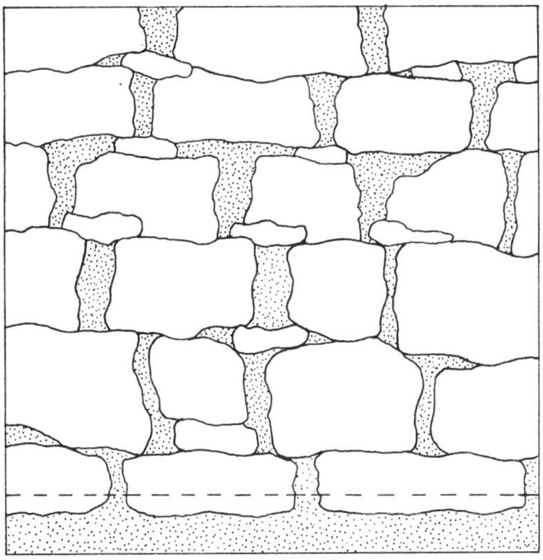

Rock wall or garden construction: (front view): Rocks at base must rest firmly below soil level. Ample soil pockets for plants result when occasional smaller stones are used to separate larger rocks.

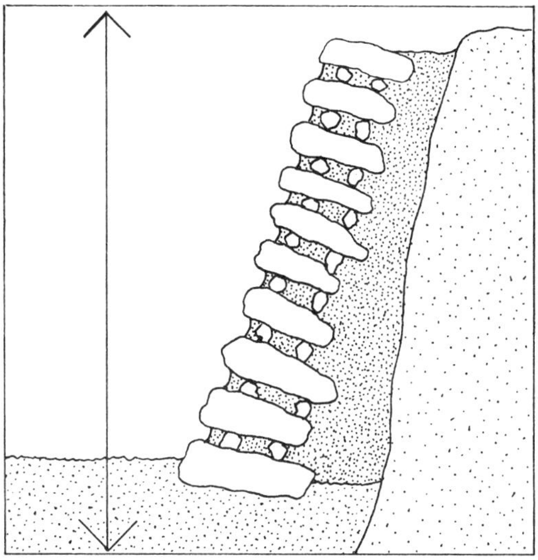

Rock wall or garden construction (profile): Vertical line contrasts with proper slant of wall. Wall face should have a slope of two to three inches to each vertical foot. Place larger stones toward base; let each stone protrude beyond one above to catch water for later plantings.

you are building a wall garden, and even then, broken courses add to the charm. Enough stone must be used to keep the ground from washing, but by using smaller pieces of stone between to block these washes, a large amount of soil can safely be exposed. Avoid unnatural tilting of stones and show the correct "faces." Generally at least one-third of the stone should be buried. The soil between the crevices should be firmly compacted.

Remember, you cannot reach under the rocks and condition the soil when it has once been placed. See that it contains plenty of vegetable matter before using. If necessary, bring in a load or some wheelbarrowsful of rich soil with which to build a rock garden "for keeps." It is better to build one square yard with the proper soil than a larger one with the improper soil. Avoid chemical fertilizers. While it is true that some rock garden plants like moderately alkaline soil and others acid soil, the majority of plants will thrive in average garden soil—one that is slightly acid, neutral, or slightly alkaline. Soil pockets for plants that require special conditions can be handled separately.

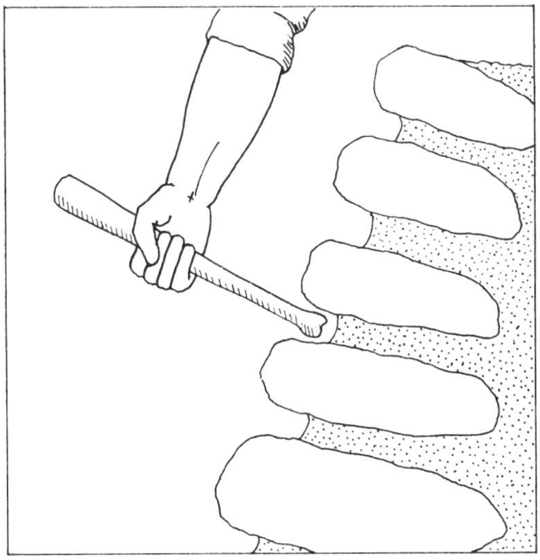

Rock wall or garden construction: Ram soil in firmly between each rock.

Building a Wall Garden

A retaining wall garden is essentially artificial and need not be an imitation of any natural setting. However, an appearance of ruggedness and informality is essential; it must not look like a brick wall. Most of the rules concerning stonework that apply to

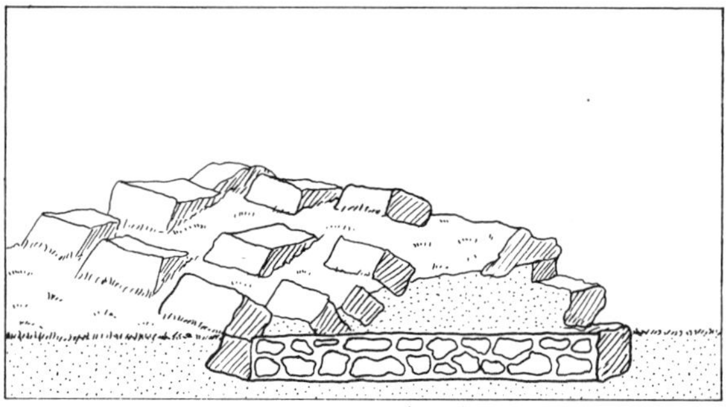

A rock garden can be constructed on level ground to simulate effect of natural outcroppings. Smaller stones or rubble can be filled in at base for drainage and firmer foundation.

One existing rock, well fissured, can be planted and thereby become a rock garden.

rock gardens also apply to a retaining or dry wall. The wall must come into the garden in a natural-appearing manner. If you have a gentle slope which supports an easily maintained lawn, do not deliberately cut it up to form a wall. If, however, you have a sudden change of grade or a steep bank, which washes and is hard to keep presentable, it may be best to turn it into a wall garden.

A good retaining wall, in common with a rock garden, must be built from below the ground up to the top. The higher the wall, the larger the stones should be at the base. A wall 3 feet high may have stones 12 inches square if there are some thick ones

More of the rock should be buried than should protrude. Rocks should be embedded to form plateaus – planting pockets – with the tops of the rocks nearly level or slightly slanting in toward slope. (Dotted line shows original slope before rocks were laid.)

at the bottom and a few larger ones to use as bonding stones. Five feet is the maximum height at which these planted walls look or act well. The taller ones need stones 18 inches square for at least half their height. Stones at the top do not need to be as large and heavy as those at the bottom.

The soil in which the plants grow should be open enough to allow excess water to drain through readily, but must hold water properly for plant use during dry spells. If you are building against a clay bank or location damp in ordinary weather, a 4-inch layer of cinders should run up this bank. The first stone should be a large, heavy one and should sit at least 4 inches below grade on top of the cinders.

Other building details: First, grade your banks, and firm them well. Then start the building, compacting the soil by pounding it in place behind each stone as it is laid. Use a board to keep materials separate. Fill in one side of the board with cinders and the other with soil. After tamping each side well, remove the board, then tamp again. This method can also be applied to keep

Rock garden plants such as pinks and pearlwort (Sagina) *can be planted among large flagstones of terrace.*

A retaining wall that is also a rock garden. Violets, alyssum and Kenilworth-ivy spill from rock joints; aubrieta *grows at base of wall.*

Natural rock outcroppings usually need only addition of a few steppingstones and rock plants to become a garden.

This planted retaining wall gives special pleasure because its plants can be enjoyed leisurely at eye level.

growing soil from mixing with the soil used for filling. (In most cases, the cinders will not be necessary.)

The majority of rock garden plants bloom in spring but an exception is this summer-flowering astilbe.

Plants for Rock and Wall Gardens

Shade plants will bear sunshine, whereas, most sun-loving plants will not do well even in partial shade. It is, therefore, necessary that the major part of the area be in the open with only shade-loving plants in the unexposed portions.

To become familiar with suitable plants, visit places where rock or alpine plants grow, or are offered for sale in bloom. Study nursery catalogs. Attempt to group plants according to foliage and color of bloom; separate rampant growers from slow-growing plants. Trailing plants should have room to spread or hang down from projecting ledges. Do not be afraid to weed out the quick growers to keep them from strangling others. Plant in early spring or in the fall; container-grown plants anytime.

VIGOROUS PLANTS FOR THE BEGINNER'S ROCK GARDEN

Achillea tomentosa (Yarrow)
Ajuga reptans (Bugle-weed)
Alyssum saxatile (Goldentuft)
Aquilegia vulgaris (Columbine)
Arabis alpina (Rockcress)
Artemisia schmidtiana nana (Silver mound)
Campanula carpatica (Bellflower)
Campanula rotundifolia (Harebell)
Cerastium tomentosum (Snow-in-summer)
Dianthus caesius (Cheddar pink)
Dianthus deltoides (Maiden pink)
Geranium grandiflorum (Cranesbill)
Geum borisi (Avens)
Gypsophila repens (Creeping gypsophila)
Helianthemum nummularium (Sunrose)
Iberis sempervirens (Candytuft)
Iris pumila (Dwarf bearded iris)
Lamium maculatum (Dead nettle)
Linum perenne (Flax)
Myosotis scorpioides (Forget-me-not)
Nepeta mussini (Catmint)
Phlox subulata (Moss-pink)
Primula polyantha (Primrose)
Polemonium reptans (Creeping polemonium)
Pulmonaria saccharata (Lungwort)
Santolina chamaecy-parissus (Lavender-cotton)
Saponaria ocymoides (Rock soapwort)
Sedum album (White stonecrop)
Sedum spurium (Stonecrop)
Sempervivum soboliferum (Hen and chickens)
Sempervivum tectorum (Roof houseleek)
Teucrium chamaedrys (Germander)
Thymus serpyllum (Thyme)
Tunica saxifraga (Tunic flower)
Veronica incana (Speedwell)
Veronica latifolia (Speedwell)
Viola cornuta (Viola)

CHOICE BUT MORE DIFFICULT ROCK PLANTS

Aethionema pulchellum (Stonecress)
Anemone pulsatilla (Pasqueflower)
Armeria maritima (Sea-thrift)
Aubrieta deltoidea (Purple-rockcress)
Campanula garganica (Bellflower)
Ceratostigma plumbaginoides (Plumbago)
Dicentra eximia (Wild bleeding-heart)
Draba sibirica (Whitlow grass)
Hypericum repens (St. Johnswort)
Myosotis alpestris (Alpine forget-me-not)

This man-made rock garden is planted with dwarf conifers and several kinds of mosses in the Japanese manner.

Papaver nudicaule (Iceland poppy)
Primula japonica (Japanese primrose)
Saxifraga macnabiana (Saxifrage)
Sedum dasyphyllum (Stonecrop)
Sedum middendorfianum (Stonecrop)
Sedum sieboldi (Stonecrop)
Sempervivum arachnoideum (Spiderweb houseleek)
Sempervivum blandum (Houseleek)
Silene alpestris (Alpine catchfly)
Silene maritima (Catchfly)
Talinum calycinum (Fame-flower)
Thymus serpyllum (Creeping thyme)
Veronica pectinata (Speedwell)
Viola pedata (Birdsfoot violet)

SHRUBS FOR ROCK GARDENS

Berberis thunbergi minor (Barberry)
Cotoneaster microphylla (Rockspray)
Cytisus kewensis (Broom)
Potentilla fruticosa (Cinquefoil)
Spiraea bullata (Spirea)

DWARF EVERGREENS FOR ROCK GARDENS

Calluna vulgaris (Heather)
Chamaecyparis obtusa nana (Dwarf Hinoki cypress)
Daphne cneorum (Garland-flower)
Erica carnea (Heath)
Euonymus fortunei minimus (Dwarf winter-creeper)
Juniperus horizontalis (Creeping juniper)
Juniperus procumbens nana (Creeping juniper)
Picea abies nidiformis (Bird's nest spruce)
Pinus mugo compacta (Swiss mountain pine)
Rhododendron ferrugeneum (Alpenrose)
Rhododendron impeditum (Rhododendron)
Rhododendron racemosum (Rhododendron)

PLANTS SUITABLE FOR THE SHADED ROCK GARDEN

(Most rock garden and alpine plants demand virtually full sun, thereby indicating that a sunny situation is best for the average rock garden. Circumstances, however, may be

A modern version of a rock garden is achieved when two boulders and a dwarf pine are casually combined.

such that the garden must be placed in the shade, and then the following plants, a number of them native wild flowers, will be found satisfactory.)

Adonis vernalis (Spring Adonis)
Ajuga reptans (Carpet bugle)
Allium moly (Lilyleek)
Anchusa myosotodiflora (Bugloss)
Anemone canadensis (Meadow anemone)
Aquilegia coerulea (Colorado columbine)
Asarum canadense (Wild ginger)
Asperula odorata (Sweet woodruff)
Asplenium trichomanes (Maidenhair spleenwort)
Camassia esculenta (Camass)
Campanula rotundifolia (Bluebell)
Cypripedium parviflora pubescens (Lady's slipper)
Dentaria diphylla (Toothwort)
Dicentra eximia (Fringed bleeding-heart)
Dodecatheon meadia (Shooting-star)
Epimedium macranthum (Epimedium)
Hepatica triloba (Hepatica)
Iris cristata (Crested iris)
Lamium maculatum (Dead nettle)
Mentha requieni (Corsican mint)
Mertensia virginica (Virginia bluebells)
Mitchella repens (Partridgeberry)
Myosotis scorpioides semperflorens (Forget-me-not)
Oxalis violacea (Violet wood-sorrel)
Phlox divaricata (Blue phlox)
Polypodium vulgare (Common polypody)
Polystichum acrostichoides (Christmas fern)
Primula various (Primrose)
Pulmonaria saccharata (Lungwort)
Sanguinaria canadensis (Bloodroot)
Saxifraga virginiensis (Virginia saxifrage)
Sedum pulchellum (Stonecrop)
Sedum ternatum (Stonecrop)
Silene caroliniana (Wild pink)
Silene virginica (Fire pink)
Trillium grandiflorum (Snow or Large-flowered trillium)
Viola various (Violet)

GROUND COVER PLANTS FOR ROCK GARDENS

Ajuga reptans (Carpet bugle)
Arctostaphylos uva-ursi (Bearberry)
Asperula odorata (Sweet woodruff)
Cerastium tomentosum (Snow-in-summer)
Euonymus fortunei minimus (Dwarf winter-creeper)
Dianthus deltoides (Maiden pink)
Erica carnea (Heath)
Phlox subulata (Moss-pink)
Sedum album (Stonecrop)
Sedum spurium (Stonecrop)
Thymus serpyllum (Thyme)
Veronica filiformis (Speedwell)

Among the more popular rock garden plants are sea thrift (Armeria), *left, and* Phlox subulata, *center.*

A colony of sempervivums *spreads itself below an equally entrenched grouping of bog andromeda.*

BULBS FOR THE ROCK GARDEN

Camassia esculenta (Camass)
Chionodoxa luciliae (Glory-of-the-snow)
Colchicum autumnale (Autumn crocus)
Crocus various (Crocus)
Eranthis hyemalis (Winter-aconite)
Fritillaria meleagris (Guinea hen flower)
Galanthus nivalis (Snowdrop)
Lilium tenuifolium (Coral lily)
Muscari botryoides (Grape-hyacinth)
Narcissus species and smaller varieties (Daffodil)
Puschkinia scilloides (Puschkinia)
Scilla hispanica (Spanish-bluebell)
Scilla nonscripta (English-bluebell)
Scilla siberica (Siberian squill)
Tulipa clusiana (Lady or Candystick tulip)
Tulipa greigi
Tulipa kaufmanniana

ROCK PLANTS FOR WALKS AND STEPPING-STONES

Arenaria verna caespitosa (Tufted sandwort)
Cymbalaria aequitriloba
Herniaria glabra (Burstwort)
Mazus reptans
Mentha requieni (Creeping or Corsican mint)
Sagina subulata (Pearlwort)
Thymus serpyllum (Creeping thyme)
Veronica filiformis (Speedwell)
Veronica repens (Creeping speedwell)

Reeds and rushes, and traditional tropical water-lilies add special interest to this informal pool.

CHAPTER 13

Water Gardening and Garden Pools

Broad water-lilies lay tremulously,
And starry river-buds glimmered by,
And around them the soft stream did glide and dance
With a motion of sweet sound and radiance.

– *Shelley*

Water gardening gives more in results for the time expended on it than any other type of gardening. It has no special requirements – only full sunshine if you wish to grow water-lilies. There are several ways to provide for the presence of water in today's gardens: a small, concrete reflecting pool only a few inches deep; a large saucer or shallow container on the terrace to serve as sculpture and bird bath; a true water garden – a concrete pool for water-lilies and other aquatics.

Pool Construction

Plastics are playing an important part here, too, as in the larger swimming pool field. Prefabricated fiberglass pools are available in different sizes and shapes. One small, inexpensive type is sold together with a miniature pump for the making of waterfalls and brooks. It economizes by circulating the same water until evaporation calls for replenishing. A depression lined with sheets of the flexible plastic sheeting also provides a satisfactory temporary water feature.

Sheet lead has proved an excellent material since it can be shaped to conform to any excavation and made watertight by simple folded and hammered seams. In color, it blends well into natural surroundings, and, being practically indestructible, it is not necessarily as expensive in the long run as its first cost might suggest. The lead can be bought in sheets one-sixteenth of an inch thick from plumbing supply outlets.

Nevertheless, most pools in the home garden are constructed of concrete. Whether you wish to build a formal pool or an irregularly shaped pool, the construction is basically the same. (Formal pools, circular, semicircular or rectangular, can be handsome water features; but to look right, they must be part of an elegant, equally formal setting. Informal pools, loosely pear-shaped or crescent in outline or in any shape appropriate to their site are much more adaptable for today's simplified landscapes.)

First, mark the shape of your pool with stakes, connecting them with twine, or use a length of garden hose so you can visualize the pool and how it will fit into your garden. A formal pool of geometric outline may require a wooden form, much like that used in the construction of poured concrete foundations for houses. The informal pool can usually be constructed without forms. It requires a hole with sloping sides which should be firmed and smoothed with a

The combination of sculpture and a millstone made into a bubbling birdbath are intriguing feature in this garden scene.

A flawless garden pool is the perfect mirror for this carefully constructed and planted rockery.

An example of a prefabricated fiberglass garden pool available from many water-lily nurseries.

Pool made from a wooden tub holds one pygmy water-lily. Surrounding plantings need moist soil.

tamper to form a good foundation for the concrete. The walls of all kinds of pools (except the smallest or shallow basins made for birds or to serve as reflecting pools) should be about 6 inches thick, the bottoms, 8 inches. Therefore, the excavation for the pool will always be about 6 inches wider all around as well as deeper than the final effect. Most of the prefabricated fiberglass pools that you can buy are about 16-20 inches deep. Water-lily pools should be about 24 inches deep. Make the bottom of the pool slope to the middle or one end, so that when you empty or clean it, the water will collect at one point.

For filling a small pool, a garden hose is usually sufficient. Therefore, no intake water connections need be provided. However, in most pools of fair size, an overflow pipe is essential unless you don't mind flooding the surrounding area when the pool overflows. In small pools, the water may be siphoned out with a hose by attaching the hose to the faucet of a laundry tub; fill the hose with water until it starts running into the pool, then remove the end from the faucet and allow it to drain into the tub.

Pools can be constructed with no further reinforcing than a close-mesh wire netting pressed into the cavity. However, although concrete reinforcing is a little intricate, most authorities recommend that three-eighths-inch deformed reinforcing rods be used and spaced 8 inches apart to form a network in both informal and formal pools. They should be wired into the forms so as to be in the center of the concrete when

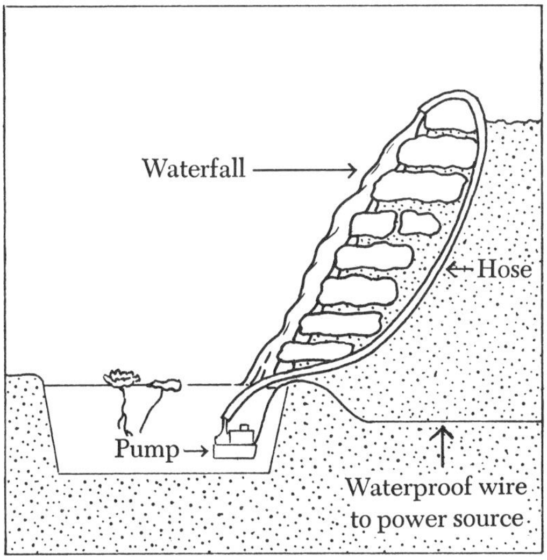

Waterfall can be made part of any pool by use of small pump that recirculates water.

poured. Care must be taken that all bars are well covered with concrete. As the top of the pool receives the most severe strain due to the pressure of ice in the winter, it is well to run 2 half-inch reinforcing bars around the entire pool. Place them about 3 to 4 inches from the top, and keep them close to the outside surface of the wall, being sure that they are covered at all points with at least 1 inch of concrete.

Example of a formal pool with a few water-lilies and shallow-water plants growing in corners.

Strengthen the joints by allowing the rods to run past each other about 6 inches. About 8 inches from the top, poke into the wall through the forms some pieces of reinforcing bars about 10 to 12 inches long. On these may be constructed around all or a part of the pool, a shelf or a ledge to form pockets of soil for shallow water aquatics.

The standard mixture for concrete is 1 part cement, 2 parts sand, and 3 parts crushed stone or gravel. These ingredients should be mixed dry before adding water (use an old metal wheelbarrow or wooden or metal trough procured for the purpose). It is important to end with a firm mixture, not so stiff that it won't pour, but not soupy. Reliable and convenient for small pools are bags of premixed dry concrete sold now in hardware and lumber stores. All you have to do is follow directions on the bag – and add water. The usual procedure is to cement the bottom of the excavation first, then the sides. The edges of pools can be a problem, and there is no one solution that will fit all pool designs. A formal pool is frankly artificial, so it can be edged with raised cement or outlined with

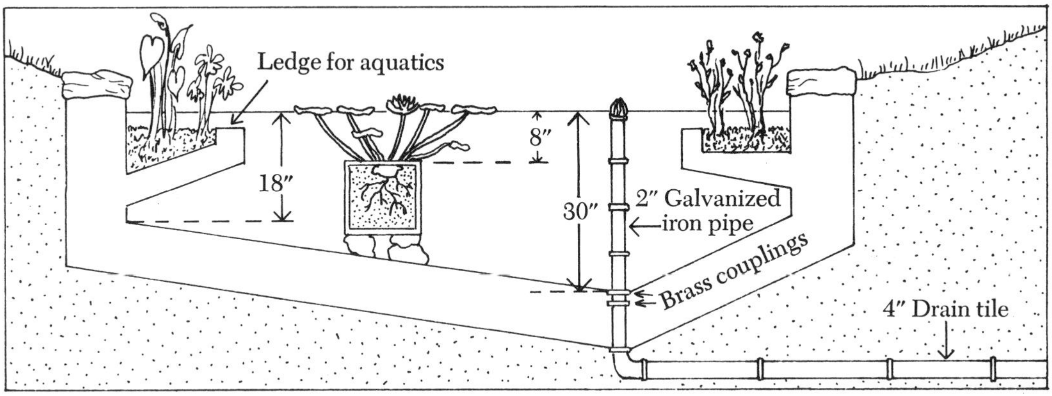

Profile of a formal pool showing overflow pipe and ledges for shallow-water plants. Such a pool must be built with forms and addition of reinforcing rods in concrete for added strength.

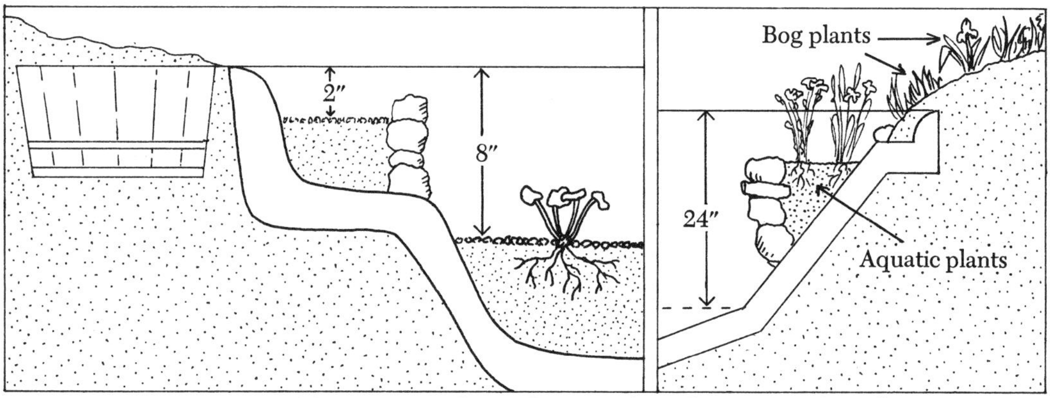

Two ideas for more informal concrete pools. Sunken barrel can be used for bog plants.

a coping of brick or flagstone. An informal pool should look as natural as possible and blend with its surroundings.

One of the best ways to finish off a natural pool is to let the lawn grow to its edge. A few stones or boulders as carefully used as in the construction of a rock garden can be appropriate. If the pool is in shade, rely on woodland plants, such as ferns, around the edges.

After the concrete has hardened (during hardening period, keep concrete covered with damp burlap), it must be allowed to season for about three weeks before plants or fish are added. The water must be changed three or four times during this period to remove alkali from the concrete which are harmful to both plants and fish. A sensible time to make a water-lily pool is in late summer. Plants are added the following spring. Leave the water in over winter and float a log in it to reduce pressure from ice.

You can have bog plants, shallow-water aquatics, and deep-water plants, such as water-lilies, all in the same pool with an equal depth if you put all plants in boxes or pots and use stones or other props to maintain them at the correct water depth.

A better method for shallow water and bog plants is to incorporate a ledge or shelf at the edge of the pools at the time of construction.

Water-lilies need space to spread: 3 feet all around the plant is the minimum and 5 feet each way is better. Plant them in strong boxes, 2 feet square and 1 foot deep or in tubs made of old barrels, first soaking the barrels with sal soda to remove acid. About 8 inches below the surface is the

The use of suitable plants and the right stones around its edges make this small pool seem natural.

Informal pool, shallow and made without forms, has been built between two large, imbedded rocks.

The elegance of a formal pool (made of sheet lead) is not marred by too many water plants.

right depth. Bog plants should have the bottom of their containers in water, and shallow aquatics should be 2 inches under water.

A few fish should be placed in the water as well as frogs and snails. These scavengers keep out mosquitoes and help keep the pool in balance. Goldfish often live over winter in water under the ice.

Do not have running water in your pool to any great extent if you want to grow plants. The plants thrive best in still, warm water. Fountains or falls should be constructed to make a maximum of fuss with a minimum of water. A trickle of water falling 18 inches or more gives the effect of motion desired, the same as a larger volume. Replace the evaporated water by spraying the plants after the sun has gone down in the evening. They appreciate water from the top the same as other plants. If green scum accumulates, sweep it off into the overflow pipe with a hose spray.

Growing Water-lilies

Hardy water-lilies and other aquatics may be set out any time in the spring after the weather starts to warm up and the danger of freezing is over. Tropical plants, however, should not be planted until late spring – from the 20th of May to the 1st of June in most areas. If it is possible, plant them a little closer to the surface when they are small. Their containers may be lowered as they grow larger. However, this is not necessary.

For soil to fill the boxes, use good garden soil (mixed with well-rotted cow manure if you have it). If manure is used, it must be well rotted. Blood meal or some all-purpose chemical fertilizer may be added during the plants' growing season by lowering the water to the top of the tub, making holes with a piece of pipe, inserting the fertilizer, and covering these holes with sand. This will encourage the plants to make new growth.

This combination of statuary, rockwork and pool is a superb example of landscaping creativity.

Water-lilies should be planted with the crown of the plant even with the surface of the soil in the container. Cover the soil in the containers with about 1 to 2 inches of pebbles or sand, but do not smother the plants with it. This will prevent the water from becoming muddy when the containers are put into the pool.

Tropical water-lilies are the most easily grown and give, under favorable conditions, much larger and more colorful blooms than the hardier varieties. If you are going to the trouble of making a nice pool, a small expenditure each year will make it more beautiful and will be more satisfactory than trying to run it on a strictly hardy plant basis.

Plants recommended for trial are:

Tropical Water-Lilies – Night Blooming

Bisset (pink)
Juno (white), sometimes listed as Dentata superba
Rubra Rosea (rosy carmine)

Day Blooming

August Koch (blue)
Blue Beauty (also listed as Pennsylvania)

Garden pools best serve their purpose when their water surface is not completely hidden by plants.

Dauben (blue – very small plant suitable for small pools and those made from tubs)
General Pershing (pink)
Panama-Pacific (purple)

Hardy Water-Lilies

Chromatella (yellow)
Gladstone (white)
Gloriosa (deep red)
Marliac Rose

Perennial or Hardy Plants for Shallow Water

Cattail
Giant arrowhead
Pickerel-weed
Variegated sweet flag
Water arum
Yellow and purple water iris

For the damp ground at the edge where water may wash over, especially if there is not an overflow drain, use:

Cardinal flower
Forget-me-not
Japanese primrose
Marsh marigold
Parrot feather
Pickerel-weed
Sweet flag
Water iris
(See additional lists in Chapter 9, "The Flower Garden.")

Storing away the harvest is not the least of the pleasures of vegetable gardening, whether done, as here, in a cool garage or basement, or in the home freezer or preserve cupboard.

CHAPTER 14

The Vegetable Garden

Make ready a plot
For seeds for the pot.
– Thomas Tusser

No matter how varied an assortment modern markets can offer, and no matter how high the quality of frozen foods, there are four outstanding reasons for devoting garden space to home-grown crops. First, a garden can supply you with fresher vegetables than you can buy; second, it can give you most vegetables in the finest stage of development, impossible when they are bought; third, you can grow higher quality varieties than commercial growers usually attempt; and, fourth, you can grow kinds that are never, or rarely, offered for sale.

When seed catalogs do not specifically point them out, the commercial kinds of vegetables can be recognized (and avoided) by descriptions that suggest business returns – for instance: "immense cropper," "highly prolific," "excellent shipper," "stands up well," "extra early," "long keeper," and so on. Look instead for "ideal for the home garden," "long season of ripening," and the like.

Checklist of Gourmet Vegetables

As to actual kinds of vegetables you plant, here adventure enters. The so-called Jerusalem artichoke (a native American plant!) is rarely seen in the markets. Yet it is one of the most delectable of vegetables escalloped, or steamed and served with Hollandaise or cream sauce. How many gardeners have tried the newer Chinese vegetables, Chinese cabbage and wong-bok? Have you ever grown these Mediterranean vegetables – finocchio (the Italian fennel that looks like celery but tastes like licorice), cherry and plum tomatoes (so useful in any recipe that calls for tomato sauce), roquette or rucola (a leaf vegetable in the mustard family that gives piquant zest to salads), or globe artichoke? Most of these gourmet vegetables are no more difficult to grow than the more mundane kinds.

Freshness and quality are important in home-grown vegetables and fruits, but so is their preparation in the kitchen. The group below have special appeal, whether they are cooked in the most simple fashion or made into delectable dishes that would please even the most creative chefs. With the exception of asparagus and snap beans, most do not take up much garden space for very long.

Asparagus: A perennial – once planted, it lasts for years. Needs room. Buy plants in spring, set 3 to 4 inches deep, 18 inches apart in sun in well-drained, rich soil. Feed

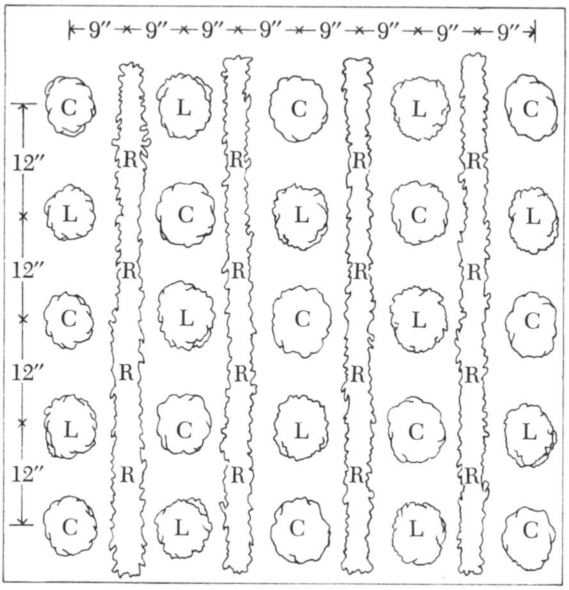

Companion cropping makes good use of space. C - cabbage, L - lettuce, R - radish. Lettuce and radishes will have been gathered by the time the cabbage requires their space.

and weed with Aero Cyanamid. Harvest for 2 months. Freeze surplus.

Beans: There are bush and pole varieties of snap beans as well as those with yellow (wax) and green or purple pods. Even short rows (10 feet or so) of bush beans are worth growing. Make 3 sowings, 2 weeks apart. Superb for freezing.

Herbs: Only a few plants of each are needed. Most useful: parsley (seed germinates slowly); basil (for tomato recipes); tarragon (tender perennial to grow in pots – use leaves in vinegar and with chicken); rosemary (tender perennial also to grow in pots for pork, beef, chicken, lamb); thyme (hardy perennial, a basic seasoning); chives (very hardy perennial with decorative flowers and onion-flavored leaves); sage (perennial, a basic flavoring).

Lettuce: Be selective. Grow kinds rarely seen in the market. Examples: 'Bibb,' 'Ruby' (red leaves and heat resistant), 'Oak Leaf' (for summer), 'Tom Thumb,' 'Matchless' (for summer). Start in early spring, continue sowing every 10 days or so for succession. Feed and water generously.

Globe artichoke is an epicure's delight. A perennial, it does best in mild-winter regions.

Rhubarb: A large perennial. Two or three plants are enough. They are quite ornamental.

Spinach: No market spinach, either fresh or frozen, matches a home-grown crop. Sow in very early spring in rich, limed soil. If space is limited, sow in flower garden, and use like lettuce in spring salads.

Squash: Many kinds. Quick, easy, and prolific are Italian bush varieties known as zucchini.

Tomatoes: Many kinds and many ways to grow them. A dozen plants of mixed varieties take care of a family of 4, but less will do. Tomato plants are very tender. If spring frosts can still be expected, plants must be protected by Hotkaps (little paper tents). Mix a handful of 5-10-5 or similar

Sage, a perennial, is a favorite culinary herb. Some sages are green, others gold or purple.

Metal edging sunk around clumps of mint keep this invasive plant within bounds.

A small herb and salad garden. An early sowing of radishes might precede basil. Part of basil row could be given to parsley or another herb.

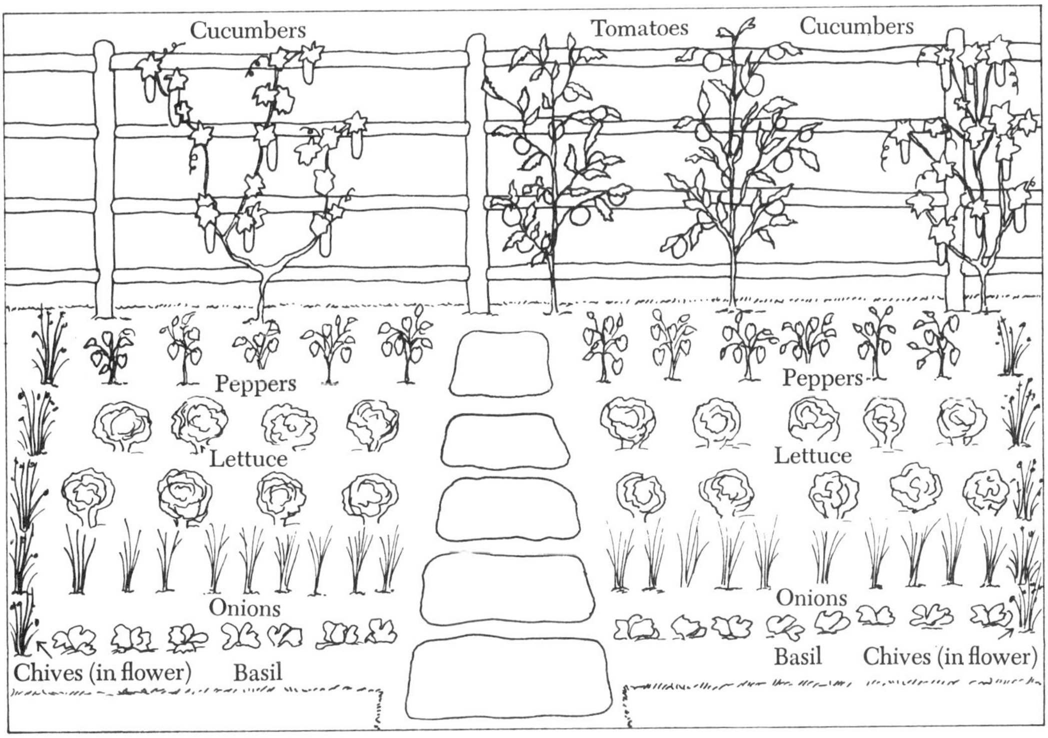

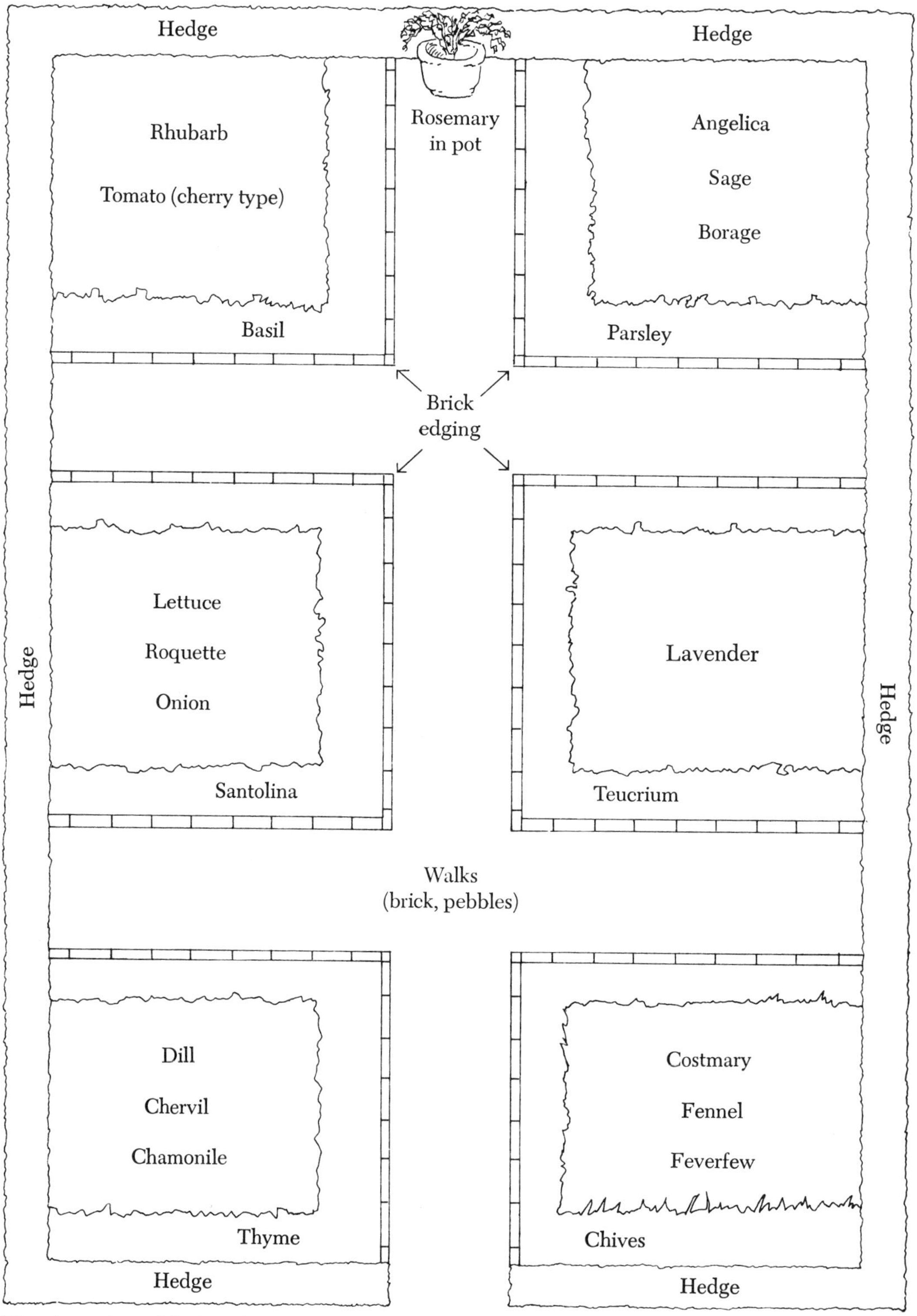

Plan for a formal herb salad garden about 20 by 34 feet. Beds could be permanently edged with bricks or low boards. Plants in centers of beds can be arranged in rows for formality.

Rhubarb can be forced in the garden. A drain tile is set over crown and covered with inverted flower pot. Pot is removed when leaves fill it.

Visual interest is added to a small garden by dividing it into triangular beds. All plants will be within easy reach from paths.

Edibles can be ornamental: this terrace garden has flowers and vegetables in its angled rows.

fertilizer in hole at time of planting. Avoid overfeeding.

To stake tomatoes, use sturdy, 6-foot poles set deep by plant at planting time. Remove side shoots to keep single stem. Tie stem to pole with cloth strips or soft twine that won't cut into plant. If strong stakes set a good foot deep are used, plants should stay upright. Other method is to mulch (hay, straw, rough compost, black plastic, anything available), and let plants sprawl. Planting distances vary according to variety or method: about 2 feet apart for staked plants; 3 feet for unstaked. There are compact varieties, especially those with small fruits, that shouldn't be staked and can be planted about 1½ to 2 feet apart.

Planning Comes Before Planting

When making up a list of vegetable kinds (not varieties) to grow, it is a good plan to follow a typical seed catalog index so as not to overlook any. You might use a filing card for each kind and under the name (bean, corn, pea, and the like) write the variety or varieties you plan to grow and any cultural notes. Your choice will depend on: first, the family appetite; second, the amount of space the plants require (sweet corn and winter squash need more room than you may be able to give them); third, those that you can obtain in just as good quality elsewhere – onions, potatoes, and winter cabbage; fourth, your ability and willingness to meet the requirements of certain fussy sorts or others especially susceptible to pests or diseases; and fifth, the family vacation schedule. If you plan to be away in August, you'll want to grow spring and early summer crops.

SOIL TEMPERATURES FOR SEED GERMINATION

Kind	*Soil temperature – Degrees F.* *Optimum*	*Minimum*
Cucumber, muskmelon, okra, pumpkin, squash, watermelon	95	60
Snap bean, eggplant, pepper	85	60
Sweet corn, tomato	85	50
Beet, broccoli, cabbage, radish, Swiss chard, turnip	85	40
Lima bean	80	60
Carrot, cauliflower, parsley	80	40
Onion	80	32
Asparagus	75	50
Pea	75	40
Endive, lettuce, cress	75	32
Celery	70	40
Parsnip, spinach	70	32

The home vegetable gardener who wants to grow a limited number of crops in limited space can ignore for the most part the maximum spacing between rows recommended on seed packets and in many publications that are directed to the farmer and market gardener. Common sense and experience will show him that if he plans to walk between rows, most crops will require a distance of 18 to 24 inches between the rows. But if his rows are short, say only a few feet long, the crops, in many cases, can be spaced much closer together. Radishes, certain lettuce varieties (the delectable Bibb types) can be planted in short rows about 8 inches apart. Where space isn't limited, and especially if power equipment is to be used for cultivation, the distance between rows must be greater – up to 3 feet or more, depending on the vegetable.

Except for the most modest of postage-stamp-sized vegetable plots, a plan on paper (made at the time of ordering seed packets) is a great help. Here are some plant groupings arranged according to the time the vegetable is planted and the time it will occupy the ground:

Annual Crops: 1. *Early spring to late spring:* Radish, lettuce, onion sets, garden cress, mustard, corn salad, spinach. 2. *Long-season vegetables, early spring to late fall:* Parsnip, salsify, scorzonera, chickory, chard, celeriac, leek, parsley. 3. *Early spring to midsummer or early fall:* Beet, early cabbage, carrot, onion, kohlrabi, early celery, pea, turnip. 4. *Late spring to* *early fall:* Tomato, okra, pepper, eggplant, sweet potato, bean, corn, muskmelon, watermelon, pumpkin, squash, cucumber, gourd. 5. *Midsummer to late fall:* Turnip, rutabaga, beet, carrot, kohlrabi, broccoli, Brussels sprouts, kale, cauliflower, endive, late cabbage, late celery. 6. *Late summer to late fall:* Lettuce, spinach, round-seeded pea, winter radish, mustard, garden cress. 7. *To be sown in late summer or early fall for late fall or early spring use:* Dandelion, spinach, sorrel, corn salad.

Perennial Crops: Besides the annual crops mentioned, there are several perennials, asparagus and rhubarb being the best known. Others are French (or globe) artichoke, dock, cardoon, sea kale, and Jerusalem (or American) artichoke. They occupy the same area permanently. But, even so, quick-maturing crops can be sown broadcast among them in early spring, and allowed to take their chances; these mature and are used before the perennials need all the space. Among those often grown in asparagus beds are spinach, lettuce, and radishes. If, in late summer, seed of spinach or corn salad is scattered over the asparagus bed, enough of the hardy seedlings should survive the winter to give an early cutting the following spring – several weeks before a spring-sown crop could be expected.

This spacious garden has been laid out with room for succeeding plantings of crops already well advanced. Parsley is a handsome edging.

Where rabbits are a nuisance, fencing the salad garden is a solution. Rows can be reached over low fence for harvesting. Edible-podded peas are at left.

Planting Schedule

Vegetables to plant early when the ground is still cool

Asparagus	Leek
Broad beans	Lettuce (all kinds)
Broccoli	Mustard
Brussels sprouts	Onion (seeds, sets, and plants)
Cabbage	Parsley
Carrots	Parsnip
Cauliflower	Peas
Celery	Radish
Cress	Roquette
Collards	Salsify
Endive	Spinach
Kale	Turnip
Kohlrabi	

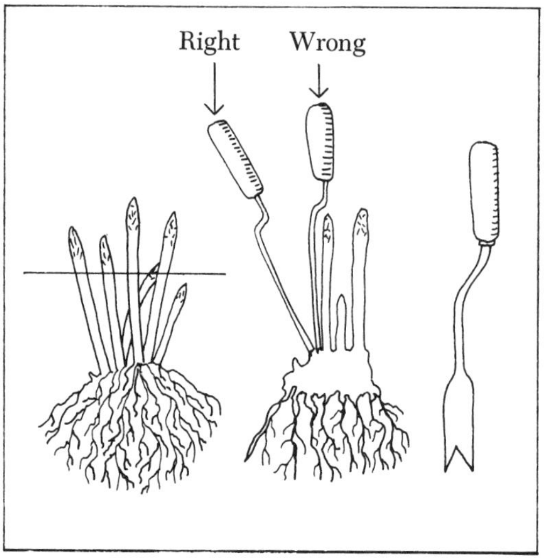

Left, how asparagus grows from crown. Right, the correct way and the wrong way to cut stalks with an asparagus knife.

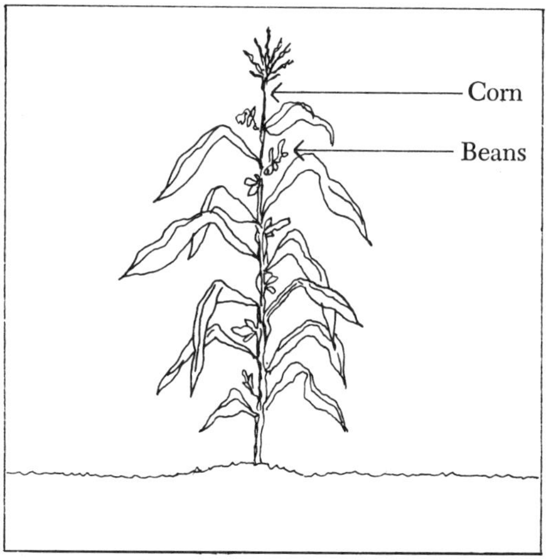

In partnership cropping, a late variety of corn supports pole beans.

Vegetables to plant when the ground becomes warm

Beans, lima	Peanuts
Beans, snap	Peppers (plants)
Corn	Pumpkin
Cucumber	Squash
Eggplant (plants)	Sweet potato (plants)
Melons	Tomato (plants)
Okra	

Vegetables to plant in midsummer for fall

If seeds of these vegetables are planted about 60 days before your first fall frost (see Table of Killing Frosts), they should all mature satisfactorily. Where plants are indicated, they should be started earlier from seed so the plants will be ready to set out 60 days before frost.

Beets	Kale
Broccoli (plants)	Kohlrabi
Brussels sprouts (plants)	Lettuce
Bush beans	Mustard
Cabbage (plants)	Onions (green)
Cauliflower (plants)	Radish
Collards	Spinach
Cress	Tampala
Endive	Turnip

Crop rotation is less practicable in small gardens than in large-scale farming. Nevertheless, whenever possible, group the plants that require similar cultural treatment, and shift them about from year to year.

Try to have a following crop as different as possible from the preceding one. If the 2 are botanically related (as mustard, cabbage, and turnips), insects and plant diseases that attack the first are likely to be more troublesome on the others.

Making the Vegetable Garden

When choice is possible, the vegetable garden should be fully exposed to the sun and longer from north to south than from east to west. If the rows can run north and south and the long way of the area, this will favor the even distribution of sunlight. Some shade, especially late in the day, will not seriously hamper the growth of most vegetables. The soil should always be well drained, because vegetables fail to grow well in poorly drained ground and because slow evaporation of excess water keeps the ground cold and "late" in spring.

The best soil for vegetable gardens is a combination of sand, clay, and humus. It holds moisture and fertility better than a

Chrysanthemums fill autumn's gardens with dependable, long-lasting color, in bright as well as pastel hues.

Fruit of snowberry, an easily-grown, hardy shrub.

Autumn

Golden maple leaves light up neighboring countrysides and home landscapes.

Many annuals, such as the calendula, prosper in the cool evenings of fall, making the best display at this time.

Left: *Many kinds of heath* (Erica) *and heather* (Calluna), *low, shrubby plants, are at their peak in early fall.*

Giant marigolds, in yellow and orange, are effective with the blue spikes of salvia. Both are cut-flower material.

There are many shapes and sizes among dahlia blooms. This is a cactus-flowered variety with quilled petals.

The vine Virginia creeper gives fall foliage color in even the most rugged climate.

Foliage house plants, summered outdoors, should be brought inside in early fall.

A yard planting effective in all seasons. Basically a green garden, it needs only occasional color.

Right: *The black locust, whose leaves turn yellow in fall, is drought resistant and suggested for the Rocky Mountain regions.*

The winged euonymous is called "burning bush" in fall when its leaves turn red.

Potted chrysanthemums transform an enclosed porch into a garden room. The brick wall and flagstone floor help to maintain a higher humidity and cool atmosphere.

Peas are one of the earliest crops to be sowed, traditionally on St. Patrick's Day. Twigs support row.

Even when space is limited, some gardeners raise a few potatoes for an early-summer taste treat.

sandy soil and is more easily worked than a predominantly clay soil. Sand can be built up by adding humus-forming materials such as manure, compost, leaf mold, peat moss or green manure; or in case of stiff clay, as follows: in late autumn spread fresh manure or any kind of humus-forming material available, and plow or dig it under, leaving the ground rough; in spring, smooth down the clods, add limestone or wood ashes (about a pound to the square yard) and more compost or other organic matter, if the soil still seems stiff, and rake in before planting. Repeat the program annually (except that lime need be added only once every 5 years unless soil tests indicate otherwise) until the soil is rich and friable.

The best source of humus is stable manure. It is famous for its magical effects on plant growth – actually due not so much to magic as to bacteria that help release plant food and in decaying, supply plant food elements discarded by animals. If a local supply is not available, it can be bought in dried, pulverized, easy-to-use form that is also free of weed seeds. When you want to

Starting a trench for cucumbers. Soil has first been cultivated with a tiller to make digging easy.

Finished trench is partly filled with seaweed gathered nearby. Compost could also be used.

improve a heavy clay, turn under fresh manure in autumn so it can decay over winter; when a light soil is to be enriched, apply well-decayed manure in spring as the plant food in it will quickly become available.

Green manures are crops grown solely to be turned under while green and soft to improve the soil. Their use is far more practical for farmers and commercial growers, but often the home gardener finds them of value. Crops used for these purposes are of two classes: those that gather nitrogen from the air and add it to the soil, and those that cannot do this but merely protect the surface and conserve what food is already present. Crimson clover (sow an ounce to 200 square feet), winter vetch (an ounce to about 60 square feet), and Canada field peas (an ounce to about 40 square feet) are the most suitable nitrogen-gathering crops for home gardens. Sow them on any vacant land from July until mid-autumn.

Crops of the other type include: Buckwheat (1 ounce to about 60 square feet), ryegrass, winter rye, barley, and oats (an ounce to about 30 square feet). A good combination is buckwheat, crimson clover, rye, and winter vetch sown all at once in mid-July, either on empty ground or between rows of late vegetables. The first frost will kill the buckwheat, and perhaps the crimson clover won't live over winter; but the rye and vetch will; they will continue growing in spring until dug or plowed under.

Quick, easy compost to take the place of or supplement hard-to-come-by animal manure can be made as follows: Heap straw, cut weeds, lawn clippings, and other waste vegetable matter in loose, flat-topped piles, 3 to 6 feet high on ground fully exposed to the weather. On top of each 4- to 6-inch layer, sprinkle evenly a mixture of 45 percent ammonium sulfate, 40 percent finely ground limestone and 15 percent superphosphate at the rate of 7 or 8 pounds to approximately 100 pounds of the vegetable material. Wet the pile as it is built and often enough thereafter to keep it moist, and the material will usually decay in three or four months, especially if it is forked over once or twice so as to throw the outside layer into the interior. The resulting compost is well worth making to improve the soil, to get rid of waste vegetable matter, and to avoid paying for as much high-

Bed of seaweed is thoroughly soaked, then covered with several inches of soil.

Sown several seeds to a hill, cucumbers are covered with Hotkaps for a "greenhouse" effect.

priced fertilizer as would otherwise be needed.

Commercial fertilizers can be organic and inorganic. Various materials of each type are often bought separately and mixed for use in farming and commercial vegetable growing, but it is generally advisable and more convenient in small gardens to use prepared plant foods; that is, complete, balanced mixtures carrying analysis figures showing the percentage content of nitrogen, phosphate, and potash. Fertilizer recommendations are usually made on an acre basis. To find the corresponding amount to apply to a small garden, divide the number of square feet in an acre (43,560) by the recommended amount to apply (say 1,000 pounds). The answer (43 and a fraction in this case) is the number of square feet on which one pound of the mixture should be spread.

The preceding information on manures, commercial fertilizer and compost is to help you in determining what the soil of your vegetable garden may need. Unless you have special problem soil, your garden may not require the addition of much material (perhaps compost or all-purpose fertilizer, according to the crops' require-

Given a good (and early) start, plants show strong growth, begin to climb fence. Pipe leads down to seaweed for underground watering.

ments) to make it suitable for growing vegetables. If it is a new garden, it is wise to have the soil tested (consult your county agent or your state agricultural experiment station for further information), or do it yourself according to directions given with the kit which can be purchased in a garden center or through a mail-order nursery. If your soil needs lime, add it in spring or fall according to the amounts indicated by the test. If your soil lacks sufficient organic matter, incorporate it in whatever form is most available (follow previous recommendations in this chapter).

For the new vegetable garden or land that has been in sod for several years, if possible, till or dig soil in the fall and leave it rough or "ungroomed" over winter. Or till the soil in spring as soon as it is dry enough to work. Soil can be safely worked in spring without spoiling its texture when it has lost its wet, glistening appearance, or when a squeezed handful breaks apart at a slight touch.

Strong twine stretched between posts is a guide for marking seed furrow.

Planting the Vegetable Garden

Before planting any seeds or setting out plants, go over the soil with a heavy rake to remove excessive debris and to level the surface. But it is certainly not necessary to approximate a ballroom floor in your vegetable garden! If lime or dry fertilizers have been broadcast over the soil, be sure to rake them well into the top few inches of soil.

In the spring garden, the first seeds to be planted are those of peas – traditionally on St. Patrick's Day over a large portion of the country. Pea seeds are exceptionally hardy and take in their stride weather that daunts even the most eager gardener. Next in hardiness are radishes, onions, and the leaf vegetables – lettuce, spinach, and cabbage. Beans and the vine crops require warm weather to germinate and grow. (See the previous suggestions on plant groupings arranged according to planting season.)

For ready germination, vermiculite (which is sterile) is spread in row before seeds are sowed.

Follow the planting directions on the seed packets and the chart in this chapter. Don't be afraid to make innovations dictated by your circumstances. There are really very few hard-and-fast rules in gardening, and this is especially true when it comes to growing vegetables.

As soon as the young plants have developed their second or third true leaves, thin them to the required distance for good development. Some of the thinnings, espe-

Cold frame offers a harvest of lettuce before it could be ready in the open ground.

some form of power tiller can be a great time and labor saver; for a smaller plot the Dutch or scuffle hoe (worked while walking backward) and other similar hand tools are excellent because they obviate walking on the freshly loosened ground.

During drought, vegetables need extra watering and benefit from an inch a week or less. When sowing seeds in very dry soil, irrigate the furrow before sowing the seeds.

A mulch between rows of vegetables keeps weeds down, and helps to conserve moisture in the soil during a drought. It also provides a path so that plants can be tended and picked without compacting the soil. It prevents a runoff of heavy rains on a slope so that the water soaks into the soil.

Almost any material is suitable to mulch the vegetable garden: grass clippings, pulled weeds, withered plant debris, or leaves. Wood chips, straw, or hay are more attractive. (Wood chips obtained from util-

cially those of lettuce, if large enough, can be eaten.

In all but the warmest climates, some vegetables are always started under glass, or in sheltered beds, and transplanted when they reach suitable size and when conditions in the open are favorable. Sown in flats, the seedlings are transplanted to stand 2 inches apart each way in other flats as soon as they can be handled; then, after being gradually exposed to cold weather they are planted outdoors, the soil being well firmed around them. The more tender kinds – eggplant, pepper, and tomato – are often put in peat pots so that pot and plant can be set out together. If cutworms are abundant, wrap a "collar" of paper around each stem so it will extend an inch above and below soil level when setting out the plants.

Throughout the growing season, cultivation of the soil between rows and plants should be carried on frequently to kill weeds. For a garden 50 by 50 feet or larger,

When soil is dry, soak furrow before sowing seed.

KILLING FROSTS AND GROWING SEASONS

(Courtesy of U. S. Weather Bureau)

City	*Growing Season (Days)*	*Last Frost Spring*	*First Frost Fall*
Lander, Wyo.	123	May 18	Sept. 18
Bismarck, N.D.	133	May 11	Sept. 21
Alpena, Mich.	141	May 13	Oct. 1
Helena, Mont.	145	May 7	Sept. 29
Reno, Nev.	145	May 14	Oct. 6
Marquette, Mich.	149	May 13	Oct. 9
Concord, N.H.	149	May 7	Oct. 3
Duluth, Minn.	152	May 6	Oct. 5
Green Bay, Wisc.	157	May 5	Oct. 9
Pocatello, Ida.	160	Apr. 29	Oct. 6
Denver, Colo.	160	May 3	Oct. 10
Pierre, S. Dak.	160	Apr. 30	Oct. 7
Minneapolis	166	Apr. 27	Oct. 10
Detroit, Mich.	170	Apr. 28	Oct. 15
Des Moines, Ia.	171	Apr. 21	Oct. 9
Fort Wayne, Ind.	171	Apr. 25	Oct. 13
Ludington, Mich.	172	May 2	Oct. 21
Albany, N.Y.	174	Apr. 24	Oct. 15
Madison, Wisc.	174	Apr. 26	Oct. 17
Santa Fe, N.M.	177	Apr. 25	Oct. 19
Hartford, Conn.	177	Apr. 20	Oct. 13
Toledo, Ohio	179	Apr. 22	Oct. 18
Portland, Maine	181	Apr. 19	Oct. 17
Spokane, Wash.	182	Apr. 14	Oct. 13
Parkersburg, W. Va.	184	Apr. 17	Oct. 18
Omaha, Nebr.	184	Apr. 14	Oct. 15
Salt Lake City	185	Apr. 18	Oct. 20
Chicago, Ill.	186	Apr. 16	Oct. 19
St. Joseph, Mo.	191	Apr. 9	Oct. 17
Trenton, N.J.	191	Apr. 16	Oct. 24
Springfield, Mo.	193	Apr. 12	Oct. 22
Boston, Mass.	195	Apr. 14	Oct. 26
Wichita, Kans.	197	Apr. 9	Oct. 23
Cincinnati, Ohio	198	Apr. 8	Oct. 23
Lewiston, Ida.	201	Apr. 6	Oct. 24
Harrisburg, Pa.	202	Apr. 9	Oct. 28
Evansville, Ind.	207	Apr. 5	Oct. 29
Cairo, Ill.	212	Mar. 31	Oct. 29
Richmond, Va.	216	Mar. 31	Nov. 2
Roseburg, Ore.	217	Apr. 8	Nov. 11
Oklahoma City	218	Mar. 30	Nov. 3
Chattanooga	220	Mar. 29	Nov. 4
Raleigh, N.C.	223	Mar. 27	Nov. 5
Little Rock, Ark.	241	Mar. 18	Nov. 14
El Paso, Tex.	242	Mar. 19	Nov. 16
Tucson, Ariz.	243	Mar. 11	Nov. 9
Macon, Ga.	245	Mar. 14	Nov. 14
Columbia, S.C.	246	Mar. 17	Nov. 18
Montgomery, Ala.	250	Mar. 8	Nov. 13
Shreveport, La.	251	Mar. 6	Nov. 12
Portland, Ore.	251	Mar. 15	Nov. 21
San Bernardino	259	Mar. 8	Nov. 22
Eureka, Calif.	277	Mar. 16	Dec. 18
Del Rio, Tex.	277	Feb. 23	Nov. 27
Sacramento	283	Feb. 19	Nov. 29
Phoenix, Ariz.	296	Feb. 10	Dec. 3
Yuma, Ariz.	334	Jan. 20	Dec. 20
San Francisco	350	Jan. 13	Dec. 29
Los Angeles	*	*	*
Miami, Fla.	*	*	*
San Diego	*	*	*

* Frosts do not occur every year.

Baled hay is pulled apart and applied loosely as mulch around young plants, thickly between rows.

A gold-medal winner in the 1969 All-America Selections is broccoli 'Green Comet,' an F_1 hybrid.

ity companies are sometimes dumped along highways, free for the collecting but are likely, these days, to end up in nurseries out of reach of the home gardener.)

Black plastic is a modern mulching material that comes in rolls from 12 to 36 inches wide. Holes are punched for the seeds or plants, or the strips can be laid on each side of the row. Soil underneath the plastic retains heat up to 10 to 15 degrees F. higher overnight than in exposed soil. The plastic is inexpensive and will last for several seasons. It should be carefully laid and weighted down with soil at the edges and a little soil in the middle to hold it in place.

Control of plant enemies begins with the disposal of weeds and crop residues that harbor diseases and insects between seasons. Compost these materials promptly. Rotating crops helps to prevent the spread of various soil-borne diseases such as club root of cabbage and related plants. Dust or spray with rotenone or pyrethrum to control Mexican bean beetles on beans and flea beetles on tomatoes, peppers, and eggplant. In general try to avoid using poisonous sprays or dusts on vegetables close to harvest. Always follow directions. If particularly troublesome problems arise, appeal for advice to your county agent or state agricultural experiment station.

After harvesting a crop, put the rest in the compost heap. Then prepare, plant, or sow the vacant ground to some other crop or green manure so as to keep it actively producing something other than weeds all season. Harvesting really starts when lettuce thinnings and cuttings can first be used in early spring. It continues until the last turnip, cabbage, celery, and broccoli are gathered for winter use. As most crops of various kinds mature more rapidly than they can be consumed, a part of each can usually be frozen.

Mulch (this is straw) virtually eliminates weeding, helps soil retain moisture longer.

"Tiny Dwarf" patio tomato is a dwarf plant suitable for pot culture; fruits are 1½ inches across.

VEGETABLE

FAIRLY FAST MATURING PLANTS

Name	*Seed Required for 50 ft. Row*	*Time to Start Seed in Hotbed or Greenhouse*	*Time to Transplant Seedlings to Garden*	*Time to Sow Seed in Open Garden*	*Rows Apart (in feet)*	*Plants Apart in Row (In.)*	*Depth of Planting (In.)*
Beans – (Bush)	½ lb.	....	....	April–May	1½–2	4	1½
Beans – (Pole)	½ lb.	....	....	May	4	36	1½–2
Beans – Lima (Bush)	½ lb.	....	....	May 15	1½–2	4	1½–2
Beans – Lima (Pole)	½ lb.	....	....	May 15	4	36	1½–2
Beets (Early)	1 oz.	....	....	April	1½	4	½
Beets (Late)	1 oz.	....	....	June–July	1½	4	½
Carrot (Early)	½ oz.	....	....	April	1½–2	2–4	½
Carrot (Late)	½ oz.	....	....	July–August	1½–2	2–4	½
Chard (Swiss)	1 oz.	....	....	April	1½	6–8	¾
Cress, Garden		....	....	April–May	1–1½	2–3	½
Dill		....	....	April	1½	4–6	½
Endive	¼ oz.	....	....	April	1½–2	8–12	½
Lettuce	¼ oz.	Feb.–Mar.	April 15	April	1½–2	8–12	¼
Mustard	1 oz.	....	....	April	1½–2	8–10	½
Onions (Sets)	1 qt.	....	....	April	1–1½	2–3	½
Peas	1 lb.	....	....	April	6–8	6	2
Potato (Early)	4–5 lbs.	....	....	April	*Double Row* 3	6–8	4
Radish	½ oz.	Feb.–Mar.	....	April	1½–2	1–3	½
Spinach	½ oz.	....	....	April	1–1½	6	½
LONG SEASON PLANTS							
Broccoli	¼ oz.	....	....	April–May	2½–3	24	½–1
Brussels Sprouts	¼ oz.	March	May	April	2½–3	18–24	½
Cabbage (Early)	¼ oz.	Feb.–Mar.	May	April	2–3	24	½
Cabbage (Late)	¼ oz.	....	....	May	2–3	24	½
Cabbage (Savoy)	¼ oz.	....	....	May	2–3	24	½
Cardoon	¼ oz.	Feb.–Mar.	May	....	3	18	½
Cauliflower	¼ oz.	Jan.–Feb.	May	....	2–3	15	½
Celeriac	¼ oz.	March	May	April	2	9	¼
Celery	¼ oz.	Feb.–Mar.	May–June	April	2–3	6–8	¼
Chicory	.....	....	....	April	1–2	10–12	½
Collards	¼ oz.	Feb.–Mar.	....	May	3	24–36	½
Corn (Sweet)	½ pt.	....	....	May	3	24–36	1
Cucumbers	½ oz.	....	....	May–June	3–4	36–48	1
Eggplant	¼ oz.	Feb.–Mar.	May	....	3	24	½
Kale (see Broccoli)	(above)	....	....	....	.....	.....	.....
Kohlrabi	¼ oz.	....	....	April	1½–2	8–12	½
Leek	½ oz.	....	....	April	1¼–2	4–6	½
Muskmelon	¼ oz.	....	....	May	3–4	36–48	1
New Zealand Spinach	¼ oz.	....	....	May	3	12–18	½
Okra	1 oz.	April	June	May	3	12	½
Onion (Seed)	½ oz.	Feb.	April	April	1	3	½
Parsley	½ oz.	....	....	April	1	4–6	½
Parsnip	¼ oz.	....	....	April	1½	4	½
Peppers	¼ oz.	Feb.–Mar.	May	May	2	24	½
Potato (Late)	4–5 lbs.	....	....	May–June	3	6–8	½
Pumpkins	½ oz.	....	....	May	4–5	36–48	4
Rutabaga	½ oz.	....	....	April	2½	8–12	1
Salsify	1 oz.	....	....	April	1½	4	½
Squash	½ oz.	....	....	May–June	4–5	48–60	½
Sweet Potato	50 roots	March	May–June	....	3–5	14	3–4
Tomato	¼ oz.	March	May	....	2½–3	30–36	½
Turnip	½ oz.	....	....	April	1½–2	3–4	½
Watermelon	1 oz.	....	....	May	8–10	80–90	1
PERENNIAL PLANTS							
Artichoke, Globe	½ oz.	Feb.–Mar.	May	....	3–4	24	½
Asparagus	40 plants	....	....	....	1½–3	14	4–5
Dandelion	½ oz.	....	....	April–May	1½	8–10	½
Horseradish	50 roots	....	....	....	2	8–12	2
Rhubarb	25 roots	....	....	....	2½–3	24	¾

PLANTING CHART

(Note: Planting dates are for Northeast and North Central regions.)

Degree of Hardiness	*Successive Plantings (Days Apart)*	*Days to Mature*	*Important Suggestions*
Tender	14 days to July	60	Early plantings can be followed by fall vegetables.
Very tender	Season	60	Longer bearing than above. Use poles 6–8 ft. long; plant 6 seeds per pole and later thin to three.
Very tender	10 days to July	60	Cultivate as for Bush Snap Beans above.
Very tender	Season		Plant and thin as for Pole Snap Beans above.
Hardy	14 days	40–70	Late plantings for winter use should use turnip varieties.
Hardy	....	90	Before freezing, dig and store in cellar or pit.
Hardy	14 days	100	Hoe deeply and frequently – keep clean of weeds.
Hardy	....	120	Give plenty of water and keep soil well cultivated.
Hardy	20–30	60–70	Can replant until September for fall and winter use.
Hardy	14 days to Sept.	35	Easily grown in winter in greenhouse, hotbed, or window box.
Tender	Fall use in June	100–120	Tie outer leaves over center bud when 6 to 8 inches long.
Hardy	August	70–90	Fertilize heavily – plant on rich soil and supply abundant moisture.
Hardy	7 days	30–40	Can be grown in window boxes in spring.
Hardy	14 days	50–60	Till top soil frequently and keep free of weeds.
Hardy	7–14 days	60	Do best in cool weather, so plant as early as possible.
Hardy	June for Fall	90	Apply fertilizer between rows several times during season.
Hardy	7–10 days	30	For fall use long, white varieties.
Hardy	....	3 mos.	Apply nitrate of soda between rows to stimulate growth.

Hardy	....	4–5 mos.	Winter crop may be started in May.
Hardy	14 days	5–6 mos.	When small sprouts begin to appear, cut large leaves off to favor sprouts.
Hardy	....	4–5 mos.	Fertilize and cultivate freely – hill up slightly as growth progresses.
Hardy	....	4–5 mos.	
Hardy	....	4–5 mos.	
Tender	....	5–6 mos.	Leaves bunched for blanching in early fall.
Tender	....	4–5 mos.	Never allow plants to become checked in growth.
Hardy	....	5–6 mos.	Roots remain in ground until wanted.
Hardy	....	5–6 mos.	Mound with soil to remove green coloring.
Hardy	....	6–7 mos.	Then raised and transplanted in trench and covered with manure – after 4 to 5 weeks ready for use.
Hardy	June	3–4 mos.	Stands hot weather better than cabbage or kale. Grown widely in southern states.
Tender	10 days to June	2–3 mos.	Deep soil and frequent cultivation make best crop.
Tender	....	2–3 mos.	Plant in low hills for perfect drainage while young.
Tender	....	4–5 mos.	Grow best in well drained, warm soil.
....	....	....	....
Hardy	....	2½–3 mos.	Quite hardy and does well where cauliflower cannot be grown.
Very Hardy	....	3–4 mos.	Plant in open furrow 5 or 6 inches deep – draw in earth as plants grow.
Tender	....	3–4 mos.	Plant in hills, 10 to 12 seed, thin to 4 plants.
Hardy	....	3–4 mos.	Soak seed 2 hours in hot water.
Tender	June	3 mos.	Requires frequent cultivation until plants cover the ground.
Very Hardy	....	Varies	Onions from seed are edible at almost any stage.
Hardy	May–June	3–4 mos.	Seed germinate very slowly – mark rows with radish seeds.
Hardy	....	4–5 mos.	Better flavored if subjected to early frosts.
Tender	....	4–5 mos.	Top dress soil between rows when plants 6 inches high.
Hardy	....	4–5 mos.	Dig before hard freezing.
Tender	....	4–5 mos.	Plant on hills and cultivate as for cucumbers.
Hardy	....	4–5 mos.	Pull roots before freezing, cut off tops and store in cellar.
Hardy	....	4–5 mos.	Dig roots in fall or winter as required.
Very Tender	....	2–4 mos.	Winter squash may be planted later and stored.
Tender	....	5–6 mos.	Dig when vines have been killed by frost.
Tender	June	4–5 mos.	Protect from frost when first set out in garden.
Hardy	June–July	2–3 mos.	Crowding or weeds make poorly flavored roots.
Tender	....	4–5 mos.	Top dress with fertilizer high in nitrogen and potash.

Tender	....	Aug.–Sept.	If crowns get too large after two or three years – divide and reset.
Hardy	....	May–June	In northern states mulch asparagus to prevent heaving of the roots during winter.
Hardy	....	Sept. (1st. yr.)	Blanch by covering with straw or leaves.
Hardy	....	Any time	Tends to become rank weed – cultivate closely and root out volunteers.
Hardy	....	2nd spring	Keep blossom stalks cut back – flowers and seed exhaust plant.

These pear trees are a mist of white in the spring garden. This is one of the many fruits worth growing for its beauty alone.

CHAPTER 15

Fruits and Berries

Beauty.
Like the sweet apple which
reddens upon the topmost bough.
– Sappho

Fruit plants offer more than food-producing value. They cost no more, generally, than shrubs, trees, and vines that are planted solely for ornament. Yet, most of them are attractive enough in foliage and flower to serve as ornamentals in the garden. They are easy to manage, and their enemies are not beyond control.

Apricot trees are conspicuous for their beautiful rose-pink flowers in early spring; the large-flowered varieties of peaches soon follow; then come the plums, sweet and sour cherries, apples, and pears. All can be used as specimen or shade trees except along the street front where their dropping fruits may be a nuisance. The bramble fruits may serve as hedges along a fence or in place of it. For an informal, unclipped hedge about 5 feet high, the black raspberry is excellent because it "stays put" (red raspberries spread to adjacent ground by suckers); it bears snowbanks of bloom in May and delicious fruit in July. Even strawberries in well-tended beds are pleasing to look at throughout the growing season.

As an accent, few shrubs equal a well-grown quince bush in full flower; none approach it in early autumn when laden with golden fruit. One bush is sufficient both as a specimen and as a source of fruit. In soil naturally or purposely made acid, blueberries may be grown in the garden. Their foliage is brilliant in its autumn color, and during winter the red branches are conspicuous. Blueberries make an even more presentable informal hedge than do the bramble fruits. These shrubs grow under the same conditions as do rhododendrons and azaleas, and interesting landscape groupings of the three kinds of shrubs can be made.

Only on large properties is there space for sweet cherries because mature trees often spread to 50 feet, whereas sour cherry trees rarely reach half that diameter and are easily kept within bounds by judicious pruning. Standard apple and pear trees also are too large for the small place, but dwarf trees are easily adapted to small quarters – whether in natural, round-head form or trained as espaliers.

Dwarf Fruit Trees

The perfection of the dwarf fruit tree today makes it possible for every home gardener to be a fruit farmer, even if he gardens on the skimpiest of suburban plots. Even home gardeners who have space for standard orchard-size fruit trees are grow-

The landscape value of high-bush blueberries is excellent. Attractive while in flower and in fruit, they have brilliant autumn foliage.

In a tiny dooryard, a flowering fruit tree is an effective screen for entrance and window.

ing the dwarfs. (And so now are farmers and commercial growers who used to scoff at any but standard trees.) Much research has been done and is continuing at state agricultural experiment stations as well as larger nurseries to find ideal root stocks that determine the degree of dwarfness.

And except for their smaller plant sizes, dwarf fruit trees are just like their larger counterparts – same size (or even larger) fruit and leaves and same shape. Dwarf fruit trees need the identical attention that large trees must receive – recognition of pollination requirements, annual pruning and regular spraying or dusting to control pests – and in general, the same growing conditions. One difference, and an important one for most homeowners, is that dwarf fruit trees start bearing the second or third year after planting.

Planting and Spacing of Fruit Trees

Most fruit trees, no matter what kind, are planted when dormant, either in late fall or early spring. In mild-climate regions, fall is an ideal time, but spring is preferable where winters are severe, especially for apple trees. The same rules apply to fruits as to other nursery stock. When your order arrives, keep it from extreme heat or cold and unpack as soon as possible. If you can't plant at once, dig a shallow hole or trench away from wind and bright sun in which to set the plants temporarily until they can be put in their permanent positions. Before planting, it is a good idea to soak the roots in a pail of water for several hours.

Here are proper distances (in feet) to allow between plants, based on the space a full-grown plant will cover:

Apple, dwarf, 8 to 12
Apple, standard, 30 to 40
Apricot, dwarf, 10
Apricot, standard, 20
Blackberry, 8
Blueberry, high bush, 4 to 5
Boysenberry, 8
Cherry, dwarf, 6 to 8
Cherry, hybrid bush, 6

Cherry, sour, 20
Cherry, sweet, 25 to 30
Currant, 3 to 5
Dewberry, 6 to 8
Gooseberry, 3 to 5
Grape, 8
Loganberry, 8
Nectarine, 20
Peach, dwarf, 10
Peach, standard, 12 to 15
Pear, dwarf, 8 to 10
Pear, standard, 20
Plum, dwarf, 8
Plum, standard, 20
Quince, 15
Raspberry, black, 4
Raspberry, purple, 3
Raspberry, red, 2
Strawberry, 1½
Youngberry, 8

Superphosphate or bone meal, cottonseed meal, and dried blood are safe to mix with the soil. Damp peat moss mixed with the soil will help the roots to start growth. Break up the soil so it will sift down among the roots and when they are covered, pack it thoroughly by tramping. When the hole is full, leave a bowl-like depression in which to apply water. Give the same planting depth as the plant had previously. Dwarf fruit trees should have their graft points above ground, otherwise the wrong stock will form roots and change the dwarf character of the tree.

After planting, cut back the top one-third to one-half so as to create a balance between it and the root system. When doing this, loosen the wires holding any labels or hang them by large loops around the trunk or a main branch.

Feeding

The first year after planting, the feeding roots extend only a little way from the base of the plant, but thereafter they forage farther and farther in all directions, the main root branches becoming mere carriers of moisture and food. Hence, annual applications of a complete fertilizer should be applied to an encircling zone that extends from about halfway between the trunk and the limit of the branch spread to about twice that distance. Nonbearing fruit trees that are making good yearly progress should not be given too much nitrogen, if any. On sod land, fertilizer should be doubled so both the grass and the fruit plants will be fed. Clean cultivation is preferable for tree and bush fruits grown in rows; but if they are planted along fences, heavy mulching is usually better as it conserves moisture, keeps down weeds, and adds humus.

Pruning and Training Fruit Trees

When you buy a fruit tree, the ideal is one whose straight stem has never been cut or broken. If its branches are far apart on the trunk with the three largest pointing in different directions, you will have no difficulty in developing a symmetrical, strong specimen. More likely, your tree will be a "whip," or branchless, yearling tree on which, by suppressing undesired shoots and encouraging well-placed branches, you can develop a symmetrical tree.

Avoid a tree with a Y-crotch formation – two erect stems of equal size and vigor. If both grow, chances are they will sooner or later split apart. But this fault can be corrected by: (1) cutting back one branch severely and the other little or not at all; (2) cutting one back to a 6-inch stub to be left for 2 or 3 years, then removed cleanly

After pruning fruit trees, use a tree-wound compound to promote healing.

(this plan is best with newly planted trees); (3) if the tree is a sapling with a well-established root system, not a newly planted one, you can cut off one branch at once, at its base.

More specific suggestions for pruning each kind of fruit tree are given later on in this chapter. (The pruning of fruit trees and all kinds of plants is such a specialized practice that readers can benefit from two books devoted solely to the subject: *Pruning Made Easy* by Edwin F. Steffek, published by Holt; and *The Pruning Manual* by Everett P. Christopher, published by Macmillan.)

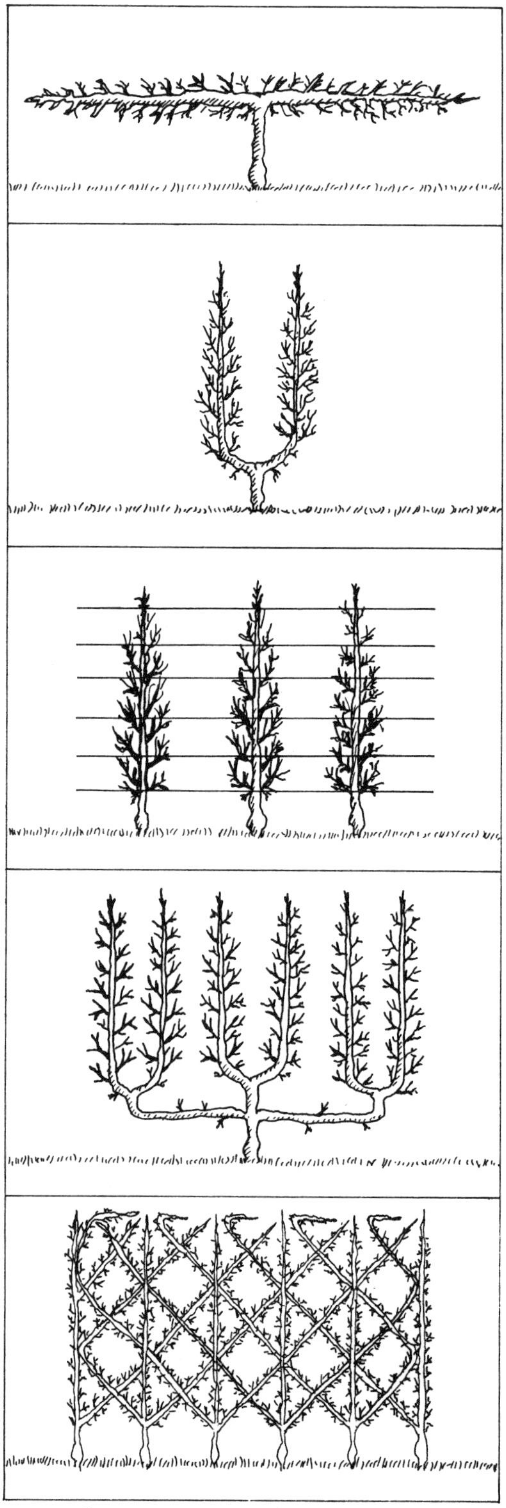

Some shapes for espaliered fruit trees.

Pest Control in the Fruit Garden

The one drawback to growing fruit trees in the home garden is the pest problem and the subsequent spraying and dusting. Of course if you are growing fruits mainly as ornamentals and consider any harvest of fruit incidental or at best, a small bonus, you can ignore the control of pests or do a hit-or-miss job with any of the all-purpose sprays now available. While the fruits harvested under such methods may be far from unblemished (apples and peaches may suffer the most), the results will be quite satisfactory for some.

Far better is to follow a prescribed series of sprayings, all timed to control the various insects and diseases when the trees are most vulnerable. Several mail-order nurseries and most garden centers stock a multipurpose spray suitable for home orchards. It may contain Captan, a chemical control for most major fungus diseases, and Malathion and Methoxychlor, two insecticides for such pests as curculio, codling moth, Oriental fruit moth, aphids, canker worm, Japanese beetle, and many others. Such a spray can usually be applied as a dormant spray (in early spring as the buds begin to swell) to kill scales and other over-wintering pests that hatch early.

Pest control is really a regional problem. Consult your county agent; write to your state agricultural experiment station for bulletins. Above all, don't throw poisonous

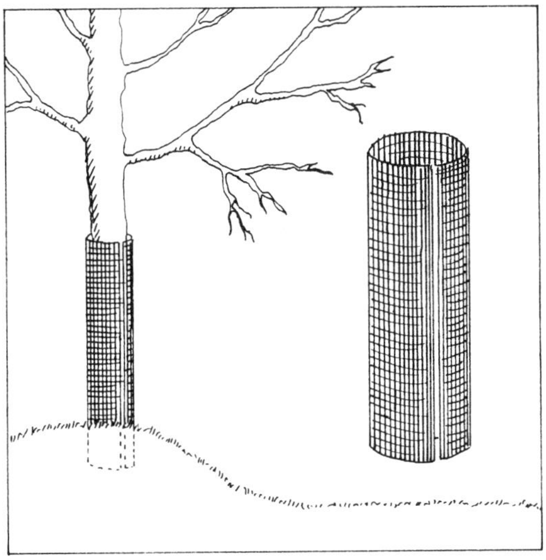

Young fruit trees need protection against gnawing rabbits and mice. This is a cylinder of hardware cloth (wire mesh).

sprays or dusts about haphazardly. Always follow directions. You may find you can get along on less than the maximum amount of spraying. The fewer poisons we add to the earth, the atmosphere, and our food, the better.

Favorite Fruits for Home Gardens

Apple (***Malus***)**:** Before you plant even one standard apple tree, make sure you can spare the space it will need – a circle at least 40 feet in diameter. If you can't, use dwarf trees which are often planted 10 feet apart.

In the space that one standard apple tree would occupy, you can plant a miniature orchard of dwarf fruit trees by setting apple (or pear) trees 20 feet apart. Put smaller-growing, shorter-lived kinds alternating in each direction between them – peach, nectarine, apricot, plum, and cherry. In this way 25 dwarf trees can fit in the space that 1 standard apple tree would occupy. As the trees become crowded, take out the shortest-lived kinds first. While the trees are small, it is advisable to devote the surrounding ground to annual vegetables or strawberries, or else to keep the ground in a 2-foot circle around each tree cultivated clean so as to reduce the danger of attacks by borers.

When the trees begin to bear fruit, apply a complete fertilizer such as 5-10-5, about a pound for each year of the tree's age, in early spring. Too much nitrogen for a young tree may postpone its bearing of fruit.

The principles of pruning are the same for standard or dwarf apple trees. Yet because of their size, dwarf trees are easier to

A comparison of the space needed by one standard fruit tree (large circle) and space needed by 25 dwarf trees. Plot is 20 by 20 feet.

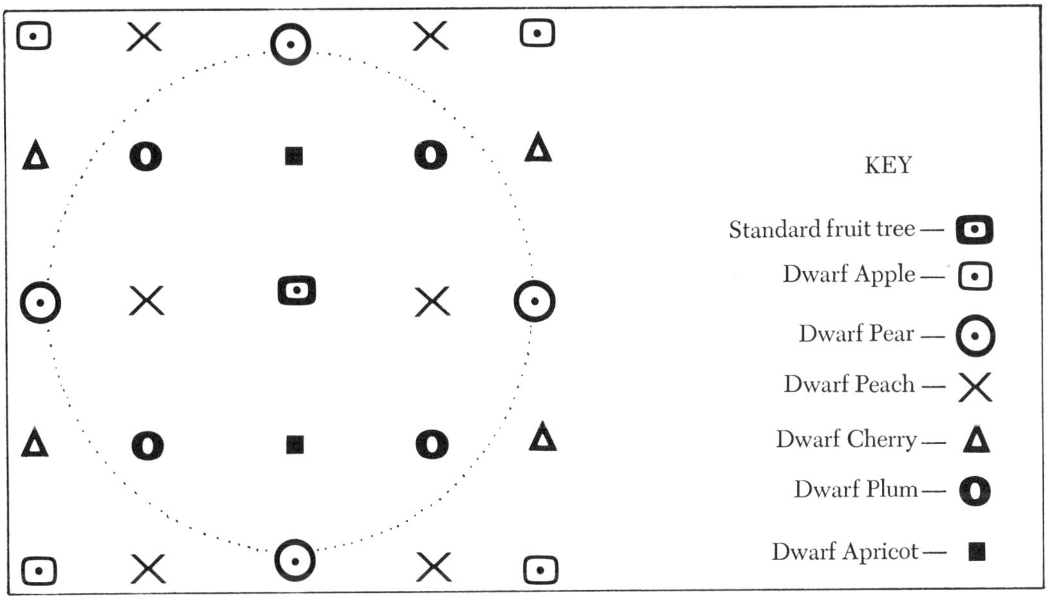

prune and require less than their standard counterparts. The first few years after a tree has been planted are the critical ones. The young tree, usually an unpromising-looking long, rooted stick (called a whip) should be cut back about one-third to force growth of side branches. In the spring of the following year, the home gardener can determine the future frame of his tree by removing all but four to seven side branches. From then on annual pruning will be concerned only with maintaining shape and removal of any crowding or crossing branches.

Old, neglected fruit trees, especially apples and pears, can be given new life by drastic pruning. Such trees are often a maze of suckers, water sprouts, dead and crisscrossing branches. When this extraneous material is removed, these old trees may bear a good harvest of fruit and assume a picturesque role in the landscape as well. Such trees are often found when old orchards have been turned into residential communities.

Apple pests include the larvae of the codling moth (responsible for wormy apples), canker worms, scale, scab, maggots, and aphids. See suggestions on spraying and dusting given earlier in this chapter.

Apricot (***Prunus armeniaca***): The beauty of its blossoms alone entitles the apricot to a place in the home garden. In addition, its early varieties ripen fully 6 weeks ahead of good peach varieties, and its delightful flavor differs from those of all other fruits. Many gardeners know only the commercial California product, picked before it is ripe; if they could once eat freshly gathered, ripe fruits, they would need no coaxing to plant their own. Contrary to belief, the tree is hardy, though buds, blossoms, or newly set fruits are sometimes injured by spring frosts in northern areas if they receive eastern and southern exposure.

Apricots want deep, rich soils, well-drained below as well as on the surface. Start with a year-old tree, either standard or dwarf, and allow about 5 main branches to develop.

A much-loved old apple tree, rejuvenated by pruning and propping, is picturesque and productive.

The fruit usually sets heavily and should be thinned when it reaches three-fourths of an inch in size. Apricot pests include curculio, brown rot, and scale. Two varieties should be planted for cross-pollination.

Blackberry (***Rubus***): Only in the home garden can the blackberry (it ripens after the raspberry) be allowed to reach full ripeness and deliciousness. Wait to gather the fruits until they will drop into your hand at a touch, eat them within an hour, and you will never regret allowing space for them. But if you don't boss them they will boss you, for blackberries send up "suckers" (new stems) from their roots, and unless you pull them up when they are about 10 inches tall they will create an impenetrable, thorny jungle. Cutting the shoots simply tends to make more suckers grow from the stumps.

Blackberries grow in average garden soil with plenty of humus. Each spring reduce

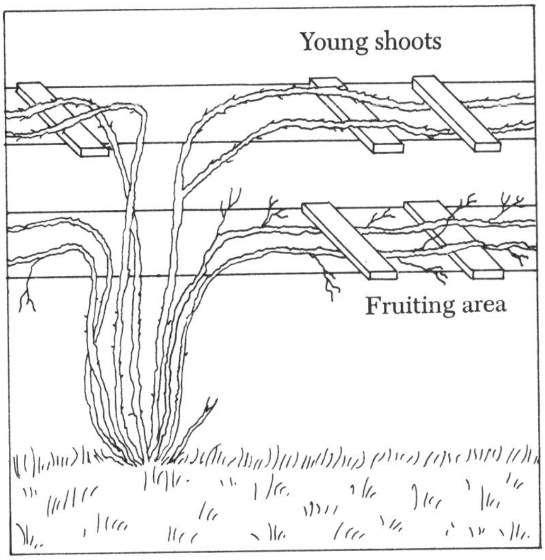

A good trellis for a blackberry plant.

the canes in the rows (7 to 8 feet apart) to one every 2 feet or so by pulling up the others; then either pinch off the tips of the growing stems when they are 30 inches tall to make them branch low, or fasten them to a wire when about 3 feet high. Better than one wire are two wires, stretched the length of the row and fastened to cross pieces nailed to posts set 25 or 30 feet apart. Young stems can be fastened to one wire one year and allowed to fruit the next season, while new stems are being fastened to the other wire. Cut the canes close to the ground as soon as they have borne, and burn them. In spring, shorten the branches of bushes trained the first way to about 18 inches, or cut back the canes of unpinched plants to about 3½ feet. Blackberries start to bear the second season; if cared for they should continue to bear for 10 or 15 years.

Blueberry (*Vaccinium corymbosum*): These attractive shrubs have high landscape value because of their rugged, twiggy form and foliage that becomes orange, scarlet, and red in autumn. They need acid soil (pH 4 to 4.8) with a high content of organic material to maintain moisture. The home gardener can best supply this necessary humus by adding great quantities of peat moss (at least one pail per plant) to the soil when planting. Leaf mold, sawdust (well rotted), or compost

Allowed to ripen until they drop into the hand, blackberries are a delicacy fresh or preserved.

are good mulching materials. Set the shrubs from 4 to 6 feet apart, either as a hedge or as a landscape group. Two or 3 varieties must be planted for cross-pollination. (Early, midseason, and late varieties – all with huge berries – are offered by most nurseries.) Cover the bushes with plastic fruit netting or the birds will snatch most of the berries. The berries, by the way, are not always fully ripe when they first turn blue. The ripening process for blueberries is much slower than for most other berry fruits. Once the shrubs are established, some annual pruning in spring is necessary to remove old wood.

Boysenberry (*Rubus*): A hybrid evolved from loganberry, blackberry, and dewberry, the boysenberry resembles the last named and should be handled like it. The fruit may be 2 inches long. Boysenberry is not reliably winter-hardy in northern states.

Bush cherry (*Prunus besseyi*): This low-growing, hardy shrub, native to the Great Plains, bears large, sweet fruits, es-

Small fruits may need protection against birds. A covering of plastic filaments is being tried on blueberries; at right, mesh protects raspberries.

pecially good for cooking. Hybrids developed from it by Professor N. E. Hansen of North Dakota have been a boon to gardeners in cold regions. Prune and train like the currant, and stimulate the growth of new shoots by rigorous reduction of old stems. To insure cross-pollination for fruit production, plant several varieties.

Cherry (***Prunus***)**:** Tree cherries are of two classes: sweet, borne on large trees; and sour, on small ones. An intermediate group of hybrids called "dukes" bears fruit of halfway tartness on smallish trees. They are mostly self-sterile and should be planted with both sour and sweet varieties to insure pollination.

Sweet cherries do better in lighter soils than the sour kinds, and require more space – 30 feet as against 20 or less. Sour cherries are the hardier and more adaptable, succeeding from Newfoundland to British Columbia, and over most if not all of the United States.

Today the homeowner has a greater choice in cherry trees than standard sweet or sour varieties as the result of research, especially in the central and northern states and Canada, to produce hardier and more compact or true dwarf forms. Most of these newer cherries do not grow taller than 8 or 10 feet and while most bear fruit classified as sour, some produce cherries sweet enough to eat fresh. They are sold by major mail-order nurseries.

Chinese chestnut (***Castanea mollissima***)**:** This tree is quite a good substitute for the virtually extinct American chestnut. It starts bearing 2 or 3 years after planting. At least 2 trees should be planted 15 feet apart for better fruit production. These chestnut trees may eventually reach 35 feet or more so they can be utilized for shade and ornament as well as nut production.

Currant (***Ribes sativum***)**:** This very hardy plant thrives in heavy, well-drained but moist loams. Its roots are close to the surface, so cultivation must be shallow. It is a gross feeder and needs an annual fertilizing with a complete fertilizer such as 5-10-5. On light soils, extra feedings with a high nitrogen fertilizer may be needed. Buy 1- or 2-year plants, and set them 5 feet apart. Keep the plants mulched.

After stems have borne 3 or 4 times, cut them off at the ground and burn immediately. In spring cut out all the young, light-colored shoots but the 2 strongest. Thus each bush should start the season with 8 stems, the 2 oldest of which are removed in midsummer after bearing.

Pick the fruit when it is dry, or it will spoil quickly. Shallow trays with perforated bottoms are better for picking than close-bottomed boxes. Half-mature currants make excellent tarts and pies; mature, but not over-ripe ones are best for jelly; for dessert use, best leave them several weeks longer until fully ripe. They may need protection from birds.

Dewberry (***Rubus flagellaris***)**:** A trailing plant that resembles a relative, the blackberry, in its fruit. It multiplies, like the black raspberry, by rooting tips. Its fruit ripens between the strawberry and the blackberry seasons. 'Lucretia' is the standard variety.

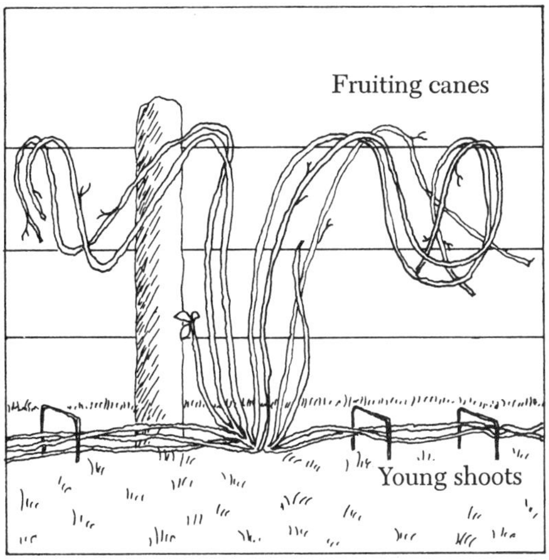

A trellis for dewberries.

Moderately fertile, light, well-drained soils suit it best. Plant early in spring slightly below ground level to allow for soil settling, but not so the crown is covered. Plants to be trained on stakes should stand 5 by 5 feet; those to be grown on trellises, 3 feet apart in rows 6 feet apart.

The favorite way to train the stems is to let the young ones sprawl lengthwise on the rows the first year. The following spring they are fastened to posts or trellises with wires 18 and 30 inches from the ground; or as described under blackberry, but a bit lower. As soon as a cane has fruited, it is cut and burned. Fertilize in late autumn or early spring.

Gooseberry (*Ribes grossularia*): See section on currants. Gooseberries are managed the same way.

Grape (*Vitis*): No other fruit plant has so wide a tolerance for climate and soil, and is so quick to begin bearing so bountiful a crop as the classic grape. But to handle grapes successfully, their natural habits must be understood and treated accordingly. All fruit is borne on green shoots that grow in spring from buds formed the previous year; never on the woody "canes." The tendency, therefore, is for the bearing parts to get farther away from the roots each year and to become less productive; pruning must be done to prevent this. Winter pruning should reduce the tops about 75 percent by cutting off completely all the puny and rank canes which never would bear, and by shortening the normal canes by at least 50 percent.

After planting first-class, 2-year vines, cut off all puny growths and reduce the strongest stem to three good bud-bearing joints. Allow a shoot to grow from each bud until (about June) the strongest becomes woody at its base; then shorten the other two to one joint apiece with a leaf at each joint. The strong shoot will become stronger, and the next year, develop side shoots, some of which should bear fruit. The following winter shorten this main stem a third to a half, and cut off all other growths. The second winter either cut back all the 1-year canes on this main trunk to "spurs" of 2 or 3 joints and allow the buds on these to produce bearing shoots; or cut off all but the 2 strongest canes, leaving these to become "arms" to be stretched on a trellis or other support. Plants should be set 8 or 10 feet apart, with posts 30 feet apart. Most trellises are of 2 or 3 wires, the lowest 24 inches from the ground, the next 18 to 24 inches higher.

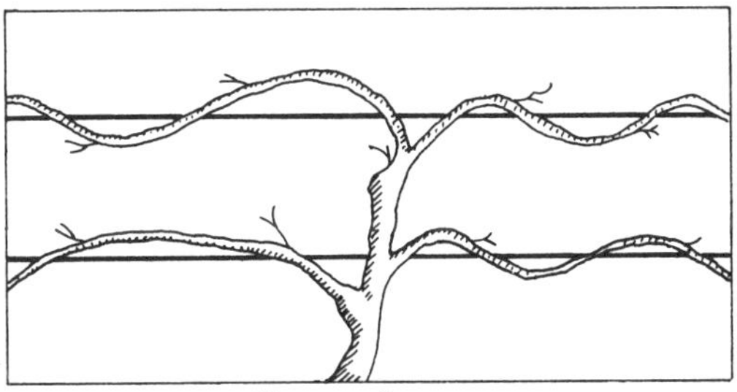

A well-pruned grapevine.

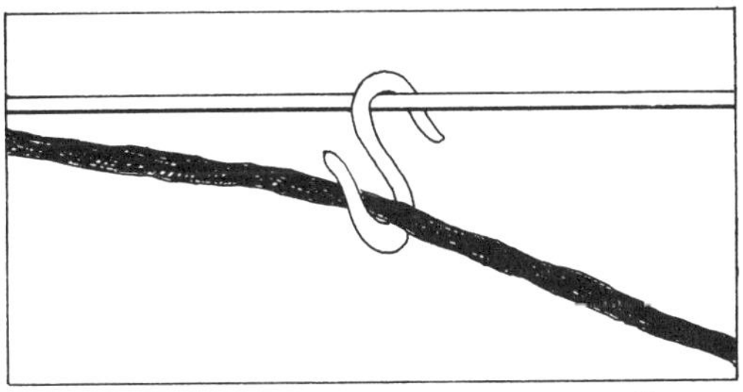

A handy hook supports grapes on a trellis or fence.

Loganberry (***Rubus ursinus***): A trailing blackberry of California with the dewberry habit. It bears large, purple fruit, tart even when fully ripe. It is too tender to be grown where winter temperatures reach zero. Plants are set 8 to 10 feet apart, and propagation and training are as for the dewberry.

Mulberry (***Morus***): Too large for small gardens, and unsuitable for use on lawns or near walks and drives because the soft, purplish-black fruit falls readily and messes up the ground beneath. Nevertheless this tree is a fine ornamental, excellent as a decoy to keep birds away from the more valued cherries and raspberries. There are several delicious, large-fruited mulberry varieties, excellent for dessert, juice, or wine-making and for canning with other tart fruits.

Nectarine (***Prunus persica***): This smooth-skinned peach is managed the same way as the more familiar "fuzzy" peach below.

Peach (***Prunus persica***): Though the life limit of peach trees is popularly rated at about 10 years, it can reach 20 or 30 if pests like borers don't interfere. Peaches thrive in any well-drained location, but perform best on light, moderately fertile soils.

Peach fruits are produced on the previous year's growth; ideally a tree should make at least a foot of new growth a year. A few years after planting, when the tree has formed its basic shape and has started bearing fruit, annual pruning in spring is necessary to keep the tree vigorous, low, and open in form. Cut out the oldest (2- and 3-year-old), weakest, and most vertical branches from the main ones. Never grow peaches in sod as this favors borer attacks. Keep the ground cultivated around the trunks even when the trees are planted on a lawn. Avoid overfeeding with strong manures and fertilizers, but don't be afraid to apply plant food rich in potash and phosphoric acid once the trees begin to bear fruit.

In addition to dwarf peach trees, there are also shrub peaches like the popular 'Bonanza' and 'Flory.' Both are especially suitable for tubs and are most ornamental on terraces and patios.

Pear (***Pyrus***): Though as hardy (it can live to a ripe old age – 40 to 60 years!) and almost as tolerant of soils as the apple tree, the pear does best in well-drained, heavy loams. Avoid the use of manures and rich fertilizers as lush growth is more subject to the fire blight disease.

Pears are available both as standards and as dwarfs. A good number of main limbs and branches is desirable so that if some are hit by blight, others will remain to carry on. Keep weak, puny shoots cut off the main branches, and disinfect the wounds.

Do little or no pruning until the trees have begun to bear; thereafter, the annual growth can be shortened 30 to 50 percent each year to reduce the amount, but improve the quality, of the fruit.

Plum (***Prunus***): Cultivated plums are derived from several species so they vary in

Purple-fruited raspberry variety "Amethyst." It is hardy as far north as southern Minnesota.

their characteristics and adaptability to soil and other conditions. In general, all require well-drained soil. Some varieties are self-sterile so 2 or more, alike or different, varieties should be planted near each other for fruit formation.

After developing the main scaffold branches as described earlier, less pruning will start the trees bearing sooner. Dwarf plums come into bearing quickly, often the second year after planting. A famous, very hardy dwarf plum is 'Sapa.' It is self-fruitful, grows only 6 to 8 feet and is especially recommended for the far North.

Under favorable conditions plum trees in the East may continue to be fruitful for 30 to 40 years; in the Central States, half as long is good performance. Thinning is important for fruit of good quality.

Quince (*Cydonia oblonga*): Because it is even more susceptible to fire blight and borers than are apples or pears, quinces should be treated as bushes rather than as trees so new stems can be grown to replace the ones attacked by those enemies.

The quince grows best, yields best, and lasts longest in well-drained, deep, warm, but only moderately fertile soil. As the roots spread widely, set plants not closer than 15 feet and keep cultivation shallow to avoid damaging the roots.

Quince flowers are borne at the tip of short shoots, so unpruned bushes become crooked and choked with worthless wood. The aim in pruning is to cut out old, superfluous twigs and branches while the plants are in flower or even after the fruits have set. The standard variety is 'Orange.' It is self-fruitful so only 1 plant is needed.

Raspberry (*Rubus*): This is a superb fruit for home gardeners in northern areas who have the space. The fruit is much too soft and perishable for modern markets, but a double row of red raspberries about 30 feet long will supply the average family enough fruit to eat fresh and to freeze. Where space is limited, use the raspberry as a boundary hedge. Unwelcome visitors will certainly not walk through it and the heavy foliage is fine for summer privacy. One problem is birds: bearing plants should be covered with a plastic fruit net to keep them out.

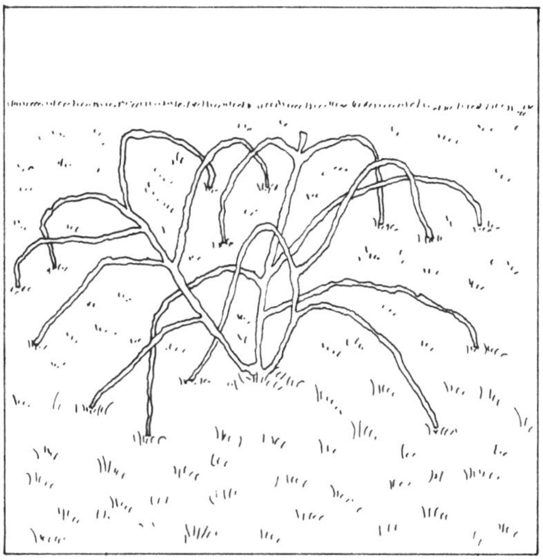

Tip rooting in the black raspberry. New plants arise where shoots touch the ground.

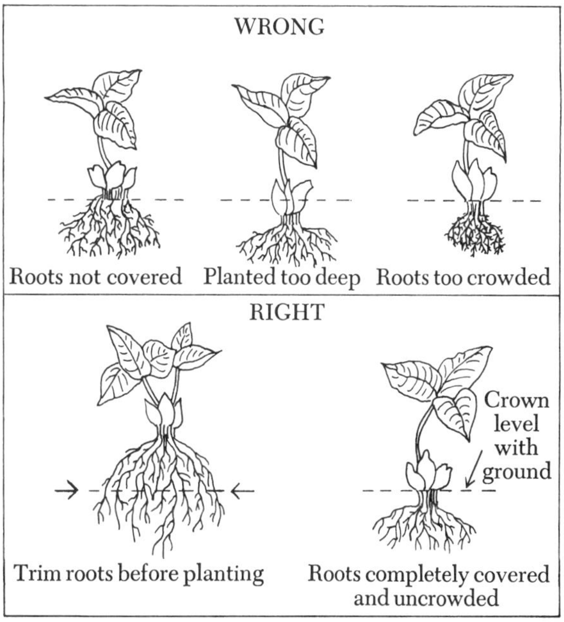

Wrong way (top) *and right way* (bottom) *to plant strawberries.*

Plant raspberries in spring or fall in well-drained, moderately fertile soil. Usually an application of a complete ferti-

A good start is needed for good strawberries. Tilled bed is enriched by compost.

Stakes and a straightedge are useful in making strawberry rows a uniform 18 inches apart.

A healthy, well-established strawberry bed. Chickenwire is placed to discourage birds.

Stakes guide the spacing of strawberries 12 inches apart. Roots should be spread and plants set with their crowns level with the soil.

lizer like 5-10-5 (a large handful to each clump) is given in the spring. Red raspberries are planted about 2 feet apart in rows 6 feet apart. They sucker freely. The suckers are easily transplanted for new plantings. The fruit is borne on second-year canes. After fruiting, these canes should be removed and burned. In everbearing varieties, the canes bear in the fall on new growth made the same summer, then bear again on the same canes the following summer.

Purple and black raspberries are usually more vigorous. Plant them about 4 feet apart in the row, the rows 8 feet apart. New shoots (allow 3 canes per plant) should have their tops pinched off when they are 18 inches tall to make strong, branching plants. These branches are cut back the next spring to leave 3 or 4 buds.

Strawberry (*Fragaria*): Like the brambles, the strawberry is an excellent home garden fruit. Its culture is as easy as that of most vegetables. Strawberry plants need well-drained soil that contains a good proportion of organic material to keep it from drying out. Purchased plants are usually shipped in bundles in spring. Set the plants out as soon as possible, and be sure they do not suffer from dryness before their roots take hold. Do not cover the crown of a plant nor leave it so high that the roots are exposed to the air. Pinch the flowers from spring-planted varieties the first season to build up the plants; do the same with everbearing kinds until late June or early July.

Ideal plant spacing in the rows is from 1½ to 2½ feet apart, but home gardeners can get good results by spacing plants about 1 foot apart. Thus an area about 10 by 10 feet becomes a strawberry "patch" when 100 plants are set.

Beginning in June, the plants will send out "runners" which, if allowed to, will take root and become new plants. The first rosette on a runner makes the best plant because it has more time in which to grow before winter. By anchoring rosettes where wanted, rows can be kept narrow; by cutting them off before they root, the original plants can be developed into single rows or hills (which produce the largest, finest fruit but less of it); by allowing them to root promiscuously, you develop "matted" rows which produce smaller berries but in greater number.

Mulching with marsh hay, straw, and pine needles maintains moisture and keeps down weeds. Usually the mulch is renewed in the fall for winter protection and in the spring is lightly pulled off the crowns to make a cushion for the fruit later.

Youngberry (*Rubus*): A trailing blackberry similar to the dewberry. It bears abundant maroon or wine-colored, nearly seedless raspberry-flavored fruits highly valued for dessert, jams, and juice. It is hardy in most areas south of Washington, D.C. and does well on the Pacific Coast west of the Cascades.

Planting and training are the same as for the dewberry. There is a thornless variety, considered hardier but less prolific.

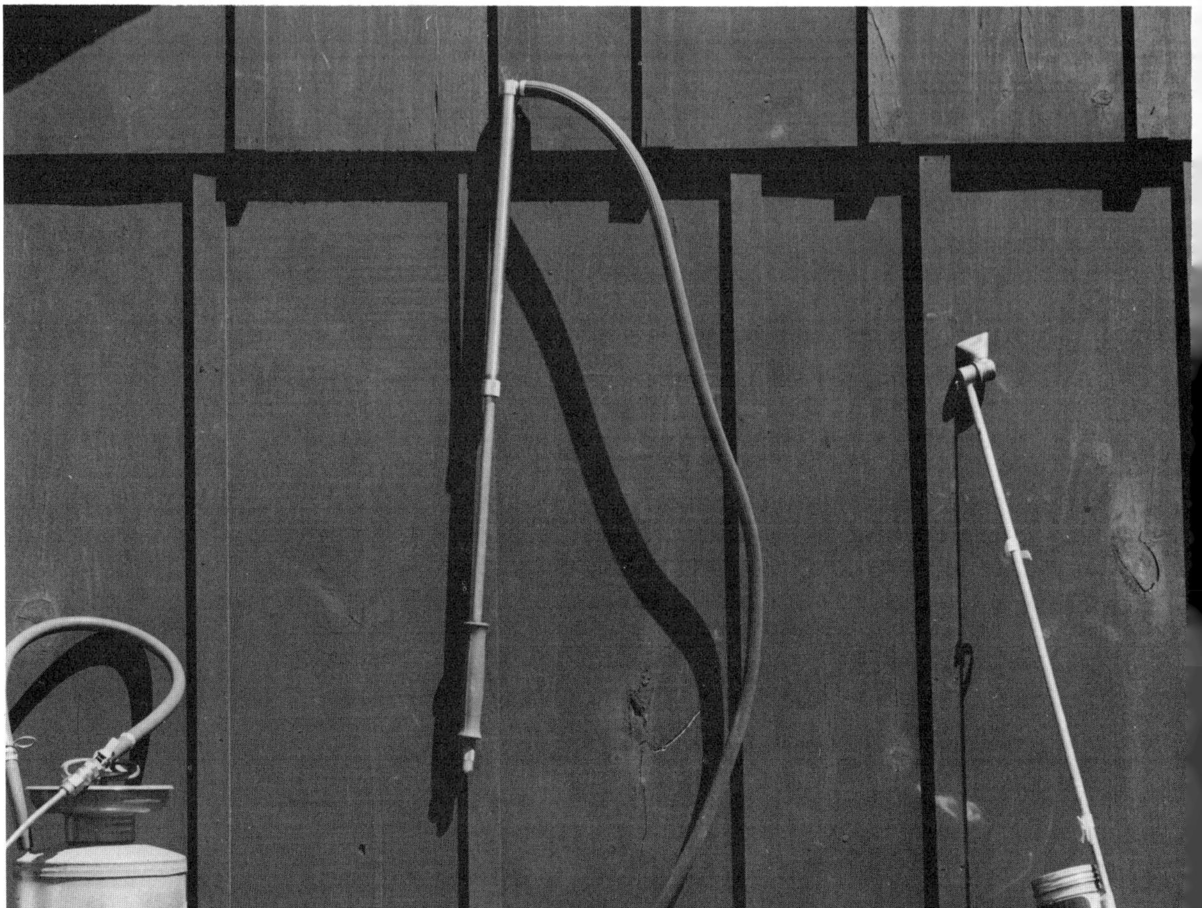

The gardener's arsenal: Some items of equipment used in the control of diseases and insect pests. From left, a tank-type sprayer; a hand sprayer; a slide-type sprayer and bucket; an aerosol weed killer for poison ivy; a hose-end sprayer and hose; rose dust; a hand duster.

CHAPTER 16

Plant Diseases and Pests

O Rose, thou art sick!
The invisible worm
Has found out thy bed
Of crimson joy.

– *William Blake*

It would be very convenient if the birds could take care of all our garden pests. There is no doubt that they do a considerable amount of good, especially when encouraged to stay in the area by the presence of suitable nesting sites and water. But as birds can't do all the work of keeping a garden free of pests, it is only sensible to use chemical sprays and dusts to control certain insects and diseases.

Yet common sense must guide the home gardener in the ways he applies poisonous chemicals and certainly in the amounts he uses. One doesn't have to be a fanatic to agree with the late Rachel Carson that the fewer poisons we release, the better for all kinds of life.

The list of garden enemies seems bewildering and discouraging at first – but soon you learn that no one garden is ever attacked by all of them. Fortunately, quite the opposite can be expected, with the gardener usually only having to contend with a few common pests that are readily controlled. Some pests, aphids for instance, are common and constant; but many other insect pests are cyclical and, in the years when they are prevalent, can cause severe damage.

While some pests – the spring canker worm, a kind of inchworm that sails through the air on a slender thread, is an example – can be destructive or distressing in the home garden, usually by the time the gardener is ready to take action, the pest has disappeared. Forbearance and patience coupled with prompt, sensible use of chemicals only when their need seems important should be the code of the modern gardener, rather than a practice of mass drenching of his premises with deadly poisons to knock out a handful of marauders.

Insects

Most insect injury results directly or indirectly from the insects' attempts to secure food. Some insects are most destructive in adult stages, others, in larval (worm) stages. Feeding habits generally determine the control methods.

There are three general classes of insects:

1. Chewing or biting insects, which get their food supply by eating plant, flower, or fruit. They are controlled by contact poisons, such as Sevin; or by stomach poisons, such as arsenate of lead or also Sevin, sprayed on the foliage. The insect

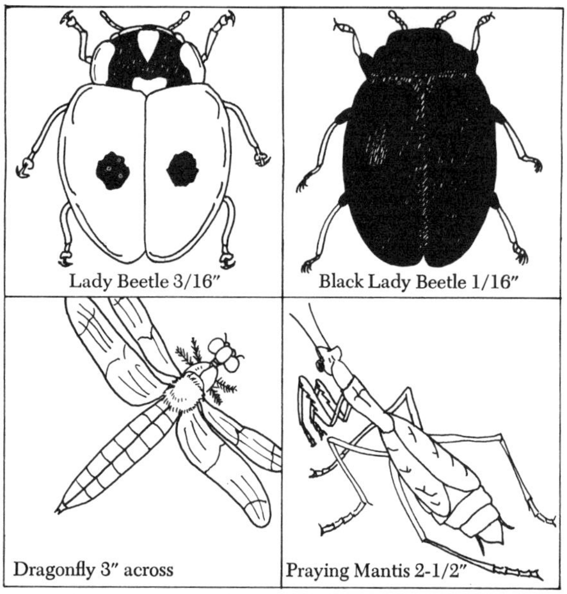

Some insects that are helpful to the gardener. Lady beetles feed on orchard mites and scale insects. Dragonflies devour mosquitoes and other small insects while in flight. The praying mantis feeds on a variety of insect pests.

is killed when it eats the poison. In this class of insects are: beetles, bulb fly larvae, caterpillars, cutworms, grasshoppers, leaf tiers, leaf rollers, rose chafers, and bagworms.

2. Some types of pests live or start their life cycle in the soil. An example is the grub of the Japanese beetle that in this stage feeds on turf roots. Pests, like slugs and snails, that live on the surface are controlled by placing poison baits on the soil.

Other pests which operate underground (nematodes, for example) are generally controlled by use of fumigants or soil treatment methods.

3. Sucking insects get their food supply by sucking plant juices. As they do not eat the plant parts, the usual stomach poisons are of no value in their control. They are killed by contact insecticides (nicotine sulfate is one) which clog their breathing pores or penetrate to their vital organs.

In this class of pests are aphid (plant louse), cyclamen mite, chrysanthemum midge, lace bug, leafhopper, mealybug, red spider mite, scale, thrips, and white fly.

Diseases

Plant diseases may be of bacterial, fungus, or virus origin.

1. Fungus diseases are the most serious to the home gardener, but they can generally be controlled with Bordeaux mixture, sulfur, or the newer Captan, Phaltan, Ferban, or Dithane. Fungus diseases include: brown rot, black spot of roses, leaf spot, mildew, mold, rust, shot hole fungus, and crown rot.

2. Bacterial diseases are difficult to control. Fire blight of certain fruit trees – pear, quince, apple – is an example of a bacterial disease.

3. Virus diseases are still not fully understood. They are systemic and are frequently transmitted by sucking insects, and in such cases control of the insect will control the disease. They can also be carried from plant to plant by budding or grafting.

General Control

One of the first steps in the control of insects or diseases is to keep the garden clean. Carefully gather and burn all diseased leaves; pull out sickly or wilted plants; and clean up and destroy any stalks of last year's garden.

The digging or power tilling of a vegetable garden in the fall or winter exposes many soil pests to freezing temperatures as well as to the sun and birds.

Sometimes it is best to cut back portions or all of a plant in order to get rid of borers, or some other problem. When cyclamen mites have ravaged a delphinium plant, the best treatment is to lift the plant and discard it in the trash can. Less drastic is to cut it off at the ground; and if new growth appears, start spraying regularly (every four or five days) with a miticide.

Spraying versus Dusting

Protecting the home garden from insect and disease attacks does not demand expensive equipment. In most cases one has the choice of spraying or dusting as a

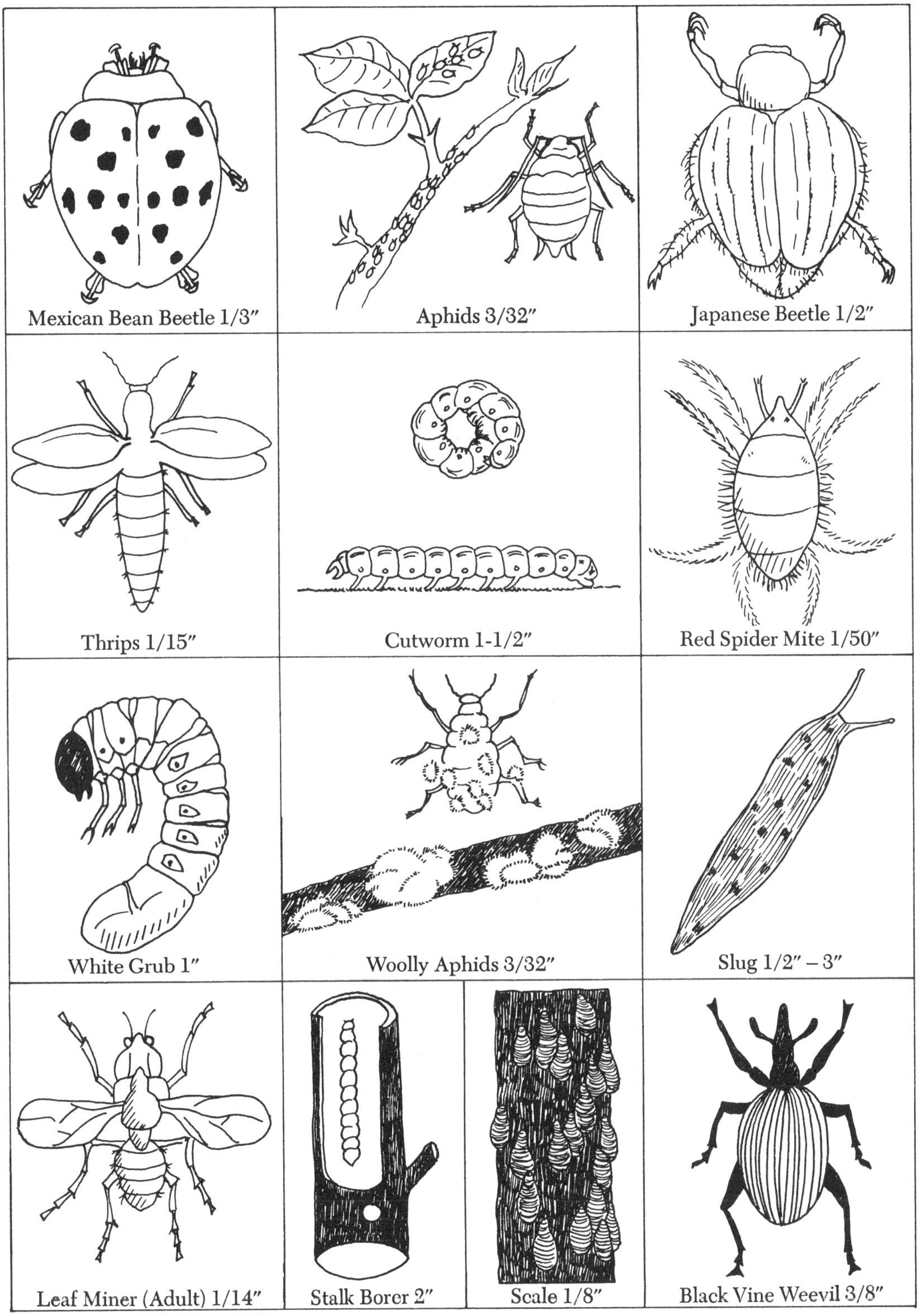

Some of the most troublesome garden pests.

The hand-operated sprayer is fine for "spot" applications or small areas.

method to use. Each method has its merits, and the choice will depend upon the preference of the individual.

Spraying is preferred by many because the material adheres to foliage better than when dusted, and fewer applications are necessary to protect crops. It can be done under such weather conditions as light wind, which make dusting impracticable. Less material is wasted in spraying than in dusting.

Less time and labor are required for dusting than for spraying. There is less danger of burning foliage than with spraying, and it is more efficient in killing aphids that attack leaves of low-growing crops, where it is impossible to force liquid spray against the bodies of the insects.

Whether spraying, dusting, or a combination of both methods are followed, good equipment should be used; and thoroughness of application is essential if control is to be secured. It is also necessary to cover the entire plant, both the stems and underside of the leaves as well as the top. A partial killing off of the pests is of little advantage, as they reproduce so fast that the condition soon reverts to its original state unless a thorough job is done.

When buying sprayers or dusting equipment, don't be tempted by junk offers. Both spraying and dusting are tedious enough without having to cope with equipment breakdown in the middle of the operation! Take the time to examine the equipment. Many insecticides and fungicides are available in aerosol bombs; and although they are expensive and don't go very far, they are convenient for the home gardener with only a few plants (or few bugs!) to tend.

Once purchased and used, it is important that the working parts of the sprayer be kept in good condition. A little lubricant placed upon the plunger of the air pump will keep the washer from drying out. The nozzle must be equipped to deliver a fine mist-like spray. Many spray heads can be clogged by the most minute foreign particle or undissolved chemical. Mix the chemicals thoroughly, and to be on the safe side, strain the mixture through a fine cheesecloth when pouring it into the sprayer.

The strength of the spray materials now available has been determined carefully in their manufacture; and if any burning of the foliage appears, the cause is usually the manner or timing of application. Perhaps you were careless with proportions in mixing and made the solution too strong. Then, too, spraying should not be done when the temperature is above 85 degrees or when the ground is dry and the plants wilted. Under such conditions the plant may draw in through its leaves some of the poisonous material. *Remember,* all sprays and dusts are poisonous to man and other animals too, and thus should be kept under lock and key or on a shelf inaccessible to children.

Avoid inhaling vapors or dust, conveying any of the materials to the mouth, or permitting them to come in contact with sores or injuries. When spraying up into trees, remember that much of the material must

For application of spray to extensive plantings, a hose-end sprayer is efficient; water from the hose dilutes the concentrated solution in the jar.

Using a tank sprayer on lawn weeds. Wand makes application to small spots feasible.

Spraying tall trees demands high-powered equipment which is used by professionals in tree maintenance.

fall down – perhaps onto a careless operator or on anything else under or around the tree. Always wash your hands after handling or applying these chemicals. In treating plants, be thorough, but do not use so copiously that quantities of the material will coat the ground beneath. After spraying, destroy or plainly label and securely store in a cool, dry place any remaining material. Carefully clean and dry the spraying apparatus, and destroy or properly dispose of any residue.

Materials to Use

As bewildering as the number of pests that are sometimes listed are the proprietary materials on the market that control them. In many sprays, soap or some other material is added as a spreader to keep the mixture from "crawling off" the plant surfaces. Care must be exercised in mixing to use the proper proportions and the directions on the package should be followed carefully.

Aramite: A miticide, effective for red spiders and mites. Usual recommendation is 1 tablespoon to 1 gallon of water.

Arsenate of lead: Arsenate of lead is a stomach poison for killing leaf-eating insects. It had been generally superseded by DDT, but now that DDT has been banned (as of 1971) by government agencies, this old remedy may come back in use. (one of the many objections to the continued use of DDT was the increase in mites, which arsenate of lead does not cause.) Arsenate of lead can be combined with Bordeaux mixture.

Bordeaux mixture: This mixture of copper sulfate and lime was for years the most widely used spray for protecting garden crops against fungus diseases. It is used in different strengths for different purposes, and these strengths are indicated by directions on the package.

Captan: Fungicide; a control for black spot and many other fungus diseases.

Chlordane: Contact soil insecticide for ants, beetles, grubs, weevils, and other under-the-ground pests.

D-D soil fumigant: It controls nematodes and wireworms, but is difficult to use in small gardens. A more simple remedy is to grow marigolds each year. Their roots release a chemical which is toxic to nematodes.

DDT: Its use has been banned as of 1971.

Demeton: A systemic insecticide usually sold as Systox. It is applied in liquid form to soil around plant so that it can be taken by roots to leaves and stems. Effective against mites, sucking insects. Use on ornamentals only.

Diazinon (sold as Spectracide): Insecticide effective against mites, European pine shoot moth, chinch bugs, leafhoppers, ants, and mosquitoes. Safe on fruits and vegetables up to 14 days before harvest.

Dieldrin: Soil insecticide (Aldrin is similar) for ants, chinch bugs, and grubs. Both very poisonous.

Dimite: A miticide especially effective against the cyclamen mite at rate of 1 teaspoon to 1 gallon of water.

Ferbam (sold as Fermate): Fungicide, effective against black spot but not mildew.

Karathane: Fungicide for powdery mildew. (Also sold as Mildex.)

Kelthane: Miticide, very effective against red spider and cyclamen mites. Do not use on food crops.

Lindane: Insecticide for aphids, thrips, and some beetles.

Malathion: Insecticide for use against aphids, scale, and many other chewing and sucking insects. Also kills bees. Do not apply on food plants within 2 weeks of harvest.

Maneb: Fungicide (also sold as Dithane D-14) for black spot, leaf spot, and tomato and potato late blights.

Metaldehyde: Poison bait available under different trade names for slugs and snails.

Methoxychlor: Insecticide that is considered "safer" than DDT, but it is of course still a powerful poison. Use on food crops up to 2 weeks before harvest. Effective against most chewing pests, especially the Mexican bean beetle.

Miscible oil: An oil (usually sold under trade name of Volck) that can be used for spray because it breaks up and forms an emulsion with water. It is used for control of scale insects on dormant plants, also at lower strengths for summer spraying for scale and red spider.

Nicotine sprays: Contact concentrated tobacco (nicotine sulfate) solution for spraying against plant lice. When nicotine sulfate is used, soap should be added at the rate of 1 cubic inch to each gallon of water, or 2 to 3 pounds to 50 gallons. Dissolve the soap in a little hot water before adding to the spray. Safe on food crops up to 7 days before harvest.

Nicotine dust: A finely powdered material containing a small percentage of nicotine mixed with a sulfur, talc, lime, or other carrier. It is used on plant lice and other soft-bodied insects, provided the material carries enough nicotine and the dust can be brought in contact with their bodies. It can also be mixed in or washed into soil to kill root aphids.

Paradichlorobenzine: Insecticide in crystal form mostly for control of the peach tree borer. Apply ¾ oz. in circle 2 inches from trunk after removing debris from area. Cover with 3 inches of soil for 3-4 weeks. If weather has been rainy, wait 5-6 weeks.

Phaltan: Fungicide highly effective for control of black spot and mildew.

Pyrethrum: Insecticide derived from a plant that is not toxic to humans. It is very toxic to chewing and sucking insects when it strikes them and kills by paralyzing. Follow strengths recommended by the manufacturer. Insects must be hit by the liquid; and there is no lasting protection, so it must be applied frequently. It is a sensible spray for home vegetable and fruit gardens.

Rotenone: An insecticide also derived from plants that is similar in action and safety to pyrethrum, and the two are often combined. Rotenone is a stomach poison, as well as a contact insecticide. (Can kill fish in ponds.)

Streptomycin: Antibiotic effective for bacterial and some fungus diseases, such as fire blight.

Sevin: Insecticide (Carbaryl) especially effective against the Japanese beetle. Also aphids, many beetles, leafhoppers, scale, and leaf miner. It destroys bees. May be used on food crops up to about a day before harvest.

Sulfur: An excellent fungicide. On evergreens it acts as a fumigant to destroy red spider. The sulfur used for dusting purposes should be finely ground so that a large portion of it will pass through a 300-mesh-per-inch sieve.

V-C 13: For nematodes. Use as a soil fumigant. It is safe to apply around living plants.

Zineb: Fungicide (sold as Dithane Z-78) for rose black spot and azalea petal blight.

Ziram: Fungicide for vegetables. Also sold as Zerlate. Controls early blight of tomatoes.

A Few Preventive Measures

Some soil fungi and bacteria which infect young seedlings can be best killed by soil sterilization. Young seedlings may be attacked and killed before they come through the soil. This is not due to poor seed, but to the sudden rotting by a fungus disease called "damping off." Disinfecting the seeds by coating them with a protectant, such as Spergon or Semesan (available from mail-order seed houses and garden centers) before sowing helps to control damping off. Many companies now ship their seeds precoated.

Small amounts of soil for seed sowing can be treated with Pano Drench. For larger amounts, use Formalin (a liquid form of formaldehyde), 1 part to 49 parts of water, at the rate of ½ to 1 gallon to each square foot of pulverized soil. The treated soil area must be covered by a heavy layer of newspaper or other material to hold the gas in the soil for about 10 days. The treated soil will be safe to use after that period. The process can be speeded up for indoor seed sowing by pouring a mixture of 2½ tablespoons of Formalin in a cup of water over a bushel of soil. The soil and solution must be carefully mixed together. Then put the soil into the containers (flats, pots) and cover with newspapers. After 24 hours, give the soil a good soaking, then sow the seeds.

Much of this fuss may be avoided by treating the seeds and/or using a sterile growing medium such as sphagnum moss.

Another form of prevention is preventive spraying, virtually a must for the home gardener who grows fruit trees. A dormant spray before the buds show any sign of green in spring is necessary for apple, peach, and plum trees. You can use miscible oil or lime-sulfur, but the newer chemicals (Captan, Methoxychlor and Malathion, often prepackaged together and sold by mail-order nurseries and garden centers) can also be used.

Not too long ago the accepted practice was for the home gardener to spray every plant in his garden once a week whether there was evidence of trouble or not. While a blanket preventive spraying program may not be necessary or even advisable, there is no question that in most localities, certain plants (like the fruit trees mentioned above) should be sprayed or dusted *before* troubles appear. The number of plants in this category is so few that it should be no hardship to spray or dust them once a week or at least that often during the period when their enemy is ready to strike. Otherwise the gardener can take his chances – he may be lucky! – or forego growing these plants at all. A few common ones include roses, hybrid teas, climbers, and tree forms; delphinium and its near relative monkshood (*Aconitum*); peony; certain vegetables like tomato and beans that can be ravaged by various pests and diseases, but fortunately, rarely fatally; birch tree and American holly, both of which can be disfigured by leaf miners; and gladiolus. A secondary group might include chrysanthemum, dahlia, iris (for borer), and phlox.

When a plant becomes sickly, many beginners understandably enough, assume that the plant is either starving or is afflicted by a disease or victimized by a pest. Rarely is the first assumption correct, and smothering a suffering plant with a heavy dose of fertilizer may finish it altogether. Nor may pests or a disease be the primary complaint. The problem may be the result of poor growing conditions (and it's quite true that certain diseases and pests are more likely to appear when a plant's environment is wrong). A number of factors may be involved: lack of adequate moisture or the opposite – poor drainage, bad air circulation, or bad air, especially such as is found in cities; too much or too little sun, depending on the plant's individual preference; the wrong soil reaction such as too alkaline a soil, often found near a foundation, for an acid-loving plant like an azalea or rhododendron. The broad-leaved evergreen andromeda (*Pieris*) is often sickly and preyed upon by the lace wing insect when it grows in full sun; when moved to a shadier site, it soon perks up and lace wing infestation is greatly reduced or disappears entirely. Yellow foliage, a condition called chlorosis, often indicates a lack of available iron in the soil. A treatment with the commercial product, iron chelates, applied according to directions may improve or cure the condition.

Of course when all of one's plants are sickly, something is drastically wrong! A good deal of soul searching on the part of the gardener is needed: he should reexamine all his gardening procedures, the sites and soil in which the plants are languishing. And a call for help to a friendly county agent may be in order.

Some Common Pests and Diseases

Ants: Ants swarming over plants are usually after honeydew secreted by aphids and other insects. Their nests in lawns or garden can be sprinkled with 5 percent chlordane dust.

Aphids: Aphids are the small insects – green, red, black, yellow, and white – usually found in clusters on stems or leaves and at one time or another on almost any kind of plant, indoors and outdoors. They are killed by a number of chemicals, such as nicotine sulfate, pyrethrum, rotenone (all of which are preferred for food crops), Malathion and others. Most general-purpose sprays (more efficient than dusts) include a chemical that will kill aphids. Lady beetles are their enemy and are often imported in huge numbers for the purpose of destroying them. The indiscriminate use of DDT, which kills the natural aphid enemies, has been blamed for their increase in some areas.

Bagworms: These worms, chiefly infesting evergreens such as arborvitae and juniper, hatch out in the spring and make a bag or nest of silk and twigs which they drag around with them while eating. Handpicking in fall and winter is most effective, but arsenate of lead (3 tablespoons to a gallon of water) or Sevin (2 tablespoons to 1 gallon of water) applied about May 1st will save much damage.

Beetles: There are many kinds of these chewing insects, and their damage can vary from total destruction of plants to merely marring and disfiguring them. Each region has its own beetle problems (the Japanese beetle, for instance, is still mostly confined to the eastern part of the country), and gardeners who want specific information on the beetles of their areas should write to their state agricultural experiment stations for bulletins. The grubs of most beetles are as destructive as the adults, chewing turf and plant roots during their sojourn in the soil before emerging as beetles. Controls vary: handpicking is as good – and safe – as any when beetle infestations are not too severe; keep a jar of kerosene at various points in the garden so you can drop the beetles into it as you admire your plants; among beetle sprays, all the new very poisonous chemicals will kill beetles, but Sevin is especially recommended. Others: rotenone, Malathion,

Methoxychlor, and arsenate of lead. Mexican bean beetles and flea beetles in vegetable gardens can be controlled with rotenone or pyrethrum.

In the grub stage in turf, chlordane as 5 percent dust can be applied at the rate of 5 pounds to 1,000 square feet. Such a treatment also eliminates the mole problem, as the grubs the moles are searching for are killed. The milky spore disease is a biological means of killing off the grub population in lawns. Unfortunately, it is not a quick control, but it is an excellent solution for those who do not want to apply chemicals to their lawns.

Borers: Borers cause tops of plants to wilt or break off above the surface of the ground. In early stages they are killed by inserting fine wire into their holes in the stalk. In advanced stages there is no cure on smaller plants.

The iris borer can be killed in spring before it reaches the rhizome, by pressing the leaves together. Weekly spraying with Malathion or Thimet, according to directions, from spring until flower buds form, is effective.

On trees, try the wire method for borers; or if the tree is healthy, dig them out, if not too deep, with a thin-bladed knife. Afterward seal the hole with grafting wax or tar. In deep drills, squirt special borer-killing preparations (obtainable at garden centers) in the holes, and immediately plug them with grafting wax, putty or wet clay. The best protection against borers on susceptible trees like the peach is to spray their trunk area with Malathion beginning in early July and continuing every 2 weeks for a total of 3 sprayings.

Caterpillars: Caterpillars and budworms are to the butterfly and moth as the grub is to the beetle. Caterpillars of various kinds and colors are especially associated with the vegetable garden: they can swarm over cabbage, broccoli, cauliflower, and kale and do drastic damage to the foliage unless the plants are dusted with rotenone at

Caterpillars, such as this green-and-black celery worm shown devouring carrot foliage, can best be controlled in the home garden by hand-picking.

The tomato hornworm, a green caterpillar which may grow to four inches long, swiftly strips branches as he feeds. Hand-picking is easiest control.

once; the tomato hornworm, a rather handsome monster, can partially defoliate a number of tomato plants unless sharp eyes find him.

Cankerworms, both spring and fall

A tent caterpillar feeding. It prefers wild cherry trees, but feeds on other fruits and ornamentals.

Caterpillars with completed tent. Since these pests sally forth to forage in the morning, tents should be removed and burned at night to destroy insects.

kinds, are more popularly known as inchworms because of their peculiar motions as they move. The usual treatment is banding tree trunks with a sticky substance to prevent the adult moths from crawling up the trunk to lay their eggs, but this is hardly practical where a number of trees are involved. Spraying with arsenate of lead or Sevin, as soon as the caterpillars are noticed, is recommended but this means virtually drenching one's premises with the spray. In those years when infestations are severe, cankerworms can move in from all directions on their silken threads.

The tent caterpillar is another example of a pest that is much worse some springs than others. It is useless to burn their nests in cherry trees and other trees during the day as most of the caterpillars are out foraging for food. They return to their nests at night and can be destroyed there very early in the morning.

Chiggers: Chiggers do not properly belong in the discussion of plant troubles, but they are sometimes very troublesome to the gardener. At a picnic or to rid the lawn of them, spray with Diazinon (Spectracide), following the manufacturer's directions.

Cutworms: When plants are cut off at the ground the most probable reason is a night crawler, the cutworm. It is rather difficult to find, but any short, dingy-colored, fat worms near the soil surface are probably the culprits. Protect tomatoes and other young, tender plants with a collar of paper around their stems.

Dogs: Dogs and other animals sometimes injure plants and become a neighborhood nuisance. Certain scents are repugnant to some animals even when so faint as to hardly be noticeable to man. This principle has been used recently in preparing a number of sprays to keep dogs away from trees, evergreens, or shrubs. A nicotine spray made at ordinary strength without a soap spreader may be partially successful.

Leaf miner: There are several kinds of leaf miners, caterpillars, or maggots that tunnel between leaf layers, but the ones most troublesome for some suburban gardeners are those found in birch trees, boxwood, and evergreen holly trees. A few leaf miners pick on herbaceous perennials, the columbine and delphinium, for instance.

Revolutionary control for the birch leaf miner, a pest that can completely disfigure the foliage and thus greatly debilitate the tree eventually, can be achieved by using one of the new systemic insecticides, such as Scope. This chemical is applied dry in a circular area on the ground under the tree and then watered into the soil so it can be absorbed into the tree's system. It is very poisonous and should be used strictly according to directions. A second method is to spray with Lindane or Sevin according to directions when the leaves are half developed. A second application of the spray should be made in about 10 to 14 days.

The boxwood leaf miner causes the leaves to become cup-shaped and blistered and can be very disfiguring to an otherwise beautiful evergreen. Spray with Lindane, Malathion, or a systemic such as Dimethoate, according to directions, when the maggots emerge as flies, usually in late April or early May in the North. In the South the timing must be earlier, of course. If you're unsure, check with a local authority such as a county agent.

Holly leaf miners are also disfiguring, although they are a bigger nuisance on American holly (*Ilex opaca*) than on some of the shinier leaved kinds. Spray with Sevin or Dimethoate as new leaves begin to unfurl in spring; or spray with Lindane or Dimethoate in early summer to kill larvae.

For the columbine leaf miner, spray foliage with Lindane or nicotine sulphate a few times as it develops in the spring. Destroy infested leaves as noticed during summer.

Moles burrow under lawns in search of grubs and other insects; best control is to eliminate their food supply.

A mole trap being placed across a burrow.

Mice and moles: Mice, field and pine, can be a greater menace to the gardener in regions where they abound, than almost any other pest. Just ask any gardener who has to contend with them! There is no certain cure or control. Both kinds of mice (the field mouse has a longer tail than the slightly more compact pine mouse) are vegetarians (as opposed to the mole) and eat bulbs, underground roots, and swollen stems. Above ground, they will gnaw trunks and stems in winter, especially when those parts are protected by leaves or a mulch or snow. In some areas, the gardener can count on rabbits and deer to eat the above-the-snow woody parts of trees and shrubs while the mice under the snow are feasting away at roots and stem bases!

Both kinds of mice are worse some winters than others. Field mice are bad enough, but most authorities agree that the pine mice will do the most damage. A partial list of plants they may favor and destroy are: pine, dogwood, holly, rose, pachistima, astilbe, phlox, bleeding-heart, babys-breath, tulip, crocus, hyacinth, trillium, certain native orchids, dahlia, potato, shallot, and strawberry. They will not touch daffodil bulbs.

The home gardener who has only a few plants and lives in pine mouse country can wrap a close mesh hardware cloth about the swollen root and crown of young trees like holly at planting time. But this is hardly practical for large specimens, especially when balled and burlapped. A collar of hardware cloth can be wrapped around the stems of all trees to protect them above ground from all mice, rabbits, and sometimes young deer.

Tulip bulbs can be planted in close mesh baskets, but sooner or later the mice may find the bulbs by entering the baskets at the top. One recommendation is to dip tulips and other susceptible bulbs in water at planting time then roll them in red lead powder. Poison baits are suggested by many state agricultural experiment stations, but they must be used with great caution. One bait is made with small apple cubes dusted lightly with zinc phosphide and then dropped in the underground runs at various intervals. If you live in mouse country, get a few good cats; or consult your county agent for current advice.

Moles do not eat bulbs or plants but insects like Japanese beetle grubs in lawns. (Mice may find their runs very convenient, though!) See recommendations for grubproofing a lawn under Beetles, above.

Mildew: White or grayish powdery spots or blotches on foliage are the indication of mildew. Lilac, phlox, and zinnia are ornamentals especially susceptible.

There are two types: powdery mildew and downy mildew, and both are fungus diseases. Dust with sulfur or spray with some of the commercial preparations such as Mildew or Karathane for powdery mildew. Spray with Zineb or Bordeaux mixture for downy mildew.

Mites: Red spider mites infest evergreens, phlox, English ivy (especially indoors in hot, dry rooms), and many other plants, causing them to turn light gray or brownish. The undersides of the leaves become dingy or dusty looking and a network of fine webbing is usually apparent. Arborvitae and other evergreens seem to dry up. This spider is tiny but can be seen with the naked eye, whereas the cyclamen mite is microscopic. Often a forceful spray from the hose will wash off red spiders, and many potted plants can be washed off under the faucet. Or spray with Kelthane or Dimite or other miticides.

The cyclamen mite is also a common problem on certain ornamentals, both in the greenhouse and outdoors. It can attack cyclamen, African-violet, delphinium, and *aconitum* (monkshood). It is also a pest of strawberries. In all cases, growth, especially new, unfolding crowns or tips, become gnarled and distorted. In delphinium and monkshood, the flower spikes often become blackened and never develop properly. Spray with Dimite, 1 teaspoonful to 1 gallon of water, weekly, and in the case of delphinium, start as soon as new growth appears in the spring. (Badly infested plants should be destroyed.) Kelthane is another recommendation. On strawberries, use it at the rate of 2 teaspoons to 1 gallon of water in spring and later as needed. Never use within 7 days of harvesting the fruit.

Rabbits and deer: High collars of wire netting around fruit tree trunks will help prevent rabbits from gnawing them in the winter. Fencing is the best way to keep both rabbits or deer out of a vegetable garden; but it must be high, or deer will sail over. Some of the repellants may help; also dried blood and tobacco dust.

Weed killer being used in a hose-end sprayer. Always be scrupulous in cleaning sprayers; never use equipment contaminated with weed killer (or deadly insect poisons) for spraying other solutions for fertilizing.

Poison ivy may be eradicated by spraying with Ammate. Reserve sprayer used for weed-control chemicals for that use only.

Root or crown rot: When plants like delphinium rot off at the ground (there are "white strings" – the mycelium threads of the fungus—apparent on the ground and among the roots) it may be caused by this disease. There is no cure, but after destroying the plant the ground can be disinfected for future plantings by soaking with corrosive sublimate (one tablet to a pint of water) or Formalin.

Rust: When powdery brown spots appear on the bottom of leaves, such as snapdragon and hollyhock, dust with sulfur; or spray with Dithane Z-78, or Zineb, every 10 days or so until flowers appear. Destroy affected leaves, especially in the fall. Plant rust-resistant strains of snapdragon.

Scale: Scale may be discovered on lilac, poplar, ash tree, and euonymus. There are many types of scale, one of the most common being in the shape of an oyster shell. It is best controlled by a dormant spray of oil or lime-sulfur. Other scale insects may be killed with Malathion when they emerge from their covering during the summer. Inspect infested plants at frequent intervals, perhaps with a magnifying glass to ascertain when this occurs.

Snails and slugs: They usually leave a silvery streak across the soil as they feed upon succulent, spring growth, usually seedlings, leaf vegetables, perennial and rock plants. They do not like lime, and a dusting helps to keep them away. Poison baits containing Metaldehyde, used according to directions, are the standard cure. They can also be trapped under boards where they often hide during the daytime.

Thrips: These small insects, about one-sixteenth inch long, produce bleached spots on gladiolus, roses, iris, and occasionally day-lilies and also cause defective bloom. They may be easily controlled by spraying with Diazinon, nicotine sulphate or pyrethrum. Before storing gladiolus, treat corms with naphthalene flakes.

Weevils: Really beetles with snouts, there are several kinds, including the taxus or black vine weevil, the strawberry root weevil, and white pine weevil. The adult black beetles are night feeders, crawling out of the debris on top of the soil to feed on a variety of plants, especially evergreens – yew, rhododendron. In the grub stage they are destructive of the roots of many plants: strawberry, bramble fruits, and many others. Controls vary according to the type of weevil, region where encountered, and crop under attack. To control the black vine weevil around rhododendrons and other evergreens, apply 5 percent chlordane dust to the soil at the rate of 1 pound to 200 square feet. Water it in at once. The powder can be mixed with the soil at planting time. Spray with Malathion to control the adults in late spring and early summer. When other types of weevils are suspected to be present, consult your county agent for local recommendations.

An outdoor potting bench is a pleasant place for seed sowing and preparation of cuttings for rooting. Bench top slopes forward for drainage. Bins hold soil, sand, and peat moss or other humus.

CHAPTER 17

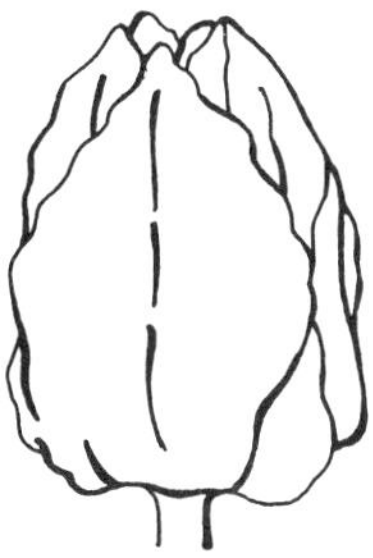

Propagation

Ah, yet, ere I descend to th' grave
May I a small house and large garden have!
– Abraham Cowley

Propagation is the raising of plants from seeds, divisions, cuttings, and layers. (Other methods of propagation, budding and grafting, most commonly practiced in the propagation of hybrid roses and fruit trees, are of more importance to the professional grower than to the home gardener.)

Most people think of seed sowing as being a spring activity, but many perennials and biennials can be sown during early summer. Other perennials need the freezing effect of winter before germinating, hence are planted in the fall. The seeds of many shrubs, like rhododendron, are usually planted in winter. Seeds can be sown in the open ground, "under glass" in cold frames or greenhouse, or in your home in a sunny window or under artificial light when sunlight is inadequate or missing.

Sowing Seeds Indoors

By sowing seeds indoors early in the spring you are able to gain from 3 to 6 weeks over those sown outdoors. Almost any sort of container will do for starting the seeds. If only a few seeds are to be sown, a large flower pot or bulb pan is adequate, but there is no rule on the kind of container to use. You can choose from discarded kitchen items (aluminum-foil baking pans and plastic trays that contained frozen foods, milk cartons cut open lengthwise), or you can buy plastic, molded fiber, or peat trays, flats, or pots designed for the purpose. Look in mail-order seed catalogs, or visit a garden center.

New clay pots must be soaked in water for a few hours so that they will not absorb the moisture from the soil. Cover the hole in the bottom with a bottle cap or pieces of broken clay pot. Small holes can be pierced in other watertight containers to permit excess water to drain out.

Damping-off is the chief enemy of indoor plant culture. It is a stem rot caused by a fungus that grows best where there is too much moisture and too little ventilation. Therefore, a sterile mixture is important for the seedbed. The nuisance of indoor soil sterilizing by steaming or even baking, just about a necessity if ordinary soil mixtures are used, can be eliminated by using vermiculite (a mica substance) and sphagnum moss.

Screened sphagnum moss, which is sterile, is an ideal seed-starting medium. If it is used alone, seedlings will need nourishment after true leaves form, as there are no nutrients in it. Either transplant the seedlings or use a liquid plant food according to directions.

Filling a standard wooden seed flat. Soil is leveled with a board, then tamped down firmly.

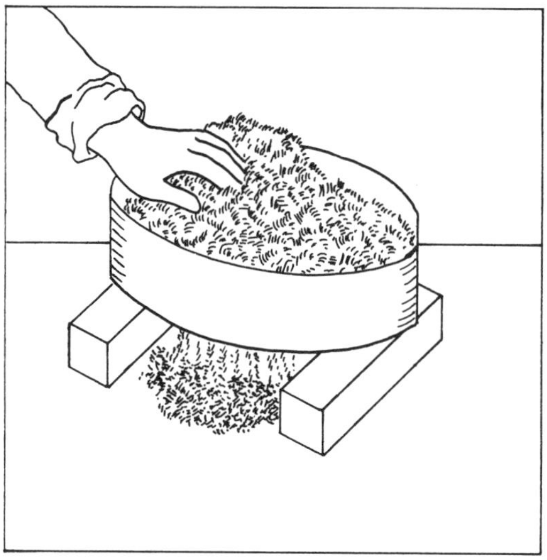

Sphagnum moss can be rubbed through a sieve to insure uniform texture. It can also be bought pre-milled.

Another sterile medium is Perlite, a volcanic ash product. It is a popular ingredient of prepackaged soil mixes, but can be bought separately. A standard sterile mix for most seeds is made up of equal parts of Perlite, Vermiculite, and milled sphagnum moss. As when the moss is used alone or with Vermiculite, a liquid fertilizer will be needed after the seedlings show their true leaves.

If a regular soil mixture (2 parts garden soil, 1 part sand, 1 part peat moss) is used, it can be sterilized in the oven for about an hour at 350 degrees. Or use a chemical such as Pano-Drench, formulated expressly for sterilizing the soil. After filling the containers with the mixture, set them in pans of water until the soil is thoroughly saturated. Pots and containers should be filled to within one-half inch of the top, and it may be necessary to add more soil after the mixture settles.

Very fine seeds like petunia, snapdragon, and verbena should be sprinkled on top of the soil and firmed into contact with the soil, but not covered. The usual rule is to cover the seeds to a depth of about three times their diameter. Cover pots with plastic bags, and keep in a warm location (about 65–70 degrees) until seeds germinate. Flats and other containers can be covered with a pane of glass; raise it one-quarter inch on 1 end after the first day, and wipe off moisture daily. A piece of newspaper laid over the glass will keep the seeds from drying out until they have germinated. Inspect the pots daily; the covering must be removed and the seedlings given a cooler temperature in a light loca-

For sowing seeds of annuals, use sterile containers and sterilized soil, milled sphagnum moss, Perlite, or Vermiculite, moistened and pressed firmly into the container.

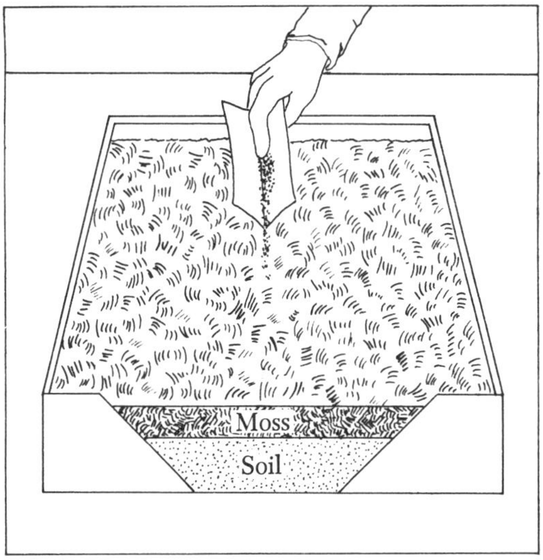

Flat has been filled with a layer of soil topped by sphagnum moss. After firming and thorough moistening, seeds are sown on moss and the flat is covered with glass or plastic.

tion as soon as they come through the soil. Give them as much light as possible, but the temperature should not go much above 60 degrees.

Seedlings growing in a window should be turned frequently, for they tend to lean toward the light. Growing seedlings indoors under fluorescent lights prevents such "leaning." The seedlings must be from 6 to 8 inches below the light tubes. The temperature should be about 70 degrees while the seed is germinating and about 50 to 60 thereafter. The lower temperature makes the plants more stocky and vigorous. Maintaining the right moisture level can be tricky. Watering after the seed has germinated should be done with a rubber bulb plant syringe with water at room temperature. The soil should not be allowed to get too wet but should be kept from getting really dry. Do not water unless the surface appears dry; then give enough water to go clear through to the bottom. The plants started in pots may be watered from below by setting the pots in water-filled saucers. When the moisture reaches the top, drain them. It is always best to water in the morning so the plants are not soaking wet at night as the temperature drops.

As the plants increase in size, they should be thinned out by pulling some from the soil. Do not break them off.

Transplanting helps the development of young plants. Shifting them to new pots, pans, or flats indoors will help strengthen them for their outdoor debut. Soil may be prepared much in the manner as for planting seed. Seedlings may be lifted from the

After sowing, seed is covered lightly. Moisten containers thoroughly with a fine mist.

Place planted containers in polyethylene bags until germination is under way.

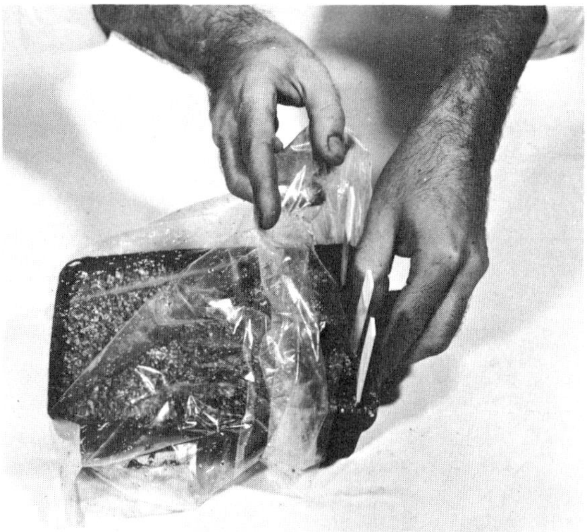

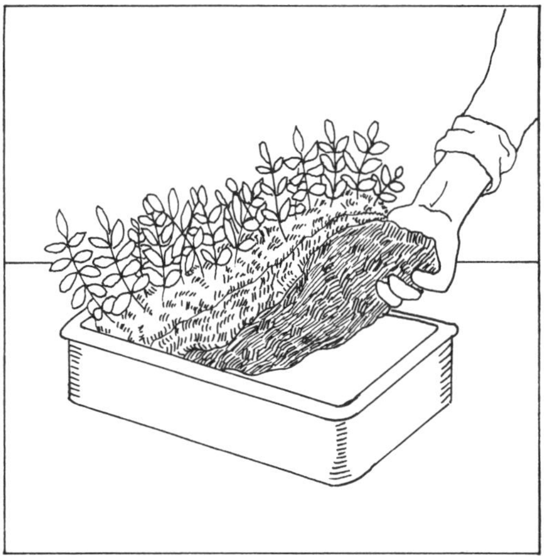

Use of sphagnum moss promotes dense root growth.

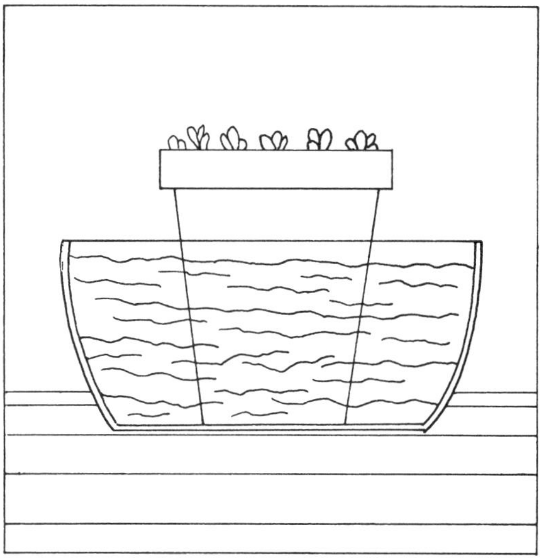

Watering seedlings by setting pot in container of water until moisture rises to surface of soil.

Seedlings on the left have two true leaves, are ready to transplant. Those on the right are too large.

How to transplant: Dig seedlings carefully with a knife blade. Pick individual plants gently from the clumps, make slit with knife in the soil in the new container, insert plant, firm soil carefully.

soil with a knife, stick, teaspoon or kitchen fork. The soil should be fairly moist in order that some soil will adhere to their roots.

Seedlings should not be transplanted until they have developed their first pair of true leaves. Do not become confused because the seed leaves which some plants put out do not look familiar; and above all, do not mistake them for weeds. Be sure to firm the soil carefully about the roots. Loose planting is dangerous. They may be hardened off by placing the flats in a cold frame before moving outdoors. Poppy, candytuft, cornflower, and portulaca are among the flowers which do not transplant well. Sow them directly where they are to bloom. They are sometimes used as ground covers and are then broadcast over the prepared garden soil between other plants and thinned out as necessary to prevent crowding after they have germinated.

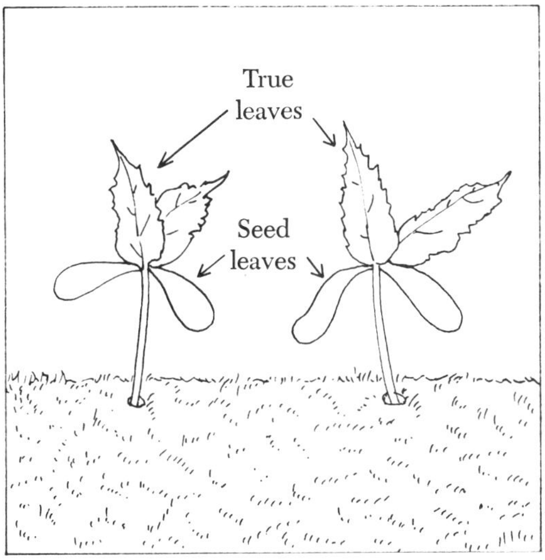

Seed leaves and true leaves. Plants are ready to transplant when true leaves develop.

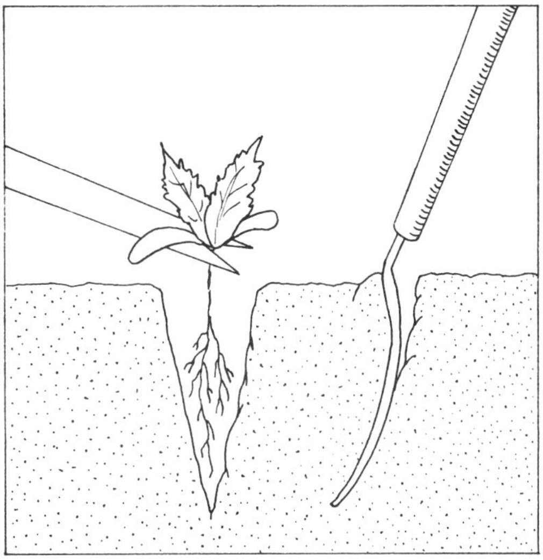

Transplanting a seedling. Make a V-shaped slit, hold seedling in place, push soil against it from side.

Marigold seedlings on left were not fertilized. Those on right were fed twice weekly.

Outdoor Seeding

Every garden should have a propagating bed or outdoor seed-bed area. Annual seeds may be planted directly here in the spring, and seedlings started indoors may be set out here temporarily.

Other uses for a seed or propagating bed include raising perennials and biennials for late spring or summer sowing. Perennials are raised during the summer for blooming the following season and a number of sea-

At eight weeks, these marigolds are ready to be set in garden, pots and all. Note roots.

Petunia on the left is correct size to set out; the one on the right is overgrown.

sons thereafter. Some, if sown in the spring, will bloom the same year if planted early enough.

Biennials differ from perennials in that they bloom the second year from seed, but usually only for a single season.

The most essential ingredients in this outdoor seedling nursery are shade, moisture, and drainage. Dry seeds will not germinate. Rich soil is not necessary, and in fact an excess of nitrogen may be harmful as it causes a rapid, soft top growth which will not stand transplanting well.

After the seedlings have appeared above ground it is necessary to protect them from the sun and from drying out, but ventilation is necessary to prevent damping-off.

First locate a sunny fence corner or other out-of-the-way area that is convenient for watering. Measure a section about 3 feet long or smaller. This will raise a lot of plants and yet be easy to reach to tend

An outdoor seedbed, with or without edging, should be spaded thoroughly and raked smooth.

Water well and allow moisture to penetrate. When surface is friable, bed is ready for seed sowing.

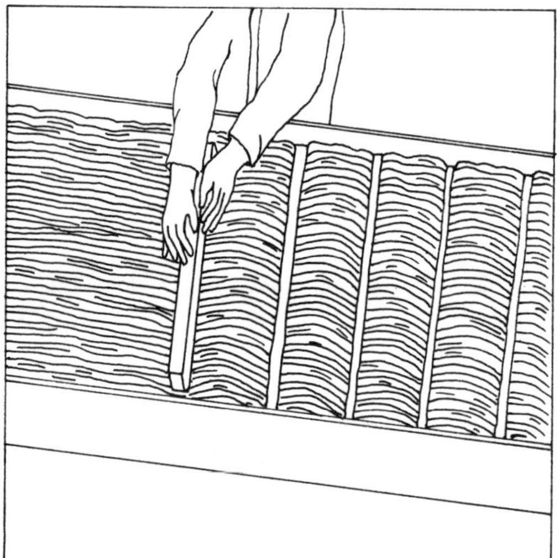

Marking seedbed rows with a straightedge.

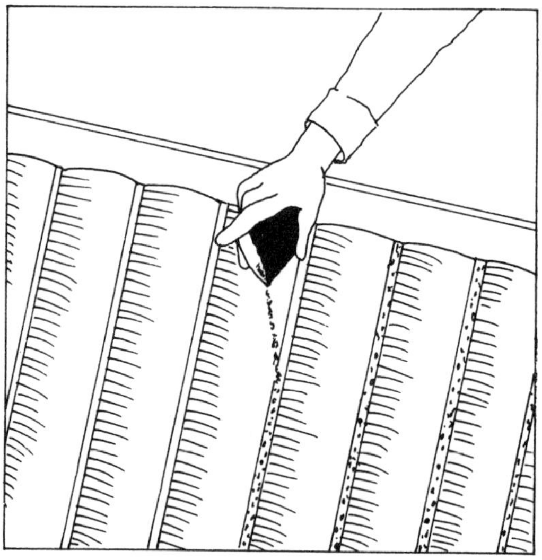

With practice, seeds can be tapped out of packet at correct spacing for their size.

them. If the bed is of ordinary lawn soil, dump on it one wheelbarrow load of sand and one of sifted leaf mold or finely granulated peat moss or both. If the soil is bad clay, these materials must be increased enough to make it friable yet still able to hold moisture. It must break up easily even when wet. Baked, cracked soil will not raise plants easily. Also it is good policy to raise the bed 4 to 6 inches above grade.

Cultivate the soil deeply, and be sure it drains well and that the surface is fine and level. A simple frame can be built around it to provide various degrees of shade for special conditions.

The day before planting seeds or seedlings, soak the bed until the water penetrates about 8 inches deep. Allow it to remain uncovered until the topsoil is readily friable, and then sow the seed in rows 4 to 6 inches apart.

Seeds large enough to be handled may be sown 2 or 3 inches apart. Most gardeners sow small seed too thickly and waste it by the necessary thinning which follows. Mix the seed with fine sand if necessary, but make it cover the space. Sow in rows – it helps you to tell seedlings from weeds while the plants are small.

Soil is sifted lightly over seed rows, then firmed with a smooth block of wood.

Sift soil lightly over seeds. Firm well with a smooth block. Water lightly with a fine mist, and cover with burlap or newspaper pegged down to the soil. Check daily for the need to water. In about ten days most of the seedlings will have appeared; remove the burlap, and cover the frame with a muslin shade, watering the seedlings gently each day with fine spray. Water pressure should be cut low, but not to the dripping point. Great loss can result from the drip of an ordinary sprinkler while the seedlings are small.

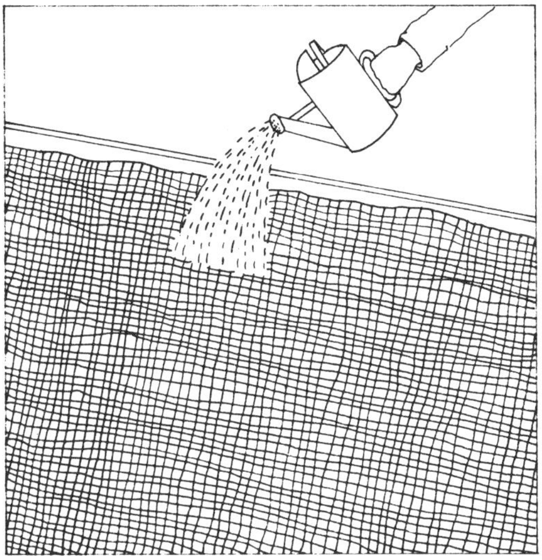

Soil, covered with burlap, is well watered whenever necessary; check daily. Remove burlap when seedlings appear and substitute a muslin shade.

As soon as the seedlings have 3 to 4 leaves, transplant them to their garden positions where they are to grow or to a nursery bed of well-drained soil mixed with sand and compost, peat moss, rotted manure, or other vegetable matter. A transplanting solution, used according to directions, will virtually prevent wilting. Care should be taken to remove plants when soil is damp but not wet. A little soil around the seedling roots will retain the fine feeding roots.

Nursery rows should be about 8 to 12 inches apart and the plants 6 to 8 inches apart in them. Water the plants well after planting.

Plants should be protected from direct, prolonged sun by a slatted screen for a few days. Cultivate often to keep weeds out and fertilize lightly until well established with liquid fertilizers used according to directions.

Do all watering in early morning or late afternoon during hot weather.

Beginner's Dozen

These plants grow easily from seed and are important in flower gardens.

Biennials (B) fill in during late May or June, when early perennials are resting, and before later ones and annuals, are blooming.

Young plants of the "variables" (V), or short-lived perennials, will replace any of the older plants that are lost.

Perennials marked (R) can be used in rock gardens or walls and as foreground plants in the flower garden. Typical perennials (P) are shasta daisy and catmint. They are staple fillers and easy to handle.

B – *Althaea rosea* (Hollyhock)
V – *Aquilegia* (Columbine)
B – *Campanula medium* (Canterbury bells)
R – *Cerastium tomentosum* (Snow-in-summer)
V – *Chrysanthemum coccineum* (Pyrethrum or Painted daisy)
P – *Chrysanthemum maximum* (Shasta daisy)
V – *Delphinium* (Chinese and hybrids)
B – *Dianthus barbatus* (Sweet William)
B – *Digitalis purpurea* (Foxglove)
R – *Linum perenne* (Blue flax)
P – *Nepeta mussini* (Catmint)
B or P – *Rudbeckia* (Gloriosa-daisy)
B – *Viola tricolor* (Pansy)

Some Tips on Germination

Some plants take so long to grow from seed to the blooming period that most home gardeners do not want to bother with them. Others have shells so hard that they must first be notched or ringed with a knife before planting. It is a safe procedure to assume that large seeds, ranging from nasturtium to lima beans, will stand soaking overnight to soften their shells for rapid germination.

Some seeds do not grow unless planted within a very short time of their ripening, but most seeds of annual plants will retain their vitality for several years. Primrose, lupine, and delphinium seeds usually germinate promptly if sown when fresh. If this is not possible (or if the seeds have not been stored properly by the seedsmen), the home gardener may be disappointed by the erratic germination results. Sometimes a week or so in the ice compartment of a refrigerator before sowing may improve germination of primrose and delphinium. The George W. Park Seed Company (Greenwood, South Carolina), which offers a wide range of seed-sowing supplies and help for home gardeners, suggests freezing primrose seeds in an ice cube for several days before sowing. This method should also work on delphinium seeds that may have gone into dormancy. Sowing seeds in late fall for spring germination usually has the same effect as the refrigerator treatment.

Many trees and shrubs that are grown from seed need a prolonged period of cold before they germinate. The holly (*Ilex opaca*) is an example. Its seeds (separated from the pulp) can be sown in a cold frame in fall after collecting. The area in which they are planted should be well marked, for they will not germinate for a year or more. Just the opposite are seeds of most rhododendrons and azaleas. They germinate quite promptly indoors when sown in a sifted mixture of sphagnum moss that is kept moist. The seed should be sprinkled on the surface of the wet moss and then the entire container should be encased in a polyethylene bag, which will keep the moss damp. The young seedlings can be transplanted into flats containing a high proportion of peat moss in the spring.

A clump of primroses in need of dividing.

Pulling off a division from the clump.

Propagation

Dividing Plants

The propagation of plants by division – separating or breaking up one clump into several – is a very common, generally easy way to increase plants. It is most often used for herbaceous perennials, especially those that are slow from seed or won't reproduce true to type from seed. Some perennials – shasta daisy, perennial aster, hardy chrysanthemum – practically fall into divisions when the gardener lifts old clumps in spring or fall. Others, like astilbe or day-lily, can be stubborn and require strength and ingenuity from the gardener to divide their clumps. One method used for them is to lift the clump, insert two spading forks back to back in the center, and then pry them apart. This usually results in two clumps – still too large, but it is then easier to divide the two into other segments. A sharp knife or pruning shears should be at hand to cut apart roots and crowns when pulling and prying methods fail.

Do not get the new clumps too small, and be sure to include in them vigorous parts from which the new plants will start. Old dead centers should be discarded. Examine the plants each year, and those

Six divisions from one overgrown plant.

which have dead centers should be divided. Replant immediately, or cover the divisions and roots with soil or burlap to prevent them from drying out until planting time. Be sure to water them well after planting.

About every 3 or 4 years is often enough to divide the majority of perennials, such as phlox, astilbe, catmint, or day-lily. But primrose and shasta daisy grow better if they are divided and replanted every other

This clump of sedum offers two ways to increase stock. Stems at left have been in contact with soil and have formed layers (new plants) that can be severed from main plant. Main clump, with buds of new growth in center, can be divided into several sections.

Prying off a division from a sedum clump.

year. Primroses should be divided immediately after flowering – in late spring or early summer. Shasta daisies can be divided in fall or early spring. The rule about timing plant division is that plants that flower in spring or early summer can be divided in fall while autumn-flowering plants (chrysanthemum and aster) are best lifted and separated in spring.

Many perennials resent disturbance and should only be lifted for division when new plants are desired. Some of these include peony, gas-plant, platycodon, bleeding-heart and babys-breath. Others, like lupine and delphinium, rarely divide well and should be increased by seed.

Growing Plants from Summer Cuttings

Softwood or greenwood cuttings ("slips") are portions of the stem growth taken from shrubs, perennials, or annuals in summer and usually consist of new or present-season growth. The method is most often used for shrubs but is also successful on certain nonwoody plants like geranium, coleus, dianthus (carnations, pinks), dahlia, candytuft, and viola.

Most deciduous (leaf-losing) shrubs can be readily rooted from cuttings taken in early summer. Among evergreen shrubs and trees the process takes longer, but the evergreen azalea is an exception. Azalea cuttings made in early July should be rooted by late summer. (But another exception is the deciduous azalea. Stem cuttings from it are difficult to root, but new plants can be obtained by layering, described later on.)

When making cuttings, cut the shoots from sturdy plants which have finished blooming. Iberis (candytuft) and arabis (rock cress) may be taken with a piece of the old stem (mallet shape); other plants, if large enough, may be cut with a heel which is a small oval piece of the outside of the old stem about one-half inch long. This is cut with a straight knife and must not be torn or pulled away from the stem of the new shoot. Roots form very quickly from heel cuttings. Small creeping plants may be cut 8 or 10 joints long and buried two-thirds their length. Care must be taken

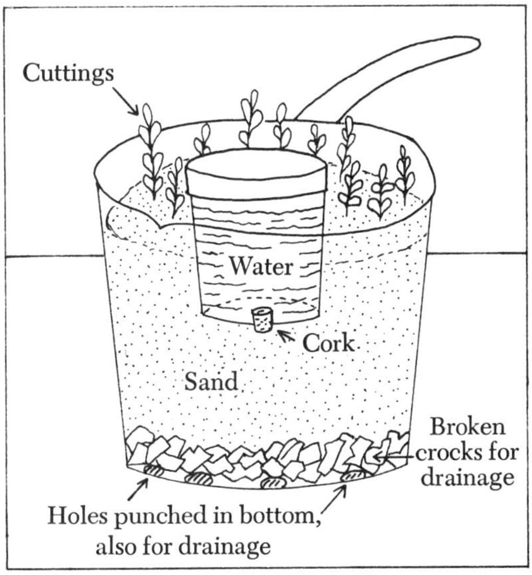

An old kitchen kettle can be used to root a few cuttings.

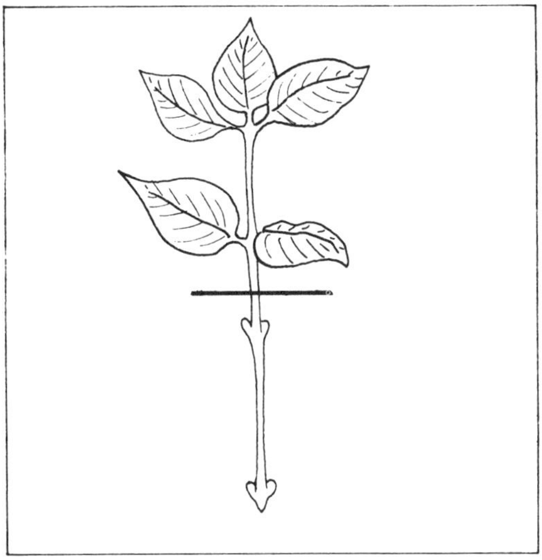

Simple softwood cutting. Lower leaves will be removed before cutting is inserted in sand.

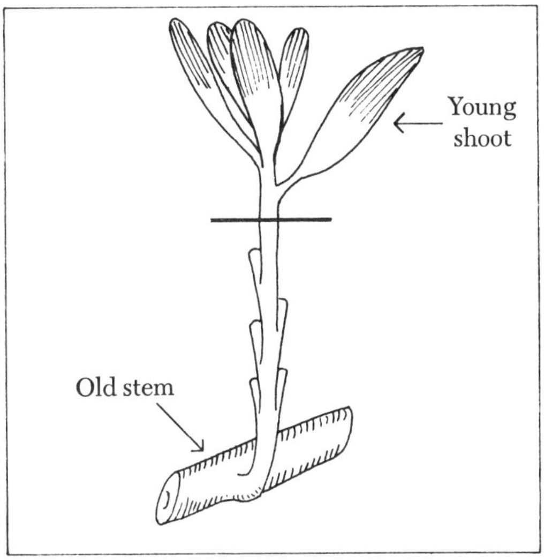

Mallet-type softwood cutting.

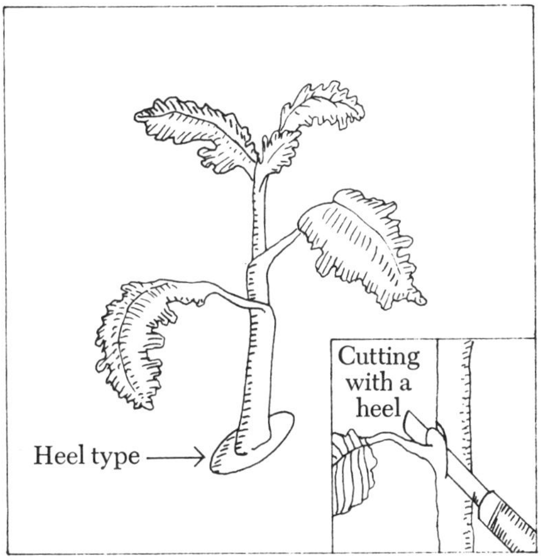

Heel cutting. "Heel" is portion cut from stem.

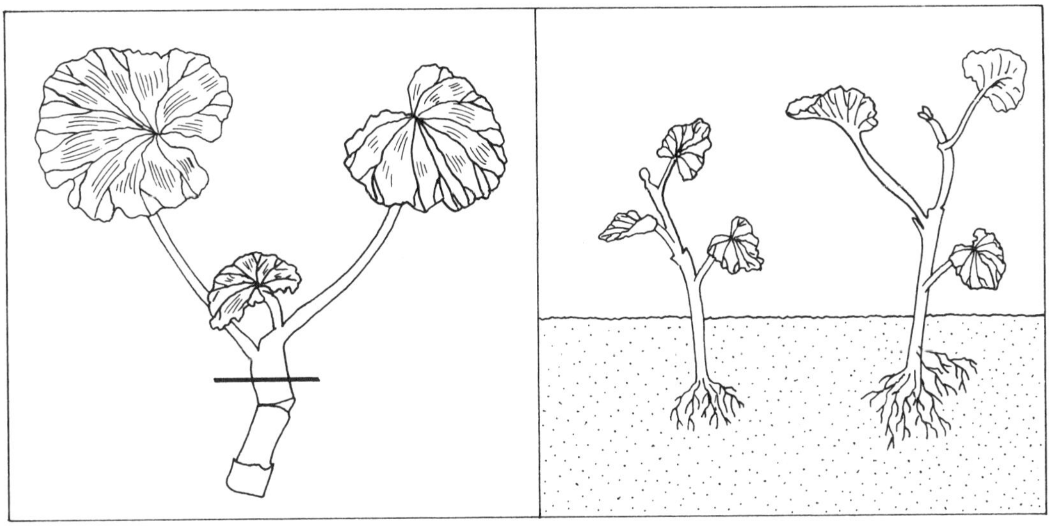

Geranium cutting, left. Right, *rooted cuttings.*

Flat containing rooting medium, well tamped down with a brick, has been provided with wire arches to hold polyethylene "tent." Other equipment for rooting cuttings: hormone powder, knife, labels, pruners.

Pruners are used to remove softwood (or greenwood) cuttings from an azalea in early summer, when new growth has matured enough to snap. Leaves will be removed from lower part of each cutting.

not to get shoots too long as weak, leggy plants will result. The best length for softwood cuttings is 3 to 6 inches. About half the leaves and all flower buds should be removed, cutting carefully without tearing.

If a heel is not obtainable, choose a terminal or lateral shoot which snaps when bent. Cut at the base of a joint except in the case of willow and clematis which root better if cut halfway between joints. Set about 1 to 1½ inches deep. Carnations are set shallow both in the rooting medium and when transplanted.

When cuttings are taken from the parent plant, they have no roots and therefore do not need nourishment. What they need most quickly is roots. Clean sharp sand or a mixture of equal parts of sand and peat moss are both good media for rooting cuttings. If sea sand is used, it should first be washed to eliminate salt. The sand-peat moss mixture is especially suitable for rooting the evergreen azalea and other acid-soil plants. (See Chapter 6.)

Propagation is hastened under the ideal conditions created by bottom heat applied in a cold frame by use of electrical cables, and in a greenhouse bench by steam pipes or an electric heating cable placed underneath. But during summer the weather in most localities is sufficiently warm to do without this.

Propagating may be done in 2 or 3 inches of sand in a section of the cold frame reserved for the purpose or in a Wardian case constructed of glass or an old aquarium. However, for most home gardeners, a box 8 inches deep (a soap box will do), open at the bottom and top is satisfactory. A small box will handle many cuttings. Remove the soil 3 inches deep and set the box in this excavation, fill to soil level with clean, sharp sand or sand and peat moss. Then wet thoroughly with clear water and tamp firmly. (Equally useful is a flat, wooden box about 3 inches deep, which becomes a sort of miniature greenhouse when polyethylene sheeting is stretched over a wire frame.)

Set the cuttings about 2 inches apart each way, carefully label and water. Cover the box snugly with a piece of glass. Shade the box with paper or cloth and keep closed for about 10 days, opening it to give light and fine spray sprinklings, but only if the top of the sand shows signs of drying

Cuttings being inserted. Base of each is dipped into hormone rooting powder, then set into a slit in the rooting medium. Flat will be watered, then covered with polyethylene and set in a light but not sunny place. No further watering should be needed.

out. It is unnecessary to water the plastic-enclosed flat after the initial soaking as the plastic prevents drying out.

After the 10 days the glass is raised during the mornings, shade being maintained and the sand kept moist at all times. If there is any sign of damping-off or other fungus, water with a solution of Pano-Drench, according to directions.

When the cuttings show signs of rooting (it may be necessary to dig 1 or 2 up), remove the glass; but maintain the shade until good root systems are established. Transplant to a growing soil of two-thirds finely sifted garden loam and one part leaf mold or peat moss. Be sure to get the soil firm around roots; water thoroughly. Shade for a day or two, and then apply semishade by using a slat cover until they can stand full sun. Apply weak chemical fertilizer (1 tablespoon to 1 gallon of water) to the plants after they have 3 or 4 new leaves. Do this only in August so that new growth will not be stimulated late in the season.

Mulch after the first good ground freeze with hardwood leaves 6 inches deep, held

These heaths and heathers have produced strong roots and are now ready to be set out in nursery rows.

For their first winter, young plants in a nursery bed require a lath shade. Deciduous azaleas in foreground are older.

loosely in place by boughs or poultry netting. Of course such tender plants as geranium and coleus must be lifted and potted for house culture as they will not stand a winter in the open in most parts of the country.

Hardwood Cuttings

Hardwood cuttings are usually taken about 8 inches long when the shrub is dormant, but not during freezing weather.

The wood should be a year old, firm, strong, and free of leaves. Each should have 2 or more eyes or nodes and be plump and thick. Thin branches have little food in them. There should be an eye at the top of each cutting.

After the cuttings have been made and tied in a bundle with a label, they are buried in damp peat moss and stored at a temperature of about 45 degrees until they have formed calluses. The time necessary for this formation varies somewhat, but generally speaking the process will take all winter. The peat should be damp enough to keep the cuttings from drying out, but not wet enough to rot them.

When the cuttings are removed from the storing medium in the spring, their butt ends will show more or less complete rings of callus. It is from these calluses that the roots will start when cuttings are planted in nursery rows outdoors. They are set vertically and quite deep in the soil with their callused ends down. In this position they will develop both roots and new top growth.

The soil and care for planting outdoors should be provided substantially as previously described for softwood transplants. All shrubs should be transplanted several times before they are placed in their permanent locations.

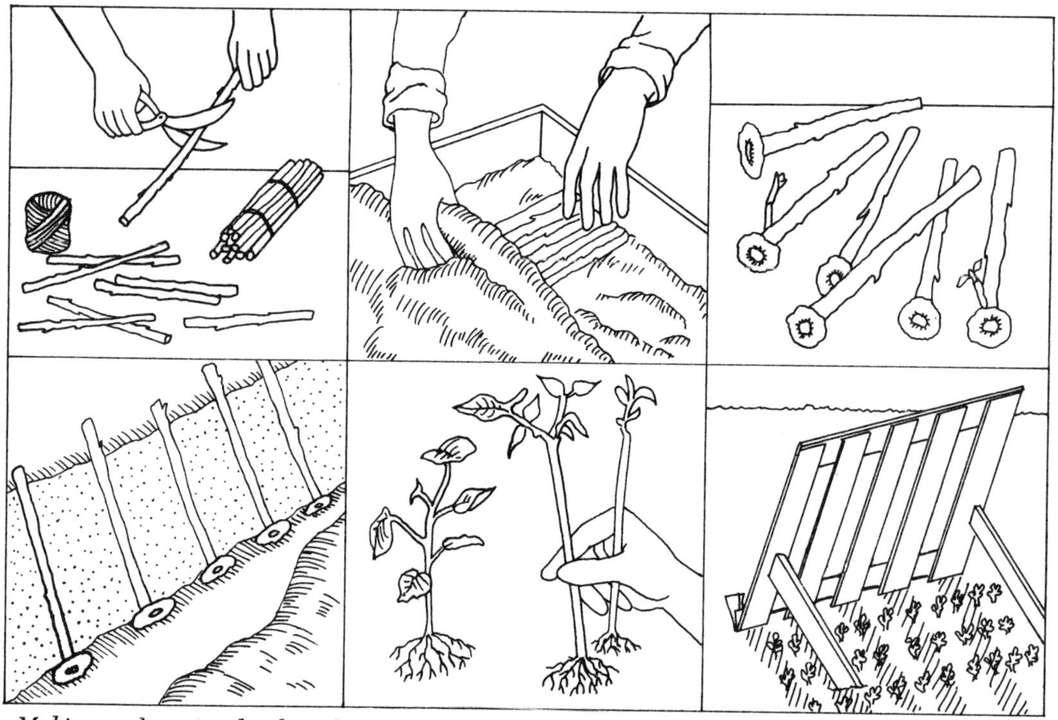

Making and rooting hardwood cuttings. Top, left to right: *Cuttings of year-old wood, with slanted ends cut between nodes, are bundled and tied, then buried in damp peat moss and stored until calluses form.* (top right). Below: *Callused cuttings are set out vertically in the spring. When root growth has been made, cuttings are set into nursery bed and given shade.*

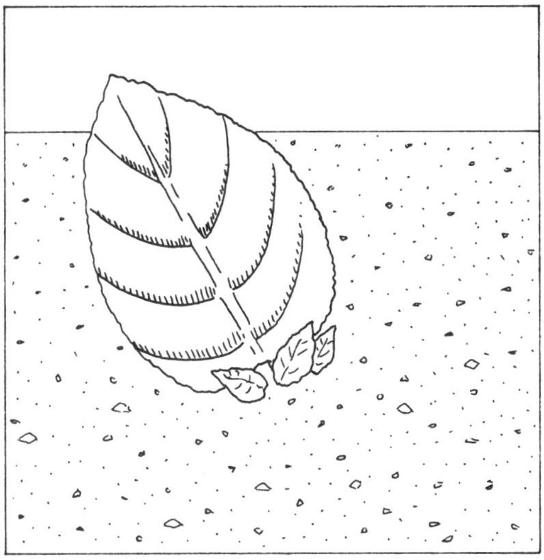

A leaf cutting of an African-violet, showing new plants around base.

Leaf Cuttings

New plants will develop from leaf cuttings in the case of some plants. Such shrubs as some kinds of rhododendron and camellia and house plants like African-violet, rex begonia, peperomia, piggyback-plant, sedum, gloxinia, and sansevieria are the best-known examples.

In the case of African-violet, take a leaf and its petiole that has been shortened to about half an inch. Insert the petiole in sand up to the base of the leaf in a pot or indoor propagating box or flat. The sand can be kept moist and the atmosphere around the cuttings humid by enclosing the container in a plastic bag. Little plants should appear at the base of leaf in from 5 to 8 weeks, depending on the variety and environment. (African-violet leaves may also be rooted in a glass jar half-filled with water. Other plants that will root in water include ivy, forsythia, willow, and box.)

If you covet a rex begonia variety owned by a friend, beg a leaf. From one leaf, it is possible to obtain several little plants.

Cut off the leaf's petiole to leave a half-inch stub, turn the leaf over and with a knife cut through several of the main veins. Then turn the leaf over and insert the petiole into the sand so that the entire leaf lies flat on it. The new plants will grow from the points that were severed, so be sure to keep the entire leaf in contact with the sand by hairpins or bent pieces of wire.

Mist Propagation

Moisture has always been a controlling factor in plant propagation, but the discovery of the advantages of mist or fog to speed up the rooting of cuttings is a recent advance. The method is most practical for nurserymen using greenhouses and outdoor frames or propagating beds, but a few devices intended for the home garden have appeared. The idea is that cuttings bathed in a fog or mist cannot lose moisture, will not wilt or dry out even if exposed to bright sunlight, and can therefore be taken with more leaves intact. Consequently, they tend to root more rapidly and successfully. The theory has been proved correct, and various devices can be obtained for producing the right sort of mist, for protecting the cuttings from wind, excessive sunlight, and the like, and for controlling the water flow. The latter can be done manually, by means of clockwork (as cook-

A cold frame being used to grow and overwinter biennials from seed—English daisies on the left, Canterbury bells on the right.

A lath house affords enough shelter from sun to be used in propagating many plants.

Misting attachments on a hose are being used for mist propagation in this portable hotbed. The bent-pipe supports may be covered with plastic film when bed is used as a miniature greenhouse.

ing operations are timed), or through rather complicated electrical hookups in which a solenoid valve turns the water on and off according to impulses transmitted from a moisture-sensitive unit placed among the cuttings, or from a sort of electric eye which reacts when the sunlight becomes strong enough to exert a drying effect.

Hormone Treatments

Scientific progress has in recent years developed materials of much value to gardeners because they stimulate the rooting of cuttings of plants formerly hard to propagate in this way, and hasten the rooting time of easily handled kinds. These hormones or growth-producing substances are obtainable in concentrated liquid form or as powders at seed stores and other garden supply houses. Following directions supplied with them, the gardener merely soaks the base half-inch or inch of his cuttings for a certain time, which may range from a few to 24 hours, then plants them in the usual way. Or, if using a powder type hormone, he sticks the moistened base end of each cutting in the powder, taps it to shake off any excess, and plants it immediately with the rest adhering. The prompt vigorous root growth that follows will not only help insure a better stand of new plants, but will also enable the plants to make rapid growth and attain planting-out size in short order.

A portable cold frame may be set over a basement window, which is a source of warmth.

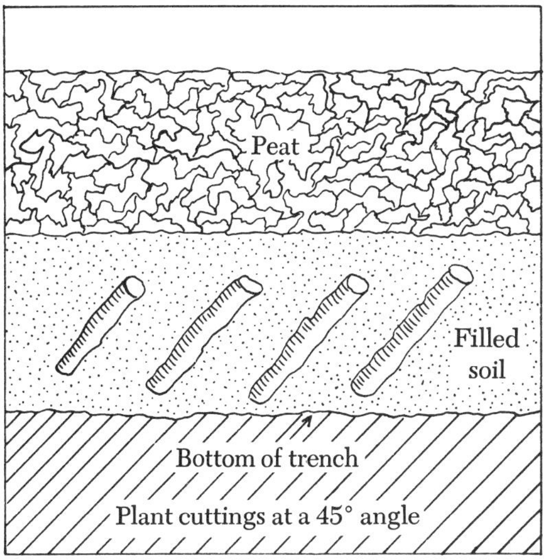

Making root cuttings.

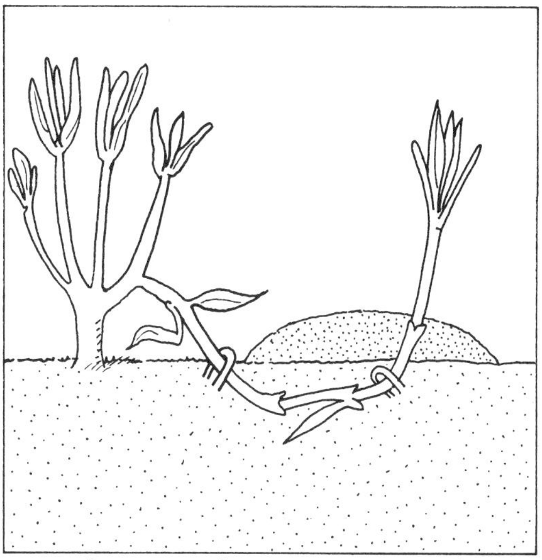

New plants from layering: Cut a notch in a stem and peg to ground; cover with soil.

Root Cuttings

Root cuttings may be used as a means of propagating some perennials. Medium fleshy roots are removed from the parent plant in the fall and are cut into 1 or 2 inch pieces and placed in soil in shallow flats or planted in well-prepared beds outside. Root pieces should be placed close together, but not overlapping, and covered with about ½ inch of soil. Mulch lightly with leaves or pine needles in late fall. In the spring, when 2 or 3 leaves have been produced, the new plants may be potted or planted directly outside in beds.

Perennials Propagated by Root Cuttings

Anchusa (Bugloss)
Anemone japonica (Windflower)
Asclepias tuberosa (Butterfly-weed)
Bocconia (Plume-poppy)
Ceratostigma (Plumbago)
Coronilla vera (Crown vetch)
Dicentra spectabilis (Bleeding-heart)
Echinops (Globe thistle)
Gypsophila paniculata (Babys-breath)
Oenothera (Evening-primrose)
Papaver orientale (Poppy)
Phlox paniculata (Summer phlox)
Polygonatum (Solomons-seal)
Stokesia (Stokes aster)
Thermopsis
Trollius (Globe-flower)
Yucca (Adams-needle)

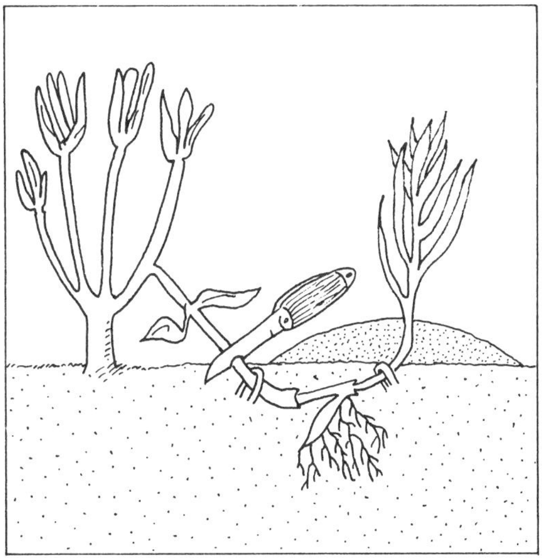

When layer (new plant) has rooted, sever stem from parent plant and set it out.

Layering

If but a few new plants are desired, many of the plants in your garden can be increased by layering. This is the process of rooting a branch without detaching it from the parent. Many plants naturally propagate themselves by this method. Many creeping plants that "walk" actually form layers first.

A branch is partially slit on the underside, and this notch is held open by a small pebble or by bending the stem. It is then

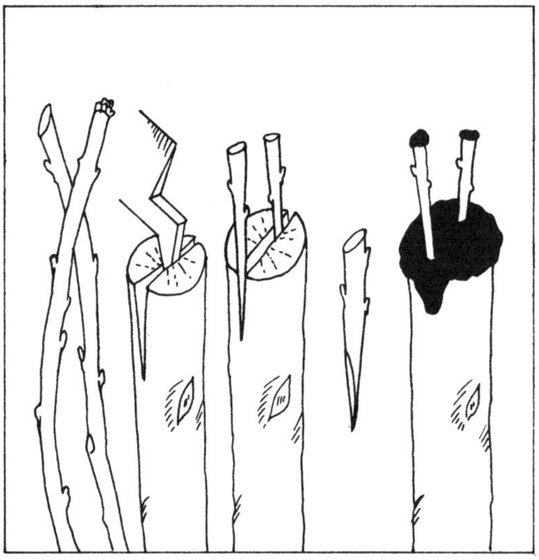

Cleft grafting. Stock is split with chisel or small axe. Scions are prepared with two slanting cuts and inserted into split stock. Wound is well covered with grafting wax.

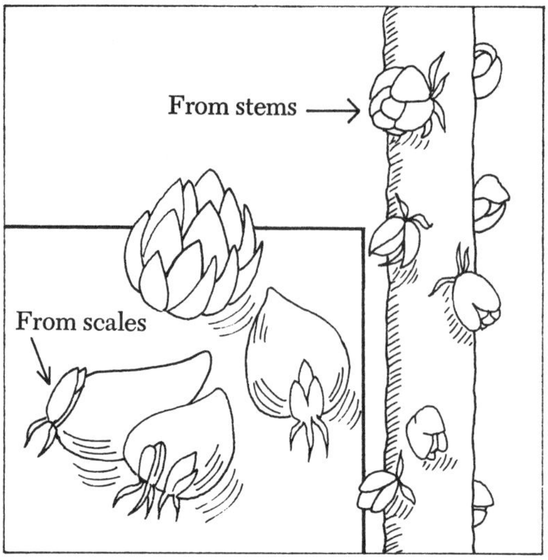

Lilies can be increased by planting out scales from the old bulb, or by planting on the bulbils from the stem.

stapled to the ground by bent pieces of heavy wire and well covered with earth. Keep it moist, and sever from the main plant when well rooted. Plants which may be easily layered are many perennials such as dianthus, strawberry, and such shrubs as rhododendron, azalea, forsythia, climbing rose, heath, and heather.

Air Layering

The ancient art of Chinese- or pot-layering has been given a boost by the use of polyethylene. It originally consisted of binding the two halves of a flower pot around a shallow cut made in a tree or shrub branch, filling the pot with soil, and keeping it moist. When roots from just above the wound filled the soil, the branch was severed below the pot and the free end, with its newly formed roots, was planted and grown as a new individual. The main difference between that procedure and the new one are that a square of flexible polyethylene can take the place of the pot; a handful of sphagnum moss soaked and then squeezed almost dry is used instead of soil; and the gardener can make a slit in the stem or remove a band of bark about as wide as the branch is thick, as in the old trick of "ringing" a grape cane to stimulate fruit production. The wounded area can be dusted with one of the root-inducing hormones before the sphagnum moss and plastic film are fastened.

Air layering is not suitable for all plants. Among house plants, the rubber plant, which may eventually lose most of its lower leaves, is the classic example of a suitable plant for air layering. Others include many hardy plants like flowering dogwood and rhododendron.

Time for Germination

Perennial Seeds

(Time can vary with temperature and moisture conditions.)

Key:

S – Seeds which can be sown in summer or spring.

F – Seeds best sown in fall.

X – Seeds sown in spring. Plants may bloom the first year.

Proper Name	Common Name	Germination Days
S – *Achillea ptarmica*	The pearl	10
F – *Aconitum napellus*	Monkshood	150-190
F – *Adonis amurensis*	Pheasants-eye	100-175
S – *Althaea rosea*	Hollyhock	10
S – *Alyssum saxatile*	Basket of gold	5-10
S – *Anchusa italica*	Bugloss	25
S – *Anemone japonica*	Windflower	20
S – *Aquilegia* various	Columbine	15
X – *Arabis alpina*	Rock cress	15
S – *Armeria maritima*	Sea pink	15
S – *Aster* various	Michaelmas daisy	15
F – *Baptisia australis*	Wild indigo	50
S – *Bellis perennis*	English daisy	10
F – *Bocconia cordata*	Plume-poppy	20
S – *Campanula carpatica*	Harebell	15
S – *Campanula medium*	Canterbury bell	15
S – *Campanula persicifolia*	Peach bell	15
S – *Campanula pyramidalis*	Chimney bell	15
F – *Catananche caerulea*	Everlasting	12
S – *Centaurea montana*	Cornflower	15
X – *Cerastium tomentosum*	Snow-in-summer	50
S – *Cheiranthus cheiri*	Wallflower	14
S – *Chrysanthemum coccineum*	Pyrethrum	20
S – *Chrysanthemum maximum*	Shasta daisy	14
X – *Chrysanthemum parthenium*	Feverfew	12
X – *Coreopsis*	Tickseed	20
F – *Delphinium chinense*	Larkspur	25
F – *Delphinium* hybrids	Larkspur	20
S – *Dianthus barbatus*	Sweet William	10
S – *Dianthus deltoides*	Maiden pink	20
F – *Dictamnus*	Gas-plant	150
S – *Digitalis purpurea*	Foxglove	10
X – *Gaillardia grandiflora*	Blanket flower	15
S – *Geum*	Avens	15
S – *Gypsophila paniculata*	Babys-breath	15
S – *Helenium*	Sneezeweed	10
S – *Helianthemum*	Sun-rose	30
S – *Heliopsis*	Sunflower	15
F – *Helleborus*	Christmas-rose	100
S – *Hesperis*	Sweet rocket	15
S – *Heuchera*	Coral-bells	15
S – *Hibiscus moscheutos*	Giant mallow	10
S – *Iberis sempervirens*	Candytuft	15
S – *Incarvillea*	Hardy gloxinia	20
F – *Iris kaempferi*	Japanese iris	25
S – *Lathyrus latifolius*	Everlasting pea	40
S – *Lavandula vera*	Sweet lavender	25
F – *Liatris*	Gayfeather	15
X – *Linum perenne*	Blue flax	15
F – *Lobelia cardinalis*	Cardinal flower	20
S – *Lupinus polyphyllus*	Lupine	25
X – *Lychnis chalcedonica*	Campion	10

Proper Name	Common Name	Germination Days
s – *Lythrum roseum superbum*	Rose loosestrife	25
x – *Myosotis*	Forget-me-not	10
s – *Nepeta mussini*	Catmint	20
s – *Nierembergia*	Cup-flower	30
F – *Oenothera*	Evening primrose	150
s – *Papaver nudicaule*	Iceland poppy	15
s – *Penstemon* various	Beard tongue	60
s – *Phlox paniculata*	Phlox	15
s – *Physostegia virginica*	False dragon head	10
s – *Platycodon*	Balloon-flower	15
x – *Polemonium*	Jacob's ladder	150
s – *Primula*	Primrose	20-150
s – *Rudbeckia*	Coneflower	15
s – *Salvia azurea*	Sage	25
s – *Scabiosa caucasica*	Bluebonnet	25
s – *Sedum*	Stonecrop	20
F – *Sidalcea*	Indian mallow	20
F – *Silene*	Catchfly	25
s – *Statice latifolia*	Sea lavender	50
s – *Stokesia laevis*	Stokes aster	25
s – *Thalictrum*	Meadow-rue	20
s – *Tritoma*	Red hot poker	30
F – *Trollius*	Globe-flower	25
x – *Tunica saxifraga*	Tunic-flower	10
s – *Valeriana*	Valerian	15
s – *Veronica* various	Speedwell	25
s – *Viola cornuta*	Violet	10
s – *Viola tricolor*	Pansy	10

Annual Seeds

Proper Name	Common Name	Germination Days
Acroclinium	Everlasting	8-10
Agathea	Blue daisy	18-20
Ageratum	Floss-flower	8-12
Amaranthus	Amaranth	20-25
Antirrhinum	Snapdragon	20-25
Arctotis	African-daisy	15-20
Argemone	Mexican poppy	20-25
Begonia sempervirens	Wax begonia	15-20
Brachycome	Swan River daisy	20-25
Browallia	Amethyst	18-20
Calceolaria	Slipper-flower	15-18
Calendula	Pot-marigold	10-12
Callistephus	China aster	8-10
Celosia	Cockscomb	20-25
Centaurea	Bachelors-button, Sweet sultan	5-20
Chrysanthemum	Chrysanthemum	5-8
Clarkia	Clarkia	8-10
Cobaea scandens	Cup and saucer vine	15-20

Proper Name	*Common Name*	*Germination Days*
Coleus	Flame nettle	20-25
Coreopsis	Tickseed	10-12
Cosmos	Cosmos	5-15
Datura	Trumpet flower	15-18
Delphinium ajacis	Larkspur	15-20
Dianthus	Pinks	5-8
Gaillardia	Blanket flower	12-15
Gloxinia	Gloxinia	15-20
Gypsophila elegans	Babys-breath	15-20
Helianthus	Sunflower	15-20
Helichrysum	Strawflower	5-10
Iberis	Annual candytuft	5-8
Impatiens	Balsam	8-12
Ipomoea	Moonflower	5-8
Kochia	Ball of fire	15-18
Lantana	Lantana	15-20
Lathyrus odoratus	Sweet peas	15-20
Linum rubrum	Scarlet flax	15-18
Lobelia erinus	Lobelia	8-10
Lupinus	Lupine	25-30
Mathiola incana	Stock	10-15
Mirabilis jalapa	Four-o'clock	12-15
Myosotis	Forget-me-not	15-20
Nicotiana	Flowering tobacco	20-25
Nigella	Love-in-a-mist	10-15
Papaver rhoeas	Poppy	15-20
Passiflora	Passion-flower	50-60
Pelargonium	Geranium	20-25
Petunia	Petunia	18-20
Phaseolus multiflorus	Scarlet runner bean	8-10
Phlox drummondi	Phlox	20-25
Portulaca	Moss rose	18-20
Ricinus	Castor-oil bean	15-20
Salpiglossis	Painted tongue	15-20
Salvia splendens	Scarlet sage	15-25
Scabiosa	Pincushion-flower	18-20
Schizanthus	Butterfly-plant	20-25
Senecio cruentus	Cineraria	5-8
Tagetes	Marigold	5-8
Thunbergia	Black-eyed Susan vine	8-10
Tropaeolum	Nasturtium	8-15
Verbena	Verbena	8-10
Viola tricolor	Pansy	8-10
Viscaria	Campion	10-12
Xeranthemum	Everlasting	8-10
Zinnia	Zinnia	5-8

The greenhouse in the garden scene. Long after outdoor flowers have faded, the glass-house and its attached workroom will come into their own as the focus of the gardener's interest.

CHAPTER 18

The Small Greenhouse

To a garden under glass –
The sun is a thousand lights.
– W. E. D.

Many people believe a greenhouse to be a luxury; but once they have owned one, they usually change their minds. As it extends the gardening season through even the nastiest winter, a greenhouse more than repays its cost by the pleasure it gives. Whether it is used as a "growing" or hobby house or as a conservatory or family room in which the plants are mainly ornamental and there is space for relaxing, reading, or even sunbathing, a modern greenhouse can be a year-round delight.

Of course there *are* greenhouses with high price tags, but among the dozens of models made by established manufacturers there are many well within the reach of average pocketbooks. A good type to start with is a sectional model which is delivered with all the members cut and fitted, even to the panes of glass. It can be made as long as desired (don't get too small a house – a common beginning mistake), and may be set up as a free-standing structure or an extension of a dwelling or other building from which heat, electricity, and water supplies may be easily extended.

Greenhouse makers' advertisements in garden magazines offer catalogs and brochures that are wonderful sources of information. Use these for guidance on what is available, and consult local officials or a contractor about building code requirements for foundations, heating, wiring, etc.

It is quite feasible for anyone who is handy with tools to build a greenhouse such as those described farther along in this chapter, or to assemble a prefabricated one. For the smallest budgets, the least costly greenhouse is a conventionally framed or quonset-hut type of structure covered with polyethylene, other plastic material, or fiberglass. Polyethylene sheeting, although inexpensive, has to be replaced fairly often, however, as sunlight causes it to deteriorate.

The process of raising plants in a greenhouse is sometimes thought to be intricate and mysterious. Quite the contrary: anyone who is successful with gardening out-of-doors will find that the principles he has been following will apply to greenhouse gardening, too, although some techniques will be different.

A greenhouse is not a "hot house," as these structures were once called, except when the maximum desirable temperature (from 50 degrees for a "cold" house to 70 degrees for a "warm" one) is compared to the winter temperature outside. Most house plants do best at lower temperatures and with much higher humidity than we can usually maintain in our living rooms.

Space, both visual and actual, is extended by an attached lean-to greenhouse opening directly into room.

The small modern greenhouse, even without the automatic controls now available, can maintain ideal conditions with much less fussing than the plants would need if they were growing in living quarters.

The home gardener can use a "growing" greenhouse in any or all of these ways:

1. *For raising cut flowers and flowering and foliage plants; for forcing bulbs as winter decoration indoors.* Garden plants carried in before frost can be brought into bloom again after a short resting period. Bulbs potted for forcing and stored outdoors to form roots can be brought inside in relays to form top growth and bloom. Foliage plants in living rooms can be rotated into the greenhouse for building up after exposure to unfavorable conditions. Innumerable kinds of plants can be grown from seed or cuttings for ornamental use. For cut flowers, asters, chrysanthemums, carnations, snapdragons, and sweet peas are all good possibilities.

2. *For carrying over stock plants for cuttings to be made the next season.* Such plants as fuchsia, salvia, chrysanthemum, geranium, and dahlia can be stored beneath the benches as mere balls of roots. Brought to the top and watered into growth in early spring, they furnish abundant cuttings to be rooted for summer bloom.

3. *Sheltering tender shrubs or other specimens that can't be wintered over outdoors.* Dwarf citrus, lantana, bay tree, camellia, rosemary, oleander, and fuchsia are examples.

4. *For growing culinary herbs, salad greens, and even vegetables for out-of-season enjoyment.* Lettuce, herbs, radishes, and the like are grown on top of the benches. Tomatoes are sown in late March and transplanted to larger pots when warmer weather comes in April. Asparagus, rhubarb, and endive can be forced beneath the benches, where it is also quite possible to grow mushrooms. If a suitable wet spot can be maintained, excellent watercress can be grown.

5. *For raising hobby plants from seed and for sowing tender flowers and vegetables for transplanting outdoors.* See the chapter on propagation for information on sowing techniques and seedling care. Several weeks' advantage can be gained in spring by sowing tender plants in the greenhouse.

6. *For propagating favorite plants.*

7. *For experimenting with breeding new varieties as a hobby.*

What Kind of Greenhouse?

There are two principal types of greenhouses, free-standing and attached. The free-standing house can be placed anywhere desired so long as there is adequate light and no objection to the possibly greater expense of extending heat, water, and electricity to some distance. The free-standing house is always of the even-span (or full-span) type, with equal areas of roof on each side sloping away from a lengthwise ridge. The sides may be of glass to the ground or to the top of the foundation, or may be built to a height of 30 or 36 inches of concrete, masonry, or wood.

A plant room accommodates large specimens. Retractable roof is covered with rigid plastic.

A demonstration model of a sectional greenhouse that can be free-standing, as shown, or attached.

Fitted into an angle of the house, this sturdy stone-based greenhouse is an architectural asset.

The attached greenhouse may be a lean-to – that is, a lengthwise half-section of an even-span structure – built onto a dwelling or garage along its ridge line. Or it may be an even-span building attached at one end to a dwelling or other building. The attached type has convenient access and economy in its favor, as it is less costly to supply heat, light, and water to an attached building than to one at a distance. This is the type to choose, too, if the greenhouse is to double as a conservatory, living room, or play room. The attached house generally costs less to erect than a free-standing house because it has only three walls.

If the glass walls of either type of greenhouse extend to foundation level, the waist-high benches can be supplemented as growing space by using the ground beds

Greenhouse with concrete-block base is a harmonious extension of the existing lean-to because its roof continues the slope of the porch roof.

Solarium-conservatory is roomy enough to permit deck-chair lounging among the orchids and other plants.

beneath the benches. If a section of bench is omitted, it is possible to grow such tall plants as camellia and standard roses or shrubs.

The usefulness of a greenhouse is increased if it includes a shed to house a potting bench and storage space for tools, supplies, and soil mixtures. Here necessary tasks can be done without using the valuable space under glass. Barrels, galvanized cans or old oil drums make good containers for soil, sand, peat moss, and plant foods, and shelves can be added to hold pots, labels, stakes, and other supplies. When a separate gas-fired heating system is used, this is the place for the boiler, to prevent damage to plants from gas fumes.

Location and Exposure

Choosing the exact location for the greenhouse depends largely on the amount of sunlight available and the exposure of the spots being considered. A minimum of three hours' winter sunlight is necessary; more is better. It is desirable for the freestanding house to run north and south, with the potting shed to the north, and for the attached even-span house to run east and west, with the potting shed (or the dwelling) to the east. The lean-to greenhouse should face south if possible, although other exposures can be satisfactory. Even a northern exposure need not be ruled out if there is no other possible place for the greenhouse; fluorescent lights can be installed to supplement sunlight, and plants can be selected according to their relatively modest light requirements.

Equipment

Besides adequate sunlight for plant growth, greenhouse gardening requires a dependable source of heat, electricity for lights (and for automatic controls, if used), means of ventilating (and of additional cooling, if the house is used in hot climates or hot weather), shading (in certain seasons and for certain plants), a water supply, and means for maintaining high humidity (around 75 percent).

Greenhouse manufacturers and local heating contractors will be the best sources of information for the best way to heat a greenhouse in your locality. It is most economical, where feasible, to tie the greenhouse system into the heating system of the dwelling and add a separate set of controls.

Other factors being equal, hot-water heat is first choice for the greenhouse, as it doesn't dry out the soil and air as fast as steam, forced warm air, stove heat, or fan-driven electric heat. It is important to have a source of auxiliary heat, such as a small kerosene heater, in areas where storms cause occasional interruptions in electric service, unless special nonelectric thermostats are provided. An alarm system that sounds off whenever the temperature goes abnormally high or low (battery-operated so that it works even when electricity is off) is good insurance, too; it can save plants worth far more than its cost.

If a separate heating system is wanted, a standard type consists of a gas-fired copper coil water heater, equipped with a thermostat. (Oil or electricity may also be the heat source.) This supplies heat to a network of ordinary wall radiation (pipes) hung beneath the benches. The thermostat is placed upon the return to the heater, thus automatically regulating the water temperature. Keep a record of heating performance in varying weather for a short time in order to determine the exact thermostat setting required.

It is best to have as much radiation as space permits – this is economy during mild weather and a necessity under extreme conditions. Install a petcock at the highest point of the radiation to release accumulated air from time to time. Note that if gas is used, the boiler must be located outside the greenhouse (the fumes are deadly to plants), unless it is of an outside-vented type.

Probably the cheapest way to heat a greenhouse is with a small coke-burning stove placed at the north end of the freestanding house (or the far end of the attached even-span house), with its pipe slung under the ridge for the length of the house. A damper near the outlet helps preserve maximum heat. With experience in firing such a stove, attention will be needed only night and morning.

Without good – and draft-free – ventilation it would be necessary to abandon the greenhouse in summer, and heat buildup under the glass would be tremendous even in other seasons. Movable ventilation panels in roof and walls admit air as needed. These are either raised and lowered manually by push rods or gears or controlled automatically by thermostats and motor-driven controls. The latter system is virtually a necessity when the greenhouse owner isn't on hand during the day to adjust openings as necessary.

Ventilation, plus effective air cooling in hot weather, can be provided by climate-control systems consisting of various arrangements of air intakes and fans. Especially valuable in warm regions is the evaporative cooler which draws in outside air through water-soaked filters to provide both cooling and humidity, which would be reduced by a conventional air-conditioning machine.

You may wonder why a greenhouse is first built to admit a maximum of sun and then covered with whitewash or shades of slats, cloth, or tinted plastic to keep the sun out. The reason is, of course, that many plants cannot stand direct sunlight, and young plants and many mature ones need at least partial shade for best growth. Most foliage plants, as well as many flowering sorts, must have constant shading.

Shading was formerly supplied by painting the outside of the glass once or twice a year with whitewash and allowing it to weather off in the winter months when most light was needed. Nowadays most greenhouses are equipped with exterior roof curtains of slats, controlled with cords, that cast partial shade on plants. Another arrangement is to install roller shades inside. The roller ends are attached to the ridge rafter and tautly stretched wires between ridge and the plate (at the top of the wall) hold the extended shade in place.

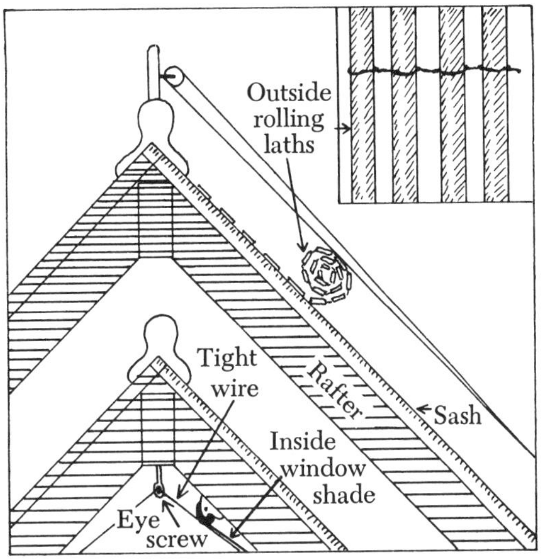

Two ways of shading the glass. Above, *exterior roof curtain of slats.* Below, *interior roller shade is mounted near ridge, held in place by wires.*

Other shading possibilities are curtains of muslin or other cloth sliding along parallel wires at the ridge and eave lines, or green-tinted plastic shading, cut to size and applied to the inside of the glass. These sheets block out around 60 percent of the sunlight and may be removed and reused repeatedly. There are also paste and powder preparations for direct application to the glass.

The necessary high humidity can be provided in the greenhouse by damping down walls, floors, and benches as often as necessary, perhaps several times a day, and by fogging the air (not the plants) with a mister or "fogger" nozzle on the garden hose. Foliage can be sprayed when it will dry off before evening, but it shouldn't be left wet for long periods or overnight.

There are available automatic humidifying devices in capacities for any size of house. Of special interest to growers of humidity-loving plants such as orchids are the automatic "foggers" that release bursts of mist at regular intervals. Humidifiers are well worth looking into for the gardener whose time is limited, as are the various automatic watering systems that are offered by manufacturers.

Equipment for watering *can* be as simple as a large barrel and a dipper, but it's obviously a great convenience to have one or more spigots in the greenhouse. Having more than one outlet will eliminate much hose-hauling in any size house but the smallest. With 2 or more hoses it is possible to keep different types of nozzles attached and ready for use.

Using the Greenhouse

The chapter on houseplants contains cultural information which applies equally well to growing the same plants in the greenhouse. Once the novice has become accustomed to his greenhouse's unique conditions, he will find that any plant that he has been growing successfully elsewhere will also thrive in the greenhouse. Attention must be given to maintaining ample humidity, to heat control, to ventilation (some is needed even in cold weather), and to finding just the right spot – on bench, shelf, or in the ground bed – for each plant.

Don't try to pack too many plants into bench space: give them room to "breathe" and to develop properly, if necessary by adding hanging shelves or baskets, brackets, and other space-making devices. Vines can be trained up and out of the way in corners or along back walls. The unlighted underbench space can be put to good use for germinating seeds, resting plants on vacation, and even for growing certain plants with low light needs. If benches are of waterproof construction, consider installing fluorescent lights beneath them, thus virtually doubling your growing space.

Control of Pests

Control of pests and diseases in the greenhouse begins with giving plants room to breathe and good air circulation: confined conditions can breed trouble. Cleanliness and neatness pay off; have clean benches, pots, and floors; and keep corners and underbench spaces free of trash and of weeds, which can be disease carriers. Foliage should be sprayed or washed regularly – but never at a time of day or in weather when it can't dry fairly quickly. This discourages the start of pest infestation, as does regular fogging of the house with an all-purpose insecticide, which can be applied from an aerosol container if the house isn't a large one.

Such fogging treatment, carried out every 3 weeks or so in the evening so that the house can be left closed overnight, should be applied with attention to manufacturers' warnings and directions about the chemicals used. Wear a mask if the manufacturer advises it, and stay out of the greenhouse until at least several hours have passed since spraying.

Fumigating with smoke-producing preparations is suitable only for the detached

A walk into spring in a two-bench greenhouse. Dampening the partly flagged floor will add humidity.

French doors can close off a small lean-to adjoining a living room. Hanging plants add to capacity.

house and should not be used in any greenhouse attached to a dwelling.

When specific evidence of disease or pest infestation is seen, measures similar to those outlined in the chapter on diseases and pests can be followed.

If some of your plants start to languish despite proper care, consider whether they are in need of a resting period after their time of most vigorous performance. Very few plants will be at their best for 12 months a year; so when signs of weariness appear, it may be time to taper off watering and place the plants under the bench (or, in summer, outdoors in a shady spot) to rest.

Finally, consult some of the excellent recent books on greenhouse gardening, and investigate whether your state agricultural experiment station offers publications on the subject.

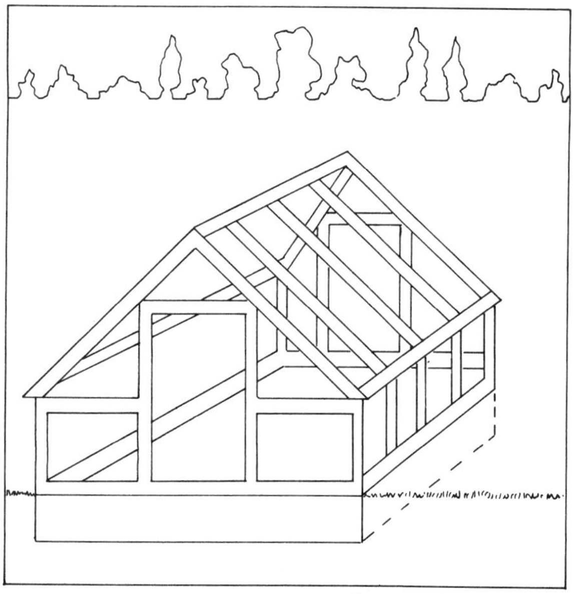

Framing of an even-span greenhouse, shown without potting-shed section. Foundation goes below frost line.

Building Your Own Greenhouse

The illustrations show sketch plans and details of some simple and fairly inexpensive greenhouses that can be built by the experienced handyman. The even-span greenhouse can be built as a free-standing structure or may be attached at one end to a dwelling; it may or may not include the potting-shed section. Different types of lean-tos are possible as are window greenhouses. There is also the sun-pit to consider as well as such an adjunct to greenhouse gardening as a lath shelter.

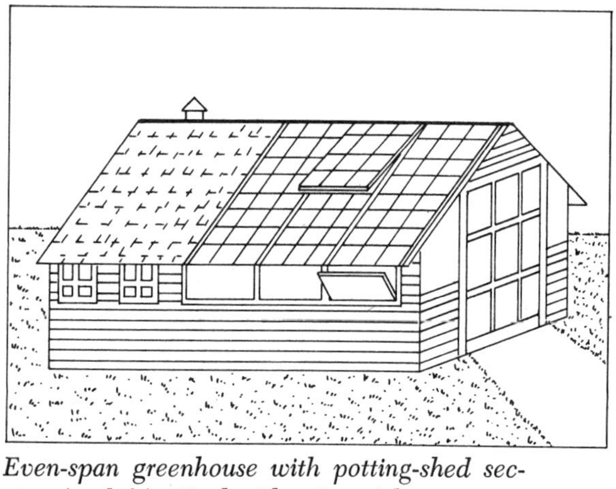

Even-span greenhouse with potting-shed section (at left). *Each side of roof has a ventilator.*

Unless construction projects are an enjoyable hobby, or cost is the first consideration, it is usually most satisfactory to buy a greenhouse from the manufacturer, perhaps doing some or all of the assembly work yourself.

The even-span house, like the lean-to, can be framed entirely of 2-by-4s. For long life, these should be of cypress wood; however, other woods will be satisfactory if properly painted. It is desirable to place the house on a foundation, which must of course be perfectly level and which should extend below the frost line, which varies from one region of the country to another. The top of the foundation should extend for 3 or 4 inches above the ground to protect the sill and framing from moisture and possible termite attack.

All elements of the frame should receive 2 coats of good ready-mixed exterior paint before being placed together. If this is not feasible, paint each side of each joint *heavily* when nailing in place; greenhouse hu-

For the handy gardener, a greenhouse to build at small cost. Ribs are of plywood.

Plastic covers the finished house. Plan No. 5946, "Plastic-Covered Greenhouse," is available from most state agricultural colleges.

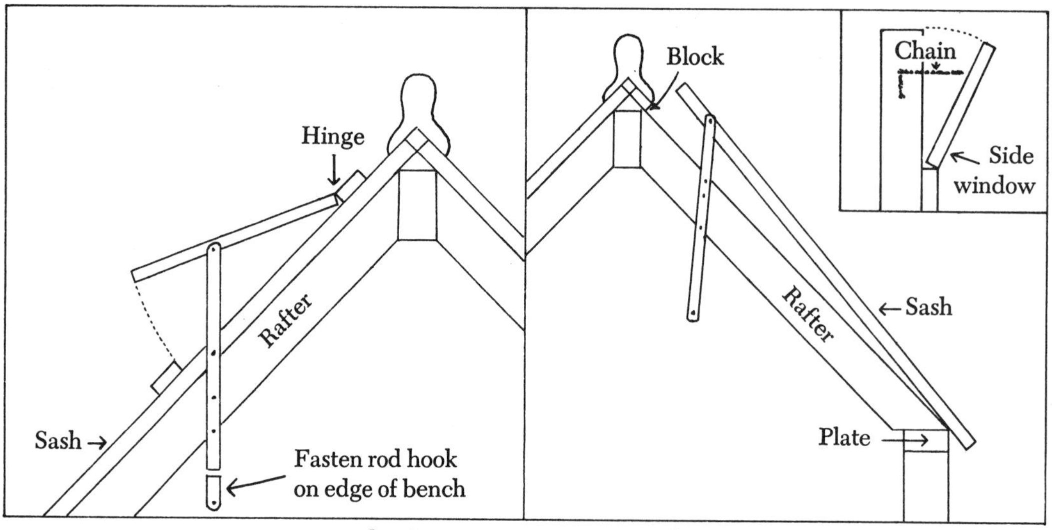

Details of two types of roof ventilators.

midity will quickly rot unprotected lumber. The sash, too, should be painted with 2 coats before being put into position.

The lower walls can be covered with roofing paper tacked directly to the studs; tongue-and-groove siding is then nailed over the paper, or another exterior finish is applied. It is well worth your while to cover the inside with sheathing and fill the space with any good insulating material.

Hotbed sash (stock size, 3 feet by 6) makes a good roof for the even-span house. The upper portion of the walls can be glazed with panes of glass held within the framing with quarter-round molding. It is a good plan to have a roof ventilator on each side of the ridge and at least one movable side window above the bench on each side. The side windows should be hinged at the bottom to open outward on a chain. Fastenings on all movable panels must be very strong, to prevent their tearing loose in a windstorm.

One way to place the ventilator is to hinge the ventilator sash to the plate, positioning its upper edge 2 or 3 inches away from the ridge. A board is inserted to fill the space above the sash and to hold the galvanized ridging. The sash is moved by a push rod consisting of a perforated piece of heavy strap iron whose holes slip over a heavy nail or screw in the side of the rafter; this permits holding the panel open as much or as little as desired.

The second method of mounting the vent sash is to remove the glass from the top half of a roof sash. Nail a cross member at the top of the remaining glass and mount a second sash on top of the open section, hinging it near the ridge. This panel is controlled by a metal rod or length of strap iron, ending in a hook which may attach to a screw eye on the bench.

To keep the roof from leaking, which would be very injurious to the plants, first coat the previously painted rafters with a mixture of white lead and oil (not too thick) and nail the prepainted sash in place while the mixture is still wet. Butt the sash together on top of the rafters, and fill any cracks completely with putty. Nail a cypress lattice strip, also bedded in white lead, over the joint. Lattice strips should also be nailed over the side edges of the movable panels, to lap over the adjoining sash. Should dripping occur along the ventilator in spite of this, an inconspicuous metal gutter can be nailed to the rafter to carry the water away from the plants to the floor, where it will do no harm.

Where the roof sashes come together above the ridge, tack a piece of heavy roofing paper. This is both for insulation and to keep out water. It is desirable to add a

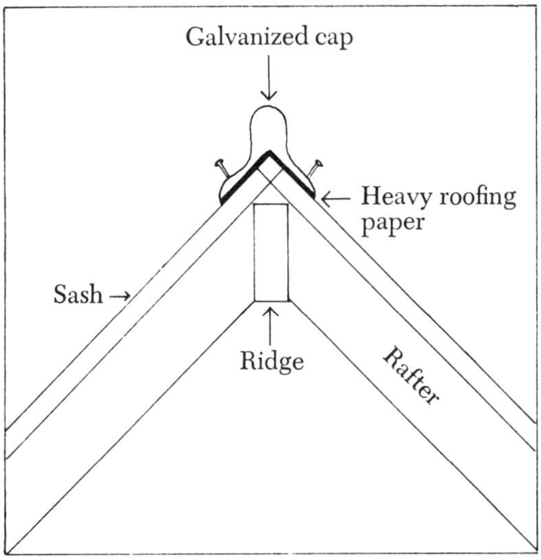

To prevent leaks at ridge, roofing paper is tacked on, then covered with galvanized cap.

strip of formed sheet metal in a stock form; this is nailed to the sash through the roofing paper, which is then trimmed off evenly.

The end of the even-span greenhouse can be fitted with another hotbed sash, attached with hooks and weather-stripped so that it may be fastened tightly in winter and removed, if desired, in summer. By admitting light clear to the ground, this sash makes under-bench space more useful. A glazed door may replace the sash and be installed on hinges to open outward.

The entire structure, once assembled, should be given a third coat of paint. It can't be overemphasized that only the best quality paint should be used on the greenhouse. Without proper painting precautions, the life expectancy of a house such as this is from 5 to 8 years; kept well-painted and caulked, it will last indefinitely.

The interior of an even-span house can consist of 2 benches, each 3 feet wide, with a 30-inch walk between. Pave the walk with stone, brick, or concrete, or leave it unpaved but provide a duckboard walk to keep your feet from the damp soil.

The benches must be strongly built, well supported, and fastened to the frame 3 feet from the ground. For long life make benches of redwood, or use asbestos cement board for the bottoms and redwood for the low sides. Place legs on concrete foundations or flat stones so that they won't sink into the ground when loaded.

The water service line, it should go without saying, must be laid below the frost line. A gas line or electric cable can often be run in the same trench; check with a local expert.

Lean-to greenhouses are even simpler to build, as each has, of course, only 3 walls. One type can be built against a house wall with, preferably, a southern exposure. The unpaved floor helps to maintain high hu-

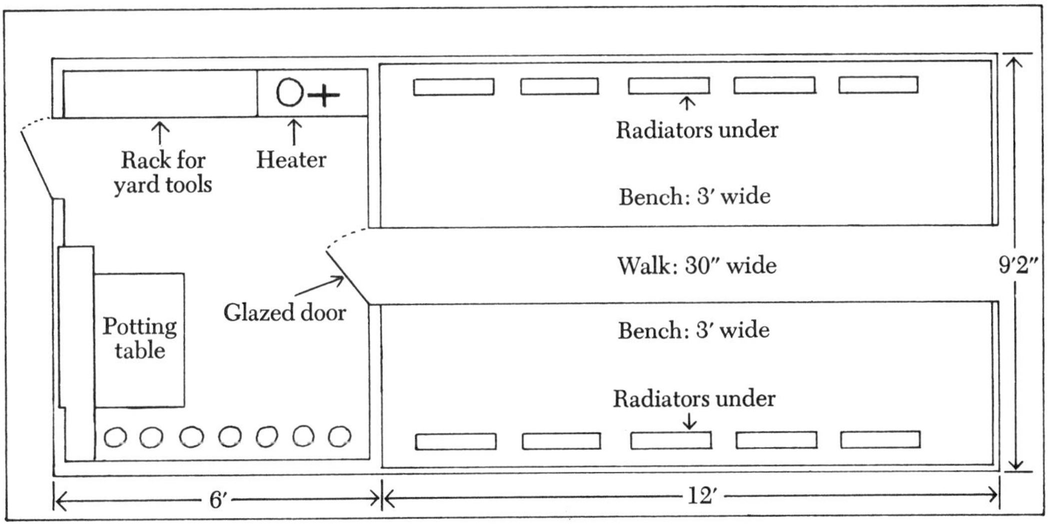

Interior plan of even-span greenhouse.

midity. The only masonry is a foundation of concrete blocks bedded in the ground and holding the wooden sill a couple of inches off the ground. The framework is 2 by 4s (ideally of cypress), and the lower walls are clapboard on the outside, sheathing on the inside, with insulation between. The only millwork required is a door and a ventilating panel in the roof, for which a large cellar sash may be used. The door is glazed or unglazed, as preferred. Any lumber yard can quote a price on materials for the whole thing, or a wrecking company will be a cheaper source. A house made of second-hand elements will need more work to make it presentable. The comments on painting as you go and on minor construction details of the even-span house apply to the lean-tos as well.

A simple lean-to greenhouse. Top, *framing plan.* Center, *interior layout; heat comes from basement window* (left). Below, *exterior of house.*

The only glass in this lean-to is in the ventilating sash. The rest of the house is covered with your choice of plastic or fiberglass material. Long in use, a material called Celloglass is still satisfactory; or use more recent materials that are available locally.

A second type of lean-to, though also simple, is larger and more substantial than the first. It is made up of multiples of hotbed sash, which come, as noted, in a standard size (6 feet by 3) and also as half sash, 3 feet by 3. The frame is constructed so that sashes of these dimensions will center on its members. The roof can be increased to any size that utilizes either or both of the basic units. One of the larger sashes may be hinged to one of the smaller (upper) ones to make a ventilator. Houses built all of hotbed sash admit light underneath the benches, doubling the growing space.

A variation of this lean-to plan would have the lower walls built solid, as previously described, and any stock sash of suitable size used for the upper walls. A portion of the solid lower wall might have a sash or two set in to admit under-bench light.

If entrance to the lean-to can be arranged from the house or garage rather than from the outdoors, bench space may be increased. A location over a cellar window allows heat to be obtained from the cellar ceiling. However, emergency heating

House plants, forced bulbs and seedlings thrive in window greenhouse, easily tended from indoors.

A window greenhouse may be built with sash hinged to board fastened to house (left). *Hooks hold sash to wall.* Right, *inside view. Glass panes are set into side walls to increase light; keep glass six inches from bottom, three inches from inside edge.*

apparatus (such as a small kerosene heater) should be on hand if the cellar is the only source of heat.

Window Greenhouses, Sun Pits, Window Hotbeds, and Lath Shelters

When it isn't possible to have a full-scale greenhouse or when you would simply like to get an early start with seed sowing without cluttering up the house, a window greenhouse may be the answer. These can easily be built at home or purchased, in a range of styles and sizes, from greenhouse manufacturers. Some are large enough to permit quite a display of flowering plants.

Controlling temperature in these structures is quite easy. The window house is hung against the window frame with gate hooks or corner irons and is weather stripped around the edges. It is ventilated by raising the hinged sash and warmed from within the room by raising the window sash. A thermometer hung in the box checks temperature, and humidity is raised by frequent misting or spraying.

Sun Pits

Another structure that is especially useful for starting seedlings in spring and for carrying over half-hardy plants in winter is an unheated, or sun pit, greenhouse. Partly sunk in the ground and glazed on only one side, the sun-pit has walls of concrete, stone, or cinder block. The glazed half of

Pleasing design makes an attractive garden feature of a lath-house shelter for plants.

the roof faces south. A small sash may also be included in the solid roof section to provide ventilation in warm weather. Most commonly heated only by the sun, the pit house may be made more useful by laying heating cables in sand under the soil beds. Many cool-temperature plants will thrive if a minimum temperature of 40 degrees can be maintained by artificial heat or by covering the glass with old rugs or mats at night in extremely cold weather.

Window Hotbeds

A basement window greenhouse is a miniature version of the pit house just described. It receives its heat from the basement and should also be covered with rugs or mats on very cold nights. Heating cable and a thermostat can be installed if more warmth is desired.

Lath Shelters

A lath house or shelter can be a utilitarian structure, serving as a growing or propagating area for plants that require the protection of partial shade or as a cool outdoor sitting room ornamented by choice plants from the shade-loving category. Such shelters are especially useful in regions of high temperatures and intense sun. Ferns, caladium, various kinds of begonia, fuchsia, and many of the more delicate bulbous subjects can be successfully grown outdoors even in difficult climates when the sunlight and the wind's force are broken.

Lath house protects begonias, fuchsias, and other shade-lovers from damage by sun and wind.

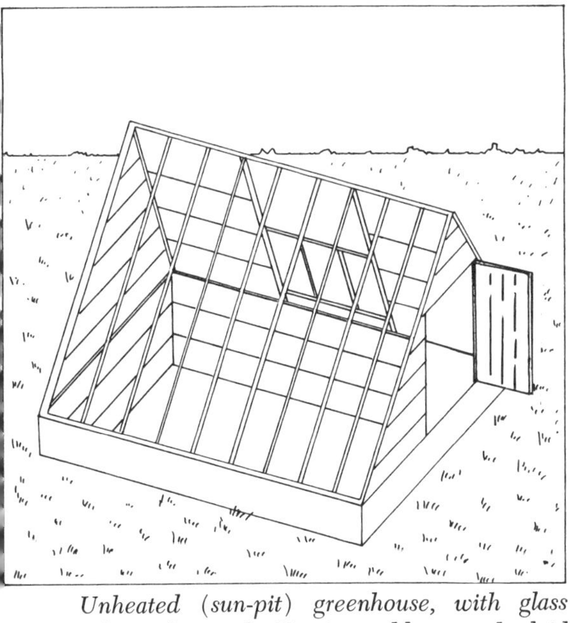

Unheated (sun-pit) greenhouse, with glass side to the south. Heating cables may be laid under soil beds to increase house's usefulness.

A delightfully inviting garden house or grotto built of lath can be created by hanging pots of ferns, other ornamentals, even orchids, along the sides and from the roof. Rock gardens or raised beds along the base of the walls make a place for a collection of choice shade-loving plants. The whole can be floored with flagstone or brick, with spaces left for planting creeping thyme or other "pavement" plants. A small recirculating fountain, electrically operated, makes it possible to have a miniature pool and waterfall to complete the effect of coolness.

Flowering plants brighten a window in late winter. Below a philodendron meandering along a wire are pots of blooming hyacinths, narcissus, African-violets, crocus, and tulips. Plants not in bloom are episcia (upper shelf) and Christmas cactus.

CHAPTER 19

Houseplants

The artist makes the house beautiful –
Growing plants give the house its spirit.
–W. E. D.

The cultivators of houseplants indoors are divided into two classes: those who raise them for love of the plants and those who have a few plants for indoor decoration. Naturally these classes overlap to some extent, and cultural needs are virtually the same no matter what category your houseplant interest falls into.

THE CHIEF REQUIREMENTS OF HOUSEPLANTS ARE:

1. Light
2. Suitable potting
3. Water (soil moisture)
4. Moist air, correct temperature and ventilation
5. Care of leaves
6. Food
7. Protection against pests

Light

It is almost safe to say that all blooming plants should be placed in the sun for at least a part of the day and turned every few days for even growth. During dark winter days there is little chance of many indoor plants being injured by too much sun. Ferns, vines, and other foliage plants do well at north and east windows but plants that produce flowers need exposure to the south and west. Ivy, philodendron and several other plants will thrive away from windows, but all must have some light.

Even some plants that are set close to or under reading lamps with incandescent bulbs make better growth. But where daylight is insufficient to support good plant growth or is lacking completely, the best results by far are obtained from fluorescent lamps. There are several kinds manufactured especially for plants; and as research continues, further innovations and improvements can be expected.

Tiered stands and carts complete with fluorescent light tubes can be purchased as can practical table-top fluorescent light stands of varying sizes. The hobbyist-handyman can build simple or elaborate set-ups for houseplants like African-violets (especially responsive to artificial light) that can also be used in the spring for starting plants from seed for later outdoor planting. Fluorescent lights make it possible to grow plants in basements and other unlighted parts of a house, the only other requirements then being proper temperature and humidity. Where more decorative effects are necessary, fluorescent tubes can be fastened inside planters and room dividers or built-in cabinets and book shelves.

Potting and Repotting

It is helpful for those who expect to do any great amount of gardening to have a potting bench. Having things handy makes tasks light. The equipment can consist of a strong table, some barrels to hold sifted soil, sand and peat moss; some large containers with covers to hold dried cow manure or sheep manure, bone meal or superphosphate, and other materials. The bench can be an old kitchen table with the legs lengthened 6 or 7 inches to make stooping unnecessary and a few boards nailed to the back and sides at the top to keep the soil from spilling off. A table 3 by 3 feet can easily be made of scrap lumber. Thirty-six inches is a good height for most people.

Where there is no garden room, it is well to appropriate a space 6 by 8 feet in the corner of the garage or cellar for this purpose. This confines the mess, and the gardener has a chance to vary his outdoor tasks on brisk, chilly days when prolonged outdoor occupation is uncomfortable.

A general purpose potting mixture for most houseplants can be composed of two parts of soil, well worked and friable, one part of sand and another of finely ground peat moss, compost or leaf mold. These ingredients, sifted through a rather fine screen, can be mixed with bone meal or superphosphate, and dried manure when a richer mixture is needed.

More attention should be paid to the condition of the soil than to its richness. Soil which has sufficient drainage and enough humus to hold moisture can easily be supplied with food in liquid or solid form. Most garden centers, nurseries, and garden departments of stores offer prepackaged bags of potting soils for various houseplants. Some contain Vermiculite or Perlite, which help retain moisture, as well as other ingredients in varying proportions.

Contrary to belief, experiments have proven that glazed decorative pots are satisfactory receptacles. If watering is carefully done, some plants, such as succulents and moisture-loving kinds, even do well in pots without bottom drainage holes.

It will be readily seen that clean pots are essential. All clay, scum, or dried slimy substances which would tend to stop the ready passage of air and water should be removed by washing and scrubbing. Soak new clay pots for a few days or boil them for a little while before using.

The potting itself is simple. First, place over the drainage hole two or three pieces of broken pots. This is important; break up a few pots if necessary with a hammer. Now put in the growing soil loosely. Do not push it down. Jar the bottom sharply against the table to settle it. When it is full enough, place the plant in position, spreading the roots over the soil toward the pot sides. More soil is now added until the pot is about full. Firm with the thumbs about the plant roots. Now water, and allow the soil to settle. When fully compacted by watering, the soil should be from ½ inch to

Checking on when to repot. 1. Removing plant from pot. 2. Plant needs larger pot. 3. Plant needs smaller pot. 4. Combing out roots lightly before repotting in fresh soil.

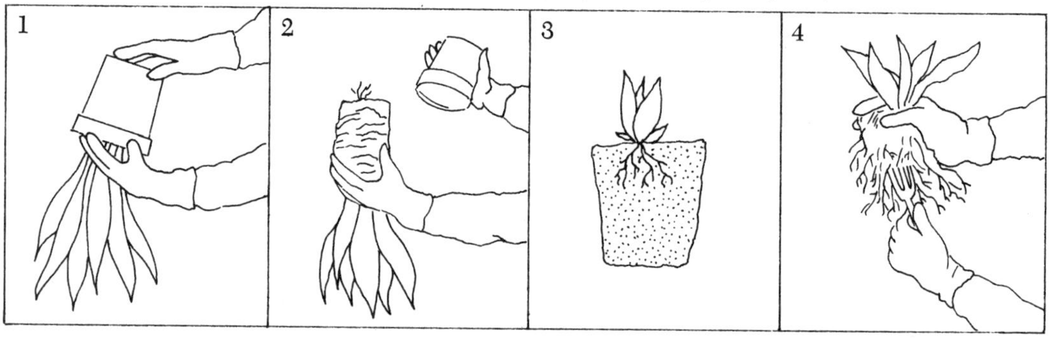

an inch below the top of the pot, according to its size, to facilitate future watering. Keep in a shady place a few days.

Repotting or shifting from one container to another is necessary to keep plants growing well. To see when this is necessary, first water well, then remove the plant from the pot by inverting and striking it upon a table while holding the soil and plant with the other hand. Sometimes a plant becomes so root-bound that the pot must be broken to get it out. This is better than injuring the roots by cutting. Do not be in a hurry to repot.

A very common error made in potting is to think that the greater the amount of soil the better for the plant. This is not the case. Flowering plants give the best bloom when they become "pot bound"; that is, their roots must nearly fill the soil mass in the pot. But then, they must receive plenty of food. Geraniums and many other plants bloom best when slightly pot-bound. Pandanus is still well potted when it thrusts its roots to the top of the pot.

There is no hard and fast rule as to when to repot. The seedling may require several changes each season while larger plants (Chinese rubber plants, azalea) need it only once every two years. But many plants need repotting in the spring, and a yearly examination of the roots is wise. After the long winter indoors the favorable conditions of summer enable them to recover from the shock of repotting better than they would at other times.

Do not hesitate, however, to repot when the plant needs it. A 3-day period in the shade, either indoors or outdoors in warm weather, usually gives the healthy plant a chance to recuperate. Sometimes the need for change is shown by a slight yellowing of the foliage and a forcing of the roots through the drainage hole. Such roots should be combed with a strong fork and broken ends cut off clean.

If upon examination the ball shows no roots at all but only a sticky mass of mud, the soil should be removed, even washed off the roots, and the plant repotted in good, fresh soil. This condition is a general indication of consistent overwatering and the need for a smaller pot.

If the ball reveals a mass of fine roots around the edge and they seem to be getting out of bounds, a larger pot is indicated. For fast, hearty growers, a pot 2 inches bigger may be required; for the slower growing, a pot 1 inch larger will be sufficient. Use a large label or stick to ram the soil mixture down between the pot and plant roots so there will be no air spaces.

Watering

Probably more plants die from overwatering each year than from any other cause. General rules are misleading, but the idea is to water well but not so often. Get enough water on the plant to thoroughly moisten all the soil in the container. Excess water must be allowed to run off freely. Plants do not like "wet feet." Jardinieres are dangerous if the plant is allowed to stand in water. There are exceptions to this rule, but not many. Fast-growing plants stand soggy conditions better than slow-growing ones. Examine the soil for about one-half inch below the surface to see if it is dry before applying more water. Larger pots require less frequent watering than

When very dry, a house plant can be watered by immersion in water to rim of pot.

smaller ones because the larger volume of soil dries out more slowly.

Daily watering is not necessary unless the soil is bone dry, but daily inspection is. Some can tell when to water by rapping a pot with the knuckles. A rap on a pot which gives a hollow sound indicates dryness, but a solid sound indicates that the soil is pressed tight against the sides of the pot by the expansion which sufficient moisture gives to its contents.

Never just sprinkle the topsoil but apply the water directly to it until it runs out the bottom. Sometimes a pot may be so dried out that the soil is cracked or shrunk away from the sides. In this instance the top water will run through to the bottom without the thorough wetting of the soil. Then place the pot in a bucket of water so that it will enter from the bottom until complete moistening takes place. Do not let water come over the rim of the pot.

A collector's cactus garden grows in a planter tray set in a sunny spot. Soil mixture has been topped with white sand.

Humidity and Temperature

Many disappointments with indoor plants result because of the hot, dry condition of the air in most homes.

A dry heat of about 75 degrees is the top for plants indoors (and for people, too!), and the list which will stand this much is quite small. Philodendron, snake plant, rubber plant, dracena are among the few. African-violet, episcia, and croton are examples of plants which will tolerate high temperature but not dry air. Most plants thrive at from 55 to 65 degrees. How to keep this in our homes is a problem, as most people feel decidedly chilly at these temperatures.

Plants do not need an even temperature maintained at all times. Cool rooms are better than those kept constantly warm; but if the temperature is high in daytime, it is a decided benefit, and flowering is prolonged, if it is reduced about 10 degrees at night. Not, however, lower than 55 degrees. Drafts and sudden changes must be prevented. Our grandmothers, who covered the plants with cloth or newspapers when the fire in the stove was permitted to run low, had the right idea. During very cold weather in winter, it may be necessary to slip several newspaper sections between the window and plants, especially at night when temperatures drop fast.

On the other hand, do not forget that fresh air is essential to all plants. See that they get some of it by opening the window farthest away from them if for only a few minutes a day. Thoroughly ventilate an adjoining room, and then open the door into the one containing the plants. No harm will be done even if the temperature goes down to 55 degrees for a short time if no drafts are allowed.

Gas is the worst enemy of houseplants. Even a small amount of it in the air is almost fatal. If you heat your rooms directly with open gas stoves, plant culture is almost an impossibility. Just laugh when anyone tells you that plants in sleeping rooms are detrimental to health. If plants

A cactus collection for an apartment window sill includes aloes, opuntia, euphorbia, haworthia, Hylocereus undatus.

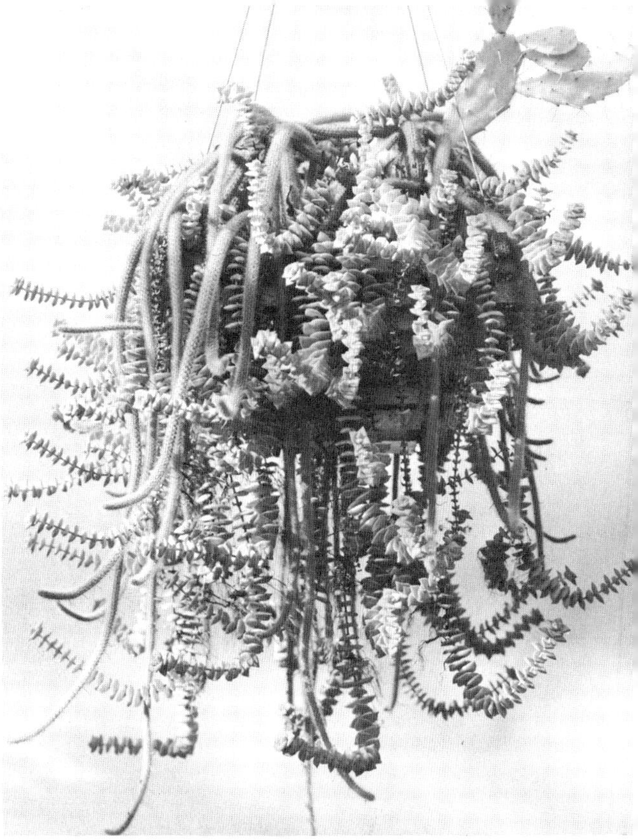

Crassula repens, *a succulent, in a hanging pottery container with opuntia and snake cactus.*

gave off injurious gas the human race would have disappeared long ago.

Along with temperature importance is that of humidity. For our own health we should use all the devices possible to obtain it in winter. Few homes have it to a sufficient degree for the health of both people and plants. In greenhouses and conservatories, humidity is attained by spraying benches, floors, and the plants themselves. Tests in well-managed greenhouses indicate that the humidity runs 75 to 85 percent, whereas in the average living room it runs 20 to 30 percent.

This condition can be somewhat overcome by keeping pans filled with water on radiators and boiling water on stoves. Room humidifiers of varying water capacity are now being sold in home appliance stores and can benefit both plants and people. Of definite value for increasing atmospheric moisture are shallow trays of peb-

A table-top or dish garden of cacti requires little care, will survive without watering during the owner's absences of a week or two.

A piece of Mexican pottery is the setting for a dish garden of cacti and succulents.

bles and water on which houseplants sit. And of course, the more plants, the greater the humidity.

Care of Leaves

Apply a fine misty spray with a bulb syringe sprinkler every day or so. It may flush off deposits of soot and dust and in any case is beneficial by helping maintain humidity. Plants with smooth, strong leaves should be sponged with lukewarm water and mild soapsuds once a month. For ferns, palms, and rubber plants, mild soapsuds (not detergents) can be used every 10 days as a spray instead of just plain water. Be sure to get the under side of the leaves in wetting and washing and do the job in the morning so that they have a chance to dry before night. Protect from direct sunlight while wet. Plants with hairy foliage (African-violets, for example) should not have water on their leaves in the sun or late in the day as the temperature drops.

Fertilizers for Houseplants

Plants with heavy roots require a heavier, more loamy soil; plants with fine, fibrous roots need a more open, sandy soil. For quick-growing plants a quart of sheep manure or dried cow manure may be incorporated in each bushel of soil. For slow-growers a quart of bone meal or superphosphate is better. (One to 3 tablespoons to each 5-inch pot.)

A few handfuls of cow, horse, or sheep manure in a bucket of water make a good liquid fertilizer for healthy plants about to bloom. Applied to a sickly or dormant plant, it does no good and may harm rather than benefit. First repot, water, and sun your plant until it starts active growth; then gradually feed it until it flourishes. Dilute the liquid manure to the color of very weak tea. Quick-growing plants may have it every 10 days; slow growers, once every 30 days.

A solution of chemical plant food, 1 tablespoon to 3 gallons of water, may be applied as a substitute for liquid manure. There are various commercial fertilizers formulated for houseplants, either to be mixed with water or applied dry, and usually all are equally valuable. Never use either liquid or dry plant food upon dry soil. Water first, then fertilize. Never permit plant food to touch leaves. Don't use lime on houseplants unless specifically directed to do so. Loosen the soil carefully on the top of the pot as frequently as possible.

Pest Problems

Healthy houseplants growing under reasonably ideal conditions are less likely to be victims of pests and related troubles. The worst problem encountered by African-violets is the cyclamen mite, the same microscopic pest that attacks such outdoor-garden plants as delphinium and straw-

In mild climates (or in the summertime in the north), house plants can be ornamental outdoors, too.

berry. It causes distorted, gnarled, and stunted growth, most apparent in an African-violet in the unnaturally tight, new growth of the rosette and imperfect flowers. Sodium selenate, a very poisonous systemic chemical, is the best control as the poison is taken up in the plant tissues where it waits to destroy any sucking pest like the mite. Whereas many gardeners are understandably loath to use the systemic poisons in their outdoor soils, using them in pots where the soil area is confined does make some sense, especially when the pest is as formidable as the cyclamen mite. A second method used by African-violet hobbyists is to dip the plants in a solution of Kelthane, 1 teaspoon to 1 gallon of water so leaves and crown are covered.

Other indoor pests likely to appear are more easily controlled. They include aphids, usually in clusters; scale insects, especially on palm, pittosporum, citrus, bromeliads; mealybug, white and wax-coated, on African-violet and many other common houseplants; red spider mite, minute web-spinning spiders that suck leaf juices to cause blotching and mottling; and white fly on heliotrope and geranium. Malathion, mixed according to directions, controls aphids, scale, white fly, and mealybug; Kelthane controls red spider mites that can also be washed off under the tap. An aerosol bomb, used according to directions so that the plants are not injured, is a quick, handy method of checking most houseplant pests. Washing strong-leaved plants with a hose spray and syringing of others will destroy many pests.

A corner of a breakfast room or sun porch is turned into a miniature conservatory by the addition of shelves and brackets. Curtains are cold-night protection for plants.

Deep window embrasures make ideal display and growing areas. Ferns, begonias, citrus, and a tree-form heliotrope grace this window.

Summer Care

After a long winter indoors and after any spring repotting, most houseplants appreciate a summer vacation outdoors in fresh air. Be careful to cxpose them to sun gradually as their soft growth is easily scorched. Provide open sun for the bloomers (slight protection for begonias), semishade for many foliage plants and the more dense shade for the ferns and orchids. Do not overlook summer watering, and before taking indoors in early fall examine the plants for insects.

Most plants can be plunged (still in their pots, of course) in open ground. Bury to the rim, placing a concave piece of pot below the drainage hole to keep it open. When ready to bring indoors, knock the clinging soil from the pot and wash it outside and around the rim so that it starts the winter clean.

Geraniums which have bloomed in late winter can be cut back or discarded in the spring as soon as 3-inch cuttings have been taken for rooting in the cold frame or propagating bed. Azaleas and other shrubby houseplants especially thrive outdoors during the summer. And of course, such bulbs as the amaryllis must be kept in active growth to renew their vitality if they are going to flower again in the winter.

A table set near a window holds a flourishing array of begonias, with flowering African-violets, daffodils and amaryllis for color.

Foliage plants chosen for variety of form and coloration make a fascinating collection for this bay window.

Some Important Foliage Plants

Copper-leaf (*Acalypha macafeana*). A colorful plant, with copper-colored leaves as its name implies. It is propagated by heel cuttings. A temperature of 65 degrees is best.

St. Bernard-lily (*Anthericum liliago*). A plant that grows rapidly from stolons like the strawberry plant. Because of its rapid growth and trailing habit, it is very useful for hanging baskets. Propagation is by stolons, although it is sometimes perpetuated by division or seeds. Usually, the plant does not suffer from the effects of overwatering.

Norfolk Island pine (*Araucaria excelsa*). This plant is a beautiful evergreen, a fairly rapid grower, and quite tolerant. As a small plant it makes an excellent table centerpiece. It requires a medium rich soil and a temperature of 70 degrees. During the summer it thrives in partial shade.

Asparagus-fern. This plant is a native of South Africa. The species *Asparagus sprengeri* and *A. plumosus* are the two most common types used as houseplants. Both produce long fronds which occasionally bear red to black berries. Overwatering and a hot, dry atmosphere will cause the leaves to drop.

Cast-iron plant (*Aspidistra elatior*). This plant easily rates as the most tolerant houseplant. It will live for months without direct sunlight; it doesn't object to too much or too little water, and it can withstand fluctuations of temperature. Because of its extreme tolerance the plant is put to many uses.

The leaves are large with long petioles arising from the rhizome. The drooping leaves give the plant a somewhat graceful appearance. Insects seldom attack it. An occasional bath will keep it attractive at all times.

Birds-nest fern (*Asplenium nidus-avis*). This fern makes an interesting houseplant. The leaves are broad and of a delicate green color. The arrangement of the crown suggests a nest for birds. Strong sunlight will spot the leaves, and too much moisture may cause a loss of color. It likes peat moss and a little lime.

Grape-ivy (*Cissus rhombifolia*). An excellent trailing, evergreen plant with 3-parted leaflets. Each leaf is about 4 inches long. New plants are grown easily from cuttings.

Coleus. *Coleus blumei* is the most commonly cultivated species. To produce a bushy, well-balanced plant the stems require frequent pinching to encourage branching. Full sunlight, high humidity, and a temperature of 70 degrees are the cultural requirements. The easiest method of propagation is by cuttings, although seeds germinate readily and provide many interesting variations in pattern. Mealybugs are the worst enemies. Frequent washing and syringing will help to keep the insects in check. Touching the insects with a wisp of cotton dipped in alcohol insures instant death.

Jade-plant (*Crassula arborescens*). A slow-growing plant with very fleshy, oval leaves and a thick stem, growing well in partial shade with moderate amounts of water. Most dish gardens contain at least one of these plants. They are propagated from the tip cuttings or the fleshy leaves. A warm temperature with moderate humidity is necessary.

Umbrella plant (*Cyperus alternifolius*). A peculiar-looking plant which derives its common name from the appearance of the foliage, a long petiole with leaves (blade) arranged similarly to the ribs of an open upright umbrella. It is native to Africa and therefore needs a warm temperature (65 degrees) and plenty of water. Fertilize occasionally. Sometimes mealybugs are a serious pest.

House hollyfern (*Cyrtomium falcatum*). This attractive plant has dark green, glossy, pinnate leaves. The fronds are long and graceful.

A dwarf lemon on the left and a gardenia plant on the right flank "kitchen plants" grown from citrus seed (second from left), a pineapple top, two avocado seeds. Grasslike plant in foreground is chlorophytum.

Bird's-nest fern (Asplenium nidus-avis).

Grape-ivy (Cissus rhombifolia).

Dumb cane (*Dieffenbachia seguine*). Grown as a potted plant because of its broad, 5- to 7-inch variegated leaves, it is propagated from short stem cuttings, planted horizontally in sand. The common name refers to the fact that if a stem is chewed, the juice will temporarily paralyze the tongue.

Dracena (*Dracaena*). Beautiful, durable plants, grown for their variegated foliage. The genus *Cordyline* is similar to *Dracaena*, differing only in the flower parts. *D. fragrans* (corn-plant) is most common, with its large corn-like leaves. *Cordyline australis* (*indivisa*) has long, drooping, narrow

Coleus, an easy and colorful plant to grow either indoors or in the garden.

leaves. The leaves of *D. godseffiana* appear in whorls on the stem, 3 to 4 inches long, with numerous white spots; flowers are greenish yellow. *C. terminalis* has large leaves (12 to 30 inches long by 3 to 4 inches wide) in many colors. *D. goldieana* is a fine foliage plant with its broad, rounded leaves (7 to 8 inches long and 4 to 5 inches wide) of white and green bands. Sponging the leaves with water at frequent intervals will improve their growth. Moderately warm temperature is necessary. The leaves will brown at the tips if overwatered.

Rubber plant (*Ficus elastica*). Magnificent foliage plants always in vogue. They are sensitive to overwatering and prefer partial shade. A temperature of 60 to 65 degrees is best. All rubber plants will do best outdoors during the summer. Frequent sponging will remove dust and eliminate clogging of the breathing pores. *Ficus pandurata* (Fiddle-leaf fig) with its large, fiddle-shaped and deeply veined leaves, is even more attractive than the common *F. elastica*. *Ficus pumila* is a dainty, trailing plant with small leaves close to the stems which cling to wall surfaces. The dense growth and rich green color make it desirable.

Silk-oak (*Grevillea robusta*). Not a particularly showy plant, but a very rapid, vigorous grower. In its native land of Australia it becomes a tree 150 feet tall. As a pot plant it produces a slender stem with long horizontal branches and feathery fern-like leaves. The usual method of propagation is by seed.

English ivy (*Hedera helix*). A very popular plant, perhaps because it does well in places receiving little sunlight and heat. It makes rapid growth under normal conditions and can be trained to supports for unusual effects. If a bushy plant is desired, the ends of the branches should be pinched off. They may be used as cuttings to propagate new plants. Occasionally aphids attack the young foliage; use a spray of nicotine sulfate or Malathion. For red spider mites, use Kelthane, according to directions. The variegated ivies are attractive but not as vigorous as the ordinary kind. A number of other kinds, self-branching or semierect, are worth a trial.

Babys-tears (*Helxine soleiroli*). A dainty creeping plant with very small leaves, forming a dense mat. It is a favorite for kitchen window sills where the high temperature and abundance of moisture are particularly favorable for its development. It thrives in partial shade. Avoid excessive watering during the winter.

Palm. Many of these decorative evergreens are frequently used as house plants. All require a temperature of about 60 to 65 degrees. Although they require plenty of moisture during the summer they will suffer if overwatered in winter. Most palms do best if not repotted too frequently. *Howea belmoreana* is a graceful plant with rather broad fan-shaped leaves. The leaves of the Phoenix palm are finer, more graceful. In its native habitat this species produces dates. *Areca lutescens* is a rapid grower with feathery foliage on long yellow stems.

Leopard plant (*Ligularia kaempferi*). This plant is used chiefly for its spotted foliage of white, yellow, or pink. New plants are started by cuttings or division.

Swiss cheese plant (*Monstera deliciosa*). Another rugged foliage plant for today's dry, overheated rooms and modern decor. However, this beautiful tropical plant makes its best growth in cool (65 degrees) rather humid rooms that are well lighted. Young plants are often sold as philodendron, some forms of which it resembles.

The Swiss-cheese plant is officially known as cut-leaved philodendron or Monstera deliciosa.

Boston ferns will thrive if given high humidity, coolness, not too much sun or water.

Nandina (*Nandina domestica*). An evergreen shrub native in China and Japan. As a houseplant it makes an excellent specimen with its thin branches, bright red berries, and delicately colored leaves. It thrives in shady or sunny positions.

Boston fern (*Nephrolepis exaltata bostoniensis*). One of the most popular houseplants, although many people find it difficult to grow satisfactorily. Ferns are sensitive and require a temperature between 65 and 70 degrees; lower or higher temperatures may cause poor growth. Poor drainage, together with overwatering, will turn the leaves yellow. Oversized pots create excessive moisture in the soil. High humidity (air moisture) is essential, which may be provided by frequent washing of the leaves. Partial shade is preferred to direct sunlight. All ferns are propagated by runners or division. Be on the lookout for white flies, aphids, and scales.

Screwpine (*Pandanus*). The most common species of the screwpine is *P. veitchi.* The leaves are long, variegated, sword-like, with sharp teeth on the margins. It objects to excessive moisture in the winter and insufficient sunlight. New plants are produced by offsets.

Philodendron (*Philodendron cordatum*). A very tolerant and rapidly growing vine. The leaves are large, bright green, and somewhat heart-shaped. It requires good light but not direct sunlight and much moisture; in fact, stems are frequently placed directly in water in ivy bowls, where they root and thrive if nutrients are occasionally supplied. There are many, many forms.

Holly fern (*Polystichum aristatum*). One of the most tolerant of all ferns for the house. It is very easily grown, requires moderate amounts of water, and prefers shade. The plant grows 12 to 18 inches tall, and each leaf is 12 to 24 inches long and 10 inches wide. Although coarser in appearance than the Boston fern, it is very vigorous in habit and stands rough treatment.

Bowstring hemp or Snake plant (*Sansevieria*). Two popular forms of this plant are *S. zeylanica,* banded with lighter green; and *S. trifasciata* variety *laurenti,* whose leaves have yellow edges. Either will exist under trying conditions. The leaves which arise from the base are of a fleshy, tough texture. They are propagated by division or leaf cuttings; however, the *laurenti* variety will not come true to color from cuttings.

Australian umbrella tree (*Schefflera actinophylla*). Large foliage plant with compound leaves; quite tolerant of dim light and fluctuating temperatures, although it performs best in good light. Sponge the leaves to keep them free from soot and dust. Do not overwater but when the soil becomes dry, give a thorough soaking.

Zebrina calathea, *like many of the tradescantias, has the common name Wandering Jew.*

Pothos (*Scindapsus*). Variegated, heart-shaped leaves more fleshy than those of philodendron. These semitrailing plants tolerate warm and dry air but need good light (not full sun).

Pick-a-back plant (*Tolmiea menziesi*). A wild flower of the Northwest that has become a popular houseplant. It is easily propagated by the plantlets that form at the ends of stems. It prefers a cool room out of direct sunlight and a humus-rich soil.

Wandering Jew (*Tradescantia fluminensis*). This is a trailing vine of succulent growth with green and white leaves. Its requirements are few: plenty of moisture, a fair amount of sunlight, and approximately a 70 degree temperature. Any type of soil will do; in fact, it will grow well in water. It is easily propagated by cuttings, placed in water, sand, or soil. Other plants called wandering Jew are in the genus *Zebrina.* Their leaves vary in color markings from purple to white.

Periwinkle (*Vinca major*). An excellent vine for window boxes and wall vases. The variety with variegated foliage is most attractive.

There are many other excellent foliage plants, both large and small. Among small plants are peperomia, artillery plant (*Pilea microphylla*) and various ferns.

Flowering Houseplants

Azalea (*Rhododendron*). Usually available at the florist at Christmas and Easter. They require ample water, a fairly cool spot, and abundant light. After the blooms fall, they should be moved into a warmer place, and given more water on soil and foliage. In May, they can be set out, still potted, in light shade, and kept moist, so that new foliage and buds will mature. In September, when brought inside, a cool sunny window and water will help bring them into bloom in winter. There are many varieties.

Begonia (*Begonia*). *B. semperflorens*, the fibrous-rooted or wax begonia, is easy to grow. The beautiful semituberous and Christmas begonias, featured by many florists ('Melior,' 'Glory of Cincinnati,' and 'Mrs. Peterson' are examples), make striking holiday gift plants, but they require cool, humid conditions and the dry, hot rooms of most homes are unsuitable. But there are many other begonia types, outstanding for both foliage and flowers, that are more tolerant. Generally, most begonias prefer a cool (65 degrees) window, well-lighted but not directly in the sun.

Cactus. (A popular name for many plant genera native to arid regions.) The growing of cacti in small bowls is popular with many people. Their peculiar shapes and habits of growth attract attention. Very few of them will bloom in the average home, but in their native habitat their flowers are extremely beautiful. An exception is the Christmas or crab cactus (*Zygocactus truncatus*), whose jointed drooping stems are topped with attractive red flowers from December to February.

Most species grow in a sandy soil, and little water is required. An occasional sprinkling of water over the plant and soil will suffice. A temperature of 65 to 70 degrees is best.

Christmas cactus (*Schlumbergera bridgesii*). This curious, crablike succulent has beautiful red flowers in the winter, often around the holidays. It needs a gritty, lean soil and only meager moisture until late fall, when the watering frequency can be increased. Many growers recommend a four- to five-week rest period out of bright light in early fall before the additional watering program is started.

Begonia 'Nellie Bly.'

Trailing begonias such as this one are excellent for wall brackets or for hanging baskets.

Lemon, Orange, and Grapefruit (*Citrus*). The most common citrus plants used as houseplants. Of all flowering plants, these

A closeup of the red flower of Christmas cactus.

The brilliant fruits of Otaheite orange (left) *are a handsome combination with yellow "Soleil d'Or" narcissus, grown in pebbles and water.*

are the most tolerant. They thrive in the high temperature of the average home. Although tolerant to partial shade they grow better in full sunlight. Overwatering is objectionable only during the winter. They react favorably to additions of complete fertilizers at regular intervals. On mature plants scales are troublesome occasionally.

Cigar-flower (*Cuphea platycentra*). A native of Mexico. The flowers resemble a cigar, with their bright red calyx and white mouth with a dark ring at the end. It is easily grown in the house and is propagated by seeds.

Cyclamen (*Cyclamen persicum*). One of the most deservedly popular houseplants, flowering from Christmas to Easter. Most plant lovers have found that new purchases each year make shapely specimens as the best blooms come from seedlings about 15 months old. Growing plants from seed is really for the specialist with a greenhouse; it is slow and difficult except in a greenhouse. And last year's bulbs can be uncertain. After flowering, the plants are gradually dried so that they rest most of the summer. In fall resume watering, and feed occasionally. Keep the plants in a cool room as described below.

Young plants may be procured very reasonably from August to November and repotted, as soon as received, in 4-inch pots. As fast as pots become filled with roots move into 5- and 6-inch pots. They do well in any soil not too heavy, but the best is made of 2 parts garden soil, 1 part fine peat moss, and 1 part sand with, to each bushel, 1 large single handful of coarse bone meal, or superphosphate, dried cow or sheep manure, and limestone. Moisten before potting. For fine blooms pinch out flowering stems that rise above foliage, before November, to conserve strength of the plant, and after this time give a weak fertilizer solution weekly.

They will continue to bloom for 3 months or more if flowers are pulled loose at the corm as soon as faded. Do not cut them; any parts of stems left will decay. Keep them in plenty of light but avoid noon sun. An even temperature is desirable; 40 to 50 degrees will prolong the blooming season. Failure can usually be traced to neglect or constant exposure to hot, dry air.

Do not splash water on the plant when watering as the center of the bulb will decay if wet. Use water at room tempera-

Star of Bethlehem (Campanula isophylla), *with white or blue flowers, is a graceful trailing plant.*

ture, and keep plant moist but not wet; empty saucer if water accumulates in it. A fine spray with a sprinkler bulb early in the day is beneficial; but keep the plant shaded until foliage dries. Wash leaves if dusty.

Freesia (*Freesia*). New colored hybrid varieties make this fragrant plant more attractive than ever. They will bloom from fall until spring under careful management. Large bulbs bloom sooner than small ones which may not flower until April.

A succession of bloom is obtained by pottings every 3 or 4 weeks from September 1st to October, but they may be potted as late as February provided cormels have not started to form on top of the old bulbs. They should bloom in 10 to 14 weeks. Bulbs are said to grow better if dried for two weeks in a sunny window. They may be planted all at one time and held back until needed in a cold frame or pit. But they are tender – they must never be put in freezing temperatures.

Plant 6 to a deep bulb pan 2 inches apart and cover tips not over 1 inch with soil made of garden loam, humusy compost, or peat moss and sand in equal parts. Moisten the soil (not wet) as mixed, and press the bulbs gently to proper depth. Place in a cool light spot (about 50 degrees). When sprouts show bring into room where temperature stays over 50 degrees and under 70 degrees. Keep close to, but not touching, the window, and avoid drafts.

As the buds show, give a little weak, liquid fertilizer when watering. Water frequently after sprouts start, but avoid water-soaked soil. Support blooms with thin stakes of wood, heavy wire, and string.

After flowering, pots can be dried out gradually and natural growth completed

One of the epiphytic orchids that will tolerate indoor conditions is Epidendrum tampense.

Winter

The warm color of geraniums contrasts with a snowy terrace.

One of winter's own favorites is the holly with long-lasting red berries and distinctive foliage.

Daffodils, hyacinths, begonias and other plants give a preview of spring in a home greenhouse.

Prayer plant is an attractive plant for well-lighted (but not sunny) rooms.

Gloxinia, a popular house plant closely related to African-violet, is grown from a bulblike root.

The yellow-flowered form of the house plant Kalanchoe is a common Christmas plant, especially in its red forms.

One of the easiest plants to grow for winter color is the amaryllis bulb, shown here with crown of thorns.

Various kinds of foliage plants in a glass bowl filled with water make a long-lasting table arrangement.

Miniature gardens, like this woodland arrangement of native plants in a terrarium, can be appealing.

For exotic fragrance from pink-tinted flowers in spring and a vining habit, choose the wax plant (Hoya carnosa).

The home greenhouse can be both an indoor garden to gladden the spirit and a source for flower arrangements.

Caladiums make superb decorations in greenhouses in winter and for patios and terraces in summer.

America's favorite house plant is the amenable, nearly ever-blooming African-violet.

In mild climates, the camellia is a beautiful shrub for gardens. In the north, it can be grown indoors in greenhouses and cool windows.

Tulips, hyacinths, and crocuses can be forced into flower for winter window gardens.

An early-winter display in a cool window that receives morning sun. Orchid is a rose-pink cymbidium. Plants below include nutmeg geranium, azalea, rosemary, amaryllis, paper-white narcissus.

until the foliage yellows. Bulbs are placed in a frost-proof sunny location to ripen, then stored until potting time. Storage is considered difficult, and it is better to buy the few bulbs needed each year.

Poinsettia (*Euphorbia pulcherrima*). The favorite Christmas flower. While the plant is in bloom, refrain from adding much water. During its growing season it requires a temperature of 65 degrees and plenty of sunlight. Avoid sudden chills. The plant is propagated by cuttings taken in early summer from plants carried from the previous winter.

Gardenia (*Gardenia jasminoides*) This evergreen shrub with fragrant white flowers is grown outdoors in warm climates. In the North it is grown in cool windows in partial sunshine. It needs ample humidity.

Amaryllis (*Hippeastrum*). A lily-like, easily managed plant for a window garden. It produces under the simplest conditions 1 to 3 spikes with 3 to 6 blooms above broad, strap-shaped leaves. Improved hybrids in many colors have increased its popularity in recent years.

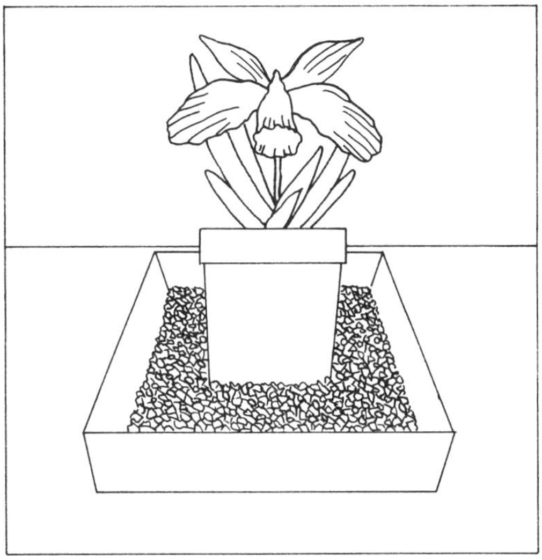

A tray of pebbles and water supplies humidity for potted orchid. Slats may also be used to keep pot above water level.

Orchid in a Wardian case, which maintains uniform humidity for the plant.

Plant bulbs as soon as received, usually October and November (any time before January), in pots 1 inch greater in diameter than the bulbs. They will not bloom if the pots are too large. Only the lower thick part is covered with soil; the long neck must be fully exposed. Use 2 parts good soil, 1 of rotted or dehydrated cow manure, and some bone meal or superphosphate. Mix this thoroughly, and water sparingly until growth is well started, but supply generously thereafter. Be careful of drainage.

A correctly potted Amaryllis bulb is set high in a pot not much larger than itself. Good drainage is vital.

Keep in a cool, shaded place but bring into light at first sign of growth.

Amaryllis need plenty of sunshine and liquid manure each week during the growing season. Flowers may appear before leaves as most of the foliage is produced after blooming. They vary greatly in time of flowering, some buds appearing in January, others not blooming until spring.

In spring, plunge the pots into soil in the open where they will get plenty of sunlight. When the leaves begin to turn yellow or frost checks them, gradually decrease watering, and store pots in a cool cellar. Look them over occasionally. Bring to light, and water regularly when they show signs of life.

Repotting is beneficial but not necessary as they will thrive for years with applications of liquid manure or chemical plant food in solution. The best time to repot is after the flowering, before new foliage appears; but no harm is done by potting in the fall at the close of the dormant season. Instead of repotting, you can remove some soil from the pots about the bulbs, and replace it with good soil, cow manure, and bone meal or superphosphate.

Hydrangea (*Hydrangea*). The French hydrangea is a gift plant for Easter and Mother's Day. It requires a cool temperature, an abundance of water, and an acid soil for blooming. Transplant to a protected place in the garden once it flowers.

Balsam or Impatiens (*Impatiens holsti*). An old-fashioned plant. The stems and leaves are quite succulent and the flowers, of various colors, are borne close to the stems. Pinching the terminal growths keeps the plant bushy and shapely. It thrives in a fertile soil in direct sunlight when supplied with plenty of water. It can be perpetuated by seeds or cuttings.

Geranium (*Pelargonium*). Includes many species and varieties. The Lady Washington pelargonium has small leaves, flowers white to red with black blotches on the two upper petals. The scented-leaf geraniums, while not outstanding for their flowers, contribute delicious, spicy aromas to otherwise scentless window gardens. All kinds of geraniums prefer plenty of sunlight and an abundance of water, although overwatering during the winter may cause the leaves to drop. A temperature between 65 and 70 degrees increases flower production. Fertilizer in fall and spring will improve the quality of the foliage and flowers.

African-violet (*Saintpaulia*). African-violets (not violets, of course, and not even related to those hardy plants) continue to grow in popularity. Perhaps the reason for their

Peppermint geranium has deliciously scented leaves with a velvety texture.

A collection of gesneriads – African-violets and episcias – thrive here with potted ferns and vines.

widespread popularity is that they require loving care! Unlike many houseplants which thrive on neglect, they demand attention and knowledge of their likes and dislikes.

Here are some of the important facts to keep in mind. African-violets grow best in a north or east window but tolerate a southern or western exposure in winter. They do not like direct sunlight as found close to the window. One should not expect heavy bloom during the short-day period in midwinter unless they are grown under fluorescent lights.

They like loamy, loose soil which should be sterilized before using. You can purchase ready-mixed soil at florists' and nursery outlets.

African-violets respond to feeding, but plants should be watered first so that the chemicals do not burn the roots. They will not tolerate excessive moisture, especially during hot, humid weather. Water should not remain in the saucer. It makes no difference if they are watered from the top or bottom, but water on the leaves will spot them if exposed to sunlight afterwards. It is important to use water at room temperature, for cold water shocks the plant.

Transplant them when the roots become crowded. Lack of bloom when the pot is overcrowded is the usual signal to transfer them to larger pots. While an expert removes additional crowns as soon as they appear around the plant, the novice may be confronted with a pot containing many crowns or plants. Sometimes they can be cut apart but keep in mind that you want at least one plant with a good root system. Cut crowns can be placed in a pan of moist sand or Vermiculite to root. It is necessary to use a hairpin or wire to hold them in place.

There are so many varieties that it would be impossible to name them. Color range includes all shades of blue and purple, pink, rose, red, and white, in single and double form. Many books have been written on the African-violet.

African-violets single, double, fringed and ruffled being grown on an attractive display stand.

Sinningia speciosa *is a tiny relative of the large gloxinias. Planter is of Featherock.*

The enormous, speckled blooms of a hybrid gloxinia are borne above velvety leaves resembling those of African-violets, another of the gesneriads.

Slipper gloxinia 'Snow Queen' has daintier blooms than the giant hybrids.

Gloxinia (*Sinningia speciosa*). An interesting plant. The flowers are large and bell-shaped, in velvety colors of violet, red, or white. It requires a warm, humid atmosphere and partial shade. After blooming, the tubers should be stored in a cool place until February when they may be started into growth. Culture is similar to that of the African-violet. Flowering plants can be produced from seeds or cuttings in about 12 months.

Spring Bulbs Indoors

Spring-flowering bulbs, sometimes referred to as Holland or Dutch bulbs, can be made to bloom indoors in winter by "forcing." Forcing does not mean quick growth at high temperature. On the contrary, bulbs for indoor bloom are raised at low temperature and very slowly. The process is so elementary that a child can master it.

Spring-flowering bulbs such as hyacinth, tulip, daffodil or narcissus – they're the same! – crocus, and a host of other small bulbs force easily if you follow a few rules.

Rule 1: Roots must be developed before any other growth. The secret of success is a pot full of roots, grown by removing all light and keeping the temperature low, imitating autumn soil conditions.

Use a garage attached to the cellar, an unheated fruit cellar, any room where you can maintain a temperature of about 50 to 60 degrees all winter. By far the best and easiest place is out-of-doors in a shaded cold frame.

Rule 2: Slow stem growth should precede bloom. Bulbs placed in direct sunlight immediately after being brought from the dark develop too fast (soft growth); the foliage flops over; and the stems may be unable to support heavy bloom. Keep them shaded for a short time in a cool room.

Rule 3: Place in a sunny window and turn daily for even growth.

Rule 4: Flowering is prolonged by moisture in the air. Outdoors they develop in cool temperature, 65 degrees or less, and moist spring air. For your own health and that of the flowers, keep the air moist.

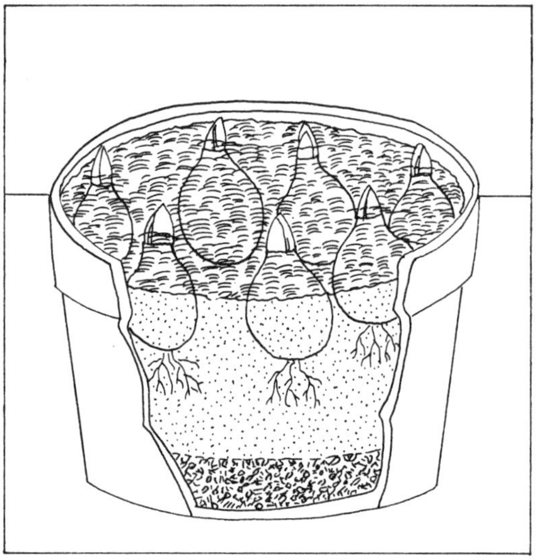

Spring-flowering bulbs potted for forcing. Good root growth is essential before top growth begins.

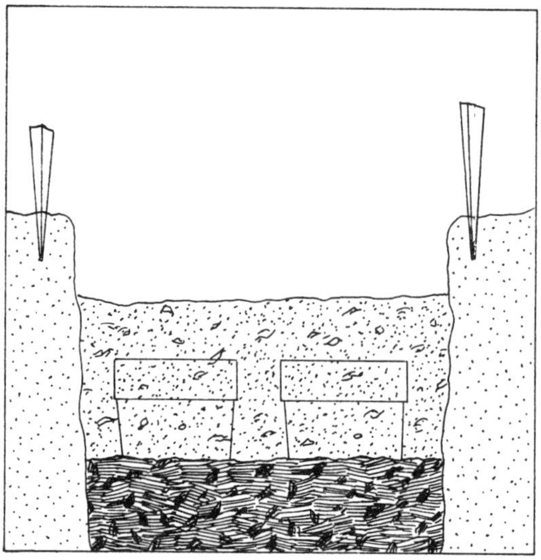

Potted-up spring bulbs plunged into storage pit outdoors for root growth before forcing. Stakes mark location for later digging.

Rule 5: Perhaps this should be rule 1. It is always best to buy good, named bulbs. They do not need to be exhibition size or expensive.

Spring-flowering bulbs can be forced in water alone, in pebbles and water, in fiber and in pots of soil, but the above rules apply to all of the methods.

Hyacinths and Narcissus in Water

Regular hyacinth jars are often sold at garden centers, but any similar jar is satisfactory. An inch or so of pebbles in the bottom gives the jars stability. Fill them with water and place the bulb on top. If it is too small to sit on the opening, three or four toothpicks or small pieces of wire stuck into it will hold it just above the surface of the water. Do not let the bulb sink deep in the water, or it may decay before roots have formed.

Put the jars in the darkest corner of your garage or in any cool dark area safe from freezing. Examine them once in a while, and add water if necessary. Temperatures should stay between 40 and 50 degrees.

In about 8 to 15 weeks, roots will have reached the bottom of the glass, and some of the best-developed bulbs may be moved to a warmer place (55 to 60 degrees is best), and covered with a paper cone until a sprout about 5 inches long has formed. The foliage will be pale, but upon removal of the cone it will turn bright green. Then set in a sunny window to bloom, and turn daily for even growth.

Paperwhite narcissus in bloom (left) *and being planted in pebbles* (right). *Roots are allowed to develop in a cool, dark spot before bowl is brought into light to start top growth.*

Good results can be had by merely bringing the jars as needed from the cool cellar into a dark corner, slightly warmer,

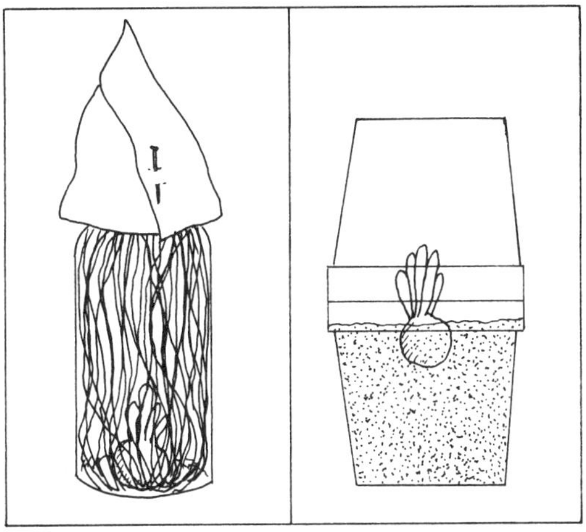

Hyacinth bulb growing in water (left) *is covered with cone of paper to encourage root growth before top sprouts.* Right, *hyacinth in soil is covered with inverted pot for the same purpose.*

until top growth is started and then to a sunny window.

Several or more jars can be rooted in this manner to be brought in as needed for a succession of bloom from January to April. The only reason for forcing hyacinths in glass containers is economy and the fun of watching the whole plant develop.

Paperwhite Narcissus and Chinese Sacred-Lilies

Paperwhite narcissus bulbs and Chinese sacred-lilies (also a kind of narcissus) can be forced in a bowl of pebbles and water. In fact they will give good results if the bowls are merely placed in the light.

They do best, however, if 6 or more bulbs are placed in a bowl of pebbles and water, which is set away in a dark closet, or better still in a cool, dark spot in the cellar, for 3 or 4 weeks. This holds back top growth until roots are established. When brought into the open, keep away from direct sun for a few days until the tops turn bright green.

It takes about 5 weeks from the time bulbs are started for them to begin to bloom. If water level is maintained, and they are kept in a temperature of about 60 degrees, the blooms will last for 2 or 3 weeks. Paperwhite bulbs bloom best if started about December 1st.

The Use of Bulb Fiber

Prepared peat or bulb fiber is usually sold at all seed stores and garden centers in the fall. This method can be successfully used on a wide range of bulbs. The bowl can be watertight so as to avoid possible injury to furniture, or it may be a regular squat bulb pot (called a bulb pan) in a saucer.

If the receptacle is watertight put a layer of charcoal in the bottom, press down firmly, but not hard, a layer of fiber. Place the bulbs in position. They should be about one-half their diameter apart, and the peak of the bulb should be just below the top of the bowl.

Now press fiber gently but firmly into place so it covers all but the tips of the bulbs which should leave it one-half inch from the top of the bowl. Pour on water slowly until the fiber has reached full absorption, and let it stand about one-half day. Tilt the bowl and drain off all water not held by the fiber; they want to drink, not swim.

If the plants are raised in a bulb pan the surplus water will drain off into the saucer, and water may be added from time to time to freshen the planting, which will make the charcoal unnecessary.

The same process of forming roots first is used with fiber as with the water method. Put bulbs in a well-ventilated place in the dark at a temperature of 40 to 50 degrees for several weeks until tops are 2 or 3 inches high. Water them occasionally, pouring off surplus as described before. If you have no cool place, put bowls in a box, and surround them with a layer of 3 or 4 inches of peat moss, slightly damp. This is fine insulation against heat and drying out.

When the bowls are filled with roots, bring them into lesser light until the sickly tops turn bright green; then they may receive bright sun for blooming.

Hyacinths, tulips, all narcissus or daffodils, crocuses, calla, freesia, grape-hyacinths, scilla, snowdrops, and Easter lilies are particularly adapted for fiber growing.

A better way to develop roots in fiber is to bury them outside (called plunging), which is described below. By this method they may all be prepared at once and brought in as needed, whereas with the cellar method it becomes impossible to suppress the top growth; and they may all start into growth at the same time.

Forcing Bulbs in Soil

Prepare soil by mixing 2 parts good garden soil with 1 part commercial humus or peat moss (mix the 2 together if you have them), and enough sand (it will usually take 1 part sand to 3 parts soil mixture) so that you cannot pack the soil into a ball when squeezed wet. Have the soil damp but not wet.

If the pots are new, they should be thoroughly soaked for at least 2 days. They will dry out too fast if this is not done.

Place a piece of broken pot over the drain hole, and fill the pots lightly. The bulbs must be placed as the pots are filled, not pushed in afterwards. They should be just even with the top of the soil which should be one-half inch from the pot rim. Do not pound soil into the pots; but fill them and tap once or twice to settle. The roots will strike down more easily in loose soil. They must have room to grow or they will force the bulb from the soil.

After a thorough watering they are ready to take to the cool cellar. Do not set them on the cement floor but bed them in sand or peat moss and if it is warm or dry cover them with sand or pack them in a 3-inch layer of peat moss. The root development for miniature hyacinths takes at least 8 weeks; first-size hyacinths, 10 to 12 weeks; tulips, 10 to 12 weeks; and narcissi (except paperwhite), 12 to 15 weeks.

The easiest and best way to root them is out-of-doors. This is known as "plunging." It is more natural and has the advantage of holding them dormant. The method is simple. Some people merely dig a trench, one spade deep, near a sheltered foundation wall. In the bottom of this is placed 2 inches of coal ashes or similar material and the pots set upon it. The soil is packed around the pots to keep the mice from making it their winter home (a layer of fine-mesh hardware cloth can be placed over the tops of the pots to keep mice from crawling in) and a layer of 2 inches of sand placed over them. The balance of the soil is then piled over it and the top mulched with about a foot of leaves.

Achimenes 'Ambrose Verschaffelt,' like other gesneriads, is adaptable to indoor conditions.

By far the easiest way to plunge is in a cold frame. An excavation is made in the loose soil, the pots set on pebbles or cinders, filled around and covered with the soil. A heavy layer of peat moss about 1 foot thick can be placed over them. The frame is not covered with the sash until severe weather. The ease with which the peat can be removed for examination makes this arrangement attractive.

At the end of the time for rooting, the pots must be examined. The soil ball may be knocked loose by gently tapping the

Planting a terrarium. Layer of gravel is laid at a slope, then covered with soil. Plants are carefully set into place, roots intact. After watering with a fine spray, cover may be placed on terrarium to maintain high humidity.

inverted pot. If the roots are well distributed through the soil, you will know they are fully developed. The best-developed should be brought indoors as needed and placed in a temperature of 50 degrees for the development of top growth.

The Art of Bonsai

Bonsai is the art of growing potted trees and shrubs as miniatures of their natural forms and, while plants so treated aren't actually "houseplants," they are meant to be displayed and enjoyed indoors on occasion. Traditionally, bonsai (the practice was originated in Japan) are grown outdoors on benches and wintered in cold frames or similar shelters; however, by choosing plants that will tolerate indoor conditions for a time, it is possible to train and keep specimens as creditable bonsai indoors all year or almost so. As with many other houseplants, the cooler the indoor temperature, the better.

It is culture alone that keeps bonsai to their relatively small size (from a few inches to perhaps 2 or 3 feet); they aren't "starved" plants, but rather plants whose root and leaf systems are kept in balance by pruning and adequate feeding, watering, and good air circulation.

The shaping of the pliable trunks and branches is achieved by winding with copper wire, softened by a flame and then wrapped in paper to avoid injury to bark. The wired trunks or branches are then bent or otherwise formed to the shape desired and left until the training is complete.

Plants for potting and training may be collected from the wild (such plants should be set outdoors in humus-rich soil for several months' recuperation before potting and training); from a nursery where container-grown shrubs will include likely possibilities, some of which with pruning may make "instant," passable bonsai; or from suppliers of seedling trees and shrubs.

In general, plants chosen for training are potted up for the first time in rather cramped containers. The roots are first pruned to encourage young fibrous growth. Then the trunk and branches are shortened if necessary. Pinching off new growth is practiced as needed to improve the form of the bonsai.

Suitable plants for bonsai include cedar, juniper, spruce, pine, and yew and most other evergreens; also maple, beech, sycamore, birch, ginkgo, hawthorne, peach, crabapple, azalea, holly, quince, and many others. Among herbs, rosemary makes a handsome bonsai.

An urban miracle: the transformation of an arid expanse of concrete into a garden. Paving of flagstones has been added, and rustic fencing (for more privacy) tops masonry walls. Well-selected plants, a fountain, and furniture complete the picture. Pavement drain permits hosing plants and pavement to eliminate soot.

CHAPTER 20

City Gardens

My eyes make pictures, when they are shut.
– Samuel T. Coleridge

A garden in today's cities can pass beyond the daydream stage. Successful gardening well within the confines of an industrial metropolis is possible. Brick, concrete, traffic, dirt and air pollution are hardly conducive to good growth and flowering of most plants, yet such bad news notwithstanding, the beauty that may be realized in a city yard or roof garden is surprising and so all the more soul enriching.

City gardens are as varied as city neighborhoods. They range from a small plot surrounded by towering buildings in a mid-town section to open yards resembling a suburban location at the edge of many large cities. Since the condition (and, usually, the depth) of soil can be altered, sunlight and air pollution are in the long run the determining factors in plant selection for a particular location.

The view from the windows is of first importance. Because most city gardens are seen the year around, it is desirable to design and plant the garden so that it presents an attractive picture with points of interest during the four seasons. Bulbs for early spring bloom give great pleasure when they can be enjoyed from windows. For summer and fall color, many kinds of annuals and chrysanthemums can be relied upon.

Finally, evergreens, interesting branch formations of deciduous trees and shrubs, and a neatly mulched ground all combine to present a pleasant winter view.

Problems of Design

A small garden, seen in its entirety at one glance, must be well designed if the effect is to be one of distinction. When a garden is framed by forbidding rear views of buildings, fire escapes and other structural ugliness, the only thing to do is to ignore them and design a garden that is a complete and separate picture in itself.

The usual city backyard contains a rectangular central plot surrounded by flagstone or cement walks. The beds adjoining the fences are narrow and permit the development of only very small plants. Although essentially formal, this basic design can be varied. Its advantages are that soil can be readily improved as necessary and plant selection can be reduced to a few kinds of ground cover plants, some shrubs and one or two small trees. Or, if there is ample sunlight and more gardening involvement rather than low maintenance is desired, a greater variety of plant material can be selected.

Ajuga and ivy take root in pavement cracks, soften the angles of a paved garden. Birdbath attracts visitors even in the heart of a city.

The smaller the garden, the more care must be given to selection of decorations. Usually only one major feature, such as a small fountain, a bird bath or a piece of sculpture, looks right.

Informal gardens, even wild-flower gardens and very simple rock gardens, are not out of place in a city. An asymmetrical design with shrubs and trees of varying heights, a curving path and groups of perennials and annuals furnishing color, is interesting because of the contrast that it offers to the city. It is a true garden where the gardener has the opportunity to be as creative as those gardening under more favorable conditions.

A city gardener gets such pleasure from seeing a plant grow and thrive that he is often tempted to delay essential pruning until the overgrown plants have spoiled the design. It is wise to avoid plants whose naturally rampant growth will result in crowding out their neighbors. With skillful pruning, forsythia as well as several other rapidly growing shrubs such as rose of Sharon, weigela, and firethorn may be trained against walls and fences. Most plants do not attain their maximum size in the city as quickly as in the country. Privet, wisteria, aralia, Japanese holly and many others, while they may be rapid growers, can be restrained by careful pruning. City gardens are planted thickly for immediate effect. Often the garden picture is complete as to plant material and scale within the first season.

There are many instances where a city garden consists primarily of architectural features, with plants used as accessories. Even a small terrace may comprise the garden. An illusion of a garden can be created with remarkably little plant material. Many city gardens are nothing but terraces with plant accents in tubs or other containers or in small beds around the terrace.

Since walls and fences around a small garden can be overpowering, their effect should be lightened and made to serve a

Neoclassical bird bath is in harmony with the city garden, with a lawn and plant beds inside brick walls.

decorative purpose. Stone or brick walls are among the best. Touches of iron grill work give dignity and elegance. Another attractive enclosure is split chestnut or cedar stake fencing. Open-mesh wire has the advantage of letting in more air. Sometimes it is possible to enclose two sides of a garden with one material and the third with brick or open-mesh wire. This treatment may make the garden look larger.

Planter boxes can create a garden in even the smallest entrance court or terrace.

Roof Gardens

More and more city dwellers are making use of above-the-ground space for attractive outdoor living rooms. Some are large enough for only a table, chair and a privet hedge. Others are spacious enough to support plant life in great variety.

Whatever the size, above-ground gardens present similar problems. The plants must be grown in containers and the soil must be hoisted up the service elevators in bags. The plants, ranging from sweet alyssum in flats to 10-foot trees, must ride up the same way. Plant material must be chosen to withstand extremes of temperatures and wind. The average roof garden gets more than enough sunshine. Many plants

Choose city-garden fencing for privacy plus good air circulation. Wovenboard fence gives both.

A small rock garden successfully meets the challenge posed by its situation on a Manhattan penthouse terrace. Plants are low to emphasize statue.

that cannot be grown in the shade of buildings on the ground can be grown in these sky gardens. The extremes of heat, wind and evaporation, however, place definite limitations on the selection. Winter sun, wind and cold account for winter-killing of all but the toughest items on the plant list. Here again, intelligent choice of plant material, proper soil and care can overcome most difficulties.

All containers (see section on window boxes and other containers in Chapter 21), whether they are made of brick, cement, stone or wood, should be as deep and as wide as possible. The more exposed the situation, the deeper the soil should be. For annuals and bedding plants, the containers should be not less than 12 inches deep. For shrubs and trees, they should be not less than 20 inches deep. The deeper the soil, the more opportunity for roots to spread and the less chance for the soil to dry out too much between waterings.

Watering on a penthouse terrace or roof is a daily chore, sometimes twice daily, during the hot, dry season. With such copious watering, much of the fertility of the soil is washed down the drain and must therefore be replaced periodically. Frequent small applications of the right kind of complete fertilizer for the various types of plantings must be given throughout the growing season. The soil, too, must be thoroughly cultivated and fertilized each spring. Winter and summer mulching is a necessity. Use any mulch – pine bark, pebbles, salt hay, aged manure – that won't blow away. Peat moss is helpful if it is mixed with the soil.

Whenever possible, penthouse or terrace plantings should be provided with windbreaks. Fences and other structures may be supplemented with hedges of rugged plants such as privet and taxus. Shielded by such a hedge, the more delicate shrubs and flowers can be grown to perfection. Brittle trees, shrubs and flowers must be eliminated unless they are thoroughly shielded from strong winds and other weather hazards. Since broadleaf evergreens grow naturally in protected areas, in humus-rich soil with ample moisture, they are seldom successful in exposed situations. But among the several hundred plants that are tolerant of the worst conditions cities have to offer, many are adaptable, hardy and showy enough to grace the finest terrace or roof garden.

The roof gardener, moreover, can have all the color he wants. Annuals that love the hot sun are especially suitable.

Window Boxes

Window boxes bring the garden almost into the room. While space for ground gardens and roof gardens may be limited, every window sill should have a window box wherever ordinances don't prohibit them. (See also section on window boxes in Chapter 21.)

Unless the boxes are very large and deep, they present a serious watering problem and the roots of closely packed plants have little room in which to expand. To have lush window-box gardens, the soil must be maintained at a very high level of fertility and the plants should never suffer from lack of water.

The soil mixture should be very light and porous. To the average good loam, peat moss and/or other moisture-retaining humus should be added up to one-third of the bulk. If the soil is heavy, sand should also be added and at planting time a 4-inch pot of bone meal or superphosphate for each bushel of soil should be well mixed with it. During the growing season the boxes should be fertilized at least once a month, but fertilizer should be given in small doses, never a lot at a time. The liquid kinds are safer in crowded plantings than dry fertilizers, as they make plant nutrients available to the roots more rapidly. After fertilizing, the boxes should be kept very well watered.

A very important detail frequently mishandled is that of filling the boxes properly. At least one inch of space must be left between the top of the soil level and the edge of the box, otherwise water will run off instead of penetrating to the roots. All too often one sees boxes with plants sitting high on top of piled-up soil, like ducks on a lake. The result is dried-out roots and wilted foliage.

Boxes may be constructed of any of several materials, but the best boxes are wooden. Metal boxes may last longer, but they heat up too much and seldom provide adequate drainage. Boxes made of tile, stone or cement can be durable and attractive. It is best that all boxes be made with drainage holes to carry off excess water. They should have a layer of broken flower pots, stones or cinders in the bottom.

Potted sempervivums add greenery to brick steps, require very little care.

Vegetables, herbs, and ornamentals thrive together here. At left are tomatoes (in sunken pots), chives, parsley, and garlic chives (Allium tuberosum) *in boxes; potted sedums are at right.*

Tall plants are to be avoided both for the sake of appearance, their height being out of proportion to the box, and because they obstruct the view through the window. The most popular edging for boxes is English ivy, which stays green until midwinter. Other good choices are *Vinca minor* and the tender *V. major, Euonymus fortunei radicans, Cissus rhombifolia* (grape ivy), and *Tradescantia fluminensis.* Balcony petunias are often used without any other trailing plants, and when well grown the ivy-leaved geranium is very effective.

For boxes in the sun, almost any of the low-growing annuals may be chosen. Besides petunias, the following look effective: lantana, dwarf marigold, annual phlox, verbena, dwarf zinnia, sweet alyssum, lobelia, impatiens, heliotrope and, of course, the ever-popular and reliable geranium. A combination of red geranium and white petunia with a border of English ivy is perennially popular. Pink geraniums combine well with blue petunia plants. Lantana and lobelia look well together.

Very unusual and easily cared for plantings may be made entirely with cacti and succulents. This class of plants can stand drought and it is possible to go away for weeks without having to worry about watering them. They literally thrive under arid conditions.

Boxes in the shade must rely mainly on interesting foliage, since few flowers can be counted on for color. Wax begonia and fuchsia will give the most satisfaction and will often bloom for several months. Many houseplants and tender greenhouse plants may be used to lend interest to an all-green box. Boston ferns thrive in the shade. Aucuba has interesting variegated foliage. Pothos (*scindapsus*), philodendron, nephthytis, anthericum, sansevieria and even small rubber plants may be combined to create an exotic effect.

For the winter, small evergreens in variety may be used. They may not be in condition to continue as ornamental plants by spring, but they add so much cheer through the cold months that they are well worth the effort and expense. The only trailing plant that will hold up throughout the winter is euonymus, but very attractive winter plantings may be made with just a prim row of small evergreens. And, of course, cut evergreen boughs can be attractive in boxes through the winter.

Soil Problems

While principles of good gardening apply to city gardening in every respect, there are some special conditions to consider: lack of air and sun, poor drainage, depleted and shallow soil, rubbish buried by builders, unattractive architectural features. It is necessary to investigate these conditions thoroughly if one is to have a garden. Fortunately, proper plant selection will make an attractive green garden in the shadiest spot and architectural ugliness can be camouflaged and rubbish disposed of. But unless the drainage is good and the soil can be reasonably improved, there is no use spending money on the new plants or muscle on the effort.

City soil tends to pack into a hard, airless mass unless considerably more humus is used than would be needed in the country. The most successful gardens are those in which the improved soil is extremely porous, rich in humus and well aerated. Most city gardens require a great deal of watering. That is another reason why the soil should be porous and the drainage good.

Soil preparation should also be deeper. City gardens get little or no natural humus. Even tree leaves that come down in the fall are likely to be so laden with soot and grime that they are more harmful than useful as a source of soil-building humus. Therefore, and because most forms of fertilizer leach away rapidly, the soil must be fertilized regularly. This is especially important for boxes, tubs and all types of elevated beds, so often used around terraces and on roof gardens. A good soil-improvement schedule consists of a late fall mulch of manure (dehydrated is suitable), leaf mold, or peat moss, the choice depending on the needs of the specific plants. This is turned under in early spring and is supplemented by an application of a complete fertilizer. During the growing season, a light monthly application of complete fertilizer will maintain fertility. This monthly schedule should be started in the year following the initial soil improvement in newly built gardens. If the soil has been well enriched in the beginning, it is not necessary to fertilize it further during the first season.

Drainage problems in a small garden require care and common sense. It is not so much a question of disposing of surplus water as of making water available to the plant roots. If the subsoil is sandy and there is no blocking by rock or hardpan, even very heavy rains will soon be absorbed by a friable soil and the roots will get the benefit. To permit the moisture to reach the roots, the planting area should be well graded with a gentle slope toward the planting. On terraces and along solidly paved walks, grading alone is seldom sufficient. Additional aid must be provided in the shape of dry wells or drain pipe or tile to take care of water which cannot be directed toward plant roots in open ground. Grading of terraces adjoining the house should always be away from the house.

Maintenance

Soot and dust are probably responsible for more casualties among city-grown plants than any other single factor. Even when resistant types of plants are selected, they will not thrive if they are not kept clean. Hosing off the foliage as frequently as is necessary to keep it shining, a chore unknown to country gardeners, is a number-one "must" on the city gardener's schedule. In locations where air pollution is extreme, it is necessary to give all evergreens a thorough "laundering" once or more in early spring in order to remove the winter's accumulation of dirt. This is best accomplished with a bucket of soapy water (use mild soap, not detergent) and a soft brush or sponge, followed by a quick, brisk hosing.

Principles and methods of watering are exactly the same as elsewhere – deep and thorough. But city gardens need more frequent watering in dry seasons. Boxes and other containers are watered at least once a day. Weeds present less of a problem. However, frequent cultivation aerates the soil and prevents packing and adds to the beauty of the garden, for freshly cultivated earth is pleasant to see.

Very shady gardens present special problems in air circulation. Because there is not sufficient evaporation, a little watering usually goes a long way. Overwatering must be avoided. Rich, acid soil is relished by such choice plants as azalea, laurel, rhododendron and other members of the heath family that thrive in the shade, but no plant likes sour, undrained soil.

Destructive insects may appear on a small terrace or in a backyard, just as elsewhere. Have a good sprayer and a supply of insecticides within reach. Because the garden space is smaller, the plants fewer

City gardening may, perforce, be indoor gardening. Light for these foliage plants comes from bank of windows; bathroom humidity is to their liking.

and a degree less rugged than in most rural or village gardens, the damage done by insects and fungi is conspicuous if this phase of gardening is neglected.

Shade and Green Gardens

It is easier to have a successful green garden in the city than to have continuous or even intermittent bloom. In a large city, few gardens get 6 or more hours of direct sunshine, surprising as this may seem. Any spot receiving less than this should be considered a shady garden. There may be sun in different parts of the garden all through the day, but often a particular bed or border gets sunshine for only 1 or 2 hours. It is obvious that in this case a lovelier garden can be created with evergreens, shade-tolerant deciduous and flowering shrubs, spring bulbs, ferns and ground covers and a few potted plants able to bloom in the shade, than with annuals which are liable to be anemic and leggy. Some of the finest gardens in the larger cities have no more color than is provided by variations in green foliage. During the torrid midsummer months a well-tended green garden can be as restful and enjoyable as anything to be found within the city limits.

Even in a shady garden, however, it is possible to have a good deal of color during the early spring. Several of the broadleaf evergreens, usually successful in the city, bear spectacular blooms. Spring-blooming bulbs – tulips, daffodils, and hyacinths – planted in the fall will furnish masses of color, at least for one season. Pansies, forget-me-nots and English daisies, all temporary but colorful, help to complete the spring display. When these are past their prime, they are taken up. Later, begonia, fuchsia, fancy-leaved caladium and calla may be purchased in pots and transplanted to spots where color is desired. Of these, wax begonias give the most in long bloom and color. Ferns, ivy, pachysandra, vinca, ajuga and euonymus may be used as ground covers in front of and underneath shrubs.

City Lawns

Lawns are difficult to maintain in congested, over-built sections. In the majority of cases, attempts to establish permanent lawns are unsuccessful. They are sadly disappointing in shady yards if air circulation is poor. But it is quite possible to have a green area where a grass lawn would be if it could be.

In the shade, ground covers, of course, are the answer. Of these, English ivy (*Hedera helix*) and its varieties are the best. *H. helix baltica,* deep green with whitish veins, is very hardy. Around New York and in similar climates, the ivy should be well mulched during the winter. The most effective manner of doing this is to shake enough peat moss between the stems of the ivy to cover the roots and lower parts of the branches. Then, after the first hard frost has occurred, a covering of evergreen branches should be placed over the whole. With such protection, the ivy will emerge in March or early April with none of the leaves browned by winter weather. However, if the Baltic variety is used, it is hardy enough to stand up without any mulching.

Vinca minor, or myrtle, makes a more refined ground cover, but requires richer soil. Pachysandra is excellent for underplanting between shrubs and for small areas, but is not very satisfactory for a smooth "lawn" effect. Ajuga, with its lavender-blue flowers, is an attractive ground cover, able to stand considerable shade. It also needs winter protection of peat moss, or peat moss and evergreen branches. None of these ground covers should be walked on.

When the opposite condition to shade has to be considered – that of a small, dry, sunny area – again grass may not be the easiest solution. Unattractive as the idea may seem at first, there is always the alternative of the crabgrass lawn! This annual grass is the bane of suburban gardeners who strive for an attractive lawn, but in the city, a crabgrass lawn, especially if fertilized, can make an acceptable patch of greenery that will be undaunted by the city's unfavorable growing conditions.

Any of the low-growing sedums, such as *Sedum album* or *S. acre* and others, will revel in the sun and spread as far as they are permitted.

Fiberglass "rocks" and pool and a small recirculating pump have been used in creating a charming waterfall to add coolness to the garden.

Recommended Plants for City Conditions

(s) indicates tolerance for shade; (c) indicates tolerance for general adverse urban conditions

Large Trees

Acer platanoides (Norway maple) Needs space. (c)

Aesculus carnea (Red horse chestnut) Beautiful flowers. Needs space.

Aesculus hippocastanum (Horse chestnut) Handsome but needs space. (s-c)

Ailanthus altissima (Tree-of-heaven) Self-sows and grows anywhere. (c)

Broussonetia papyrifera (Paper mulberry) Not hardy north of New York City. Very handsome tree but branches are brittle. (s-c)

Catalpa speciosa (Western catalpa) Graceful; lovely flowers. (s-c)

Ginkgo biloba (Maidenhair tree) One of the best for street plantings. Slender habit. Plant male tree to avoid messy fruit. (s-c)

Gleditsia triacanthos (Honey locust) Many forms.

Platanus acerifolia (London plane, Sycamore) Very tolerant. (s-c)

Populus (Lombardy and Bolleana poplars) Good for quick screening. (c)

Salix babylonica (Weeping willow) Needs moisture. Stands wind and shade well. Will grow on high terraces. (s-c)

Tilia europaea (Linden) Standard street tree.

Small Trees

Aralia spinosa (Devils-walking-stick) Unusual shape and foliage. Thorny.

Cornus florida (Flowering dogwood) Needs deep, rich soil.

Crataegus (Hawthorn) All kinds. Lovely in bloom. (c)

Elaeagnus angustifolia (Russian-olive) Slender, graceful. Wind-resistant. Good for high terraces. (s-c)

Magnolia (Magnolia) Does well even in mediocre soil but should have sun for blooms. *M. soulangeana* and *M. stellata* are popular in city. (s)

Malus (Flowering crab) Many kinds available. (c)

Morus alba pendula (Weeping white mulberry). Interesting as tub subject on terrace. (s-c)

Fruit Trees

Apple, pear, cherry and peach all do well and have pretty flowers even if fruit is mediocre or lacking. Dwarf trees and espalier forms are especially desirable. All need some sun; the more the better.

Evergreen Trees and Shrubs

Frequent replacements, especially among coniferous evergreens, may be necessary in very dense situations. Taxus or yew is more tolerant than most needle evergreens.

Euonymus Many kinds of these evergreen types do exceptionally well in the city garden. (s-c)

Ilex crenata (Japanese holly) Excellent for year-round effect. (s-c)

Kalmia latifolia (Mountain-laurel) Showy flowers for shade. (s-c)

Pieris japonica (Andromeda) Showy flowers, good foliage in shade. (s-c)

Rhododendron Evergreen azaleas very satisfactory in shade. (s-c)

Deciduous Shrubs

Abelia grandiflora (Abelia) Semi-evergreen south of New York City. Elsewhere, may die to ground in winter but comes back rapidly. Attractive flowers. (c)

Acanthopanax sieboldianus (Aralia) Useful foliage plants. (s-c)

Berberis (Barberry) Many kinds, both evergreen and deciduous. (s-c)

Buddleia davidi (Butterfly-bush) Handsome flowers in summer. (c)

Calycanthus floridus (Strawberry bush) Coarse but rugged with fragrant, late spring flowers, yellow autumn foliage. (s-c)

Chaenomeles (Japanese flowering quince) Showy red or pink flowers in spring.

Cotoneaster horizontalis Graceful plant for walls and foreground.

Deutzia gracilis Dainty white flowers on low shrub. (c)

Euonymus alatus (Burning-bush) For background. Red autumn coloring. (c)

Forsythia Several kinds. For sun and space. Can be espaliered against walls.

Hibiscus syriacus (Rose of Sharon) Needs sun. (c)

Hydrangea Most kinds where there is space. (s-c)

Kerria japonica Yellow flowers, attractive foliage and green stems. (s-c)

Ligustrum (Privet) Indispensable for hedges, boxes, tubs. (s-c)

Lonicera (Honeysuckle) Shrub forms are not for cramped quarters.

Philadelphus (Mock-orange) Needs sun. Select compact varieties. (c)

Prunus glandulosa rosea (Flowering almond) Dainty habit. Early pink flowers.

Pyracantha coccinea (Firethorn) Choice with showy orange berries. Can be espaliered. (c)

Rhodotypos tetrapetala (Jetbead) Durable, low-growing. Its white flowers appear even in shade. (s-c)

Rosa (Rose) No rose does well in shade nor in dense, polluted atmosphere. Hybrid tea roses may endure for a season in tubs in sun.

Sorbaria sorbifolia (False-spirea). Rapid growing. Handsome feathery foliage and large panicles of white flowers in summer. (s-c)

Spiraea (Spirea) Anthony Waterer, *S. vanhouttei*, *S. thunbergi* best in city.

Stephandandra incisa Low habit but spreads. For sun or shade. (s-c)

Viburnum Many species and varieties available. (s-c)

Weigela Very tough. Needs sun to flower well. (c)

Perennial Vines

Akebia quinata Graceful vine for trellises.

Ampelopsis brevipedunculata (Turquoise-berry) Handsome foliage and berries.

Clematis Only *Clematis paniculata* and *C. jackmani* will endure.

Dioscorea batatas (Cinnamon-vine) Tough. Self-seeds.

Hedera helix (English ivy) Rugged but burns in winter sun or wind. (s-c)

Lonicera halliana (Honeysuckle) Even in city can grow out-of-bounds.

Parthenocissus quinquefolia (Virginia creeper) Excellent cover. (s-c).

Parthenocissus tricuspidata (Boston ivy) Very handsome. (s-c)

Polygonum auberti (Silver lace) Long season; clean foliage; white flowers. Once established, grows rapidly. (c)

Pueraria (Kudzu-vine) Coarse foliage. Rapid growth. May winter-kill to ground. (s-c)

Wisteria sinensis Long-lived, beautiful flowering vine. Train horizontally. (c)

Annual Vines

Calonyction aculeatum (Moonflower) Its night-blooming habit one of joys of city gardening.

Dolichos lablab (Hyacinth bean) Twining habit. (c)

Echinocystis lobata (Wild cucumber) Self-seeds; may become weedy.

Humulus japonicus (Japanese hop) Same as above. (s-c)

Ipomoea (Morning glory) Needs sun, otherwise will grow and flower anywhere. (c)

Bulbs, Wild Flowers and Ferns

Among spring-flowering bulbs, tulips, daffodils and hyacinths are especially rewarding. Most of the smaller kinds, crocus, etc., are also satisfactory. It may be necessary to make new plantings each fall. Many spring wild flowers and ferns, especially in shade, are successful. Violet, trillium, Solomons-seal, and Jack-in-the-pulpit combine well with ferns and spring bulbs.

Perennials

Many perennials will succeed for a season or longer where conditions are relatively good. The following are especially tolerant.

Ajuga All kinds. (s-c)

Astilbe japonica Some shade.

Bergenia Some shade. (s-c)

Ceratostigma Fall flowers.

Chrysanthemum Buy budded plants.

Convallaria (Lily-of-the-valley) For shade.

Coreopsis For sun.

Dianthus barbatus Buy budded plants.

Dicentra eximia For shade. (s-c)

Gaillardia For sun.

Hemerocallis (Day-lily) Superior. (s-c)

Heuchera For sun.

Hosta For shade. (s)

Iris For sun. Durable.

Peony Full sun; large gardens.

Phlox divaricata (s)

Platycodon For sun.

Sedum For sun. (c)

Annuals

Ageratum

Antirrhinum (Snapdragon)

Celosia

Cleome

Coreopsis (Calliopsis)

Lobelia

Lobularia (Sweet alyssum)

Mirabilis (Four-o'clock)

Nicotiana

Petunia

Phlox

Portulaca

Salvia

Tagetes (Marigold)

Torenia (s)

Verbena

Zinnia

Miscellaneous Bedding Plants

To supplement annuals and perennials, there are caladium, wax begonia (tuberous begonia will not succeed in a poorly ventilated, smoky atmosphere), pansy, English daisy and forget-me-not. For sun only, there are geraniums and lantana plants. Coleus will succeed in partial shade.

A statue of the young Carl Linnaeus, in his garden in Uppsala, Sweden, commemorates the man whose book Species Plantarum *(1753) marked the beginning of the binomial system of naming plants.*

CHAPTER 21

A Small Treasury

Who loves a garden
Still his Eden keeps,
Perennial pleasures plants,
And wholesome harvest reaps
– *Amos Bronson Alcott*

The purpose of plant names, of course, is to identify and distinguish individual plants from one another and also indicate the botanical relationship, if any, between them. All plants have a botanical or scientific name, Latin in form (because that is the language of science the world over). Most plants also have a "common," popular, or vernacular name that varies according to the language of which it is a part, and also according to the region where it originated and is used.

Common names of plants, like nicknames of people, are largely a matter of usage or custom. A plant may be called several things in different places – cornflower, bachelors-button, and bluebottle in this country, and Kaiser-blume (or emperor's flower) in Germany, are all names referring to the plant that botanists know as *Centaurea cyanus.*

So it is easy to understand why a botanical name is the best identification: it is the same in all countries and, usually, does not change with the years. Common names may be picturesque, have sentimental or historical significance, and seem, at first, easier to use. But when you understand the form and meaning of botanical names, their usefulness becomes apparent; and it doesn't take long to get into the habit of using both kinds interchangeably. You do just that when you speak of chrysanthemum, zinnia, iris, salvia, delphinium, rhododendron, and many other familiar garden flowers – for their botanical and common names are the same.

Every plant has been given at least 2 botanical names, which correspond roughly to our surnames and given names. The first, always spelled with a capital, indicates the plant group or *genus* the plant belongs to, as *Delphinium, Rosa, Dahlia, Iris.* The second indicates the *species,* or group within a genus, to which it and its close relatives belong, as *Rosa rugosa, Iris siberica.* Within a species there may be numerous *varieties* which differ in only a single character: color, height, doubleness of flower. A variety name may be in botanical form (sometimes within quotation marks) or it may be merely a proper name like the many found in catalogs. To be especially accurate, writers often use a plant's common name followed by its botanical name, often in italics, in parentheses.

An example is the name, "Double peach-leaved bellflower (*Campanula persicifolia flore-pleno*)." *Campanula* (genus or generic name) comes from the Latin for "little bell"; *persicifolia* (species or specific name) is the combination of botanical

Latin for leaf (*folia*) and the specific name for peach (*persica*); and the varietal label *flore-pleno* is botanical Latin for "double-flowered." But whereas the English name would mean something only to one speaking that language, the botanical name would mean the same thing to all persons in all countries.

Tool Talk

With tools as in everything else, quality pays. Buy only the best of tools, and do your best to keep from lending them to your friends and neighbors. A man who is not interested enough in gardening to own the necessary tools will not take proper care of yours!

Whether you purchase a hand mower, a power mower, or an electric model will depend on the size of your lawn area and the effort you are willing to give to this chore. The electric mower is perhaps the easiest to operate but the cord may be bothersome.

The rotary type power mower has much in its favor. Since it cuts high, turfmen claim it will do more towards building up a heavy turf than any other part of a lawn maintenance program. The rotary mower will cut higher grass and weeds than the reel type and will also mow under shrubs, hedges, and trees, thus cutting down on the trimming. But in order to make a clean cut, the blades must be kept sharp. Dull blades mutilate the top of the grass and may cause severe injury to the turf.

The reel type provides a neater cut, and there is no danger connected with its use. It is self-sharpening to some extent and does not leave the mounds of clippings or duff as is the case with a rotary type. The reel-type mower must be used more often than the rotary for it will not cut high grass. Neither is it satisfactory on grades.

Few hand mowers are in use today; but if there is only a small area to mow, they serve the purpose very well. And they are comparatively quiet!

A rotary power mower is a boon when large areas, high grass, or irregular surfaces are to be mowed. This one is self-propelled.

A leaf sweeper eases the chore of removing autumn's crop from lawn, where leaves shouldn't remain.

While there is always the restriction of the budget, it is poor economy to purchase a cheap power mower. It will be the source of continual aggravation, for nothing is more frustrating than to have a mower out of order when the grass needs attention. The casing and the wheels, as well as the motor and blades, should be of quality materials, backed by a reputable company.

After soil has been pulverized by power tiller (in rear), a spreader is being used to add a measured application of lime or plant food.

Long-handled shears have uses besides hedge trimming. These help in autumn clean-up.

In addition to tilling soil on the level, a power tiller can be used to prepare planting holes.

Like any other piece of equipment, the mower will last longer if given some care. Read directions carefully, and keep them in a convenient location so that you can check back from time to time. Don't let young children play with or operate the mower; keep them at a good distance when the mower is being operated.

Many gardeners who should know better tend to turn a deaf ear to the admonition of keeping hand tools in proper condition. Yet, dull-edged, rusted, or hard clay-encased trowels and shovels do not slide through the soil cleanly or function correctly in transplanting procedures.

No matter where you store tools, cleaning cloths should always be provided to care for them after each use. First you need an oily cloth and then a dry cloth. It is surprising how much easier the tools are to use, how much more satisfaction they will give if they are kept clean.

A pail or box in the toolhouse or garage filled with sand saturated with motor oil provides a handy means of keeping hand tools in working order. The spade, shovel, fork or trowel can be plunged several times in the sand and oil after use.

Whether you have the minimum or maximum number of both power and hand tools and equipment, the matter of storage can be a concern. The advent of the pegboard has helped to solve the problem of utilizing wall space in the garage or tool-

Attached to this cupola-topped garden house are shelves where potted or cut flowers could be displayed or house plants summered over.

Dual duty is done by a pool house with dressing rooms backed up by tool and supply storage.

house, thus providing a convenient storage for many tools.

A toolhouse or shed, attractive enough to resemble the more traditional garden house, sometimes is the only solution for storage of garden tools and equipment. It should be practical as well as attractive – no one wants to look at an eyesore. Don't make it too small, or in a few years you'll have to solve the storage problem all over again. There should be space for the necessary tools as well as chemical supplies, bags of fertilizer, and any other gardening adjuncts.

Cold Frames

The cold frame is merely a glass-topped box set in or upon the ground which, while protecting its contents from wind and frost, is heated by the sun in the daytime. This heat may be retained at night by a mat covering.

The cold frame's uses are many. Every gardener will find it adaptable to some need. It has been estimated that the flowering season may be prolonged outdoors for 60 days by using it to start flowers earlier and to mature the late ones in the fall. Spring-flowering bulbs potted for winter bloom may be easily buried here to be taken indoors as needed.

For wintering half-hardy plants such as foxglove, campanula, and pansy, its value cannot be overestimated. Gourmet cooks can grow winter onion, chives, parsley, and thyme for seasoning all winter, not to mention the early onion, radish, and lettuce, whose flavor cannot be duplicated in stores.

The messy business of trying to start seedling plants indoors in the spring is to a great extent made unnecessary by a cold frame. Seeds started early may be hardened to fit outdoor conditions, and the chances of success are multiplied many times.

A practical selection of plants which can easily be started in cold frames in March in most areas would include: China aster, cardinal flower, chrysanthemum (annual), cosmos, dahlia, phlox (annual), snapdragon, stock (10 weeks), sweet William, blue salvia, and delphinium. Both hotbeds (see below) and cold frames should be located in a sheltered place, where they will be protected from north and northwest winds by shrubbery, a fence, building, or higher ground. They should also be placed on ground with a southern and an eastern exposure, so that the plants will receive the maximum amount of light and heat. The frames should be handy to the house and garden so that they can be given constant attention. The soil in and about the frame should be well drained. The water supply should be close to the frame, for watering is an essential factor in the production of good plants.

Do not be in too big a hurry to construct your cold frame of concrete. A wooden one will last for years. After you have used it for a while you may want to move it.

The frame may be constructed up on top of the ground but a better way is to dig a pit and extend the wooden frame to the bottom; then after conditioning the soil replace it in the pit. The wooden frame insulates the soil in the bed from the surrounding conditions and enables you to control it more easily.

The frame should be made of tight boards, and it is better to bank the soil around as a further protection. The sash comes in standard size (3 feet wide and 6 feet long). Half-size sash (3 feet by 3 feet) is made for small frames. A third size (2 feet by 4 feet) is easier to handle and suitable for most home gardeners. (Small cold frames can also be purchased ready-made.) The sash must be painted each year and stored on end, in the shade, where it is fairly dry, when not in use, as the sun and continual moisture rot them.

The sash is made as light as possible for handling and because of this sags quickly. It must be supported by a 2 by 4 on edge at each end of the frame and by 2 by 4 bars set flat between each 2 sashes. The sash is allowed to rest upon these bars 1 inch on either side. Upon the bars are nailed 1-inch strips to keep the sashes from interfering when moved and to make them fit tightly. Close fitting is essential as a slight draft at the wrong time will harm the plants.

While not as durable as glass, plastics can be used to cover the cold frame. The plastic should be of a heavy quality, preferably with thin wire running through it. The plastic should be fastened on a reinforced frame with molding or strips so that the nails do not come through. A plastic cover is light in weight; hence it is important to use fasteners like screen-door hooks and eyes.

A lath screen for shading seedlings after the sash or cover is removed is a necessity. It will also prevent pets from digging and children from tramping in the frame. More important, it will keep hard rains from washing the seeds away and will shade the plants from the hot sun. Laths are sold in bundles. Merely tack them onto stakes the

Two views of a conventional cold frame.

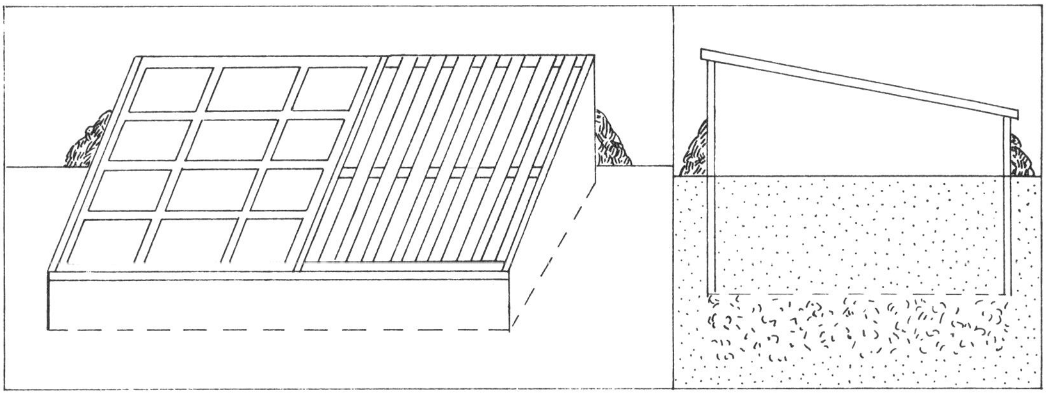

A simple homemade cold frame set over a basement window is being covered with plastic.

Plastic sheeting is held firmly in place by wood strips. Oakum should be used for caulking where frame doesn't fit closely against house.

Hotkaps function like miniature greenhouses, giving an early start to tender vegetables. Once growth is well under way, a small hole is torn in each.

length of the frame. The screen will last longer and be less conspicuous if painted.

Cold frame soil depends upon the use to which the frame is being put. For growing more mature plants, fertility is necessary; but for starting seed and maturing seedlings a rich soil is a detriment. Seeds and cuttings must first have their roots developed in what is known as a sterile medium, usually sand for drainage and peat moss for holding moisture.

Whatever the use, the soil at all times must drain well. The enemy of all propagation, indoors or under glass, is a fungus disease called "damping-off" that feeds on an excess of moisture in soil and air. The soil must be allowed to hold only what can be absorbed by it, and the excess must run off freely.

When wintering plants in a cold frame the sash may be left on most of the time; but when young plants are being raised, ventilation is necessary every day. Otherwise, the air is damp and confined and the inside climate changeable. This results in the fatal damping-off. Steam of moisture upon the glass is a danger signal. Open the sash a tiny crack for a short time in cold weather and more in warmer. Always open on the side away from the wind.

On sunny days water each day in the morning so that plants dry off before the cold of night. In cloudy weather, they may need watering only once every two or three days.

For sudden changes or cold nights late in spring, it is well to have a mat made of an old rug or quilted burlap bags, to cover the entire frame. Be sure to remove it during the daytime. Strong mats made for the purpose can be purchased.

Hotbeds

A hotbed differs from a cold frame only in that it is artificially heated from below by the fermentation of manure or otherwise. It is a miniature greenhouse. Electricity is the key to modern hotbed operation. It does away with the delay and mess of using fresh manure, which is becoming harder and harder to obtain in cities and suburbs. It is easy and inexpensive to install, and it provides steady heat where most needed (just below seeds or plants) and, with the help of a simple automatic thermostat, to whatever extent is desired. Assuming that an ordinary light socket is close by the hotbed, or that you can rig up (or have installed) the necessary wiring, all that is needed is (1) a length of lead-covered heating cable to be laid back and forth on a bed of sand in the hotbed and covered with another layer of sand and then soil; (2) the thermostat which turns the current on when heat is needed and off when it is not; and (3) a soil thermometer connected with the thermostat and inserted in the soil. The whole business can be bought from greenhouse manufacturing firms and should last a good many years. For more information write to your state experiment station for bulletins.

Planters, Window Boxes, and Containers

Though there is nothing new to using potted plants to dress up the outdoors, today's architecture and landscaping trends make the use of planters and all kinds of containers especially valid. Without them the terrace or patio may appear unfurnished and uninviting.

The boxes or planters need not always match the architecture of the house, but they should harmonize in color and form. Do not make the planters or boxes too small. Keep in mind that living plants will be confined in them, and roots will not be able to go down deep where there is moisture, the way they would if planted in the garden.

An iron frame supports this portable "window box" containing cut evergreens and artificial poinsettias.

Window boxes should extend past the opening 4 to 6 inches on either side of the window rather than be fitted to the sill. This will add considerably to their appearance. During the winter, small living evergreens will thrive in a large planter if adequate moisture is provided. As for smaller boxes, branches of evergreens will remain fresh in appearance over a long period.

Large-leaved tropical plants are dramatic for terrace boxes and planters during the summer in cold climates. Cacti and succulents may be effective on very sunny terraces where other plants would require too frequent watering. Cacti and succulents demand a gritty soil – about half sand and half soil mixture. Actually, almost any kind of plant can be put in a container, either permanently or temporarily, depending on the container and the climate. Penthouse garden plants are all container-grown, of course, with small flowering trees, birches, and evergreens confined to larger tubs, and smaller shrubs, perennials, and annuals growing in large planters.

A change in garden level – a flight of shallow steps – is marked by an Italian clay pot containing a dracena.

A "step garden" of marguerites and marigolds in painted wooden tubs of various sizes.

Even vegetables like the tomato can successfully be grown in pots and planters.

In container gardening, the same rules apply as in arranging plants in the open ground. Avoid the use of too many different plants; group a few of the same kinds together. Don't use too many exotic or accent plants without the unifying effect of other plants of less dramatic habit.

Exposure and climate must also be considered (some plants, tropical or perhaps only half-hardy, must be brought into a cool but frost-free shelter during winter unless they are considered expendable), as well as the soil requirements of some plants. Fortunately, the majority of plants will thrive in containers in an average garden soil well fortified with peat moss to hold moisture. Yet the requirement of adequate drainage is as important as the need for soil that does not bake dry and hard every sunny day.

Boxes should have holes in the bottom for drainage, and about 2 inches of coarse gravel below the soil mixture. Keep in mind that the soil will dry out rapidly in hot or windy weather. It may need watering at least once a day. Also, plants must be fed at regular intervals. The soil in the planters and pots should be revitalized with peat moss, superphosphate, and other materials each year. In deep planters only about a foot of the soil need be improved.

Garden centers and nurseries display a wide variety of pots and containers of clay, cement, plastic, and wood. Home craftsmen can make planters of oak, redwood, and other materials fastened with screws rather than nails (which won't hold), according to their own designs or those found in books and magazines.

The following plants are suggested for containers but there are many more. In fact, most plants can be used, though not all are hardy in cold regions.

TREES AND SHRUBS

Acacia, various
Acer palmatum (Japanese maple)

This Camellia japonica, *which spends its winters indoors, is planted in plastic and wire for easy transfer from a container or indoor bed to its outdoor summer quarters.*

Classic formal urns needn't be restricted to large gardens if kept in scale with their surroundings.

Aucuba japonica (Golddust tree)
Bambusa, various (Bamboo)
Berberis, various (Barberry)
Betula, various white forms (White birch)
Buxus koreana and *B. sempervirens* (Box)
Camellia, various (Camellia)
Citrus, dwarf kinds
Cornus florida (Flowering dogwood)
Crataegus, various (Hawthorn)
Cryptomeria japonica

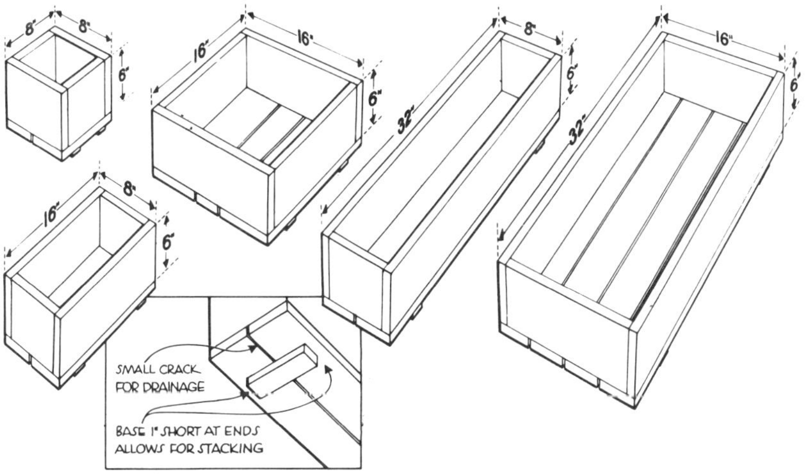

Measurements and construction details for planter boxes of convenient dimensions.

As redwood contains its own natural preservatives, it is ideal wood for containers such as this.

Six-sided planters of various heights can be combined in groups or used individually. Made of a double thickness of boards, these are reinforced with galvanized metal strips at joints.

Forsythia various (Forsythia)
Gardenia various (Gardenia)
Hedera helix (English ivy)
Hibiscus syriacus (Rose of Sharon)
Hydrangea macrophylla (French hydrangea)
Hydrangea petiolaris (Climbing hydrangea)
Ilex various (Holly)
Juniperus various (Juniper)
Laburnum wateri (Golden chain)
Laurus nobilis (Sweet bay)
Lavendula officinalis (Lavender)
Ligustrum various (Privet)
Magnolia soulangeana (Saucer magnolia)
Magnolia stellata (Star magnolia)
Malus, both dwarf and espalier forms (Apple, Crabapple)
Nandina domestica (Heavenly bamboo)
Nerium oleander (Oleander)
Osmanthus ilicifolius (Tea-olive)
Pinus various (Pine)
Pittosporum tobira (Pittosporum)
Poncirus trifoliata (Trifoliate orange)
Prunus various (Japanese cherry, Plum, Flowering almond)
Prunus persica 'Flory' and 'Bonanza' (Flowering dwarf peach)
Pyracantha various (Firethorn)
Raphiolepis indica (India-hawthorn)
Rhododendron, evergreen azaleas are best
Rosmarinus officinalis (Rosemary)
Skimmia japonica (Skimmia)
Syringa various (Lilac)
Taxus various (Yew)
Thuja various (Arborvitae)
Wisteria, tree or standard forms (Wisteria)

ANNUALS AND PERENNIALS

Acanthus
Agapanthus (Blue lily of the Nile)
Ageratum (Floss-flower)
Astilbe
Begonia, especially Wax and Tuberous
Bergenia
Browallia
Caladium
Chrysanthemum, all kinds
Clivia
Coleus
Crinum
Ferns, most kinds
Fuchsia
Heliotropium (Heliotrope)
Hemerocallis (Day-lily)
Hosta (Funkia)
Hyacinthus (Hyacinth)
Kochia (Burning-bush)
Lantana
Narcissus (Daffodil)
Pelargonium (Geranium)
Petunia
Sedum
Tagetes (Marigold)
Tropaeolum (Nasturtium)

Tulipa (Tulip)
Vinca major (Large periwinkle)
Viola tricolor (Pansy)
Yucca (Spanish bayonet)

Concrete in the Garden

Concrete in the garden? Yes, but it must be added with discretion and should never dominate the scene to the extent of drawing one's attention away from the plants and garden as a whole.

Concrete is made by mixing cement with clean, sharp sand and washed, crushed stone or pebbles. The sand is called fine aggregate; and the stone or pebbles, coarse aggregate. The cement and sand form a sort of glue or mortar which goes into the spaces between the pebbles (called "voids"), uniting them into a stone-like mass. It takes 7 cubic feet of material to form 4½ cubic feet of concrete.

Large masses of concrete may use coarse pebbles or stone, but small objects, such as stepping-stones or garden pottery, use fine pebbles, usually called pea gravel or torpedo sand.

In the making of small objects such as boxes and benches, it is important that the cement be fresh. Cement is very sensitive to moisture; and if exposed to rain, fogs, dew or moisture of any kind it receives its first set or "hydration." This destroys its usefulness for fine work although it may work very well in walls or mass.

Its freshness may be tested by examining the sack to see that there are no hard lumps in it. Fresh cement will feel slippery when rubbed between the fingertips.

All materials should be accurately measured. A large scoop shovel is good for this purpose. Also, a pail may be used. Thus a standard mixture known as 1:2:4 would be measured: 1 pail of cement, 2 of sand, and 4 of pebbles. A sack of cement contains approximately 1 cubic foot.

Lay the proportioned materials on a watertight platform of boards; first spread the sand and cement in layers, and cut them each way until no streaks of gray show.

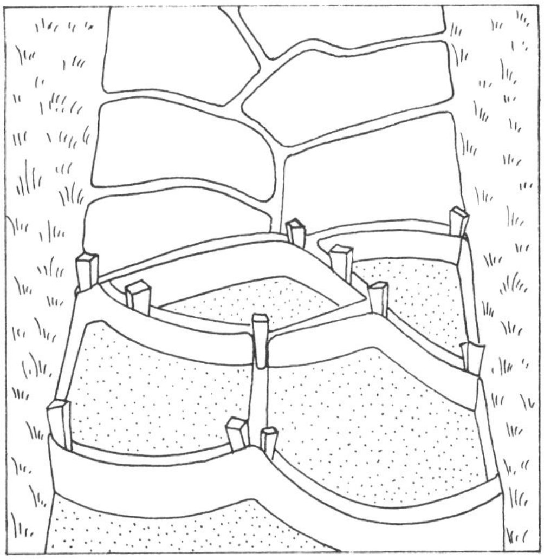

Using sheet-metal forms to cast a stepping-stone path in place.

Careful preparation of foundations and unhurried workmanship give good results in garden masonry or concrete work.

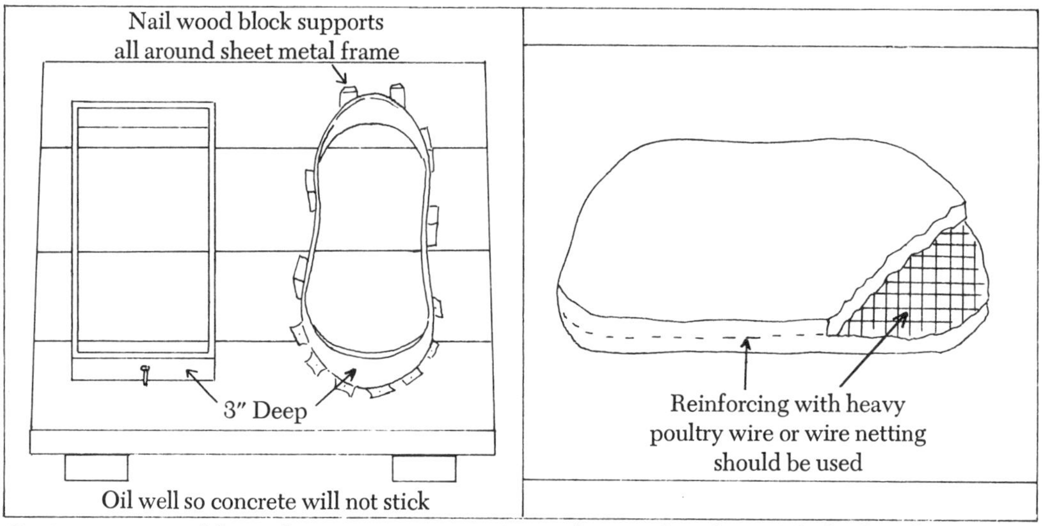

Casting concrete slabs and stepping-stones in forms three inches deep. Oil the board base and forms well. Right, *heavy poultry wire or wire netting is used as interior reinforcement.*

Both good design and good sense: the half-round well left around the tree will admit water and air to roots.

Over this spread the pebbles, and mix thoroughly. It is well to have a second person apply the water (after the dry materials are mixed together) with a hose, gradually obtaining the proper moisture; or it may be applied in a depression or hollow in the top of the pile as it is mixed. When the process is completed, every pebble should be coated with a mortar of sand and cement. Try to achieve a mixture wet enough to form a pasty or jelly-like mass but not soupy enough to flow or run.

When cement is mixed with water alone, it is called "neat." Neat cement is used for coating surfaces of pottery boxes and other objects to make them very smooth. When a rough or pebbled finish, similar to stucco, is desired use a very wet or soupy mortar and apply it by spattering it over the object. Dip a whisk broom into the mortar, and throw it in fine particles against the slightly dampened surface of the object to be covered. The usual mixture for stucco is 1:2 (1 part cement to 2 parts sand).

Any objects made of concrete which do not come out of their form well finished can be pointed up with a mortar mixture of 1 part cement to 2 parts of sand. This same mixture can be plastered on the inside of a pool to make it waterproof. Cement paints are for sale in white and other colors for yearly freshening, or the cement can be colored as it is mixed by using special cement tints.

For objects such as stepping-stones, slabs, benches, bird baths, and fence posts use a 1:2:3 mixture, meaning 1 part cement, 2 of sand, and 3 parts pebbles. The pebbles should be fine (torpedo sand or pea gravel). A standard mixture of 1:2:4 in which the pebbles may be fairly large is used for walls, walks, structures, floors, and foundations.

Most objects of concrete require a form but small, free-form pools and shallow bird baths and many kinds of stepping-stones are exceptions. Forms are made of metal, wood, and in some cases plaster of Paris. In mass work (walls, piers), it is important that the forms be strongly made. The extreme weight of the material causes great pressure against the form walls. If they are not well braced and wired together, they will bulge and cause irregular work. They must be true and level. Spreader blocks are placed to keep the form faces the right distance apart; they are removed as the concrete is placed up to them. The wires are twisted as the form is made to true it up and keep the blocks in place. The weight of the mass as placed loosens them for easy removal.

Whether you are building a wall or a vase, your finished surface will be no smoother than your forms. Good forms are not battered or rough. All of them should be coated with oil before placing concrete in them to prevent adhesion and to make their removal easy. If the form is to slide out of, or away from the concrete, it must be slightly tapered; and if made of metal, it must be free from dents which would impede this process.

The concrete mixture should be poured into the forms as soon as possible; in no case more than 30 minutes after mixing. In walls, place it in layers 6 inches thick, thoroughly spaded. (Spading means working with a spade or chisel board into the concrete against the forms up and down and

A pattern for setting pre-cast concrete slabs.

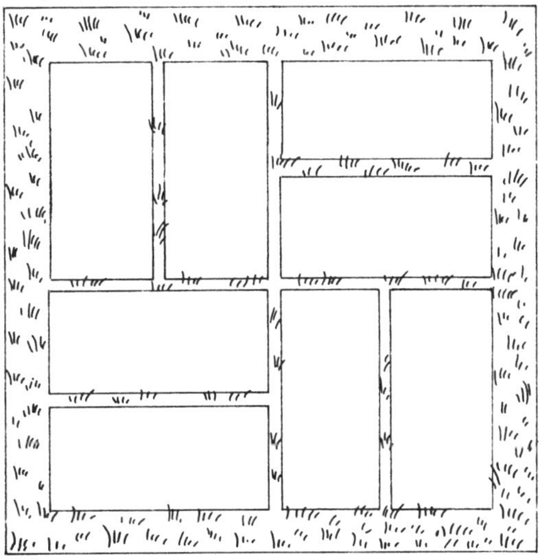

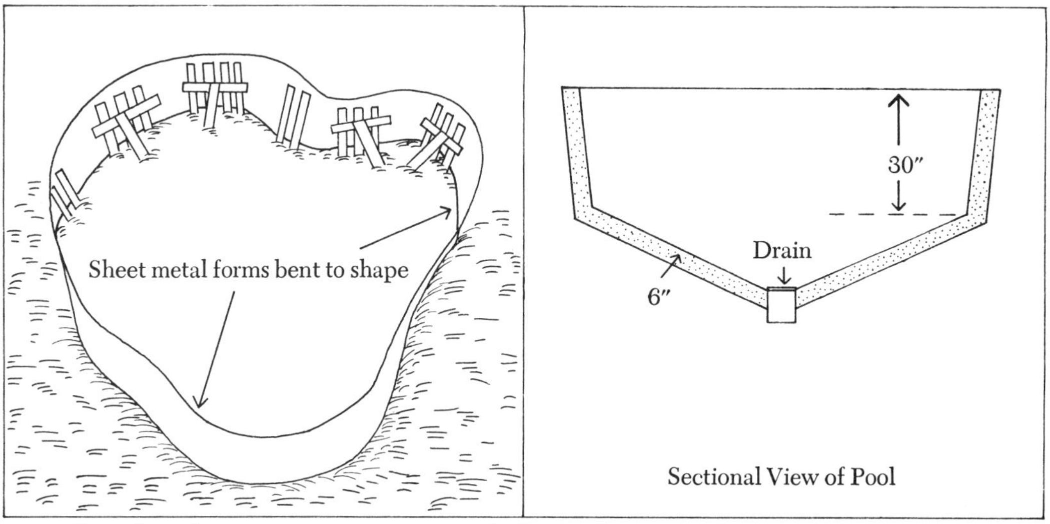

A small pool can be cast in an excavation, with sheet-metal forms bent to shape for the sides.

to and fro, to remove any air spaces and force large pebbles away from the forms into the mass. This insures an even, dense surface when finished.)

Concrete in smaller objects is thoroughly worked with a chisel-edged stick or trowel to see that all corners are completely filled and the coarser particles kept away from the faces of the form.

In making a lawn roller, a piece of iron pipe is cast in the exact center to act as an axle sleeve or boxing. A smaller piece of pipe threaded at each end is run through this to be used as an axle. Pipe flanges or nuts are used to fasten it tightly to the handle. Some prefer to cast the axle solidly into the concrete, allowing it to turn in the handle.

Flat work, such as walks and floors, is not spaded. A foundation layer of cinders is tamped on ground which has been thoroughly compacted, and the concrete is placed and leveled off with a "strike board." This concrete is then firmed into place by tamping it lightly and finishing with a float or trowel. If a smooth surface is desired, it is finished with a steel tool which draws the water and cement to the surface. This is called "flowing it" or "floating it" to the top. This cement lacks wearing qualities so that excessive manipulation of the surface will cause hair cracks after the concrete hardens. A surface finished under a wooden float wears better and is not so liable to be slippery.

After pouring the concrete it should be allowed to harden before removing the forms. In summer it takes from 2 to 4 days and in winter from 4 to 7 days. It must never be allowed to freeze until it is thoroughly set. Heat hastens and cold delays setting; thus it can be hastened by using warm water and, in cases of smaller objects, adding a very small quantity of washing soda to the water.

Properly prepared concrete will harden with age. If it is exposed to the sun or wind the water necessary for its hardening will dry out too quickly, causing cracking or shrinkage. The hardening is a chemical change which takes place slowly in the presence of water. Keeping the object damp for 10 days to 2 weeks is good practice. The objects may be covered with damp straw or canvas and wet by sprinkling. Walks and flat surfaces may be covered with earth after hardening and small objects made very hard by immersing in water for 4 or 5 days. After the forms have been removed, all rough spots should be pointed.

Reinforcing is necessary for many major

A good use of concrete block for a low retaining wall. Low-growing plants soften its outlines.

concrete construction projects and in any considerable job should be designed by an engineer. Reinforcing is necessary because concrete is strong under compression and is capable of bearing great loads but is comparatively weak in tensile strength. Steel rods properly placed increase its power to resist strains and keep it from pulling apart. Improperly placed they are wasted.

In smaller objects, use one-half-inch wire-net reinforcement to resist cracks due to shrinkage. Poultry netting or fine fence wire can also be used. All joints should be lapped or run past each other, and care must be used to keep the reinforcing material equally distant from the 2 surfaces. In making slabs, the concrete can be poured into the molds and firmed down, after which the reinforcing mesh or rods can be laid upon it and the rest of the concrete poured.

In walls or piers which do not have to stand any great strain but are reinforced to avoid cracks or shrinkage, three-eighths-inch deformed rods should be spaced 8 inches apart each way to form a network. They should be wired together into place midway between the form faces as the forms are built. They must stay in exact position as the concrete is spaded around them.

The rod sizes can be increased slightly if the ground to be supported is filled; but, if beams or walls are to be cast and are expected to hold great loads, it is better to hire an engineer to design properly the steel placement than to risk the loss of all the work.

All walks, steps, walls, and pools must be placed on solid ground. Any settling will cause them to crack or fall. Stepping-stones do not divide a garden layout and make it seem smaller as a solid concrete path does.

The wires support pyracantha espaliers on this neatly built wall of concrete block.

They can be tinted an earthy brown to resemble stones.

The effect of stone can also be obtained in the following manner: Crumble a long sheet of the heaviest brown paper into a barrel or tub of water, and let it soak for a few minutes. Then spread it out carefully on a wood or concrete platform, and set a single mold or multiple wooden molds upon it. The creases of the paper will make a pattern that suggests stone on the concrete as it hardens. For a walk, build an oblong mold of wood, the width of the walk and long enough to represent one section of the pattern desired. The finished blocks can be set on cinders or tamped ground and the joints filled with sand, or fine soil in which seed can be sown, or thyme and sedums planted.

By using molds of 2 different shapes and then using the slabs in as many different positions as possible the danger of monotony can be avoided. They should be laid just a trifle higher than the soil level and then tamped with a 2 by 4 to grade. Repeat the tamping several times after rains if necessary.

One important detail in laying steppingstones and, in fact, all walks, is that the outside edges be comparatively parallel. The path should be planned by placing a cord or a row of stakes before setting. If wide and narrow stones are laid at random it will not produce a pleasing design. Curves also must be broad and graceful.

To Help with Regional Problems

Each state maintains its own state agricultural experiment station, which can be a great help in solving specific regional problems. When writing, send questions to State Agricultural Experiment Station, followed by address for your state as given below.

Alabama: Auburn Univ., Auburn 36830.
Alaska: Univ. of Alaska, College 99735.
Arizona: Univ. of Arizona, Tucson 85721.
Arkansas: Univ. of Arkansas, Fayetteville 72701.
California: Univ. of California, 2200 University Ave., Berkeley 94720.
Colorado: Colorado State Univ., Fort Collins 80521.
Connecticut: Univ. of Connecticut, Storrs 06268.
Delaware: Univ. of Delaware, Newark 19711.
Florida: Univ. of Florida, Gainesville 32603.
Georgia: Univ. of Georgia, Athens 30601.
Hawaii: Univ. of Hawaii, Honolulu 96822.
Idaho: Univ. of Idaho, Moscow 83843.
Illinois: Univ. of Illinois, Urbana 61803.
Indiana: Purdue Univ., Lafayette 47907.
Iowa: Iowa State Univ., Ames 50010.
Kansas: Kansas State Univ., Manhattan 66504.
Kentucky: Univ. of Kentucky, Lexington 40506.
Louisiana: Louisiana State Univ., Baton Rouge 70803.
Maine: Univ. of Maine, Orono 04473.
Maryland: Univ. of Maryland, College Park 20742.
Massachusetts: Univ. of Massachusetts, Amherst 01003.
Michigan: Michigan State Univ., East Lansing 48823.

A graceful gate and wrought-iron lamps make an inviting entrance to a kitchen garden (raspberries are in view) surrounded by a painted concrete-block wall.

Minnesota: Univ. of Minnesota, St. Paul 55101.
Mississippi: Mississippi State Univ., State College 39762.
Missouri: Univ. of Missouri, Columbia 65201.
Montana: Montana State Univ., Bozeman 59715.
Nebraska: Univ. of Nebraska, Lincoln 68503.
Nevada: Univ. of Nevada, Reno 89507.
New Hampshire: Univ. of New Hampshire, Durham 03824.
New Jersey: Rutgers Univ., New Brunswick 08903.
New Mexico: New Mexico State Univ., University Park 88070.
New York: New York State Col. of Agr., Ithaca 14850.
North Carolina: North Carolina State Univ., Raleigh 27607.
North Dakota: North Dakota State Univ., Fargo 58103.
Ohio: Ohio State Univ., 2120 Fyffe Rd., Columbus 43210.
Oklahoma: Oklahoma State Univ., Stillwater 74075.
Oregon: Oregon State Univ., Corvallis 97331.
Pennsylvania: Pennsylvania State Univ., University Park 16802.
Rhode Island: Univ. of Rhode Island, Kingston 02881.
South Carolina: Clemson Univ., Clemson 29631.
South Dakota: South Dakota State Univ., Brookings 57007.
Tennessee: Univ. of Tennessee, Box 1071, Knoxville 37901.
Texas: Texas A&M Univ., College Station 77841.
Utah: Utah State Univ., Logan 84321.
Vermont: Univ. of Vermont, Burlington 05401.
Virginia: Virginia Polytechnic Inst., Blacksburg 24061.
Washington: Washington State Univ., Pullman 99163.
West Virginia: Nesius, Mineral Industries Bldg., West Virginia Univ., Morgantown 26506.
Wisconsin: Univ. of Wisconsin, Madison 53706.
Wyoming: Univ. of Wyoming, Box 3354, Univ. Station, Laramie 82071.

Begin the new year with at least one good foliage house plant. This is the bird's-nest fern.

CHAPTER 22

Garden Calendar

The Gardener's January

See, not one tree but what has lost its leaves –
And yet the landscape wears a pleasing hue. –*John Clare*

General: January is a time of dreaming and planning for most gardeners, many of whom have gardens submerged under snow. Gardeners in mild climates are an exception. They are spared these winter months of waiting and may continue to enjoy most outdoor activity, including planting. For one and all, the arrival of seed catalogs is a reminder of the magic stored in a tiny brown seed.

Make an inventory of garden tools and supplies. Discard those that are no longer useful. Old tools with dull edges can be sharpened for the coming season. Wrap friction tape around split wood sections which pinch fingers or leave slivers. Paint handles bright colors so you can find them easily and to help you remember to take them in at night.

If your garage is beginning to bulge from an abundance of power and hand tools, bicycles, and assorted items, consider the addition of a toolhouse. Many garden centers and department stores offer prefabricated metal houses of varying sizes. Before making a selection, think of your neighbors as some designs are hardly attractive. Building your own of a design in harmony with your house and surroundings may be a better solution.

In milder areas, it may be possible to dig up your garden if the soil is not wet, and expose it to the beneficial effects of freezing which breaks apart the heavy clods, causing them to crumble. The turning also exposes the eggs of many insect pests to the effects of sun, wind, freezing, and the food-hunting birds.

Birds: The best way to become acquainted with the winter as well as all-year residents among the birds is to feed them. Feeders, of course, should be near windows and should contain a variety of seeds to attract as many different birds as possible. Scatter some seed on the ground for birds that are naturally ground feeders. Suggested reading: any of the Roger Tory Peterson Field Guides to the Birds, and *Handtaming Wild Birds at the Feeder* by Alfred G. Martin.

Both coniferous and broadleaved evergreens considerably soften the stark outlines of winter landscapes.

Bulbs: The bulbs outdoors sometimes poke their noses through the ground during a warm spell; in such case, cover them with soil or peat moss, or draw the covering of boughs or straw a bit closer. An excellent use for discarded Christmas trees is to cover such early adventurers.

Evergreens: Shake off the snow (or use a broom) from evergreen trees and shrubs to keep the branches from breaking or bending out of shape. Light, fluffy snow does not pose too serious a threat to most evergreens, but if the weather changes so that the snow eventually freezes, the branches may be injured.

Evergreens are most important to the winter landscape. Do you have enough, and are they situated where you can enjoy them? If not, January is as good a time as any to correct that omission as far as planning is concerned. If your discarded Christmas tree is at hand, move it about to help you plan future evergreen plantings.

Pretty but potentially dangerous! Evergreens and other plants can be injured by deposits of snow or ice.

Feed the birds for more winter enjoyment. Make your own containers or buy elaborate, larger feeders.

Greenhouse and Cold Frame: Tilt the sash on cold frames on sunny days to ventilate. But be sure to cover them up again at night!

Greenhouse plants must be sprayed frequently with a strong force of water to keep red spider mite in check. This is one of the worst greenhouse pests if neglected, yet easy enough to keep under control. It is a case of frequent inspection and prompt action when necessary.

Houseplants: Soap and water work wonders with dust-clogged leaf pores of houseplants. Washing the foliage under the tap also rids plants like ivy of red spider mites. Actively-growing plants will benefit from a feeding of liquid fertilizer. Do everything you can to maintain humidity around houseplants, but don't syringe the foliage at night.

It is also a good practice to pull down the blinds behind plants on very cold nights or if necessary cover them with newspapers.

Christmas gift plants will last for weeks if given the right care. Protect the poinsettia from drafts, keeping it in a temperature of 70 degrees in the daytime and not lower than about 63 at night. Water daily or as often as needed with tepid or slightly warm water from above to keep the soil damp. When it has finished blooming and begins to drop its leaves, discard it, or set it aside; and give only enough water to keep it from drying out. In May, the plants are pruned back to leave stubs about 4 to 5 inches and repotted in a rich light soil. They are kept growing in a light position and in early June are plunged in the garden, where they may remain until late September. Professional growers always take cuttings from the new growth but home gardeners may be satisfied by following the above method.

The Christmas begonia remains a long time in bloom if given reasonable care and temperature conditions similar to those advised for poinsettia.

The Christmas cherry is long-lasting and less delicate than either begonia or poinsettia, thriving well in a cooler room and withstanding greater variations of temperature. During summer it can be planted in the open garden.

The cyclamen is a beautiful winter-blooming plant but don't be tempted to give it to anyone who can't provide a cool window for it. This plant needs more moisture than some. A daily watering may be necessary in dry rooms.

If you have rooted bulbs, you are now enjoying bloom aplenty but if you haven't, lily-of-the-valley pips may be obtained from your seed store or florist. All that is necessary is to add water. Hyacinths, Chinese sacred-lilies, and paperwhite narcissus can still be forced in bowls of water if bulbs are available.

Rock Garden: Sunny days bring out life in the rock garden. If snow is absent as a protector, see that surface soil has not been washed away from the crowns of plants. Press any lifted ones back in their pockets and sprinkle around more stone chips or gritty soil. Use leaves, evergreen boughs or marsh hay or straw as a light covering over low evergreens, heaths, and heathers to prevent winter burn of the foliage.

Seeds: Seed-sowing time will soon be here. Have you all the material ready–growing media, stones or broken flower pots for drainage, moss, boxes, seed pans, labels? Have you ordered your seeds and nursery stock?

Getting Started in February

Brother, joy to you!
I've brought some snowdrops; only just a few,
But quite enough to prove the world awake.
–Christina Rossetti

General: Start anything that will make spring tasks easier. Have you sprayed fruit trees for scale with miscible oil or lime-sulfur solution? (If you are in doubt as to proper timing for this activity in your area, call your county agent.)

Have you ordered your seeds and plants? February is the time to do it, when you have leisure to let the selections rattle around in your mind before making a final choice. Many gardens are spoiled by snap

This outdoor-living court with Douglas fir decking didn't just happen – it was carefully planned in advance.

Midwinter planning can pay. Decide now whether your terrace area makes sense for your family's needs.

decisions which the gardener makes in the heat of a busy season.

You may be one of those who has a tendency to crowd too much into your garden. Study some of the principles of planting in making your plan this year and don't attempt too great a variety in every plant grouping. Suggested reading: *On Gardening* by Gertrude Jekyll. You will marvel at the degree of planning and knowledge that was considered customary rather than exceptional when gardens were planned in the golden age of gardening.

If you must grow exotic plants not hardy in the region in which you live, remember that they are museum pieces rather than the backbone of your garden and treat them as such.

It is much easier to have your lawn mower taken care of now than it will be when you want to cut grass. You will then be in competition with everyone else, and the service may be hurried and uncertain. Plant stakes and labels are a necessary evil. If you expect to make some, get them ready now so that your staking may begin before your plant gets out of shape. Your seedsman can supply you with many label varieties in wood or metal. Bamboo stakes are fine for most perennials, although you will want some of the hoop or circular wire supports, too.

Consider an underground irrigation system for your lawn and garden this summer. Water is the life-giving force of the garden. An automatic system for the lawn is a great convenience and labor saver. You can install some of the systems yourself; others may require the work of a professional.

Annual Flowers: The time for selecting annual seeds is at hand. For all-round general use and beauty, nothing can equal petunia, marigold, nasturtium, zinnia, and snapdragon. The zinnia comes in so many sizes, colors, and shapes from the lilliput to the dahlia-flowered that a large space might be devoted to it alone without monotony.

So much can be achieved in handsome effects as well as nearly all-summer color that it is only sensible to plan before ordering annual seeds. Here are a few dependable combinations:

For Background: Lavender giant zinnia ('Lilac Time' or similar) and flowering tobacco ('Sensation,' 'Daylight') in red, pink, white. Lemon-yellow marigold and burnt-orange zinnia. Pale-yellow marigold with pink and white cosmos and blue salvia (*Salvia farinacea*). Globe-amaranth (magenta and white) with large-type zinnia. Pink cleome and pink or white cosmos.

Middle Border: Of course, plants for the middle border must be selected with a view to what is immediately behind and in front of them. In front of the flowering tobacco and the lilac zinnia, place shell-pink zinnia. In front of the lemon-yellow marigold and burnt-orange zinnia, place snapdragon (yellow or white), Chinese forget-me-not (*Cynoglossum*), and Unwin dwarf dahlia. Rose-colored zinnias also look well in front of the flowering tobacco. 'Pink Feather' cockscomb does well in front of the pale-yellow marigold and white cosmos, as also do pink and white China asters.

For the Front Border: Ageratum, dwarf French marigold (yellow), or dwarf 'Thumbelina' zinnia (mixed), dark-red dwarf nasturtium, petunia in many colors, sweet-alyssum, and lavender annual phlox (*Phlox drummondi*).

Now, while it is still winter, is a good time to appreciate the value of everlasting bouquets for winter decorations. Some of these may be brought indoors from the shrubbery border or the woods, but the majority of them require careful planning in the garden. Many catalogs devote space to the descriptions of these plants. You will find some of them fit into your borders very well while others are too stiff or sturdy in their texture and must be grown by themselves. By all means include some of them in your seed order. Instructions for drying them are found in the May calendar.

The middle of February is the traditional time to plant indoors seeds of slow-growing plants such as lobelia, ageratum, verbena, petunia, vinca, blue salvia, and scabiosa. Most other seeds can be started indoors in March. Unless you plan to move your seedlings later to a cold frame, it is a mistake to start most annuals indoors too early.

Bulbs: All the summer-flowering bulbs, such as canna, dahlia, and gladiolus, are subject to damage. See that they have not been started into growth by heat or dampness. They should be stored in a thoroughly dry place at a temperature of about 45 degrees. If the tubers have shriveled, place them in very slightly damp peat moss, but keep them cool so that they will not start into premature growth.

Evergreens: Giving them a dormant spray now will help control the red spider as well as scale and other pests. Check now for bagworm cocoons. They can be cut off and burned.

Shake off with care any heavy snow which clings to them, as the shape of the plant can be spoiled beyond remedy if it is left on too long.

Fruits: Prune grape vines. The fruit is borne near the beginning of shoots which will develop during the present season. These shoots come from last year's growth. In order to keep the strength of the plant from developing foliage instead of fruit, trim away the oldest wood, leaving only a few principal stems. Each of these old stems should retain 2 to 6 of the canes which grew last year. These previous year's canes must be cut back to 3 to 10 buds each.

Cut out the canes of raspberries (except everbearers) and blackberries which bore fruit last year. On currants, prune out the wood which is over 3 years old. Get supports of wire or tightly stretched wire fencing ready for the berries so that the new canes may be fastened to them for the best exposure to sun and air.

Have you studied the merits of a fruit border? Raspberries, currants, gooseberries, blackberries, grapes – all these make excellent border plants for the garden if kept within bounds and upon decent-looking supports.

Fruit trees can be pruned within the next few weeks. Of course, they will bear if they are not pruned, but will do much better if given attention. Good fruit is the product of intelligent pruning and spraying. The product of trees which do not have this care is usually wormy and knotty. Spray with lime-sulfur at dormant strength or use miscible oil (lime-sulfur will stain) if close to your house. All this pruning and spraying should be done before the sap starts to rise. Consider dwarf fruit trees for bloom and fruit if your place is small.

Houseplants: Sponge the leaves of houseplants occasionally with clean water. Give them plenty of fresh air, but not direct drafts. Now that the turn of the winter has passed, use a little fertilizer on any houseplants which have begun to show new growth.

Certain kinds of indoor bulbous houseplants (freesia, amaryllis, veltheimia, nerine) must be kept growing for a period after they have flowered and before their bulbs are rested. Amaryllis requires a long growth period during which time the foliage must be preserved if the bulb is to flower the next year. Hyacinth bulbs that have been forced indoors can be kept growing after flowering and planted outdoors when the ground warms up in late March.

It is a mistake to repot orange and other citrus trees too often; keep them potbound. Feed once a month during the growing period.

Red spider, aphid, white fly, mealybug, and scale can well compose the list of 5 most unwanted houseplant pests. (If you grow African-violets, you must watch for signs of the cyclamen mite. You won't see him, but his damage – distortion of growth, especially the centers – is very obvious.) For aphids and mealybug, use thick, mild soapsuds, and rinse off after an hour; or wipe off with a soft cloth dipped in mild soapsuds. Scale must be scraped off by hand with cloth or brush and the foliage rinsed off later. Red spider is very difficult to get rid of and very easy to acquire. Remember that it cannot live in moist, cool conditions and that the underside of the leaf is especially affected. Wash the leaves often with water as a preventive, and keep the air moist and cool. White fly sucks the plant juices. Use an aerosol bomb for all these pests, except cyclamen mite. Don't get the spray too close to the plants, or there will be leaf injury. Use sodium selenate treatment for African-violets. Follow directions when using any insecticides – indoors or outdoors! (Recommended reading: *The Complete Book of Gardening Under Lights* by Elvin McDonald.)

This apple tree is part of a small dwarf fruit orchard adjacent to a suburban property. Note how easily the fruit can be reached compared to large trees.

Pruning: Are you anxious to use new pruning shears or saw? Fruits, as suggested above, should get first attention. Then, any deadwood and branch trimming previously noticed on shade trees can be tackled. It is best not to cut live wood now of trees that "bleed" such as maple or elm. Wait until September or until their leaves are developed.

You can prune leaf-losing shrubs now, but keep in mind you may sacrifice some flower display – as in most cases, flower buds are now formed. Prune the peegee and snowhill hydrangea to very short stubs of branches.

Vegetables: Have you ordered your vegetable seeds? Some vegetables can be started earlier than you may realize. Some even *demand* an early start: peas, broad beans, onion, spinach, endive, radish, roquette, corn salad, and cress are the main cold-weather crops. In many areas of the South and West Coast, these crops are already growing or about to be sown. In colder regions, the seeds should be on hand, ready to go into the ground in March.

The Busy Month of March

In the wind of windy March
The catkins drop down,
Curly, caterpillar-like,
Curious green and brown.
– *Christina Rossetti*

General: The fickle weather of spring makes absolute dates for planting an impossibility. Many operations can be done during February or March when spring is early and the weather dry, whereas the next year may find them impossible until later in the season.

With the first warm days of March it is a temptation to start to remove winter mulches from flower beds. Don't do it in one fell swoop, but loosen them gradually over a period of days to permit air and some light to penetrate.

The purpose of a winter mulch is to serve as protection from wind and sudden changes in temperature. When you do your early spring cultivation, rake off the rougher material to be burned or composted. Dig the finer mulch into the beds. Always remember it is better to be too late with this removal than too early.

On the other hand, the hardiest bulbs and early perennials shouldn't remain hidden from now on. Early kinds of crocus and snowdrops are examples of plants that will bloom through cold, wet weather and late snow storms without damage (see following paragraph).

In many parts of the country, March means the opening of such intrepid bulbs as snowflake (Leocojum).

Bulbs: Daffodils will be pushing through the ground, and very early varieties ('Peeping Tom,' 'February Gold,' 'March Sunshine') will soon be in bloom. Tulips and hyacinths are slower to appear, a good thing, too, as they are more sensitive to late periods of freezing than daffodils. Loosen the mulch to keep them well covered, and add some more mulch to those over-valiant shoots which insist on coming through. A cold night wind will dry them out and injure the bulb. The longer you hold them back with a loose airy mulch, the more sure you will be of the results later.

Dahlia roots should be started into growth late in the month so that they may be easily divided or so that you can take cuttings from them if you wish. Lay the roots upon a few inches of sand, and water freely to start them into growth. Do not do this too early or give them too warm a temperature. (A greenhouse is ideal for this process.) Tuberous begonia and caladium may be embedded in flats of peat moss about the middle of the month.

Forcing: The forcing of flowering branches like forsythia, pussy willow, white forsythia (*Abeliophyllum*), February daphne, cornelian-cherry, and dogwood works like magic now, and you need wait only a few days for them to flower. You may also enjoy your own indoor spring flower show this season. Many spring-blooming plants may be forced by bringing them indoors in clumps. Select a day when the ground is still frozen but not hard enough to prevent you from digging clumps of dwarf iris, violet, crocus, scilla and a few other bulbs to be planted in bowls or pots. Water them well and remember to keep them cool at first so that they may acclimatize themselves to indoor conditions. The cooler you keep them, the longer they will last.

Greenhouse and Cold Frame: At this time of the year a cold frame is almost a necessity. Plants may be started indoors by various means, but many more can be started outdoors in a cold frame. Also the indoor plants must be hardened to the weather before being placed in permanent position. A cold frame is excellent protection from late frosts or cold, dank days.

In the greenhouse, cuttings of all the various types of bedding plants should be started in sand early this month. Coleus, geranium, lantana, heliotrope, and ageratum are some of those which come under this general heading and are suitable for many situations. Chrysanthemums for next fall may be propagated at this time, if the space is available. It is good practice to put in a batch of cuttings every four weeks from now until early June so as to assure a long period of bloom that will extend well into the autumn. (Recommended reading: *Greenhouse Gardening for Fun* by Clare L. Blake.)

Houseplants: An early Easter may mean the problem of how best to take care of gift plants in overheated, dry rooms. Potted azalea plants should be kept as cool as possible. If the variety is a hardy one or you live in a mild climate, the plant can be put permanently in the shrub border after frost danger has passed. If the variety is not reliably winter hardy, in cold climates, the potted plant can be summered outdoors and watered as needed. Bring indoors again in late fall. (Recommended reading: *Foliage Plants for Indoor Gardening* by James V. Crockett.)

Lawn: In most parts of the country, March is not too soon to give attention to your lawn. Too many people postpone work on their lawns until the balmy, sunny days of May. This is a mistake – for the lawn, anyway – as by the time the weather suits you, it is often too late in spring to sow seed, catch crabgrass in its preemergent stage, and give your grass a good start that only an early feeding can accomplish.

Don't just sprinkle lime on an established lawn because your neighbor is doing it. Test your soil, and, if pH results are below 6, apply lime at the rate of ½ to 1 pound per square yard. In most situations, lawns benefit from an application of lime about every 3 years or so.

Before applying one of the many commercial "weed-and-feed" lawn products available, it may be a good idea to rent a thatching machine, especially if your lawn is made primarily of Merion bluegrass or one of the other tight-growing grasses. Thatch, the dead grass clippings of the previous season, tends to suffocate the living grass and should be raked out in the spring. There are special rakes designed for the purpose that can be used when lawn areas are small. Otherwise a thatching machine will save time and labor.

Don't be in a hurry to roll your lawn with a heavy roller. Heavy rolling when the ground is wet compacts the soil. Clay soil, especially, puddles into a sticky, putty-like mass that makes it crack and bake in drier weather. Soil texture is destroyed. Light rollings are good for certain lawns to force any clumps of heaved sod back into contact with the soil, but reserve heavy rolling, necessary to smooth the lawn, until a dry spell after the frost is definitely out of the ground. A water-weight roller is a great

'Peeping Tom' daffodil is one of the first of the clan to appear. Its blossoms last for several weeks.

advantage in regulating light and heavy rollings. Rolling the soil after new seedings (before sprinkling the soil) is a good practice.

Seed must be kept wet for at least 2 weeks to germinate, and after that seedlings will die if the soil is dried out. Altogether it requires about 30 days of moisture to grow successfully. This is easy if the seed is sown about March 15th but harder a month later.

Perennials: Have you ordered new perennials from your favorite nursery? Mail-order nurseries may ship plants from storage that will be dormant when you receive them; or they may ship fresh field-dug or cold frame plants which may be only semi-dormant or already making new growth. In any case, the packages should be opened at once and any wilted plants revived by plunging in a pail of water. Keep from extremes of heat and cold if you can't plant at once. Such plants can be kept for a short time in temporary positions in the garden until you can plant them permanently. They should be protected from wind and strong sunshine at first.

Pests: Dormant spraying may be safely carried on in most localities until March 15th. After that, the strength of the solution must be cut down considerably in order to keep it from injuring the swelling buds. The best time is a dull, still day when the weather is over 40 degrees. Use lime-sulfur for fruit trees and lilacs if they are far enough away from the house to avoid splattering paint or brick. Miscible oil (from your seed store) is the best general-purpose dormant spray. It will not discolor buildings, walks, or trellises.

Rock Garden: Look it over often during the spring thaws to see that the tiny plants have not been heaved or washed out of the soil. When frost is past, see that they are firmly settled and well covered. Force some small stones about their crowns to hold them down.

Roses: In the rose garden, the hardy polyantha, hybrid perpetual, and rambler roses can be pruned of dead and broken branches the latter part of the month, but the tender hybrid tea roses should be left until later before being either pruned or uncovered. The best time to prune or uncover them is just before they start to unfold their leaves.

Seed: Most of the gardener's attention during the early spring is devoted to seeds and what to do about them. Annuals may be divided into 3 general groups. (1) Those extremely hardy ones that may be planted in the fall or even sow themselves. (Examples are larkspur, California-poppy, and stock, and March is not too soon to sow them outside.) (2) Other plants are so tender that they should not be sown until all danger of frost is past. (Examples are zinnia and marigold.) (3) The last group requires a long time to mature and should be sown indoors in March or they will miss a lot of their best season. (Examples are ageratum, petunia, and snapdragon.)

Many people have become discouraged with seed sowing indoors because it has not been understood. The chief requirement is a high temperature (70 to 80 degrees) before germination, followed by lower temperature when growing. Light is not required until after the plants start to grow. Slip small seed pans or pots into kitchen plastic bags to keep the soil moist until germination. After they germinate, they need a temperature of 50 degrees to make them stocky and healthy. High temperatures too early will make them shoot up too fast and they will acquire what is known as "legginess": top growth without sufficient roots to support them. This causes the plants to flop over and die.

The chief enemy of all seedlings indoors is a fungus disease known as damping-off. It is prevented by proper drainage, ventilation, and, above all, the disinfecting of seeds and soil before a start is made. Use sterile growing media like sphagnum moss or Vermiculite, or bake small amounts of soil in an oven at a temperature over 212 degrees for 2 hours; or the soil may be disinfected with preparations obtained at a seed store.

All receptacles must be thoroughly scrubbed. Seed flats can be scalded with hot water or, better still, disinfected. New flower pots must be boiled to get the alkali out of them and soaked in water for several hours. Old pots must be scoured inside and out. Better yet, each year start afresh by purchasing the various seed trays, peat pots, and the like that are manufactured for the purpose.

Plant the seeds which take the same time for germination in the same receptacles. This will make the care much easier as you will thin them at the same time and avoid having large and small plants in the same tray. Sterilized soil germinates many more plants from a packet of seeds.

The seedlings may be kept in a little-used bedroom, attic, or hall to obtain the low temperature necessary, but probably the best place to mature them is in a box made to hang outside a window so that it fits tightly to the frame and may be heated by raising the window. Ventilate by manipulating the hinged sash top, which lets in the light to the plants.

Do not sow too thickly, or you will lose many plants when thinning out. Also, there is the danger of injuring the plants that you want to save because the roots become entangled. Thin them out early, and then keep thinning them until you have the size you want.

Shrubs and Trees: Move or plant any shrubs and trees as early as you can work the ground without trying to plant them with frozen clumps of soil. Now and during the next few weeks you can plant hedges, fruit trees, grapes, evergreens, dormant roses, and other bare-root plants.

If you are not ready to plant new nursery stock as soon as it arrives, lay the plants, slanting, in a shallow trench and cover the roots deeply with soil. Be sure the soil remains moist. Treated in this way both shrubs and trees may be kept in good condition for several weeks if absolutely necessary. Whether you are planting new stock or moving the old, see that roots are not dried out by wind or sun and that you do not plant any broken or bruised roots. Plant at the same depth at which the plant was previously growing.

Sweet Peas: The traditional time for planting sweet peas out of doors is March 17th. They require a rich, deeply worked soil which contains clay but has excellent drainage. Extremely thin soils are not suitable as they dry out too quickly. Open sunny locations are best. The best plan is to prepare the trench deeply in autumn, mulch heavily to exclude frost; and plant the seed in March. If this has not been done, however, dig trenches about 2 feet deep and the width of a spade. Fill the trench with good topsoil and manure well mixed and sow the seed about 2 inches below the surface and 1 to 3 inches apart. The young plants can be hilled up occasionally as they grow.

Seeds grown indoors in peat pots in an inch of sand on top of well-drained soil may be planted in this trench without disturbing the roots by planting pot and plant. This may secure a blooming date 3 to 6 weeks earlier than those sown outside.

Try planting vegetables close together to save space. In rows above, lettuce and spinach will soon be harvested and yield their place to snap beans.

Vegetables: If you are to have your first vegetable garden this spring, make a plan or at least some sort of rough guide on paper first so you won't have your rows or plots going every which way. If space is limited, be daring, and try planting closer together. There is some evidence that close planting increases yield.

To be planted early: peas, radishes, onion, lettuce.

Planning and Working in April

When daffodils begin to peer,
With heigh! the doxy over the dale,
Why, then comes in the sweet o' the year;
For the red blood reigns in the winter's pale.

– *William Shakespeare*

General: The gardening fever rises in April, and so much activity beckons in every direction that it is difficult to choose where to start. Yet with all that needs doing, it is necessary to dream a little, too, to pause and enjoy the effects of previous efforts – for in spring the evidence of garden magic is everywhere.

Remove the oldest and most rotted parts of the compost for renovation in flower beds and when planting new shrubs. Early in the month begin to prepare the seed beds by digging and letting them settle. Turn under the cover crops which you planted last fall. Be careful to do all digging when the ground is fairly dry so that you will not destroy its structure.

Bulbs: Daffodils should be full bloom now, and most hyacinths, too. This is the

Traditional flower borders of formal patterns with equally traditional gazebo at Sturbridge, Mass. Iberis blooms along with daffodils and tulips.

Japanese-style garden house has modern appeal and is especially suitable for year-long outdoor living of West Coast and other mild climates.

time to check on labels and decide where a few more varieties can be planted in the fall. Make a note of which daffodils must be divided – they are the ones that produce more foliage than flowers.

Have you ordered gladiolus corms for planting next month? For continual cutting material, gladiolus can be planted every 10 days up to early summer.

Flowers: Once the winter mulch has been removed from the main flower garden, the next step is to clean around each plant – remove dead foliage and stalks and any other debris too close to the plant to catch with a rake. Plants that may need this individual attention include day-lily, various kinds of iris, tritoma, nepeta, and other perennials.

If you have a supply of manure, by all means dig it carefully into the soil around the plants. If you are one of those gardeners who believes in the magical properties of bone meal, now is the time to scatter it and scratch it into the soil. Or apply superphosphate – a loose peppering of the entire flower bed is of benefit every few years – in spring or in fall. Wood ashes from the fireplace are welcome in the perennial garden, especially among bearded iris, delphinium, monkshood, and babysbreath.

When all other fertilizers are in short supply, there is always good old 5-10-5. This all-purpose commercial fertilizer can be scattered over the entire flower garden. Do not apply it when the soil is especially wet, nor let it strike or settle on tender green foliage and new growth. Burning is bound to result if it is not washed off fresh growth of plants. To be on the safe side, sprinkle the entire garden thoroughly after its application.

Many perennials can be divided in the spring. They include delphinium, helenium, windflower (*Anemone japonica*), aster, chrysanthemum, monkshood, shasta daisy, phlox, day-lily. Day-lily should be divided in early spring, otherwise the summer bloom will be sacrificed until the following year. Lift the clumps with a fork; place the clump on firm ground, and insert two forks back to back in the center of the clump. Then pry them apart. The resulting 2 divisions can then be divided again. When dividing most perennials, discard the woody center portions, and save only the outer, more succulent sections.

Delphinium definitely respond to limestone, about a handful per clump worked well into the soil. Delphinium also need rich soil that is full of humus and deeply prepared. As soon as new shoots appear at the crowns in the spring – and these weather-hardy plants are among the first to begin growing – commence a weekly spray program to control the cyclamen mite. Dimite is very effective.

As the weather becomes settled, set out the plants which have been wintered in a cold frame: pansy, forget-me-not, Canterbury bells, aquilegia, and foxglove. Rampant plants which try to overrun the garden such as achillea, goldenglow, boltonia, certain kinds of artemisia, bee balm, physostegia should be thinned out so that those left will have room for new growth.

Most perennials can be safely transplanted in early spring although there are a few exceptions. Peony, platycodon, Oriental poppy, babys-breath, and gas-plant should not be disturbed in the spring. Most perennials will not even know they have been moved if the job is done quickly and is followed by a good soaking.

Many primroses are in bloom now, and they are very tolerant of being shifted about – even while in bloom.

Fruits: Dormant (before buds show green) sprays can still be applied in many cold regions although the spray known as "prebloom" (a trace of flower bud color shows) is more likely in order. Homeowners growing fruit trees should check with their county agent or write their state experimental stations for pertinent local schedules.

Most brambles and bush fruits can be fertilized in spring. Use a commercial 5-10-5 formula except on blueberry bushes. For those, any fertilizer for acid-soil plants (azalea, rhododendron, and the like) can be used, though sulfate of ammonia, about a half pound to each bush, is the more usual fertilizer. Some blueberry specialists claim that commercial fertilizers spoil the taste of the berries. They prefer to use organic fertilizers like cottonseed meal. Whichever fertilizer you use, always keep a leaf mold mulch present around the shrubs.

The roots of grape vines are close to the surface so when applying fertilizer, barely scratch it in to avoid injuring them.

Greenhouse and Cold Frame: Start hardening off bedding plants in the greenhouse or frame. It is certain death to set out coleus, geranium, and others unless they have been gradually accustomed to the marked change in temperature. Give more and more cool, fresh air to them each pleasant day.

Many flowering plants as well as vegetables are easily started in greenhouse or cold frame now in individual peat pots sold for the purpose. Early sweet corn, beans, eggplant, okra, pepper, and tomato work well this way. Plant lima beans with the eye down. Withhold water (after soaking soil) until germination starts or they will rot. Plant twice as many seeds as you want and thin them as soon as they are well started. Water thoroughly a day in advance of planting, and water sparingly before the plants are up. Do not set out any of these plants until the ground has warmed. Stake them until they become firm in the soil. See also seeds below.

Herbs: Most of the major culinary herbs can be grown from seed. Thyme, sage, dill, marjoram, basil, and chervil can be sown directly in the open ground in open spots in flower or shrub borders if you don't have a vegetable or cutting garden. Basil is tender – sow after frost possibilities have

Organic gardeners, who generally use no poisonous sprays, claim a border of chives chases aphids from roses.

passed. It is decorative enough to use as a low hedge around a terrace. (Recommended reading: *Herbs for Every Garden* by Gertrude B. Foster.)

Houseplants: Some houseplants may need repotting at this time. Place them out-of-doors but sheltered from strong sun or wind during the day, and help them recuperate from the hardships of the winter. Palm, rubber plant, dracena, and all other foliage plants usually need renewal, especially if they have outgrown their pots.

The African-violet is an exception to the plants that like to summer out-of-doors. Unless you have a lath house or an especially sheltered area free from wind and excessive light, these plants are best kept indoors.

Lawn: Same advice as suggested in March. There is no reason today why anyone should have a poor lawn.

Do not be in too much of a hurry for the first mowing. Let the grasses get off to a good start so they can better survive the hot, dry weather of summer. Do not cut lower than 1½ inches, even if this means mowing every few days or so during the peak spring season.

Pruning: If you have not already done so, prune grape vines and orchard fruits at once. Rub water sprouts from fruit and other trees. Box and privet hedges should be trimmed before they start into growth. Evergreens in need of shaping and thickening may be sheared advantageously as the new growth gets under way. Cut spirea 'Anthony Waterer' close to the ground to stimulate new growth. After the plants are in leaf you may be able to find indications of weakness. Cut back the weak plants, and fertilize for a fresh start. Fertilize all trees and shrubs while they are leafing out, and see that they do not lack for water. If

One or two plants of English lavender perfume the air. The flower spikes are especially long lasting.

pruning of your early-flowering shrubs is necessary, prepare to do it soon after they have bloomed. Forsythia is probably the earliest one.

Rhododendrons: All broad-leaved evergreens (rhododendron, azalea, pieris, mountain laurel, camellia) may be fertilized with cottonseed meal or any commercial fertilizer formulated for acid-soil plants. Do not remove windbreaks until strong spring winds are past. Maintain a thick mulch around the plants. Use compost, leaf mold, decayed wood chips, or decayed sawdust. Peat moss can be mixed with any of these but is too sponge-like in its action to be used as a mulch alone. It is fine mixed in the soil, though.

Roses: Prune hybrid tea roses to 3 eyes. Pruning of roses is largely to develop new wood and to make them grow so that there will be open air and sunlight in the center.

Prune to buds which point toward the outside of the plants. The new wood will grow from these in the right direction. The weaker the rose, the more it needs pruning. The first of April is about the best time in spring to plant dormant roses. Heap soil or peat moss (it must be damp) around the newly planted bushes, and keep it there for about 2 weeks. Remove it on a cloudy day. This prevents the bottom of the canes from drying out until the roots have a chance to take hold.

Seed: Seedlings started indoors should be gradually accustomed to outdoor conditions to harden them off. Some seeds that can be sown outdoors toward the end of the month are snapdragon, aster, sweet alyssum, calendula, centaurea, viola, scabiosa, mignonette, dianthus, cosmos, gypsophila, nasturtium, annual phlox, and verbena.

Tender annuals like zinnia, marigold,

Dahlias, which can be grown from seed or tubers, and African marigolds make a colorful combination.

and ageratum can still be started in a cold frame or indoors. Soak nasturtium seeds overnight in water before planting. All of the various morning glory and moonflower clan are good subjects for receiving a head-start sowing in peat pots indoors. Before sowing, lightly notch the seed, and then soak overnight, as with nasturtium, to soften their hard seed coats. These annual vines resent root disturbance, so any of the organic pots are especially appropriate for them, as the pot is planted, too, thus preventing root disturbance.

Shrubs and Trees: Early planting is best for woody stock. Try to get all deciduous trees and shrubs planted before foliage starts. The exception is the magnolia, which can be transplanted during May while it is in leaf.

Evergreens should be set early so that there will be plenty of rain while they are establishing themselves. Stake all newly planted trees to prevent them from swaying in high winds. Don't neglect new stock – liberal watering once a week in dry weather is essential, and a heavy mulching of manure or compost a little later is excellent. Do not remove stakes or guy wires until the plant is thoroughly established. Wrap the trunks of newly planted trees (especially the smooth-bark type) with burlap or kraft paper made for the purpose, to prevent sunscald. Fasten securely with twine at the top and bottom.

Trees and shrubs that prefer spring planting are birch, magnolia, tulip tree, sweet gum, Japanese maple, large-flowering dogwood, althea, flowering almond, ornamental cherry, peach, buddleia, hawthorn, and weigela.

If you have sprays of pussy willows in the house, they will probably have made roots in water. Later in the month plant them outdoors in a damp spot, and they will form bushes.

Soil Testing: Many plants have a decided preference as to the degree of acidity in the soil. Soil can be changed to suit the needs of the plants and their successful culture enhanced. All that is needed is the knowledge. This can be gained by the use of a soil-testing outfit for sale at seed stores. Its operation is nontechnical, and a kit, which can be had for about $2.00, usually contains a booklet of instruction.

Staking: A plant staked early in its growth is much easier to handle than when it becomes a tangled mass later on. Nearly all tall flowers will benefit by staking against the pressure of high winds and heavy rains. This is particularly true of larkspur, hollyhock, foxglove, garden heliotrope, dahlia, delphinium, peony, babysbreath, and gladioli. Use strong stakes, and tie firmly with raffia or soft coarse cord in several places. Small flowers also deserve attention. Old coat hangers cut into sections make excellent small plant supports. Bend 2 to 4 inches over at right angles at the proper distance from the ground and form into a semicircle or corkscrew so that the plant may be loosely encircled to keep it from being broken off in the wind. Galvanized wire can be used for the same purpose.

Vegetables: Make several plantings of lettuce, radish, and other salad ingredients; otherwise, they will all be ready at the same time – and finished at the same time. Order some lettuce varieties for sowing next month and thereafter to harvest in summer. Reliable hot-weather lettuce types include 'Ruby,' 'Matchless,' 'Hot Weather,' and 'Oak Leaf.'

Wild Flowers: Do your little bit toward conservation by reserving a small area of your garden for native plants. Many plants can safely be dug when they are in bloom – often the only time they are in evidence. Look along back roads and open woodlands, and especially in areas you know are marked for real estate developments.

Give them the same growing situations that you found them in. Incorporate leaf mold and/or peat moss in the soil, and water well to help them become established. If you live in a completely built-up region, there are many wild flower nurseries that sell native plants. (Suggested reading: *The Concise Encyclopedia of Favorite Wild Flowers* by Marjorie J. Dietz.)

The Home Garden in May

There is no time like Spring,
When life's alive in everything . . .
– *Christina Rossetti*

General: If yours is mainly a spring garden, you'll find one way to keep up is to record planting and blooming dates in a diary. Weekend gardeners will especially benefit from keeping such a year-to-year record.

There are enough tools and gadgets on the market to make one's head spin. Which ones are junk and not worth the space in the garage to store them? Which ones will really increase gardening efficiency? Alas, generally there are no magical answers to these questions, and the home gardener must be his own tester and use his own common sense. For beginners, especially, this can be a bewildering and frustrating experience.

The lovely month of May. Color is everywhere but especially dominant in rock gardens.

For a start among hand tools: A long-handled spade, a spading fork, a lawn rake (bamboo and a flexible metal rake are both useful tools), several trowels, a soil rake, and a hoe.

Among power tools, you will certainly want a lawn mower, rotary or reel. The elaborateness of the mower depends to a great degree on the size of your lawn. If you have a large vegetable garden and plan on extensive garden projects, you will want to investigate the practicality of buying a power cultivator.

For hedges, you will want an electric hedge trimmer. Other tools to think about include a lawn sweeper, especially essential for those surrounded by shade trees, perhaps a one-wheel lawn mower to use around garden beds and close to walls, and a grass whip swung like a golf club and cutting both ways to get close to fences and shrubbery without stooping.

Flowers which are staked early in the season are easy to train and also make disease more easily detected.

Weed killers used strictly according to directions on walks and drives, while the weeds are young, will prevent work later.

Everything that is being transplanted, from tiny seedlings to young trees, must have roots protected against drying while out of the ground. Unless this is done, these highly sensitive and vital parts will be severely injured if not killed. Try to transplant on cloudy days.

Annual Flowers: A great boon has been the development of peat pots, available in several sizes. The advantage of these pots, of course, is that both pot and plant go into the ground together, eliminating any setback to the roots of the plants as well as the fuss and time of knocking the plant out of the plastic or clay pot.

One caution to observe with peat pots is to be sure that the plant and soil do not dry out. The peat is a thirsty fiber and can quickly draw moisture from the soil. After setting out pot and plant, be sure to give a good soaking – and do it often, until you are certain the plant's roots have penetrated the soil outside the pot.

When transplanting annual plants from flats or seedbed rows, it will help them to recover faster if they are dipped in a transplanting solution. This can be a solution formulated for the purpose and offered by most seed sources and garden centers or a liquid made from a water-soluble fertilizer according to directions on the package.

May is about the last call for sowing annuals in the open ground. Sow marigold, zinnia, sweet alyssum, impatiens, amaranth, gomphrena, celosia, cosmos, portulaca, nicotiana, morning glory, gourds, and China aster.

Before planting asters try an application of wood ashes to the soil. Contrary to popular belief they do not thrive well in poor soil. Dig in rotted manure or compost

For a rainbow effect, plant a mixture of Darwin and Cottage tulips in a long, informal border.

deeply, and give the surface a finely raked finish. Plant seed 2 inches apart in rows spaced 10 inches apart. Planting half an inch deep will give later flowers but better plants. Get early and late blooming varieties and set them out about May 15th. Apply liquid manure or fertilizer to the wet ground just before and during bloom. Watch the soil for root aphids, and control by liberal applications of tobacco dust well worked and watered in.

Bulbs: Start planting gladiolus May 15th, and plant every two weeks until July 10th to get bloom through to October. Control thrips by spraying with Dimethoate, nicotine sulphate or pyrethrum.

Plant the summer-flowering bulbs before the end of the month. Canna, begonia, tuberose, and ismene are all very satisfactory. Daffodils do not need to be disturbed for several years; but when any bulbs are naturalized in the lawn, the grass should not be cut until their leaves begin to turn yellow. It is best not to dig any spring-flowering bulbs until the leaves ripen, but with care, daffodils can be lifted and di-

One of the largest of early-flowering tulips is 'Red Emperor,' with long-lasting flowers.

vided before their foliage disappears. Treat them as growing plants – keeping the foliage intact and the roots on the bulbs as little mangled as possible. After replanting, give a good soaking.

Fall planting is best for most lilies but regal lily (*Lilium regale*), goldband lily of Japan (*L. auratum*) and any of the show lilies (*L. speciosum*) do very well with early-spring planting.

Dahlia roots may be planted as soon as the weather is settled. Stake large dahlias when you plant. Doing so later when they are ready for support may injure the roots.

Houseplants: Examine your plants to see if they need repotting before being set outdoors for summer recuperation. Amaryllis foliage must be kept in growth all summer, but such bulbous plants as nerine, freesia, and veltheimia should be rested.

Tubbed plants of all kinds may be taken from their winter quarters and moved into place on the terrace now that danger of severe frost is past. They should be given liquid manure or fertilizer; and, as growth becomes active, loosen the surface of the

White tulip varieties bring a special magic to the spring garden.

Daffodil variety 'Early Splendor' is well suited to naturalizing in open woodlands.

soil in their containers. Keep well watered. Bring out the poinsettia plants to start them into growth (see January calendar).

Lawns: Good lawns are the result of liberal fertilization. It is not too late to apply any of the many special lawn fertilizers, but don't delay any longer. Newly seeded lawns should be cut high until the grass has begun to grow vigorously and thickened.

Perennial Flowers: You can now see clearly what you need in the way of replacement. You may still be receiving plants from mail-order nurseries (and it's getting late as most will be in active growth). Provide shade for plants if the weather is warm. Newspapers may be used, but all shade should be removed at night. Do not overcrowd. Plant firmly – press the soil around the edges of the plant, rather than the top of the plant itself – spread the roots naturally and fill the spaces between them. Each root must be surrounded with soil free from air pockets. Set the crowns as they were in the nursery. Newly planted perennials must be watered regularly, in early morning or just before sundown.

Most local nurseries now offer perennials in containers. The later the season, the safer and easier it is to set out such plants.

Peonies require an abundance of water while buds are being formed. A large flower pot or a piece of 4-inch farm tile sunk about a foot away from each peony plant (and covered with a stone), enables you to get water down where it is most needed. The flowers may be removed while in the bud and opened in water. Remove some of the buds to give larger flowers. Peonies should be staked before the buds start to weigh down the stalks. An encircling support is better than stakes. Do not neglect the plants after they have bloomed. They are preparing for next year. Don't cut off their foliage.

Columbine (*Aquilegia*) is one of the most popular plants in the garden, but often it disappears after the second year. Keep a supply coming along from seed sown in a propagating bed in spring or early summer. April and May are good months for sowing as it is easier to keep the seedbed moist.

Columbine likes a light, rich soil which must be moist but have good drainage. A heavy wet soil will not suit them at all. They grow fairly well in full sunlight but benefit from shade for a few hours during the heat of the day. If given this shade, they will grow larger and bloom over a longer period. Space them 9 to 10 inches apart when transplanting them in fall or very early spring.

The beautiful, candle-like blooms of lupine can add a most dramatic effect to a flower garden. Since the advent of Russell lupine hybrids from England, the color range has broadened far beyond the more usual pinks and purples. Now there are yellow, bronze, brown, salmon, maroon, red, and purple and often bicolor varieties, all of which can be grown from seed packets in the home garden. Many mail-order nurseries offer ready-to-bloom plants in spring or fall for those who don't want to start their own plants from seed.

Perennial lupines require an acid soil, contrary to some belief, and once the long tap roots are established, it is best not to try to transplant or divide the clumps. Give them a well-prepared soil of leaf mold, peat moss, or compost. Perfect drainage is a necessity.

The annual lupine, *Lupinus hartwegi,* is quite easy to grow if the seed is sown in early spring in the open ground and the plants are not transplanted. It is also a useful greenhouse plant for winter cutting.

Roses: You may take the protection completely off of roses. Remember extreme vigilance is the price of a good rose garden – keep it dusted or sprayed. A last-minute rose garden can be made in the next month or so if you buy container or potted plants. They can be transferred in full leaf and even bud without harmful root disturbance. Be sure that the soil into which they go is well-drained and rich, and keep them regularly watered during dry weather. (Suggested reading: *The Complete Book of Roses* by F. F. Rockwell and Esther C. Grayson.)

Vegetables: All the warm-weather crops like eggplant, tomato, and pepper can be set out in the seedling stage at the beginning of this month, and earlier in many areas, if those little protective tents called Hotkaps are placed over them as protection from late frosts and too-cool nights.

Most vegetables grown from seed in the open ground – bean, squash, okra, cucumber, melon, and others – can be planted about the middle of the month.

Window Boxes and Other Containers: They are back in style but more often around terraces, outdoor living areas, swimming pools, and decks than windows. The petunia is a most satisfactory plant for such use and may provide more continual color than geranium.

The Perfect Month of June

So here are strawberries,
Sun-flushed and sweet, as many as you please;
And here are full-blown roses by the score,
More roses, and yet more.
– *Christina Rossetti*

General: The sun dial should be chosen according to the degree of latitude in which the garden is located. That which fits the garden in a distant city will not do for yours. Nor can a sun dial keep up with daylight savings time. The time to set it is on June 15th, and place it so that the shadow falls on 12:00 at exactly noon on this date.

Unless you especially enjoy weeding, you had better provide some sort of mulch in its stead. (Even with a mulch, there will be some hand weeding necessary, espe-

A simple planter, ideal for pansies in spring, has been formed by large stone slabs.

cially in flower gardens.) Mulching is essential to the well-being of broad-leaved evergreens like rhododendron, azalea, and is of benefit to most wild-flower gardens. Pine needles, a combination of compost and peat moss (better than peat moss alone), rotted manure, rotted sawdust, leaf mold, rotted wood chips, and other natural materials are suitable. In the vegetable garden such practical materials as black plastic mulch, newspaper, straw, and hay can all be used and in addition to smothering weed seeds, they retain soil moisture.

Flowers: Thinning of all kinds of seedlings should be done when the plants are very small and before the roots interlock. Thinning of rampant-growing plants to permit air circulation in the center of the clumps, as well as around the outer edges, must be done all season. Do not confine your staking operations to dahlia, peony, and the plants which seem to cry for it. Attend to the little fellows, also.

Try to clip the blossoms of all flowers as they are about to fade. There may be some that will not benefit by this process, but most of them will respond. It is essential if annuals are to continue blooming. All plants grow to produce seed. The longer you prevent seeding, the longer they will bloom. Many perennials will give a second blooming if the old stalks are removed. Removal of bloomed-out stalks is necessary on delphinium and many others to keep them sending new flowering growth from the bottom. One caution for delphinium: don't cut back the fading flower stem directly at ground level until the main leaves on the stalk have ripened. Just cut off the top of the stem that has flowered. Remove the entire stem when the leaves have withered and new shoots have appeared at the base.

Pinch off the tops of many plants to make them branch. Cosmos is one plant which needs it this month, but many others also benefit. Try pinching a few of all kinds of plants so that you may learn which will do best. Use your fingernails or a knife or scissors.

Mark the areas occupied by such plants as bleeding-heart, trillium, spring bulbs, and mertensia, which will soon be going dormant. Continue this process all summer. Mark all your plants with permanent labels. It is a tedious business but pays.

Sow seeds of perennials and biennials for next year's garden.

Plant chrysanthemums before the end of the month. Other flowers which endure early frost should not be overlooked now. That beautiful late season is an interesting period in the garden if you provide it with bloom. In addition to such perennials as delphinium and achillea which may give scattered fall effect, especially if watered well and given an application of plant food, there are Japanese anemone, aster, boltonia, ceratostigma, cimicifuga, coreopsis, late lilies, monkshood, and phlox.

Pests: Continue regularly to spray or dust roses and delphinium. In the vegetable garden, the flea beetle may pepper the leaves of tomato; Mexican bean beetles may be congregating on bean vines; and rose chafers and Japanese beetles may be swarming over rose bushes. Sevin is recommended for all the beetles; rotenone or pyrethrum may be preferred for vegetables. Most complete rose sprays or dusts are formulated to control all rose problems – from beetles to the dreaded black spot, a fungus disease. While delphinium may be plagued by fungus problems, its major enemy is cyclamen mite. Spray with Dimite.

Shrubs, Trees, and Vines: As soon as spring-flowering shrubs have finished blooming, cut all unnecessary wood to the ground. Don't lop the branches off at the top or midway, but choose old branches and chop them off at the base. Leave younger stems to take their places.

All hedge trimming should be done now; a second shearing may be needed in August. Frequent trimming of hedges makes a thick green surface growth and avoids unsightly open spots. Break or cut all seed pods from azalea, rhododendron, and lilac, but be careful as next year's blooming buds are already being formed.

Take care that newly planted materials receive a thorough soaking each week. Soak; do not sprinkle. Mulch them and wash the leaves.

Roses: Climbing roses should be looked over carefully and any heavy growth firmly tied into the proper position. Prune them after blossoming.

Vegetables: If space permits, make another sowing of bush bean and summer lettuce.

July Calendar

Shall not July bring fresh delight,
As underneath green trees ye sit?
– William Morris

General: July is one of those gardening months when the amount of activity indulged in by the gardener can vary from little to a good deal. Watering time is certainly at hand, but during some summers nature takes care of much of it. When the rains fail, the gardener must help out with the hose, watering thoroughly and deeply. Almost all plants alike need attention, but

This shell serves as sculpture in the garden as well as watering place for birds.

Old millstone makes an attractive adjunct to the garden terrace.

Sundials and other inanimate features can be interesting additions to the garden when chosen with care.

lawns, broad-leaved evergreens, and flower gardens head the list. Lawns are helped by practicing high mowing, and, of course, mulches of all kinds elsewhere lessen the need for frequent watering. The mulch acts as a parasol and an insulating seal: it keeps the soil cool and moist. It must be light to admit air, but in turn its air spaces keep out excess heat.

Cut Flowers: Cut with a very sharp flower shears or knife, to avoid injury to the growing plant. A special pair of cutting scissors may be bought which holds the cut-off stem, allowing the removal to be a one-handed operation. Carry a bucket of water to the garden to plunge the cut stems into at once.

After cutting, remove lower leaves and any excess foliage, and recut stems under water. Wilted flowers can often be revived by this treatment or by placing them in fairly hot water for a few minutes.

Woody stems (shrubs, peony) should have the ends slit or a little bark peeled away. Chrysanthemum and stock stems do best when slightly battered, but the stems of plants which exude a sticky or milky sap after cutting (dahlia, Oriental poppy, heliotrope, poinsettia) must be sealed by searing with the flame of a match, or gas, or dipping the tips in boiling water.

An important step in making bouquets last is cutting at the proper stage of development. Most flowers fade immediately after pollination. It is best to cut them just as they begin to mature and where possible remove the stamens to prevent pollination. This is quite easy on many flowers, such as lily or amaryllis. Cut gladiolus as the first bud opens; peony as the outer petals develop; roses in the soft bud; dahlia in full bloom after the sun goes down; poppies the night before, and allow them to open in the water. Iris, if being transported a distance, should be cut in the bud.

Late afternoon, when the stems are empty of sap, is a good time to cut flowers with hollow stems, such as gladiolus and zinnia. They will fill quickly when plunged deep in water and be in prime condition the next morning. Flowers can be too fresh: calendula, chrysanthemum, euphorbia, mignonette, rose, stock, and snapdragon need 24 hours to fill and harden off.

Flowers should never be crowded into a small-mouthed vase. Air should easily reach the water. Water must remain clean, cool and pure.

Flowers: Cut back most of the top growth of *Viola cornuta,* forget-me-not, and nepeta, and fertilize for August bloom. Phlox, veronica, and hollyhock may bloom again if kept from seeding. Pinch back pink and white boltonia and New England aster to 5 inches, early in July, to keep them bushy. Pinch back chrysanthemum and poinsettia, and remove surplus shoots. Order colchicum and autumn crocus for August planting. Sow perennial seeds, especially fresh lupine and delphinium.

The main stems of dahlia should be kept free of side shoots. In larger varieties, maintain a single stalk. An adequate support must be provided to prevent storm breakage. Water well, and fertilize.

Bearded iris should be divided if over 3 years old and if roots are crowded. Replace the more common varieties with new ones.

Water Japanese iris well before flowering, and give less afterwards. Divide every 3 years after they have flowered, lifting and separating carefully with a sharp knife. Set much deeper than bearded kinds, and water sparingly after transplanting.

Propagation: When growth has stopped and vanished foliage indicates a dormant condition, dig a root each of bleeding-heart, anchusa, and Oriental poppy. Cut these long roots into inch pieces, and plant them in a mixture of sand and rich loam. Keep the area fairly moist, and soon tiny leaves will shoot up. The new plants will be ready for permanent quarters in the spring.

Verbena, pinks, euonymus, pachysandra, ivy, *Daphne cneorum,* climbing roses, rhododendron, azalea, and many shrubs, in fact, all those with bending stems, will probably take root if fastened down with a wire hairpin and covered with good soil.

This is softwood cutting time for most shrubs. Evergreen azalea cuttings root quickly in flats of peat moss and sand that are enclosed in a plastic tent after a thorough watering. So do cuttings of heath (*Erica*) and heather (*Calluna*).

Plant seeds of biennial plants like sweet William (*Dianthus barbatus*), Canterbury bells (*Campanula medium*), and hollyhock (*Althaea rosea*). Pansy seeds should be ordered for early August sowing.

Vegetables: Early this month, make last sowing of bush beans. If you have empty space in your garden, sow a cover crop (cereal rye, clover, vetch, and the like) to turn under later to return humus and nitrates to soil.

Things To Do in August

At length the finished garden to the view
Its vistas opens and its alleys green.
– James Thomson the Elder

General: The wise gardener who wants spring bulbs for fall planting orders them early. The stock of many varieties is often limited.

Keep the bird bath filled, especially if a drought comes. The contents evaporate rapidly in such weather, to say nothing of what the birds themselves spatter about.

Flowers: Don't let your flower garden run down this season. Water well when water is needed.

For rows of plants like chrysanthemum and gladiolus, the best way to stake is to use lines of twine on both sides of the row, stretched tight between stakes set 10 feet or so apart, forming an alley.

Oriental poppies can be transplanted, divided, or new varieties planted this month.

Cut strawflowers intended for winter bouquets before the blossoms are fully open. Dry them in the shade, hanging head downward in the small, uncrowded bunches. In handling, be especially careful not to crack the stems near the blossoms.

Phlox gives definite and beautiful mass effects in the garden in August provided it is well grown. It needs full sun, deep rich soil, and plenty of moisture at roots, especially during droughts. Don't let flowers go to seed. Plants must be divided as soon as they get too thick, every 3 years or so, in fall or early spring. For the largest florets, never leave more than 4 or 5 stalks to a plant. Keep plants sprayed or dusted with a general purpose chemical. They should be grown in groups of no less than 5 plants. Phlox is used for masses of color rather than individual flower form effects. Snip off flower heads when they have finished blooming, and feed the plants.

Much complaint comes from the so-called reverting of red and pink phlox to lavender and magenta. This is not a true reversion but a case of the parent stock being replaced by seedlings which seldom come true to parent color and are usually poor bloomers.

Greenhouse and Cold Frame: Cuttings can be taken of bedding plants such as coleus and geranium. If these are carried in a cool greenhouse through the winter, they will make good stock for setting out next spring.

This arrangement by Margot Cochrane Cole is expressive of summer's bountiful flowers – marigolds, helenium and the contrasting seed heads of dock.

Sow annuals for winter flowering indoors. Calendula blooms well and keeps long. Browallia, mignonette, sweet pea, annual lupine, ageratum, marigold, stock, snapdragon, and many others are good subjects. Small plants may be purchased from growers who specialize in supplying such material.

Buds will be forming on most of the greenhouse chrysanthemums by this time, and strong feedings will be necessary if you want highest quality flowers.

Lawn: Follow nature's tip and do your lawn seeding now. This applies to spot renovation as well as complete renovation and planting brand new lawns. Although days are now hot, evenings are cooler. With any luck, natural rainfall will take care of nursing the young seedlings through the fall. This magic time for lawn making extends through September in most areas, but the earlier the start, the better.

Seed: Pansy, forget-me-not, and English daisies are sturdier plants if sown this month rather than earlier in the summer.

Certain vegetables that will not succumb to fall's frosts can be sown. They include lettuce, fall broccoli, Chinese cabbage, and Chinese white winter radish.

Trees and Shrubs: Deciduous trees and shrubs and evergreens, both broad-leaved and coniferous, can be planted from now to the middle of next month and later in many areas. They need a great deal of water. Where possible, too, let them be protected somewhat from the sweep of drying summer winds.

The scholar-tree (*Sophora japonica*) is a beautiful tree found around temples and pagodas in Japan. Its creamy white flowers appear in large panicles in August when few trees are blooming. It is a graceful tree, low branching where it has room. The foliage is similar to that of the locust and turns yellow in the fall and persists late.

The tree has a tremendous taproot. It is slow-growing – slower than its relative, the yellow-wood – and does not flower when young. Old trees flower freely, especially in the hot season in August and September. It will stand drought. Plant in well-drained sandy soil.

Our common summersweet (*Clethra alnifolia*) makes the hedgerows fragrant in July and August with its white flowers in upright panicles. It likes a moist peaty or sandy soil, but will thrive in ordinary garden soil. Plant it in groups and as background for azalea to give later color. It averages 4 to 6 feet tall, and sometimes grows to 10 feet.

The Arnold hawthorn (*Crataegus arnoldiana*) is one of the earliest among the hawthorns to fruit and is popular on that account. It flowers in May. It has bright red fruit, about an inch in diameter, in August, and this also falls early. The tree grows to be 20 feet tall. It is easy to transplant if pruned severely, all over, at the time. It likes lime, in common with other hawthorns. Use sandy loam enriched with well-rotted manure or compost.

Cuttings of various shrubs can be started in a shaded cold frame which can be covered with sash as cold weather comes. Use ripe, new wood with most of the foliage removed. Various combinations of sand, sand and soil, or sand and peat moss are used.

What To Do in September

In brisk wind of September
The heavy-headed fruits
Shake upon their bending boughs
And drop from the shoots.
– *Christina Rossetti*

General: Now that you have had the experience of the summer garden, were you satisfied with it? If not, start to plan for next year. Remember how fast the spring season went, and make these calm beautiful days of fall count. Many things can be planted as well in the fall as in spring and some to a lot better advantage.

Even if you have occasional rains, remember that the soil still dries out quickly. Keep propagating beds and newly planted or transplanted items moist.

Bulbs: Have you sent your order for spring bulbs – daffodils, tulips, hyacinths, and the little bulbs and summer-flowering lilies? The beginning of this month is just about the last call for sending mail orders. In fact, if you ordered last month or earlier you now have your bulbs at hand and can start planting daffodils and crocuses, the ones that should be in the ground first.

Garden centers, local nurseries, and other shops often feature spring bulbs, but you will never find the wide variety offered by mail-order specialists in bulbs.

If you are tempted to plant daffodils, crocus, scilla, and chionodoxa in the lawn, isolate the groupings in such a way that you can let the grass grow around them in the spring until their foliage has ripened. If the grass is cut before this process is completed, it will just about eliminate future bulb displays.

Field and pine mice destroy thousands of tulip bulbs annually. It helps to plant the bulbs in baskets made of half-inch mesh wire.

Lift gladiolus as soon as the foliage turns brown. Lift dahlia, canna, caladium and other tender bulbs and roots as soon as the tops are blackened by frost. Tuberous begonia corms should be taken up before the first light frost. Retain a good sized clump of soil, and place in a frost-proof but well ventilated cellar. Wait until the foliage wilts, and then cut it loose from the clump. Dry bulbs for a few days, and store in dry sand or peat moss at about 50 degrees.

Greenhouse and Cold Frame: Do any necessary painting, glazing or repairing of heating plant in the greenhouse. Soil for winter potting ought to be obtained and stored somewhere under cover.

Take cuttings of outdoor plants, such as chrysanthemum, coleus, geranium, and begonia before they are destroyed by frost. They may be grown all winter in the greenhouse or even on a glass-enclosed and heated sun porch.

Carnations that were planted outdoors may now be put in the greenhouse for the indoor season, before the frost has a chance to catch them. The glass should be shaded slightly until the roots again become active, after which normal light is again allowed to enter the house. Ventilate carefully, especially during the day. Try to maintain an even temperature through the 24 hours.

Freesia corms may be started late this month in pots or flats.

Transplant biennials, such as pansy, Canterbury bells, and English daisy, in the cold frames for the winter to give early bloom.

Sow annual lupine, snapdragon, sweet pea, schizanthus, annual larkspur, gypsophila, stock, calendula, pansy seeds for later display and cutting in the greenhouse.

Houseplants: Start bringing in houseplants while the windows may still be left open so that they will gradually become inured to the dry house air.

Such bulbous window plants as nerine and veltheimia can be watered now. The nerine should be about to flower. Amaryllis bulbs can be rested so they will flower later in the winter. Keep the bulbs (in their pots) in a frost-free room and do not water.

Lawn: Keep cutting the grass as long as it grows vigorously. This is about the last chance for properly seeding lawns; most weed growth is over, and the grass will get a sufficient start to carry it through the winter. You must be prepared, however, to water it abundantly in case the fall rains fail to put in an appearance.

Perennial Flowers: When the results of fall planting are unsatisfactory it is generally either because the plants were put in too late in the fall or because they were plants of uncertain hardiness. Plants in the latter category should always be transplanted in the spring. Any planting done in the fall should be early enough to let the roots get properly established before winter. Otherwise they are practically only heeled in during this period and are more apt to be winter killed.

Perennial asters – they and chrysanthemums give glory to the fall garden – need constant division in order not to deteriorate in the garden. Clumps should be divided every year (in the spring) leaving not over 4 or 5 stalks to a plant. Stake them early in the season. Later on, a few branches of asters staked to grow horizontally will help fill up the vacant spaces.

Try transplanting peony clumps in rotation – a few each year. In this way you will not risk loss of bloom on all of them. The middle of this month marks about the last opportunity for transplanting or planting peonies.

A method which will avoid the usual 2-year void of bloom that usually results after peony division is to dig a trench around one-half of a large clump, then separate one-half of the main plant for division, leaving just half of the established peony clump in place. The hole, if filled with rich soil, will supply new life to the old established peony and give you bloom until the new divisions are ready. If your clumps are extra large you may even remove three-fourths for division.

September is also your last chance to successfully divide iris this year. Divide gaillardia clumps over 2 years old. They tend to stop blooming after 3 years.

Pansies may be wintered in the open ground if covered with straw or excelsior just before frost. If leaves are used be sure to have a poultry wire fence to hold them in place without letting them pack down.

Delphinium is one of the exceptions among perennials to the rule against saving your own seed. Keep a few of the choicest seed capsules on the stalk until ripe. Then plant them at once in a garden seedbed. They will grow into husky little plants that winter well where they are, ready to transplant into permanent quarters in the spring.

Roses: It will not be necessary to feed roses from now on, but they should be sprayed after each rain to prevent black spot. Also, keep them well watered. Late fall planting of hardy garden roses is recommended for mild climates. You can prepare the bed now so it will have time to settle before actual planting time. Prune ramblers after they have finished blooming. Now is the proper time to prune all the other kinds of climbing roses.

Shrubs, Trees and Vines: As soon as the foliage colors on deciduous plants, or just before, it is safe to transplant; the earlier the better, so that the roots will have a chance to take hold before cold weather. Newly planted stock, especially if exposed to much wind, should be firmly staked for at least a year to hold it perpendicular. Be sure to protect from hot drying winds, and paint cuts immediately with tree paint. Magnolia, dogwood, birch, and some others do better if spring planted.

This is the season when evergreens are nearest dormant. Transplant now for best results.

Shape trees and shrubs now while the foliage is on them, and you can see what they will look like. Deadwood is easy to distinguish. Do not prune spring-flowering shrubs now unless next year's bloom is not important to you. (It may be better to shape the plants now and sacrifice the bloom for a year.)

When other vines begin to fade you can really appreciate the virgin's bower (*Clematis paniculata*) which remains green until November. Give some lime and a mulch of manure or compost this fall, and follow with a ration of bone meal or superphosphate next spring. It will repay you.

Vegetables: If many vegetables like tomato and pole beans can survive the first few frosts, they are likely to give several more weeks of harvest. Try to keep a check on the weather; and if a heavy frost is predicted, it may be feasible to protect a few plants overnight.

Leeks can be left in the ground all winter, to be dug as needed. Keep the soil mulched to prevent deep freezing.

What To Do in October

When Autumn comes the days are drear,
It is the downfall of the year:
We heed the wind and falling leaf
More than the golden harvest-sheaf.
– *Christina Rossetti*

General: Too many people think that gardening is over when the leaves begin to turn brown or even after the first frost. Actually in most sections planting and other outdoor activity can be continued through the autumn season.

The time for raking leaves is at hand. They are a source of humus; and if you have space enough, start a compost or leaf pile. Leaves can be kept in place if you enclose them in chicken wire. Compost and leaves decay faster if kept moist. Add some manure or peat moss if you want to increase the supply.

This is also a good time to apply soil conditioners such as manures if you can get them and forms of commercial humus. The manure does not need to be well rotted at this time if you are careful to keep it away from the plant roots. The freezing and thawing of winter will take a lot of the heat out of it before the spring season.

Bulbs: Many lily bulbs arrive late. If you intend to plant them, prepare the soil; and mulch the soil to keep it from freezing if you live in very cold areas.

Few gardeners are sufficiently impressed with the necessity of setting out spring bulbs at the proper time. Only tulips should be held until after this month. The daffodil, while much planted in October, should go in as early as possible, as it takes 3 months of warm weather to develop their roots properly. Hyacinths and many of the smaller bulbs should be planted in September or early October.

Continue to dig and store tender bulbous plants such as gladiolus and dahlia. The dahlia can be stored in boxes of very slightly moist peat moss and kept in a cool, dark but not too dry cellar. Packing is not needed for gladiolus corms but dusting them with naphthalene flakes and keeping in paper bags for two weeks will destroy thrips.

Greenhouse and Cold Frame: Cold frames in which young perennial plants are being carried through the winter should be kept closed now except on warm days. When growth ceases, cover the sash with mats to exclude the sun and stabilize the temperature. Give them air during mild winter days.

Don't neglect to get hyacinths and daffodils and other early-flowering bulbs boxed or planted in pots preparatory to forcing them in the greenhouse.

Stop feeding greenhouse chrysanthemums just as soon as the buds show color. It is a good practice to shade the greenhouse slightly in order that development may be normal.

Houseplants: The first few days in the house is the critical period for indoor plants. Use great care in watering, and be sure to keep the foliage sprayed lest the plant dry too quickly. There is, of course, much difference between outdoor and indoor conditions.

A plant or so of parsley, taken from the garden and reset in a pot of good soil, will do well all winter if watered and grown in a sunny window of the kitchen. This is one herb whose appearance, odor, and flavor are all welcome through the cold weather. Chives, rose geranium, garden sage, thyme, and many other herbs can also be maintained in this manner.

Lawn: Lawn mowing is to be kept up as long as new growth is apparent. This keeps the turf looking well and also improves its condition for next year. Long matted grass that has lain on the lawn all winter is harder to manage in the spring when mowing begins. Keep the lawn free of leaves and other litter during the winter.

Perennial Flowers: Now is a good time to renovate borders to get ready for spring. Beds renovated or newly prepared now will be settled and ready for spring transplanting.

Care should be taken that plants newly set out or divided are well watered during a period of autumn drought.

It soon will be time to apply winter protection to the flower border. Mulch with hardwood leaves after the ground is frozen to avoid heaving and root breaking.

Chrysanthemum lovers who have no greenhouse may keep their plants in bloom far into the fall weather by using a few light frames, covered with cheesecloth, to form a little house. These may be made by any handy person from lath or lattice and easily fastened together with a few screen door hooks. A temporary stake or two will aid in keeping them upright.

Watch the thermometer on cold nights. A cold clear night when no wind is blowing usually means a destructive frost.

Rock Garden: Stone chips used as top dressing will not only minimize erosion in the rock garden, but also help to prevent soil heaving and resultant damage to roots. Work them close around the crowns of the plants. Get them in place now, and let them remain there permanently. Pine needles also make a good mulch. Where plants are grown which do not care for lime, use marble or granite chips which may be obtained from monument manufacturers.

Roses: The time for winter protection comes about the end of the month. The best time for fall planting of roses is just before freezing weather.

If your climbing roses are in an exposed location, tie them firmly with cloth strips so that the wind will not beat them against the trellis and bruise the bark. Have you observed the pruning rules so that there will not be a mass of useless branches to catch the wind?

Shrubs and Trees: Water evergreens just before they go into winter, if the weather is at all dry. All your evergreens will grow better if mulched with strawy manure after the ground freezes. Especially don't neglect to mulch, with manure or at least with straw or some loose material, those evergreens that were transplanted during the current year. The results will well repay you. Before applying the mulch, soak the ground to a depth of 2 or 3 feet.

A final mulching with pine needles or rotting oak leaves should be given to rhododendrons and other broad-leaved evergreens. It will maintain acidity, conserve moisture, and generally serve to protect the roots and create natural conditions favorable to growth. Where rhododendrons are growing in places exposed to strong winds and winter sunlight, give them some upright protection with evergreen boughs or even burlap screens.

Dwarf fruit trees, available in excellent quality and variety, are highly desirable features for the home grounds, large or small. They can be planted successfully now. The espalier types can be grown against walls, trellises or fences.

The planting of new trees and shrubs can continue.

The Garden in November

Praise large estates but farm a small one.
– Virgil

General: First comes the problem of leaves. Hardwood leaves, such as oak, hickory, and beech, should be put aside for winter mulching. They do not rot quickly nor pack down to smother the plants. Leaves of the quickly decaying sorts, such as maple, become humus by spring if composted. Keep the piles wet and shaded, if possible. Never burn them, for that is waste, and the smoke becomes just one more pollution for our ever-suffering atmosphere.

If you have extensive lawn areas surrounded by many leaf-shedding trees, rent or buy a lawn sweeper.

Bulbs: Tulips may be planted until December if the ground remains unfrozen. If any other outdoor bulb planting remains to be done, do not forget to apply a mulch that will exclude the frost for 5 or 6 weeks, so that proper roots can form. Otherwise, next spring's flowers will probably be unsatisfactory, and the bulbs themselves may suffer. Some of the hardy lilies are late getting into the market. Be sure to get them into the ground as quickly as possible, and mulch the ground heavily to keep it open so some root growth can begin.

If you are planning to have some hyacinths indoors, November is about the last chance to pot them. Hyacinths and many others respond especially well to various easy treatments and will bloom until April. Bring in bulbs the latter part of the month for a succession of bloom all winter.

Greenhouse and Cold Frame: Start seeds of some of the more rapid-growing annuals in the greenhouse for winter flowers. Of these may be mentioned calliopsis, candytuft, and the fragrant mignonette.

Sweet peas in the greenhouse should be fed freely with liquid fertilizers. The first flowers to appear should be pinched off to conserve the plants' strength. Keep the atmosphere dry at night.

Poinsettia, primula, and other heat-loving plants intended for Christmas bloom must be forced evenly and not too rapidly. A temperature of 75 degrees, or even 80 degrees when plenty of moisture is available, will be beneficial to them.

Carnation plants should be supported and properly disbudded. Never allow the benches to accumulate green mold. The surface of the ground should be stirred. Topdress with dehydrated manure.

Houseplants: Winter houseplants need care to help them weather generally adverse conditions. They benefit most from moist air. To secure it indoors, set each pot on a tray of pebbles which is kept filled with water almost to the top level of the stones. Of course the real remedy for too-dry air lies in the use of one of the house humidifiers. Such units are of equal benefit to your own well-being.

Lawn: Low spots in the lawn or irregularities in the surface may be topdressed now. Use good soil; and when not more than 2 inches of it is applied, the grass has a chance to come through again. Be sure to keep leaves and other heavy matter off the grass as it smothers very easily during extremely cold weather.

Perennial Flowers: The early days of November bring the last call for the safe transplanting of herbaceous perennials in most regions. Firm the clumps well after watering them. Water which collects upon the surface of the garden during the winter will freeze and may damage perennials. Little ditches will carry this off. See that the beds drain well.

When chrysanthemums are through flowering, remove the stalks at once within a few inches of the ground. This will help root development and make them send out vigorous sprouts in the spring. Some may be lifted and replanted in the cold frame. Plants for potting can be taken from the side sprouts which will develop next May.

Late this month or in early December is the time to mulch the perennial border for the winter after the ground first freezes a couple of inches deep. Winter protection of peony clumps is seldom needed after the first year; and when too thick a layer is applied, the result is flowerless stalks. At most, apply a light mulch of manure over the root area, but not the crowns. Wait to do this until the leaves die. Burn the stalks of peony, delphinium, hollyhock, and phlox.

Pests: Rabbits and mice are a nuisance of the winter season. Some of the depredations of mice are to a large extent due to too early mulching, which causes them to seek a warm winter home in the mulch and to feed upon your plants or roots while snowed in. Field mice also inhabit drains if not prevented from entering them by gratings over the open end. The abandoned burrows of moles should also be destroyed.

Rabbits gnaw the bark of young trees. Protect them with a collar of tar paper or a fence of poultry wire. Less reliable are the proprietary animal-repellent sprays obtainable at seed stores.

Roses: Hybrid tea, hybrid perpetual, and hardy climber roses will winter well in most localities if mounded with soil 6 or 8 inches and covered with leaves. Standard or tree roses are about the hardest to protect. The stems should be laid down for the winter and the tops covered with soil. Dig away the soil from one side of the crown, taking care not to expose the roots, and then bend and lay the canes in a trench, covering them with the excavated soil.

While the more severe pruning of roses should be left until spring, shortening the branches will keep them from being blown about by the wind and make them easier to protect. Do not be in too big a hurry to cover roses as it is best to have a freeze first.

Shrubs, Trees and Vines: Newly planted trees (even small ones) require some sort of steadying support against wind and storm. Stakes or guy wires are effective for this purpose, depending on the tree size. They should be securely placed at the time of planting and left for a year. Newly planted shade trees are often injured by the sun during the first winter. This is called "sun scald" and is prevented by wrapping the trunk with burlap or paper tree wrap. It is especially necessary on smooth bark trees. A collar about 18 inches high fastened about the base of the tree will keep its bark from being injured by mice or rabbits.

Late fall planting of evergreens is risky. This class of plant should always be given plenty of time to reestablish its roots before the advent of really cold weather stops underground growth. Don't forget to supply even well-established evergreens with plenty of water before freezing weather.

November and December are good months to clean out the tangle of overgrown flowering vines. Cutting out old or diseased wood will send the strength into the remaining branches.

Peegee hydrangea should be trimmed back to 2 to 4 buds on each shoot. Remove all flower heads, and cut out the old branches of the blue and pink flowered variety. The dwarf pink spirea 'Anthony Waterer' should be cut back about two-thirds and deadwood removed. Summer-flowering tamarix should be brought into shape and old growth removed. Remove the suckers which spring up from the roots of lilac bushes and snowberry. Cut out the oldest stems of mock-orange (philadelphus) to the ground – the blossoms, next year, will come on wood which grew this season. Shape up the rose of Sharon. Take out the oldest parts of untrimmed privet hedges, and shape. Hill up soil around butterfly-bush but do not cut off the tops until spring. They may live through.

Winter Protection: Mulches of leaves or other material applied to the plant before the ground is frozen often do irreparable damage. More plants are lost by smothering in this manner than by the severity of the weather. Any plant which is injured by the first light freeze of fall cannot be regarded as hardy and should be taken inside or at least wintered in a cold frame.

Many plants require cold weather and will not grow if they are not partially exposed all winter. Some alpines, for instance, are accustomed to mild summers and long severe winters. Therefore, they are difficult to handle in more southerly states. Most hardy plants do not require any protection at all.

If you mulch with the kind of leaves which get soft and pack down quickly (maple, for instance), they form a heavy mass which will retain water and exclude air over long periods. In the spring, they tend to ferment and generate heat, which coaxes the plants into activity too soon, exposing them to late frost. Hardwood leaves, such as oak, beech, and hickory, do not absorb water so readily and remain loose all winter.

Most plants with evergreen leaves cannot stand complete covering. It is therefore well to place a row of stakes or a ring of poultry netting close about the plant so that the ground can be covered to prevent sudden thawing while the evergreen leaves are free. Let the mulch be somewhat funnel-shaped inside the ring. Some alpines or fuzzy-leaved plants need the cold but do not like water upon their leaves.

Many exotic plants that are being grown out of their normal climatic range must be covered with upended baskets of leaves; to keep them from becoming damp, a piece of sheet iron may be tacked over the basket to shed water.

Garden Tips for December

Under the snow of each December
Lie buds of next year's May, remember . . .

– Douglas Malloch

No garden calendar like this can be all things to all gardeners everywhere every month of the year. Much help of a regional nature can be obtained from state agricultural experiment stations (listed in Chapter 21) and county agents. Call on them freely – generally the information they give is free.

General: Tools can be cleaned during the next 90 days until they look like new. Anyone who has adopted the policy of using only clean tools knows how much easier they work.

Give the compost heap a final turning over with a fork so as to mix in the latest additions and hasten their decomposition. A generous sprinkling of lime will help things along.

All of the ashes from the fireplace this winter ought to be saved for garden use in the spring. They are a fertile source of potash, an essential plant food. Store them in watertight containers over the winter; and keep them dry, as their strength easily leaches away. When applying them in the spring use them thinly, especially on lawns.

Rhubarb may be forced in the cellar by planting good-sized clumps that have undergone freezing for several weeks in barrels or boxes. Place them beside the furnace or chimney in a temperature of 60 degrees. The soil should be kept moderately moist. The stalks should be ready in about 3 weeks. Chicory is one of the best winter salad plants. It can be forced in any ordinary cellar by planting the roots in boxes and keeping them dark.

To lift the spirits in winter, grow the Christmas rose. It's not a true rose, but is an evergreen perennial named Helleborus niger.

If you expect to secure any landscape service this year do it now as the man you select will have more time to give you now than later in the season. Also, while your grounds are bare he can get a better idea of your problems.

Be especially sure that any garden ornaments such as urns or jars are turned over to keep them from collecting water and breaking when it freezes.

Birds: Be sure to keep water for birds in pans that can be brought inside to be thawed out. This is one of their chief needs when everything is frozen. Grit or sand is another, so have a little fine poultry grit mixed with sand accessible for them.

A supply of sunflower, hemp, and millet seed supplemented with suet scraps will take care of the food matter very nicely. Suet wired to a branch is welcome to several species. A secluded fence corner facing south makes a good feeding station. A platform located in an open position near a hemlock, spruce, or pine tree is also very good.

The junco is the most prevalent of winter bird visitors. He comes about October 1 and often stays until the last of May. The time to convince him he has reached a good stop is early in the fall before he is driven by hunger to seek other food. That is the time to teach him to feed from your window sill and insure his companionship throughout the winter. Juncos are absolutely fearless and radiate cheer in the garden. They come in tones of slate gray and are often mistaken for English sparrows except when their outer tail feathers are conspicuously flashed in the light.

Most gardeners are familiar with the whistle-call of the cardinal in spring or have seen him fluttering about the low branches of shrubs at that time. He can usually be observed at all times of the winter too. He makes no attempt at concealment but passes most of the time in the lower undergrowth, selecting a most conspicuous perch at a season when color is lacking, challenging the attention of the world.

The goldfinch, which goes by the common name of wild canary, wears a brown coat in the winter, but sheds it for his goldfinch costume in the spring, when he is ready for his song of "per-chic-o-ree."

The chickadee is an active and ever-welcome visitor to winter lunch counters and often can be coaxed to feed from one's hand. He can be identified by his clearly enunciated "chickadee" and its variations.

Traditional Christmas arrangements: topiary tree of boxwood, decorated with artificial strawberries; basket-wreath made with wire ring, balsam fir branches stuck in styrofoam, cones and ribbon; Della-Robbia wreath of artificial fruits.

Bulbs: It is not too late to pot some bulbs in soil or to force them in water. Ten or 12 weeks may seem a long time to wait for them to root but the time soon passes and, properly handled, they are easy and sure of bloom.

Christmas Decorations: It is surprising the amount of Christmas decorations that can be made in a few minutes with material from your own garden. Clippings from evergreen trees and broad-leaf evergreen plants such as mahonia and holly, and various berried shrubs lend themselves well to this purpose. This is an easy way to prune the plants, too.

Greenhouse and Cold Frame: It is a good practice to sow alpine plant seed early in December in an outdoor cold frame. They will not germinate until spring, so the frame should be kept shaded and ventilated in order that they may remain frozen until March. Seeds may also be sown in flats and placed in some convenient outdoor location where they will be shaded and well frozen. A good covering of snow seems to help.

Cold frames in which semihardy plants are being wintered, or frames that are used as growing media, should have some kind of covering. Loose hay may be used, but the best covering is a jute mat. Homemade mats of old carpet or burlap stuffed with straw also serve the purpose.

Plants such as carnation, rose, and snapdragon that are growing in greenhouse benches will respond to an application of dehydrated manure now.

Houseplants: Much common failure of houseplants is due to overwatering and poor drainage which are even more objectionable indoors than in the outdoor garden. Indoor plants must have both food and drink, but wet soggy soil is not to their liking. Apply enough water so that it drips from the drainage hole in the bottom of the pot. Then let the soil dry out (but not become bone- or dust-dry) before the next soaking. Spraying the foliage with a fine mist of room-temperature water will help to maintain humidity – of benefit to most plants.

Ferns and other foliage houseplants should be treated occasionally to some of the concentrated plant foods sold for the purpose. Keep the surface of the soil loosened so that no green scum forms. They do best at a temperature of 60 to 70 degrees and when given a frequent misting of their foliage, as described above.

Check amaryllis bulbs that are still being kept dry. If any show signs of breaking their dormancy – buds beginning – they can be brought into the light and watered.

A welcome touch on a bleak winter day is the verdant vine of a common sweet potato growing in a jar of water. Hold it suspended in the water, using some toothpicks stuck into it if necessary. Kiln-dried potatoes are not suitable for this purpose, nor are those that have been sulfured.

Rock Garden: Some of the more tender rock plants may be protected with a thin (very thin) mulch of marsh hay, or better – evergreen boughs. They are ap-

The sleeping garden. A snow cover can be the best winter protection of all.

plied as windbreaks, and the plants should be clearly visible through the mulch. Now is a good time to collect odd stones for extending the rock garden. (Suggested reading: *All About the Rock Garden* by Walter Kolaga.)

Trees and Shrubs: The planting of deciduous trees and shrubs may be continued just as long as the weather permits in most regions. Trees that are to be moved with a ball of frozen earth around their roots may now have trenches dug to encircle them and facilitate the final digging later on. To guard against the soil ball drying out, these trenches may be filled in with dead leaves or any rough litter.

The fresh nuts of hickory, butternut, and black walnut will often germinate quite readily if planted outdoors an inch or so deep and left there over the winter. The combined action of frost and moisture splits their hard shells and allows the root to emerge. You may have to enclose them in a wire basket to protect from rodents.

Tree branches that have grown so much as to cast excess shade over the flower plantings should be cut off this winter when, in falling, they can do no damage to the bed. All deciduous tree and shrub trimming may be done now; but be careful in pruning shrubbery now not to do it too severely, or you will destroy all the flowering branches for next spring. Prune the fruit trees.

The weight of wet snow upon evergreens will often bend and permanently distort or break them. Heavy sticky snow should always be removed as soon as possible.

Index